D0990609

MOLLY SPOTTED ELK

Molly as she appeared in Texas Guinan's clubs, 1928.

MOLLY SPOTTED ELK

A PENOBSCOT IN PARIS

by
Bunny McBride

Foreword by Eunice Nelson-Bauman
Postscript by Jean Archambaud Moore

University of Oklahoma Press : Norman and London

This book is dedicated to my mentor-friend Henrietta Buckmaster, whose bold and empathetic pen imparted both inspiration and aspiration.

970.3
P416m
1995

Library of Congress Cataloging-in-Publication Data

McBride, Bunny,
    Molly Spotted Elk : a Penobscot in Paris / by Bunny McBride ; foreword by Eunice Nelson-Bauman ; postscript by Jean Archambaud Moore.
        p.   cm.
    Includes bibliographical references and index.
    ISBN 0–8061–2756–2 (alk. paper)
    1. Spotted Elk. 2. Penobscot Indians—Biography. 3. Dancers—United States—Biography. 4. Dancers—France—Biography. I. Title.
    E99.P5S755   1995
    973'.04973—dc20   95-6891
                                                              CIP

Text design by Cathy Carney Imboden.

The paper in this book meets the guidelines for permanence and durability of the Committee on Production Guidelines for Book Longevity of the Council on Library Resources. ∞

1 2 3 4 5 6 7 8 9 10

CONTENTS

ILLUSTRATIONS

Unless otherwise noted, photographs are courtesy of Molly's daughter, Jean Archambaud Moore.

FOREWORD

As a child, my oldest sister Molly was told, "Curiosity killed the cat," and she immediately asked, "Whose cat?" This was one of the many family anecdotes I heard while growing up. At first, however, I did not understand what curiosity meant. I was about six years old when I finally learned, and Molly was involved in the lesson. I had accompanied her to the edge of a field behind our house where wild cherries could be found growing on trees that were only a little thicker than saplings. Molly climbed one of these, broke small branches off, and threw them down to me. As I ran back and forth to gather the branches to place them all in one pile, I caught sight of an object hanging from the branch of a nearby tree. It was shaped somewhat like a football but was flattened at both ends and appeared to be made of rough gray tissue paper. I approached the object, started patting it, and shouted, "Molly, what's this?" I never did understand how she got out of that tree so quickly, but with rapidly swelling eyes, I saw her tearing toward the house at top speed and heard her shouting, "Run!" The gray object was, of course, a hornet's nest. As my mother rubbed her gold wedding band over my numerous stings to quell the pain, she said something about "curiosity," leaving no doubt in my mind as to what that word meant.

Born twelve years before me, Molly took care of me during my childhood at least as often as my mother—so much so that I called her "Mama." She was central to my young years. Yet, reading this account of her life, I realize how little I really knew

her as a woman. By the time I had matured enough to get to
know her to any depth, she had become only an occasional
visitor for short periods of time. And when she later resettled
on our island reservation, I had moved to another corner of the
world, following my own curiosities. I did not come back to the
island to stay until after her death. On top of this, traditional
Penobscot child-rearing patterns discouraged talking about
oneself, especially talking in a way that gave any hint of
boasting. I cannot recall any instance when my sister spoke to
me about herself in terms of her career or her dreams, how she
felt about life in general or about her life in particular.

Yet, she taught me much. It was mostly from her example and
informal teachings that, in my early years, I learned to paddle
a canoe properly; to know where to look for wild strawberries,
blueberries, raspberries, and blackberries; and to enjoy time
spent in the woods, where one could find the sweet-smelling
Mayflowers, Indian pipes, lady slippers, hear the songs of the
sparrows, warblers, and mourning doves and catch an occasional glimpse of small wild creatures. She aroused my interest
in numerous and diverse matters, including the story of Atlan-
tis—which, more than a half century later, I still pursue when
new evidence of its existence surfaces. Watching her intellectual quests, I became aware of my own academic capabilities.

Her life spoke to me in other ways that are inexplicable. I
once saw her dance in a local nightclub. Words fail me when I
try to explain my reaction. I only know that as I watched her,
my heart pounded, tears streamed down my face, and my body
trembled uncontrollably. Here, in this book, I read in an
excerpt from her diary that she wanted her dancing to be
"passionate," and I can affirm that for me it was just that.

I rejoiced when I read of the relationship Molly had with
Johnny, the Frenchman she married. What a beautiful and
uncommon union it was—a many-splendored and multileveled
compatibility that, I'm convinced, most of us women hope for,
but rarely find.

I mourned Molly's death more and longer than even that of
our mother. I find no words adequate enough to express my

gratitude to the author who, through diligent and extensive research, has made available to me the story of an extraordinary woman who happened to be my sister.

EUNICE NELSON-BAUMAN

Indian Island, Old Town, Maine

PREFACE

It was 1988. I was leaving Maine for yet another trip to Africa—
this time to East Africa to research several magazine and
newspaper articles. "Why are you always going so far away
when there is so much to write about here?" my husband
asked. Then he mentioned, as he had several times before, the
life of Molly Spotted Elk. When I returned six weeks later, he
handed me an article about Molly, which had appeared in a
local newspaper during my absence. A close-up photograph of
her caught—and held—my attention. Her elegant, fine-fea-
tured face was warm, inviting. Then I was drawn to the dark
eyes. To my surprise, they were wary, impenetrable. This
ambiguous image haunted me for days, ultimately convincing
me that my husband was right.

Where to start? Seven years of work on a native rights case
with the Aroostook Band of Micmacs in northern Maine had
brought me into contact not only with Micmacs, but with
members of the state's three other tribes: the Penobscot,
Passamaquoddy, and Maliseet. Molly had been dead for a
decade, but I had met her youngest sister, Dr. Eunice Nelson-
Bauman, who lives on the Penobscot reservation on Indian
Island. I phoned Eunice and talked with her about the possibility of writing an article and perhaps a book about Molly.
Soon thereafter, Eunice spent a long weekend at our home in
Hallowell. For me time stopped as I sat on our deck overlooking
the Kennebec River, listening to her reminisce about her sister.
Molly had performed in vaudeville as a teenager, studied jour-
nalism and anthropology at the University of Pennsylvania,

danced topless in New York, starred in a classic docu-drama
chronicling traditional Ojibway Indian life, danced for royalty
in Europe, hobnobbed with well-known American literati in
Paris, lectured at the Sorbonne, married a French journalist,
and barely escaped the Nazi occupation of France by hiking
over the Pyrenees with her young daughter. Molly's life, marked
by tradition mixed with independence, professional determination, and artistic and intellectual cosmopolitanism, defied the stereotype of a woman born in the early years of this
century—particularly of an American Indian woman. By the
time Eunice left, I knew I wanted to find out more about her
sister and share my discoveries in a book.

Eunice suggested I contact Molly's daughter, Jean Archambaud Moore, who had in her keeping Molly's diaries, photographs, letters, and other memorabilia. I phoned Jean, who, at
the time, lived in Murfreesboro, Tennessee, and told her of my
desire to write about her mother. My desire grew as I listened to
this keen-witted woman talk about her mother in a deep,
earthy voice. Her recollections were vivid and brilliantly told.
She had been approached by others interested in writing
Molly's life story, so I offerred to send her samples of my work to
help her decide if she felt I was the right one for the task.

A dozen days later, Jean telephoned to invite me to Tennessee. We worked together intensely for a week, from early
morning until deep into the night, recording her recollections
of Molly and sorting through boxes of memorabilia. Jean,
indefatigable, sat hour after hour, day after day, on a wooden
chair at her desk. As afternoons gave way to evenings, she
would lean more heavily on her bureau, propping herself up
with her elbows. That desk held the tools of her fortune-telling
trade, including a crystal ball and cards. On our last evening
together, I learned that she practiced her trade personally as
well as professionally:

"Would you like to know why I chose you to tell my mother's
story? she asked.

"Indeed, I would."

"You see this painting?" she queried, pointing above her

desk to a picture of the Indian saint Kateri Tekawitha—one
of several paintings of this saint for which her mother had
posed.

"Yes, I've been looking at it all week."

"Well, two weeks before you first phoned me, I noticed it was
crooked and straightened it out. The next day, I found it had
shifted again and once more leveled it. This happened again
and again. When I straightened it on the day you telephoned, I
asked out loud, 'Mother, what are you trying to tell me?!' After
your call, the painting remained evenly hung. Apparently, my
mother felt comfortable about entrusting you with her story."

Jean's level of trust proved to be as extraordinary as this
message from her deceased mother. When I left after our first
visit, I carried with me a box of precious goods—Molly's
diaries. Since then I have been entrusted with hundreds of
family photographs and personal letters, not to mention Jean's
utterly candid recollections.

Molly was extremely private, even in her diaries. This is
evident not only in the content of the diaries, but also in the
fact that her writing was so miniscule that I had to make
enlarged photocopies of the pages in order to decipher them.
Typically, Molly chronicled her daily doings. She also provided
social commentary on a range of topics, from politics and
racism to the emptiness of high society life. She had an
anthropologist's eye and in her travels frequently recorded
culturally based values, habits, and tastes that differed from
her own. During her first months in France she devoted a half-
dozen pages to descriptions of French cheeses and eating
habits. While self-reflection, soul-searching, and personal struggle are expressed in her diaries, Molly usually used journal
writing as a means of wrestling out of, rather than plunging
into, the sorrows that plagued her. Her determination to be
cheerful and to carry on in the face of great difficulty inspired
me. But at times it left me confused about her true feelings.
When I interviewed dancer Lisan Kay, one of Molly's old friends
from both New York and Paris, she told me that Molly was
always upbeat and never depressed. Molly fooled her—and she

almost fooled me. Only after reading all (and transcribing much) of her surviving journals did I learn how to read between the lines. There I discovered the ambiguity that haunted Molly through much of her life—ambiguity toward and from dominant white society concerning her place in it. Despite the frequent masking of emotions in Molly's diaries, I found them fully reliable in terms of facts. If she noted that an article appeared about her in a magazine or newspaper, I was able to track it down. If she mentioned giving a particular performance, I could find evidence of it in reviews and promotional material. The friendships, love relationships, and work associations referred to in her daybooks were repeatedly verified through interviews with those who knew her. In short, Molly's diaries withstood an intensive veracity test when held against oral histories and personal correspondance, as well as written and photographic records unearthed in national, local, and university archives and libraries in France and the United States.

But the diaries by no means told the full story of Molly's life. Hunting down and fitting together the missing fragments challenged me considerably—and getting to Molly's soul seemed nearly impossible. For me, she was the quintessential "other." We hailed from dramatically different times and societal niches, and our personalities were strikingly different. The choices she made rarely matched my own. I remember vividly the first time I saw a pair of her size five dance moccasins. Glancing from them to my own size nine and one-half feet I thought, "I'll never be able to step into her shoes and tell her story." Nonetheless, taking my cue from her undaunted spirit, I continued my journey to the far-off land of her life. One by one, I shed the assumptions that hindered my travel. I strolled the paths and sidewalks frequented by her on Indian Island and in New York and Paris. I pored over her diaries. I devoured the impassioned love letters she received from Jean Archambaud. I stood at the foot of the stairs where she died. Finally, as I wrote my way toward the end of Molly's life and the final chapter in this book, our souls touched. The meeting, a holy happening in the

mind's eye, occurred during a walk through the Flint Hills of
eastern Kansas where I live. There, I swear, Molly gave me the
conclusion to this book. Or, perhaps, the conclusion gave me
Molly.

BUNNY MCBRIDE

ACKNOWLEDGMENTS

Molly's story could not have come to light without the help of her daughter, Jean Archambaud Moore, and her youngest sister, Eunice Nelson-Bauman. Both shared memories and memorabilia concerning Molly with generosity, trust, and candor. Plus, each time a new chapter rolled out of my printer, they reviewed it, and provided feedback that kept the facts on track and inspired me onward. My sincere thanks to them.

Two other women read an early draft of this book: my sister and my mother. For support that reaches far beyond these pages, I am indebted to them, and to my father.

Donald Smith, who authored the captivating biography of Molly's *Silent Enemy* costar Long Lance, read my chapter on the making of that film and offered a thoughtful critique. Moreover, he led me to two vital and equally helpful sources: Jean Burden Bostwick (the widow of W. Douglas Burden who produced the docu-drama), and Madeline Theriault (an Ojibwa who made many of the costumes for the movie and played a small role in it).

Although they do not appear in the coming pages, I want to acknowledge and express thanks to my Micmac Indian friends in northern Maine. Working beside them in their struggle for native rights and cultural survival affected my world view profoundly. In particular, I gleaned insights from the elder women whose oral histories I gathered—life stories of stalwart souls who have faced countless adversities with quiet determination. In many ways they prepared me to receive Molly's story.

My background research for this book was aided greatly by

access to the library of my husband, anthropologist Harald Prins—the only person I know who has read all seventy-two volumes of the *Jesuit Relations*. During our years in Maine, Harald painstakingly pored over and topically transcribed volumes of archival records relating to American Indians in the region. Of special note here are research findings he shared with me concerning the emergence of American Indians as entertainers, which provided a valuable framework in which to place Molly's vaudeville experiences. Beyond this, he celebrated the completion of each chapter by listening to me read it aloud to him and by offering essential and insightful feedback. For his perspicacity, enthusiasm, friendship, and love, I am deeply and daily grateful.

Finally, I wish to thank the staff at the Maine State Library, which, during my decade in Maine, seemed like an annex to my home office. Even after moving to Kansas I have continued to marvel at and rely upon their gracious and able assistance.

MOLLY SPOTTED ELK

CHAPTER 1

ESCAPE

Panic ahead, wonder, doubt, prayers, longing, writing—and a woman walks alone. Everywhere there are Germans. . . . There remains only one thing for me: to go home.

—Molly (Royan, France, 1940)[1]

Years before, she had hiked the steep forested slopes of the Pyrenees for pleasure, relishing the grand vistas and iced air that are the gifts of mountains.[2] But in the summer of 1940, the majestic mile-high range offered anything but pleasure. Sixty miles wide and 260 miles long, it stood like a fortress between France and Spain, hindering her escape from the horrors of Nazi occupation in France. The overland retreat from Royan was arduous, even for a woman like Molly Spotted Elk, whose legs were strong enough to dance her into the arms of international fame. She had her six-year-old daughter in tow, plus the immense heartache of making the journey without her French husband and with no knowledge of his whereabouts or safety.

They traveled by day, walking mile after mile, sometimes hitching rides in horse-drawn carts, ambulances, relief trucks. At night, she wrapped the child in her arms and, exhausted and hungry, they slept by the roadside. When German fighter planes roared overhead and startled the girl to tears, Molly comforted her with the ancient Penobscot Indian legends that had cheered her own childhood. Their immediate goal, a refugee steamer destined for New York, awaited departure in

Lisbon, Portugal, hundreds of miles away. The ultimate destination, their reservation home on Indian Island at Old Town, Maine, seemed as far away as the moon.[3]

CHAPTER 2

ROOTS

The green of the trees made me think of home.
—Molly (Paris 1934)[1]

Journeying to Indian Island meant returning to native roots that reached back beyond the horizon of memory. The wind-swept pines on this 315-acre isle whispered of bygone genera-tions of Penobscot Indians who hunted and gathered here, relying only upon nature's generosity and their own ingenuity to survive. Here, as early as nine thousand years ago, Molly's nomadic ancestors camped in birchbark wigwams under pitch-black skies filled with icechip stars.[2] They called the place *Panawahpskek*—"where the rocks spread out"—for the island lies where the river widens, just above the rocky ledges of a great falls. Eventually that name attached itself to the people who inhabited the island and to the powerful river that flows around it. When Europeans, who first sailed up this river in the early seventeenth century, wrapped their tongues around *Pan-awahpskek,* it became Penobscot. Upon learning that the island was the oldest occupied Indian settlement on the Pe-nobscot River, the newcomers called it Indian Old Town.[3]

But the river, more than the island, defined the lives of the natives. It was their lifeline, a liquid highway winding through dense forests to nature's various storehouses. Thirty-five miles downriver sprawled the ocean, rolling in and out of Penobscot Bay with its jagged rock-lined coast. The bay, a two-day paddle from Old Town, was dotted with offshore islands ideal for camping, and offered a feast of cod, seal, porpoise, and shellfish. In the other direction, the river and its east and west branches reached some two hundred miles inland, leading to countless tributaries and lakes teeming with fish. In the deep forests of hemlock, cedar, birch, and fir that flanked the watercourses, roamed a bounty of four-legged creatures: moose, deer, bear, caribou.[4]

Molly's forebears moved as needed to follow nature's shifting banquet. They traveled by canoe when the rivers flowed and by sled or snowshoe when waterways froze firm as granite and snow covered their world in a thick blanket of white.

In summer, the season of plenty, abundant food supplies enabled many families to live side by side at various encampments along the Penobscot River and the Atlantic coast without threatening each other's survival. The days were long, warm, and washed with sunlight. Men hunted the sea for fish and mammals and walked the forests looking for giant white birch trees, whose bark they used to make lightweight canoes. Women and children collected fruits, nuts, and shellfish, and prepared smoked fish and dried berries to be stored with nuts for the harsh winter months. Everyone spent much time socializing, reaffirming friendships and alliances with their Penobscot kin groups, each named for and closely associated with an animal, such as the bear, wolf, or beaver. For young people, summer offered romantic possibilities—not only with other Penobscot River inhabitants, but with members of various migratory groups who were part of their widespread social network.[5]

In autumn, when bright leaves feigned fire, most tribespeople paddled inland and dispersed into small family groups for the fall hunt. Men stalked prey and tended traplines. Women worked furs and hides into clothes and moccasins, sometimes painting them with pigments made from crushed berries or ochre or embroidering them with dyed porcupine quills.[6]

Winter was so stingy that January was known as the "moon that provides little food grudgingly."[7] At this time of year, people relied more on their indomitable spirits than on the meager offerings of nature. Temperatures plummeted well was far easier to negotiate with than Europeans, who held to the curious notion that all uncultivated land was up for grabs. White settlers and their vigorous development efforts all but destroyed traditional subsistence possibilities for the Wabanaki. Struggling to survive and to hold the settlers at bay, Penobscots relinquished aboriginal title to their vast homeland bit by bit, treaty by treaty. In return they received annuities (annual payments of corn, salt pork, blankets, ammunition, and other goods) and guarantees that their remaining refuge would not be encroached upon. The guarantees were not honored. During the last third of the eighteenth century and the first third of the nineteenth, Penobscot territory shrank from several million acres to five thousand. This remnant consisted of 140 small islands lying in the thirty-mile stretch of river from Old Town to Mattawamkeag. The last land surrender took place in 1833. It was a financial transaction—fifty thousand dollars for one hundred thousand acres. The money went into a trust fund controlled and invested by the state of Maine. In the years that followed, interest from the fund went toward an island school, remuneration for a government-appointed Indian agent, and the purchase of annuity goods promised by earlier treaties.[6]

By the time Molly's grandfather Peter Nelson was born on Indian Island in 1851, most families living there had replaced their bark wigwams and communal longhouses for modest single-family woodframe houses or shacks.[7] The town of Bangor, ten miles downstream, had swelled to twelve thousand inhabitants and become the lumber capital of the world. Above this boomtown, some 250 sawmills dotted the Penobscot River and its tributaries, including a series of enormously productive mills at the falls just below Old Town.[8] Peter's father had witnessed the building of these mills and the resulting destruction of native fisheries. So great were the changes in the land and its resources that very few tribespeople could now subsist solely by fishing and hunting. While holding to this piece of their past as an avocation, Penobscots eked out a living by taking seasonal jobs as loggers or river drivers. Some took up subsistence farming in the summer or worked as guides to a growing battalion of sporthunters. They made snowshoes and canoes for sale. In addition, they fashioned baskets, toy canoes, and moccasins. Many traveled by railroad and steamship to Boston or various tourist haunts to market their goods.[9] A few families went on the road, ranging as far as New York and Philadelphia, to perform in primitive vaudeville shows of Indian life.[10] No matter how they pieced together a living, almost all Penobscots lived close to the bone. According to Maine Governor Hubbard, in 1851, most existed "in a condition bordering upon pauperism."[11]

Henry David Thoreau made several trips to Maine about this time, expecting to commune with nature by following in the sure steps of native guides. His first trek, in 1846, took him to Katahdin, New England's second highest mountain, long sacred to the Wabanaki. He traveled by steamer from Concord, Massachusetts to Bangor, then by train to mainland Old Town. From there he took a ferry northward, passing by Indian Island.[12]

At first glance, the heartland of Penobscot life dismayed the naturalist. In his journal he described the record of these people as "a history of extinction," then elaborated:

> The island seemed deserted today, yet I observed some new houses among the weather-stained ones, as if the tribe had still a design upon life; but generally they have a very shabby, forlorn and cheerless look, being all back side and woodshed, not homesteads. . . .
> The church is the only trim-looking building, but that is not Abenaki, that was Rome's doing. . . . These were once a powerful tribe. . . . a row of wigwams, with a dance of powwows and a prisoner tortured at the stake, would be more respectable than this.[13]

On a return trip in 1853, Thoreau sketched a fuller yet more ambiguous picture of Penobscot life. This time, Penobscot Joseph Attean and a friend guided him through Moosehead and Chesuncook lakes some sixty miles north of Indian Island.[14] In Thoreau's words, Attean (an age-mate of Molly's great-grandfather and son of tribal governor John Attean) was "a good-looking Indian, twenty-four years old . . . short and stout, with a broad face and a reddish complexion, and eyes, me thinks, narrower and more turned up at the outer corners than ours. . . . He wore a red-flannel shirt, woolen pants, and a black cossuth hat, the ordinary dress of the lumberman, and, to a considerable extent, of the Penobscot Indian."[15]

Thoreau's account of this trip exudes his philospher's yearning to witness in daily life the unadulterated noble savage he cradled in his own consciousness.[16] As the three men paddled along in Attean's nineteen-foot birchbark canoe, Thoreau mused aloud about the beauty of living purely off a wilderness bounty of game, fish, and berries. Attean's response startled him: "'Yes, that's the way [my ancestors] got a living, like wild fellows, wild as bears. By George! I shan't go into the woods without provision,—hard bread, pork, etc.'" Thoreau was equally surprised to hear Attean whistling "Oh Susanna" and punctuating conversation with exclamations like "Yes, siree!"[17]

Despite these hints of acculturation, Attean seemed in Thoreau's eyes a nearly mythic figure, a link between civilized man and the mystery of the wilderness. In crystal-clear prose he described his guide blowing mournful moosecalls on a birchbark horn, striding over portages while "twirling his canoe in his hands as if it were a feather," and standing in the canoe's moonlit bow, framed by a forest that rose like "an endless succession of porticos and columns, cornices and facades, verandas and cathedrals."[18]

At night, lying by the campfire, listening to his Penobscot companions talk in an "Indian language, which the white man cannot speak or understand," Thoreau cherished the thought that "These were the sounds that issued from the wigwams of this country before Columbus was born; they have not yet died away. . . . I felt that I . . . lay as near to the primitive man of America, that night, as any of its discovers did."[19]

Following this venture Thoreau headed south to Old Town, then crossed to Indian Island in a bateau, sitting beside a Catholic priest. He described the village like this:

The Indian houses are framed, mostly of one story, and in rows one behind another at the south end of the island, with a few scattered ones. I counted about forty, not including the church and what my companion called the council-house. . . . Here and there were moose-hides stretched and drying about them. There were no cart-paths, nor tracks of horses, but footpaths; very little land cultivated, but an abundance of weeds, indigenous and naturalized; more introduced weeds than useful vegetables, as the Indian is said to cultivate the vices rather than the virtues of the white man. Yet this village was cleaner than I expected, far cleaner than such Irish villages as I have seen.[20]

As he and his companions sauntered along the footpaths, they met several little boys carrying bows and arrows. The youngsters cried, "Put up a cent!"—inviting the visitors to toss a coin in the air so the boys might win it by hitting it with an arrow. Thoreau later lamented this scene in his journal:

[T]he curiosity of the white man is insatiable and from the first he has been eager to witness this forest accomplishment. That elastic piece of wood and its feathered dart, so sure to be unstrung by contact with civilization, will serve for the type, the coat-of-arms of the savage. Alas for the Hunter Race! The white man has driven off their game, substituted a cent in its place.[21]

Yet, as Thoreau saw with Attean, despite the profound changes brought by colonization and the usurption of Wabanaki lands, some traditions held firm. Most Penobscots still moved with the seasons and knew how to read nature by its scents and sounds. They trusted traditional healers, relied on their hands, and held social exchange on a par with economic pursuits. And, as Thoreau discovered, the ancient legends that defined their relationship to the earth and all its creatures still spilled from the mouths of old-timers.

Before leaving the island, Thoreau visted former Penobscot governor John Neptune in his humble "tenfooter" woodframe home. Sitting on his bed, the eighty-nine-year-old Neptune, whose "black hair was only slightly grayed," told Thoreau of his plans to go moose hunting that fall, as he had the year before. Then, waxing nostalgic about days when moose were more plentiful and much larger, he revealed a legendary fact to

Thoreau: "'Moose was whale once. Away down Merrimack way, a whale came ashore in a shallow bay. Sea went out and left him and he came upon land a moose."[22]

So it was that age-old tales, the heart of Penobscot tradition, lived in the memories and conversations of tribal elders. The stories survived just long enough for young Molliedellis Nelson to gather them up.[23]

CHAPTER 4

ISLAND PATHS

My parents were wise. They knew my fondness for stories. Since I was a tom-boy and loved to roam the woods and swim the streams rather than do homely household tasks, they would persuade me to do my chores in exchange for stories. . . . So, many hours were spent picking berries, braiding sweet grass, weaving baskets, chopping wood or shoveling snow, and in return I gathered many a tale of my people.
—Molly (Paris 1938)[1]

She was the first of Horace and Philomene Nelson's eight children, born on Indian Island, November 17, 1903. She arrived in Maine's starkest month, a season when nature gasped in its nakedness, caught between the fiery apparel of fall and the iced white robes of winter. Like most births at that time, this one took place at home—in a small, worn-out, woodframe house just above the ferry landing under the long shadow of St. Ann's church tower. After she was pulled from the womb by her maternal grandmother,[2] her parents gave her a Christian name—Mary Alice. But they, and everyone else on the island, except the priest and nuns, pronounced it the Indian way: *Molliedellis*. For short, they called her Molliedell.

From the beginning, it appeared that this *dji'djis* (gee-gis/ infant)[3] would be a beauty with a fine delicate chin, high cheeks, rosebud mouth, blackberry eyes, and rather fair skin. She had one flaw: her little ears were oddly pointed, elf like. Perhaps her mother had briefly forgotten to heed traditional

View of Indian Island, the Penobscot reservation, from Old Town
shore, circa 1906, three years after Molly's birth. She was born in
the little white house that has two windows. A porch was added
soon after this photograph was taken. Log booms used in river
drives are visible in the river, as is a ferry bateau used to shuttle
people to and from the island. (A postcard. Courtesy of Harald
E. L. Prins.)

Penobscot warnings that a pregnant woman avert her eyes from
anything unsightly to prevent bearing a disfigured child. Tradition also required that the navel cord be burned or buried
lest the child grow up overly inquisitive. Later, witnessing the
insatiable curiosity of young Molliedell, some would speculate
this was not done.[4]

Some four hundred people lived on the island the year of
Molly's birth. About half of the households were headed by
parents who were both Penobscot. The other half were mixed
unions—primarily formed by a Penobscot marrying an Indian
from one of the other Wabanaki tribes, which followed an age-
old practice of intermarriage between native communities in
the region.[5] Molly's was a mixed family; her father, Horace
Nelson, was Penobscot-Passamaquoddy, her mother, Philomene Saulis, was Penobscot-Maliseet, with some French ancestry.

Horace's tie to Indian Island could be traced back three
generations. His great-grandfather G. W. Nelson, who belonged

to the Spider clan, which was largely Passamaquoddy,[6] married Penobscot Molly Pennewaite. They lived on the island where she gave birth to Horace's grandfather, John Weston Nelson, in 1829. John, with his first wife Hannah, who is thought to have been Penobscot, parented Horace's father, Peter, in 1851. And on February 16, 1878, Peter's wife, Mary Francis Mitchell, gave birth to Horace on the island. Mary, a Penobscot-Passamaquoddy who grew up on the Passamaquoddy reservation at Pleasant Point, came from the Bear clan, a dignified and much respected family that considered it taboo to kill bears. Legend held that an ancestor had been abducted by bears that cared for him as if he were their cub. Later, recovered by his human relatives, this man and his descendants became known as bears, and regarded this totem animal with supernatural kinship reverence.[7]

Mary died when Horace was a toddler, and after her death he joined the household of his grandfather John Nelson and his second wife Louise, along with their children, Sockus and Alice. They lived in a little green house at the southwest edge of the island near the tribal hall and common. Like most children of his generation, Horace attended the reservation gradeschool run by the Sisters of Mercy. A turn-of-the-century newspaper account hints at the benevolent racism at work at the school in Horace's day: "Under the most favorable circumstances the primary teaching of Indian children requires a deal of tact and patience—more patience than the ordinary teacher possesses. The work must be a labor of love to be successful, for these young minds are not only childish, but they are the offspring of parents whose minds are immature and untrained."[8]

After finishing primary school, Horace, like a fair number of other Penobscot children, went on to attend the Old Town junior high and high school on the mainland. Attendance was erratic because getting across the river could be a treacherous undertaking, especially during flood season, ice flows, and partial thaws. Legend held that on winter days a soft section in the ice waited to claim someone and freeze over without leaving a trace. Time and again, people disappeared some-

Molly's paternal grandparents, Peter "Dindy" Nelson and
Mary Francis Mitchell Nelson, circa 1878.

where between the island and the mainland.[9] If the river did
not steal children from the classroom, economic necessity did;
teens, including Horace, were repeatedly plucked from school
to do work to help support their families.

In 1900, at age twenty-two, Horace graduated from Old Town
High, becoming the second Penobscot to finish secondary
school. (Louis Sockalexis, whose prowess in baseball had won
him a place in a private academy, had gained a high school
diploma seven years earlier, then gone on to play ball at Notre
Dame, followed by a position with the Cleveland Spiders in the

National League.[10]) With a grade point average of seventy-seven percent, Horace placed fourteenth in a class of eighteen students—his generally excellent performance dragged down year after year by barely passing scores in French.[11] He was the only Indian among his peers.

A Cambridge, Massachusetts journalist touted the supposed benefits of an Old Town education for Penobscot youngsters: "This highschool experience is a great advantage to them, for they not only have the benefit of the advanced training, but also come in close contact with the white man's civilization and become instilled with his point of view and his ideas of citizenship and progress."[12]

While Horace had little interest in surrendering traditional views for mainstream notions of progress, he felt nonetheless curious about life beyond the island. In the fall of 1900 he entered Dartmouth College on a "trial" basis. Apparently, after Horace arrived at the college, officials deemed him unprepared for its rigors and transferred him to Hanover Highschool, where he spent a year. He returned to Dartmouth and matriculated in September 1901. Academic records of him vanish after that date, although several subsequent issues of the college's alumni magazine mention him as a member of the class of 1904. Family oral tradition holds that he stayed in Hanover two years in all, so it appears that he completed a year at the college after attending Hanover High.[13]

Although details of Horace's Dartmouth experience are foggy, something else is crystal-clear: life away from Indian Island never hooked him. The island was home, in the deepest sense of the word. It was his birthplace. A link to ancestors long gone. A refuge from the society that had undone much of the Penobscot way of life. A place where traditions could be carried on with dignity. Moreover, in terms of nature's offerings, it was simply a beautiful place to live.

In December 1902, Horace attended a dance at Tobique, a Maliseet reservation in western New Brunswick that had long been part of the social network of Indian Islanders. There he met sixteen-year-old Philomene Saulis, whose high rosy cheeks, deep-set brown eyes, and vivacious character so stirred his imagination that he determined to marry her on the spot. While Philomene was known for her beauty, Horace was rather ordinary, a man who family members say "wouldn't win first place or booby prize for looks."[14] But he had dark penetrating eyes and a keen intellect and throughout his life never had trouble wooing women. Philomene, then and later, proved to be a great challenge, however. Circumventing her, he donned his suit and stiff white collar and went to see her parents to ask for her hand.[15]

Philomene's father, Frank Saulis, was actually a Mitchell, a member of the Bear clan, like Horace's mother. When Frank was born, his Penobscot parents lived north of Indian Island on Moosehead Lake in Greenville. Somehow, Frank was orphaned at an early age, taken to the Maliseet reservation at Tobique and adopted by the Saulis family.[16] Philomene's mother, Mary Petite, had a French father and Maliseet mother.[17] It is said that Mary and her sister, who also married a Maliseet, populated Tobique almost singlehandedly, each having more than a dozen children. It is also said that Mary was a teacher and, among other things, taught the Maliseets at Tobique to use forks, knives, and spoons.[18]

Horace succeeded in convincing Frank and Mary Saulis that he was a good match for their daughter. Two months later, on February 14 1903, the young couple married.[19] Wabanaki wedding celebrations of the day inevitably included a dance, usually held in the tribal hall. The groom paid for the food, band, and dance leader. Traditionally, a series of special round dances comprised the marriage rite. But by 1903, marriage rituals had long been dictated by a priest, and these dances were simply part of a marriage celebration that followed a formal religious ceremony. People came dressed in their best, the older folks in tribal garb. A dance leader orchestrated the step-and-shuffle dances, shaking a cowhorn rattle and singing refrains. At the end of each dance he shouted *matamal e yehe!*, which symbolized marriage, and everyone echoed the cry.[20]

When Horace married Philomene, he got more than a beautiful young woman who had learned good table etiquette from

Molly's maternal grandfather, Frank Saulis, circa 1900.

her mother. His wife had only a third grade education, but she possessed a sharp mind. She read avidly, if not academically. The daily paper, detective stories, and western and romance novels were her favorites. She spoke Penobscot, Passamaquoddy-Maliseet, English, and French.[21] More significantly, she was the seventh daughter of a seventh daughter, and tradition held that this placement gave her the great healing and psychic abilities she exhibited from the time she was little. When she was a child, her mother frequently pulled her from play and took her to the bedside of an ill person. Philomene used psychic insights and the laying on of hands in her healings, and gradually began collecting wild herbs and preparing various concoctions to heal a range of ailments from stiff joints and headaches, to peptitus and gall stones. In her thirties and forties she read palms, cards, and tea leaves. Sometimes her readings were so accurate that she panicked, fearing the devil was working through her. Eventually she expressed her fears to the priest, who told her to give thanks to God for the wonderful gifts He had bestowed upon her. She could not convince herself of this, however, and stopped doing readings altogether.[22]

During her life on Indian Island, Philomene gained a reputation not only for healing, but for her industrious nature, basketry skills, and culinary know-how—and for her remarkable store of local gossip. Everyone knew that sweet-grass braiding parties hosted by Philomene Nelson offered lots of good gab and some of the best food on the island—from muskrat stew and venison mincemeat pies, to doughnuts and chokecherry wine.[23]

In the twenty-one years following Molly's birth, Philomene bore seven other children in the tiny riverside house that seemed to shrink with each new arrival. The first of these, destined to be Molly's most faithful sibling, was Winifred Gertrude.[24] She arrived at the stroke of midnight on a warm summer night in 1905, the year tribal members elected Horace's father as the Penobscot representative to the Maine State Legislature.[25] Later nicknamed *Muji Apid* ("bad woman") by her maternal grandmother, Winifred presented quite a contrast to her older sister. While Molly's personality and physical features were delicately vivacious, Apid's were big and bold. Apid remembers, "Molly was petite, but I was husky—ten pounds at birth. Had the tit till age two . . . and grew to be the biggest of the girls—nearly five feet, eight inches. Even as a kid, when my little grandmother came from Canada, I used to pick her up and kiss her in the air and her feet would be danglin' and kickin'; she was just five feet tall and ninety-five pounds."[26]

The responsibilities shouldered by Molly and Apid had nothing to do with size; simply because they were the oldest, it fell

Molly's mother, Philomene, in studio pose, circa 1914.

to both of them to care for a half-dozen brothers and sisters. The siblings included "Blun" (Francis Xavier, born 1907), "Darly" (Mildred Philomena, 1910), "Johnny" (John Weston, 1914), "Noon" (Eunice Josephine, 1915), "Naman" ("little son"— Peter Samuel, 1921), and "Bunty" (Horace Aloyisius Jr., 1924). In Apid's words, "My mother produced kids like a doughnut machine and Molly and I had to take care of them." Molly was so central to young Eunice's upbringing that from the time Eunice could speak she called Molly "Mama." She referred to Philomene as "Mother."[27]

Molly and Apid did more than look after their siblings. They picked berries for jam, sold their mother's baked goods door to door, braided yard upon yard of sweet-grass for baskets, and as soon as they were big enough to stand at the sink on a box, washed dishes, laundered enormous quantities of clothing, and did a host of other household chores. Beginning at age six, they attended the island school, which Apid remembers with little fondness: "When the nuns taught you they *taught* you. They made you stay after school and work. They made us pray three times a day, and religion was shoved down my throat till it made me sick." Philomene reinforced the rigors of their religious training: "Mama made us go to confession every Saturday even if we hadn't sinned. And Sunday we had to go to service in the morning, then to benediction in the afternoon."[28]

From the time they were eleven, Philomene "rented out" her oldest daughters. As Apid tells it, she and Molly were "slaves." In the summers they cared for other people's children. They got room and board, and Philomene got their payment—which went toward shoes and winter clothes for all the children. During the rest of the year, they scrubbed floors—up to twelve a weekend, thirty cents a job. Sometimes Philomene allowed them to keep a bit of their earnings to pay their way into vaudeville shows or nickel movie houses; she kept the balance.[29]

Philomene made equal demands upon herself. Dealing with the physical ailments of her own children and other people on the island took much of her time. Among others, she suc-

Molly and Apid in a parade on Corpus Christi day on Indian Island, circa 1911. This Catholic Eucharist festival was an annual event on the reservation.

cessfully treated Apid for peptitus and Johnny for a severe
burn. On several occasions she doctored her oldest daughter
for tuberculosis, a disease that would haunt Molly throughout
her life.[30] She helped support her burgeoning brood by taking
in laundry, cleaning houses, and making doughnuts and other
baked goods to sell. Her baskets provided a mainstay in the
family economy. In fact, throughout Molly's childhood, basketry was central to the economic well-being of most Indian
Island families. It was a rare household that was not in some
way occupied with the production or sale of woodsplint and
braided grass baskets. All winter long, the sweet earthy scents
of grass and wood filled homes as families prepared piles of
goods to sell to Maine's summer tourists. Generally, the men,
including Horace, gathered the sweet grass, and found, felled,
and prepared the brown ash trees used for splints. The women
fashioned the baskets. And both men and women sold the work,
often spending the summer months camping in tents beside
popular tourist haunts, including Camden, Searsport, Bar
Harbor, Poland Spring, and Kennebunkport. "We had a regular
tent and that's what we lived in," recalled one of Molly's
childhood friends. "We'd go to the lumber company and buy a
[floor]board so that we wouldn't be on the ground." Indian
basketmakers camped rent free, usually returning to the same
site year after year. Many made enough cash to get by throughout the winter.[31] Some families manufactured additional items
to market, such as snowshoes, bows and arrows, birchbark toy
canoes, carved war clubs, beaded leather moccasins, and
rustic furniture. Beyond crafts, Penobscots in the early 1900s
supported themselves by guiding tourists and sportsmen through
Maine's forests and waterways and by working as day laborers,
lumberjacks, riverdrivers, or as boatbuilders at Old Town
Canoe Company.[32]

Horace's work life was erratic at best. Not that he was lazy —
he chopped and split all the wood needed for cooking and
heating, he put his green thumb to use in the family garden, he
provided Philomene with basket supplies, ventured to metropolitan centers to sell baskets and other Indian crafts, and he

insulated the house every winter with a three-foot bank of dirt, then shoveled the heap away each spring. But, unlike Philomene, he was never driven by the dollar, especially if it interfered with his freedom. Also in contrast to Philomene, he liked spending time with his children—going fishing with them, taking them outside at night to teach them about the stars, encouraging them in their music.[33] Plus he liked time on his own to sit in his rocker and read or to head upriver in his canoe. He held a range of jobs in his lifetime, most of which paid modestly, lasted rather briefly, and did not tap into his education: ferry master, surveyor, musician with the Penobscot Indian Band, laborer for the Bangor and Aroostook Railroad, boatbuilder at Old Town Canoe, nightguard for Bruce and Lucy Poolaw's tourist tepee that was full of baskets and other wares. Two positions did challenge his intellectual and political finesse: during 1921 and 1922, he served as Penobscot representative to the Maine State Legislature (a position that paid $120 a year), and in 1939 the tribe elected him to a two-year term as governor of the Penobscot Nation.[34]

Like most Penobscot men of the day, Horace trapped, fished, and occasionally hunted "for the pot." And, unlike most, he kept a vegetable garden, whose harvest Philomene canned or otherwise stored.[35] The Nelson household offered no luxury and faced some painfully lean years, but the larder was usually pretty well-stocked. Apid recalls, "Mama had a lock on the walk-in closet where there were shelves of jam, twenty-gallon crocks full of pickles—and cookies. She made cookies twice a week and doled them out like dollar bills. She made doughnuts twice a week and doled them out too. I think my father had the key to that closet copied and every time my mother went to town he'd go in there and steal cookies and doughnuts and he'd stash 'em." Most families had a cold room underneath the house where they stored raw vegetables and other perishables.[36] Throughout Molly's childhood, each family on the island received government rations once a year; the main items were a half-barrel of molasses and a half-barrel of salt pork.[37]

Molly's father, Horace Nelson, as a young man in his Old Town canoe on the Penobscot River, circa 1910.

As Apid remembers it, supper at the Nelson's tended to be a tasty, if strict, affair. "Mama separated the boys and the girls on opposite sides of the table. She was at one end and my father at the other. He was served first. Mama had a big switch and if you [started on] your food before everyone had some, you got it. She wouldn't let us snack, so you stuffed your gut at the table."³⁸ The meal began with a prayer, such as this favorite of Philomene: "I thank God for the bread I have today to share with other people, and pray that tomorrow I'll have another piece to share with others."³⁹ This was no empty chant. As in other households on the island, generosity was the rule, and there was always room for extra people at the table. When one family went through a hard time, the community would have a "pound party" for them, descending on the household with canned goods or some flour, salt, or potatoes. These were not "potluck" dinners, for the guests did not eat the food they brought. Everyone just had a good visit and then left the goods on the table. Each gave what they could afford, and nobody had to say thank-you because next week it might be their turn to do the giving. Indian Island was a place where people took turns being down-and-out, and the only insurance policy they had was one another.⁴⁰

Life on the island was relatively simple in those days. There was no road, and there were no carriages or other vehicles on this mile-long strip of land, shaped like an arrowhead. Just a web of footpaths winding through the trees. One main trail looped around the island's entire perimeter. Another, nearly road-size in width, went from the boat landing, across the broad lawn surrounding the Catholic church, rectory and nunnery, and then fanned out into pathways linking several dozen homes that dotted the island's southern end. Other pathways sliced through the forested, little-inhabited land northward.⁴¹

Just about everyone bathed in the river when weather allowed, and in a big tub in the kitchen when it did not. For most, bathing was an infrequent event. Horace, who had almost no body hair except on top of his head, washed as often as he shaved—every four or six months. Philomene bathed more often—for Christmas, Easter, trips, doctor's visits, and other special occasions.⁴²

Since the island did not have a store, folks crossed the river
to the mainland if they wanted to shop or browse, or check for
mail at the post office, or go to school, a movie, a job. In the
winter, everyone walked across the river's frozen back on the
"sawdust trail." In other seasons, they reached the mainland by
private boat (most families had a canoe or rowboat), or on the
public ferry—a fourteen-passenger bateau that cost two cents
each direction. Anyone who missed the last ferry or had their
canoe snatched from behind the bushes, had to spend the night
on the mainland, swim home (a dangerous undertaking, given
the current), or stand at the shore and yell, hoping some kind
soul would paddle over and retrieve them.[43]

In pleasant weather, the lawn between the ferry landing and
the church hosted an ever-changing cast of loungers, relaxing
and chatting after a trip to town. Some brought their rocking
chairs down to the boat landing, and sat there talking and
making baskets, hoping to sell them to any tourists who
ventured across on the ferry. Philomene, with her house situated near the landing, had a prime spot for selling her work.[44]

Because basketmaking was central to economic survival on
Indian Island, the task was woven into the social fabric of the
community. During winter months in particular, women got
together for sweet-grass braiding parties, sometimes producing one hundred yards apiece in an afternoon or evening. One
night the party would be at Philomene's, the next night at
someone else's, until each person's supply of sweet grass was
ready to be woven into baskets. Hostesses usually provided
fruits, candies, or pastries, and it was common to have a little
musical entertainment—a song, a dance.[45]

Sunday afternoons, after the supper dishes were washed,
women often got together to play canasta, gin rummy, or some
other card game. Philomene's parlor was a favorite gathering
place. Here she dished up her homemade pies and chokecherry
wine, while ladies dealt their decks and lit their corncob pipes
filled with plug tobacco. Philomene, who usually kept her pipe
tucked in the pocket of her bib apron, made a point of smoking
only among family members and close friends. If someone less

familiar showed up while she was smoking, she panicked and hastily stuffed the glowing pipe behind a cushion, in her pocket, or in some other handy place. Near pyrotechnic catastrophes were not uncommon.[46] Men had their own get-togethers, when they played poker or checkers. And many, like Horace, found their pleasure in "going about"—heading out in a canoe, solo or with a friend, prepared to hunt, fish, cut wood, gather basket materials, or just gab, depending on mood and opportunity.[47]

When adults socialized inside, children were usually sent outside to play. To those with imagination, entertainment possibilities were multifarious: swimming, fishing, boat races, tree climbing, hide-and-seek in the woods. In the winter there was snowshoeing or iceskating. Apid recalls, "We each got a pair of skates one Christmas. One day I fell down and knocked myself out on the ice. Molly found me. I was stiffening out like a board so she went for my father. I was small enough that he could pick me up, carry me to a snow bank, and he rubbed snow all over me to knock the frostbite out. Father was kinda tenderhearted. Compared to my mother he was a softie."[48]

Although Molly had Apid and other age-mates to play with, when she was free from household duties, she often went off on her own—to look for books in the old jailhouse that had been converted into a library of sorts, to fish, explore the shoreline, hike through the woods, or find some tribal elder to talk to. Older people and the tales they carried in their graying heads held special appeal for her. She sat beside them for hours on end, listening and committing to memory the legends they told her. Their stories supplied her with a cultural-historical rootedness that she would carry with her for a lifetime. As an adult, she typed up the legends collected during her childhood, and wrote an introduction to accompany them. She described two storytellers in particular:

> There was old Ach-zal-leek, who spoke little English. I made a bargain with her to chop some kindling and fire wood for her kitchen stove if she told me a story. Thus I began to earn my stories. And my curiosity grew, even though my mother taught

Studio portrait of Molly and her younger sister
Apid in their Easter outfits, sewn by Philomene,
circa 1914.

me that little girls should not be curious or question the wisdom
of the old people. . . . My favorite storyteller was an old man,
Hemlock Joe. . . . He was a hopeless invalid and his greatest joys
were woodcarving and storytelling. Not only was he the greatest
storyteller I have heard, but he was the greatest natural actor I
have seen. When he told a story, he made believe he was the hero.
And as he talked in his native tongue he imitated birds, animals
and legendary Indian characters. He would puff out his wrinkled
bronzed cheeks when he became *Woch-ow-sen,* the wind-blower.

He would blow and whistle like the winds through the tall pines that protected his little one-room shack on the banks of the Penobscot.[49]

Even more than stories, Molly had a passion for music and dance—and there was plenty of both on Indian Island. Horace periodically played in the Penobscot Indian Band, which performed for special occasions on and off the island, and gave a weekly, mostly classical, concert in the gazebo on the tribal common near the church.[50] From the time his children were young, Horace encouraged their musical pursuits. Molly, like many Penobscot children, studied piano and voice with the Sisters of Mercy. Most youngsters had their first dance lessons when observing adults and teens at the many dance events on the island: weddings, holidays, minstrel shows, church fundraisers, and tribal ceremonial events, such as the inauguration of a new governor. The community's dance repertoire ranged from traditional Indian to classical and contemporary western dances. A journalist writing for a local newspaper about this time noted, "The young and old alike [on Indian Island] are always ready to get up dancing parties, which average two a week." He went on to describe a Penobscot wedding dance he attended. Like most dances, it began with traditional steps tempoed by chants and the shake of "a curiously carved bull's horn half-filled with shot." For the snake dance, traditionally used to "try the strength of the braves . . . some 20 or 30 men locked arms . . . and swung round and round increasing the speed every turn until the strain on the arms and shoulders was something tremendous. Twice the writer's arms straightened out helplessly, and he would have been disgraced by breaking the line had not the Indians on each side grasped his wrists with almost breaking force." Next, the writer continued, came:

> yankee dances, for the Penobscots like all kinds. With an Indian orchestra of piano, cornet and violin and the air resounding with happy laughter, the scene was one of charming enjoyment, for the Indians inherit a love for dancing. Chubby little children with ruddy faces were playing hide and seek around the piano legs,

and some were trying to dance together like the older ones, [but] nearly every time degenerated into a wrestling match. The girls are graceful dancers and especially enjoy a slow glide waltz.[51]

Another article of the era described the dance held to celebrate the inauguration of Penobscot Governor Joseph Francis, who "delivered an [hour-and-a-half] address that would have been considered creditable in any of our state assemblies." The dance followed the oath of office. For more than an hour, Big Thunder,

> one of the oldest men on the island. . . . dressed in the ancient costume of the tribe, his face striped with black paint and red, his head covered with a mass of iron-gray hair on which rested a head-dress of eagle plumes . . . led a company of men in the shot-horn dance and the snake dance to weird chants sung by the dancers. When the men tired of their fun, a quadrille was formed, followed by a contra dance and waltz. Music was supplied by piano, violin, and cornet, played by members of the tribe.[52]

Molly imbibed these many rhythms. Futhermore, at age nine she struck a deal with a Bangor dance instructor named Miss Rosanna Odiorne to do housework in exchange for ballet lessons. Every week she traveled the twelve miles between Old Town and Bangor by trolley to work on her hands and knees and then dance on her toes.[53]

During the summers of Molly's childhood, which brought tourists galore to Maine, a host of performance opportunities arose for Penobscots and other Indians, including children. One of Molly's contemporaries recalls that when he was a youngster, "Tourists used to come across to the island on the bateau. We'd be waiting for them, and we'd start dancing as soon as they got close. We'd get candy and small change."[54] Children who went with their parents to sell baskets near summer resorts also danced for tourists. A childhood friend of Molly's remembered: "Indian kids danced for the people [staying at the big hotels]. They'd give us money [usually a nickel]. They never threw money at us. They gave it to us in our hands. We never asked 'em but they gave it to us."[55] Summer camp directors hired Indians to teach Indian lore,

The Penobscot Band, circa 1910. Molly's father, Horace is in the first row, third from the right. He played coronet and French horn. Note that some of the men are wearing wigs and/or war paint. (Courtesy of Salt Documentary Archive, Portland, Maine.)

dances, music, and crafts. Road shows and circuses passing through town eagerly signed on "Indian numbers." Filmmakers, looking for "authentic" Indian extras for romanticized movie tales, found their way to the island. And the Penobscots, finding that showmanship helped in selling crafts, orchestrated Indian pageants to attract buyers. Indeed, summer had become the season of road shows and ballyhoo, and young Molliedell Nelson soon found herself caught up in the hoopla.

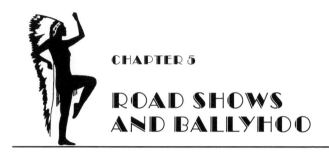

CHAPTER 5

ROAD SHOWS
AND BALLYHOO

*Played at the Scenic, a small beach theatre at Oak-
land Beach, Rhode Island, July 3–4. . . . Poor crowd.
. . . Rode around. Had to ballyhoo in my costume. So
tiresome I could leave the company. They're making
a regular little monkey out of me.*

—*Molly (Boston, 1922)*[1]

Throughout Molly's childhood, show business meant primarily
circuses, wild west shows, and, especially, vaudeville—from
the exclusive and expensive big-time productions of Keith-
Albee, to the widely popular and affordable small-time performances of the Shuberts, Marcus Loew, and William Morris.
Farther down the line were the far-traveling tiny-time shows
run by shoestring producers who organized one-night stands
in backwater towns where curtains were hung with safety pins.
A 1910 count showed the United States "knee-deep in two
thousand small-time hinterland theaters" that catered to those
who were "starved for the sight of anything that didn't squeal,
moo, or cluck." Whether big or small, vaude shows were wildly
successful. So much so that average citizens took in a show two
or three times a week—more often than they bathed.[2]

Indian Islanders were no less enchanted by such entertainment than were mainstream Americans. Bangor got the big
shows; Old Town the small ones. And when there were no
professionals in town, amateurs pulled something together.
The island put on its own share of in-house revues and musical
events whenever anyone could think up an excuse to do so: for

Saint Patrick's Day, May Day, Corpus Christi, weddings, and fundraisers for the church. Plus they produced pageants to muster up sales for baskets and other wares. There were many opportunities for Indian youngsters to perform, and Molly had her first solo at age six—an Irish jig at the Island's annual Saint Patrick's show.[3] As a young teenager she first experienced being paid to perform, beyond getting nickels from tourists for impromptu dances. Accompanied by her cousin Nelson Ranco at Amateur Night in a Bangor theater, she sang a song and won ten dollars—a hardy sum in those days.[4]

Molly and her peers also had an opportunity to perform academically. But this came at a cost: to receive an education beyond the sixth grade, they had to attend school in Old Town where discrimination against Indian students could discourage even the most determined learner. One of Molly's childhood friends described the experience of going to school in town as a "sore spot" in the memory of her youth: "Those people were hostile to us. . . . There was this little girl that used to chase me from the school to the ferryboat. She called me names and said that I should go over to my own reservation, that I was no good and would never be anything. . . . I just went there one year. I couldn't take it no more. I quit [after grade six]. A lot of the girls quit at almost the same time. The boys quit too."[5]

Molly stuck it out and graduated from Old Town Junior High in 1917 at age thirteen. Books were her treasures, and she vacillated between dreams of becoming a writer and of a life on stage, if not screen. By that time movies had infiltrated theaters and were often presented after a vaudeville show's cavalcade of minstrels, dancers, acrobats, and leaping dogs.[6] By the 1920s, many films were being made as well as shown in Maine by companies such as North Woods Films, the Edison Company, Pine Tree Pictures, Holman Day, and Dirigo Pictures.[7] A Penobscot man born in 1913 recalls

When we were kids, there were movie people here from all over the place. I was in three pictures altogether. . . . [About 1919,

Indian Island girls and women dressed for pageant, circa 1917—before the diffusion of Plains-style pan Indian costumery and culture spawned by the motion picture industry. The peeked cap of the elderly woman in the front row is traditional among Wabanaki peoples, dating back to the seventeenth century. Back row: Madas Glossian, Annie Andrews, Mamie Joseph, Ardell Nicholas, Mary Jane Mitchell and her son Robert. Middle row: Bertha Ranco, Myra Andrews, Elizabeth Andrews, Molly's sister Apid, Molly's mother Philomene. Front row: Frances Joseph, Barbara Thomas, Elizabeth Francis, Harriet Ketchum, Bertha Paul. (Courtesy of the Maine State Museum, Augusta.)

Molly's then five-year-old brother] John Nelson and I went way down to Lewiston, Maine [to be in a movie]. Us two kids and about a dozen grownups. They made us dance Indian. Danced hard as we could dance. . . . They paid us kids five dollars apiece, and drove us down there by taxi, and took us to dinner. Another time they took a big skow we had, built it into a pilgrimlike sailboat with a cardboard prow—something European settlers would come in. Then they put us in canoes, all painted up like we was attacking them. We was in blankets with bows and arrows.[8]

Although Molly registered for high school in September of 1917, she did not attend until 1920.[9] Instead, she headed south to Massachusetts, prodded by her mother to add to the family income by taking a job as a governess for a family in Swampscot. It is likely that Philomene met the family when selling baskets on the island or at one of Maine's summer resorts. Apid recalls that after some months, perhaps even a year, in Swampscot, Molly quit her job to join a small-time vaudeville outfit. She began staying in cheap boarding rooms, continued sending part of her earnings home to the family, and came home for visits whenever possible.[10]

In the fall of 1920, Molly returned to the Island to live. Two months before her seventeenth birthday, she finally began high school. That was the year the tribe elected her father to his two-year term as Penobscot representative to the Maine State Legislature in Augusta. This was the sole government representation available to the Penobscots, for, although 1920 was the year American women got the vote, American Indians, be they male or female, had no vote. Molly, keenly interested in politics, went down to the capital city with her father on at least one occasion to watch some of the proceedings and meet his colleagues.[11] In school she fared well, especially in English, French, and music, despite ongoing struggles with discrimination, which included white students warning one another that if they were friendly with Indians they would no longer consider each other as friends.[12]

Molly lasted only two terms in high school before venturing to Boston to answer the call of the stage. Her father took her to

Molly in her early vaudeville days, circa 1918, when she was fourteen or fifteen.

the Old Town train station sometime in the fall of 1921,[13] and by the end of the year she was on the road as part of an Indian revue managed by a hard-driving white man named Milton Goodhue, who, in Molly's words, led her on a "tin can circuit of small dumps."[14] It is not clear how she landed the job. Possibly through her cousin John Ranco whose time with the group overlapped with hers. Or by knocking on the doors of agent offices, which dotted the city of Boston like so many pinecones on a forest floor. She may have answered one of many newspaper advertisements calling for performers. It is also possible that an agent or producer enticed her south after spotting her at the Indian Island pageant held that summer (where she and Apid, dressed in fringed dresses banded with ribbons, and crowned with beaded necklaces, headbands and feathers, won the canoe race and posed for postcards).[15]

However Molly got the job, she was not a pioneer, for an American Indian performing in road shows was hardly something new. In one sense the tradition began in 1493 when ten Taino Indians sailed from Haiti to Spain in Christopher Columbus's caravels. After arriving in Seville, they walked eight hundred miles with Columbus to Barcelona where they were presented with great pomp to King Ferdinand and Queen Isabella. But one of the earliest genuine public performances by Indians in Europe took place in 1528, eight years after Hernando Cortes defeated Aztec emperor Montezuma. That year, the emperor's son and several other Mexican *caciques* (lords) sailed with Cortes as political envoys to the court of Spanish emperor Charles V, then at Toledo. They traveled in the company of Indian entertainers, including a dozen Aztec jugglers and acrobats—as well as several wild animals and birds of beautiful plumage. Journeying to Toledo by way of Seville, the cavalcade delighted spectators en route, presenting "a spectacle such as had not been seen since the return of Columbus [and] the Indian chieftains."[16]

In the United States, the first public performances by American Indians were part of diplomatic exchanges. For instance, in 1710, delegates of the six Iroquois nations, along with the Mohegan and Scatacook Indians, came to Boston, where they were "kindly entertained." After a conference with the General Assembly, the Indians, in turn, offered entertainment, and "thousands of spectators were present to behold and hear their barbarous singing and dancing. . . ."[17] After the U.S. govern-

Molly and her sister Apid posing for a postcard after
winning a canoe race at the Penobscot Indian Pageant,
circa 1921.

ment headquarters relocated in Washington, D.C., in 1800,
Indian delegations visiting the capital city were often asked to
dance and sing. Such performances, usually held on White
House grounds, were festive, well-publicized affairs that drew
huge crowds. The first of these shows may have been in 1804,
when "a large concourse of ladies and gentlemen, including

President Jefferson and members of his cabinet, watched the Osages perform a series of war dances to the music of an Italian band."[18]
It was during the 1800s that American Indians turned to performing as a means of economic survival. In the course of that century, it became impossible for native peoples, beginning with the eastern tribes and moving westward, to retain and rely upon their traditional modes of subsistence. Confined to ever shrinking tracts of land with inadequate resources, confronted by an unstoppable wave of white settlers whose numbers climbed to twelve million by 1830 and thirty-one million by 1860, and confounded by the plummet of their own populations due to disease, warfare, and forced relocations, native survivors found themselves subject to the control of Indian agents and the impositions of a foreign economic system that had become dominant. In an irony seemingly lost on them, white Americans eagerly paid to see native people perform the very traditions that they were destroying. The message was clear: control American Indian traditions by confining them to the stage.

Two of the first documented "for profit" performances took place in 1827 when a company of Iroquois Indians put on shows in New York at the National Hotel and Peale's Museum. Their program, announced in the *Post*, included "the marriage dance . . . the manner in which they skulk and lay in ambush and the manner of scalping an enemy . . . ceremonies used on the return of victorious warriors, and . . . [the] grand war dance. . . . "[19]

In 1842, Phineas Taylor ("PT") Barnum opened his American Museum on Broadway in New York City and quickly won fame for extravagant advertisements and a huge range of exhibits, including: exotic animals; marionette shows; "freaks" such as General Tom Thumb and Siamese twins Chang and Eng; an American painters' gallery; models of Paris, Jerusalem, and other famed cities. American Indians were also exhibited as public curiosities, fully regaled and re-enacting traditional ceremonies. For instance, in 1863, a group of fifteen

Kiowa, Cheyenne, Arapaho, and Comanche Indians performed for a fee of "good food and many gifts." The museum's doors were open from dawn until 10:00 P.M., and visitors could have a good time all day for just twenty-five cents.[20] In 1871, after the museum had drawn more than eighty million visitors and suffered two devastating fires, Barnum invested his fire insurance money in a circus, soon taking "The Greatest Show on Earth" on the road. Although it was the biggest circus to date, it was by no means the first. Circuses, part of American life since the early eighteenth century, had grown rapidly in number and size since the 1820s when improved transportation and the introduction of canvas tents enhanced their mobility.[21]

On the heels of Barnum came other big-time showmen like William F. Cody ("Buffalo Bill") who, in 1882, launched his *Wild West*—a stupendous show consisting of exhibitions of Indian and cowboy skills (foot racing, riding, lassoing, and sharp shooting) and dramatized portraits of life in the West (the Pony Express, Indian dances and ceremonies, Custer's Last Stand, and Indians hunting buffalo, burning a settler's cabin, and attacking the Deadwood mail coach). While the show glorified cowboys as true heroes of the west, it presented Indians as warring, if agile, savages.[22]

As tribes crumbled, Buffalo Bill and other producers stepped forward to claim the survivors for their shows. Even great Indian heroes, forced onto reservations by the ceaseless encroachments of white settlers, grabbed at road shows as a last straw for survival. So it was that one year after participating in the last great buffalo hunt, the famous Sioux chief Sitting Bull joined an 1884 show tour arranged by Colonel Alvaren Allen, who promoted him as "the slayer of General Custer." Treated poorly, Sitting Bull decided to quit the show. The next year, aged fifty-four, he signed on with Buffalo Bill, who offered him a decent contract: fifty dollars a week for four months, two week's advance pay, a $125 bonus, and the concession to sell photographs and autographs of himself.[23] In 1886 an Oglala Sioux holyman named Black Elk, then twenty-three years of age, began dancing in Buffalo Bill's Wild West. Years later, telling his life story to writer Richard Neihardt, he explained his decision to perform in Cody's show: "Some Wasichus [whites] [came] who wanted a band of Oglalas for a big show that the other Passhuka [Buffalo Bill] had. They told us that this show would go across the big water to strange lands, and I thought I ought to go, because I might learn some secret of the Wasichu that would help my people somehow."[24] Wabanaki tribespeople, including Penobscots, were among these nineteenth-century Indian performers. By 1820, they were marketing bits and pieces of their disintegrating cultures—peddling baskets, toy canoes, and other wares in far-flung coastal and river towns throughout the northeast. Within twenty years they were involved in traveling shows, often as a means of attracting buyers for their goods which by then included medicinal herbs.[25]

Molly's nineteenth-century Penobscot predecessors included Clara Neptune, who performed in primitive vaudeville shows midcentury, and Princess Watawaso (Lucy Nicola), who began charming high society folks from New York to Chicago at the turn of the century, singing Thurlow Lieurance's songs, which were based on the traditional melodies of various American Indian tribes.[26] But the earliest and most notorious of Penobscot entertainers was Frank Loring, known as "Chief Big Thunder." He was born in 1827, the youngest of eight children. When he was twelve, his mother died, and he and his sisters took up basketry to survive. They traveled about Maine, Pennsylvania, and New York hawking their wares. In New York City they hooked up with P. T. Barnum at the American Museum for eight months.

By 1848, twenty-one-year-old Loring had become a handsome, strapping young man, well over six feet tall. With an imagination equal to his size, he worked that year as an agent for a small touring theater or circus, putting together Indian shows. After hiring a young Micmac in Boston and escorting him by train to New York City, he went to Indian Island to check out several Indian actors who belonged to a company. He hired them, and purchased necessary costumes—plus a couple of young bears. The entourage traveled by train to Bangor, and then by steamboat to New York where the tour began. They performed *Pocahontas,* a play favored by the public for decades after its 1830 debut in New York. Loring portrayed a savage-looking Indian warrior in full regalia and painted face. He also played the role of Captain John Smith. The actors were paid well—two dollars a day, plus traveling expenses. In the following years, Loring continued to make his living as a showman, alternately as an actor, a producer, and an agent for other companies.

Eventually, Loring quit touring and settled down on Indian Island. But he remained a showman-in-residence until his dying day in 1906. Billing himself as "custodian of the tribe," he ran a little relic shop on the reservation. The birchbark sign out front read: "Big Thunder, Indian Relics and Indian Traditions Told."[27] He did just what the sign said: sold "relics" by making up tales to enhance their value.[28]

Molly, three years old when Loring died, is unique among the many American Indian performers who preceded her (and most who succeeded her), in part, because she recorded the pains and pleasures of her profession in diaries. She began these journals in 1917 when she was just thirteen, but her earliest surviving diary is from 1922. In it, she described life on the road with manager Goodhue and the other members of his small company, including "Blue Cloud" and "Chief." The troupe was based in Boston, a cultural, intellectual, industrial, and shipping center that lured the full scope of humanity—from highbrows and patricians, to sailors and laborers. Dubbed "The Hub of the Universe" by Oliver Wendell Holmes in the late nineteenth century, this city of contrasts had long been a center for Wabanaki craftspeople and performers who found that in their entrepreneurial efforts, be they crafts or shows, they could rely on the insatiable appetites of Bostonians. Even Wabanaki youngsters had fared well here, such as the Micmac boys who worked the Boston Common with Dr. Tomah's band in the mid-1800s; while Tomah sold his medicines and the other

adults hawked baskets and quill boxes, the boys earned an
"honest penny" from spectators by shooting at coins with their
bows and arrows.[29]

Molly, now eighteen, lived in a rooming house on Concord
Square, near the once-fashionable Columbus Avenue.[30] She
took her meals at Mr. and Mrs. Goodhue's or "ate a tin can
dinner" in her room. The troupe, performing with variously
skilled local pianists picked up upon arrival in each new town,
did several shows a day at schools, town halls, theaters, and
music halls in Boston and dozens of satellite towns. Sometimes
they traveled longer distances, spending several days in Rhode
Island or southern Maine. Performing on a great variety of
stages (including one only "as large as a bed"[31]), they danced
and sang to popular "Indian" songs of the day. Much of the
music was written by contemporary American composers
Thurlow Lieurance and Charles Cadman, who freely adopted
traditional Indian melodies as the bases for their work.[32]

Goodhue was rarely generous, and sometimes he was down-
right abusive. Beyond giving three or four performances a day,
Molly had to participate in daily exercise sessions and rehearsals. Goodhue sent her "ballyhooing"[33] up and down the streets
in full costume to drum up customers and regularly assigned
her to work in the ticket window before show time. She was
obliged to pay for, make, and clean her own costumes. This was
not unusual for actors in vaudeville productions, particularly
small-time. In fact, some had to bring their own scenery, for
most producers guaranteed no more than a theater, box office,
orchestra, stagehands, and ushers.[34] In addition to show work,
Molly frequently did laundry for the Goodhues and Mrs. Morris
to earn extra money to send to her family back home.

Often she felt melancholy, missing her family and yearning
for the natural world offered in the Island woods. Some days
she would escape the city's bustle by going to the Boston Public
Gardens to watch birds and "study the types of people that
frequent the inviting cool shade." Very often she made notes in
her diary such as: "Getting restless, lonesome for home"; "Sat
on front steps, a favorite past-time for city folk. But I belong in

the country"; or "How I long to be home for even a few days to see the dear faces of my loved ones."[35]

Despite the hardships, not every moment was arduous. When bookings were low or shows were cancelled because only a handful of people appeared in the audience, Molly found herself with free time. She used much of it on her own, writing poetry and stories or going to the library to replenish her supply of reading material. But she also socialized with her coactors and a string of admiring suitors who waited for her after her performances. Card playing, dining out, and going to the movies were her usual entertainments. Almost always, after seeing a film, she critically reviewed it in her diary. One of her favorite breaks while working for Goodhue came during the weeks the Sells Floto Circus performed in Boston. At every opportunity, Molly went to the circus grounds where she made friends with Sioux Indian performers Enemy-in-the-Night, Ghost Bear, and their spouses. They taught her how to spin a rope, invited her to watch the matinee and the wild west shows, and shared their "very good meals" with her in the circus tent. She, in turn, introduced them to the agent at her booking office, and took them "shopping for beads and sombreros" downtown, where they "attracted much attention for they were in regalia."[36]

Her other great pastime was letter writing. Regularly she penned missives home, enclosing money (typically five dollars) whenever possible. She cherished mail from her family and established a lifelong practice of noting its arrival in her diary. While her mother's letters were often demanding, pressing her to be frugal, work hard, and not forget her siblings, her father's were gentle and supportive. Early in 1922 he wrote to her in response to a letter and a pair of shoes she had sent to him: "Dear Daughter: . . . Did you receive the blue dress, of latest my favorite color, and the $10.00 cash? Also, fine [beaded Indian necklace], which I bought from Sockus Nelson for you. I have pawned my canoe to Ira Ballard and will have to redeem it before April 1922." Horace closed this letter by noting his appreciation for the shoes Molly had sent to him and reminding her, "I remember you in my prairs and pray for you to enjoy the blessing of good health and success, also to protect you through the world safely to a place of happiness now and here after."[37] While letters from home boosted Molly's morale, it was primarily her unwavering love for dance that sustained her during difficult times. She was a determined and self-critical performer, who regularly "reviewed" her work in her diaries as "stinking," "poor," "fair," or "good." Often she noted that her performance was "well received," or that the audience gave a "wonderful applause" and "demanded an encore." But not once would she rate herself as excellent—even in later years when well-known critics raved. Audiences during her early vaudeville years were not always gracious, and Molly sometimes recoiled when hecklers took a jab at her performance or at the fact that she was an Indian. "Cried after performance," she wrote one night. "Why? Heard a cutting remark." Other times she fought back: "A front row couple made fun of us. I flirted with the fellow and the girl became silent." In another instance, apparently after a school performance, she challenged insults by writing a "criticism on a school problem and racial feeling to the Boston Telegram."[38]

By the end of the summer of 1922, bookings had petered out, and Molly noted "I'm getting tired of Mrs. Goodhue. Too sarcastic for me. And Milton [Goodhue], he's a frump . . . a regular sissy." She quit, packed her trunk, and headed home by train. Soon thereafter she noted angrily, "They never paid me for my room." To a girl expected to help support her family, this was devastating, and Molly vowed, "As long as I live, I'll not forget that."[39] Sadly, stings like this were not uncommon in the business. *Variety* magazine disclosed that "many chiseling vaude managers were giving the road a black eye through [such] sharp practices" as paying their actors hastily in dimes, nickels and quarters just before train time, when there was not a minute to check totals. Tallying up aboard the train, performers often found themselves shortchanged.[40]

Molly's ticket home was paid for by a boyfriend named Johnny Gamage. En route to Old Town, she got off the train in

Damariscotta, where Johnny met her and took her to his family's farm in Bristol for a week-long visit. Although Molly was obviously very fond of him, affectionately nicknaming him "Jug," he was but one of several young men mentioned in her diary that year. All, except for José, a South American poet and political journalist, appear to have been white college boys. The only two whose names would continue to appear in the coming years were Jug and Roy, a Yale student whom she met when performing in New Haven.

Back home and back in high school, Molly wrestled with discrimination, rediscovering that being appreciated on stage did not translate into being accepted as a friend—especially in Old Town. She challenged the racism in her diary after attending a dance at the City Hall with Apid and their friend "Dul" (Dorothy Ranco), a trio Molly referred to as "the three muskateeresses":

> Saw Van who acted as though he were one of us. His actions were white and his gentlemanly treatment to us a rare thing, for seldom does a white chap, especially a student from University of Maine, treat an Indian girl as though she were lady. Little do they realize that the modern Indian maid has many advantages of studying and picking real gentlemen among the numerous boys with whom they come in contact, and that rarely does she choose a friend there across the river. The white boys and men [of Old Town] shun the . . . Indian girl like poison, each afraid to be seen even saying "How do you do," tipping their hats or treating an Indian girl as a "girl." All thoughts of good are thrust into the background and the ever remaining thought of not understanding their real natures, the thought of inferiority, of evil tendencies, are directed toward the Indian with little sympathy or understanding. What would the white man or woman realize when they know that it is an honored one who is invited to visit their lowly homes? That is why we admire and welcome as a friend the one who is not ashamed to be seen with us and who is bred in the real American democratic spirit of manhood to respect any lady, whether of the black, yellow, red or white race, of any class, creed or tongue—if she is a LADY or TRIES to be one.[41]

The theme of racism appeared again and again. When her friend Roy sent a letter inviting her for a visit, she wrote, "Is it possible Roy considers an Indian girl his friend to invite her to the sophomore spring dance at the College of Yale and to be his guest for two days? It is true, but how broadened and more distant the gulf of difference seems to me." To this, she added a comment typical of her writing self: "What a plot for a story . . . this potential romance across a cultural chasm would make."[42]

Despite such troubles, Molly was pleased to be home, telling her diary: "Papers are full of road show failures and bless my stars I'm lucky I kept off the road for the half season at least."[43] Later in the term she noted, "School work progressing nicely. Attitude of scholars improved toward Indian classmates."[44] Her days were filled with schoolwork and the usual heap of household duties, plus movies at the Strand or the Bijou, dances on the island, in town, and at the university, evening parlor visits on the island with card playing or singing, much writing and reading, and plenty of daydreaming about becoming a "delineator of life." One day she told her diary, "[I] made a bookshelf on the wall in our bedroom and packed my books there." Noting how "pleasing" this little shelf was, she mused, "What would the feeling be, were I to own a real book case [full of] books on philosophy, research, adventure, travel, scientific editions of animal and plant books, encyclopedia, old stories of great authors, medieval and ancient works, and novels of varied tragedies, comedies, and romance—a book room, like the one in my hero's room in [my] story of 'Snared Rabbits.'"[45]

Much time was also spent in rehearsals for several special spring events. Her repertoire for these differed greatly from the Indian fare she had performed while on the road with Goodhue. For the island's annual Saint Patrick's day "entertainments," open to the public, she taught ten little girls an Irish folk dance and brushed up on her "old song"—"When I dream of old Erin I'm Dreaming of Us." For Easter, she rehearsed *St. Leonard's Mass,* and stated triumphantly in her diary, "I'm to have a solo after all these years of being in the choir."[46] For the high school's spring physical training exhibition, Molly prepared a "Spanish number." She stayed home from school the day of that show to sew her costume. "Felt like a bundle of feathers," she confessed, for the audience included "the most prominent members of Old Town." As usual she critiqued her own performance: "Not up to my best, but received wonderful applause for repeat. Gave encore of 'drunken sailor' dance. Another applause for an encore, but just bowed and exited. . . . reminded me of my vaudeville days."[47]

The summer of 1923 presented Molly with a new performance outlet that tapped into her knowledge of Penobscot traditions. She was invited to be a special Indian counselor at Camp Overlook in Georgetown, Maine—an exclusive girls' camp catering to young ladies who attended private schools in the affluent outskirts of Boston.

"I think Molly was brought for publicity," says Dorothy Crocker Reed, a camper at Overlook that summer.[48] This was no doubt true, for having a "real Indian" at one's camp was a thing of prestige. Interest in Indian lore had grown steadily since the turn of the century with the establishment of various youth organizations that extolled activities modeled after real or putative American Indian themes: dancing, sign language, and crafts such as beadwork, basketry, and costume-making. These organizations included Boy Scouts of America, Boys' Clubs, Girl Scouts U.S.A., Camp Fire Girls, Young Men's Christian Association, and Young Men's Hebrew Association. Boy Scouts, incorporated by Congress in 1910, was the largest and most influential of these groups. Of its three cofounders, two placed particular focus on Indian lore: Daniel Carter Beard (an outdoorsman and author of children's books) and Ernest Thompson Seton (a naturalist and author). In 1911, Boy Scouts initiated the Indian Lore Merit Badge, which gave formal recognition of achievement in Indian lore activities. In 1915 Indian lore became even more popular with the founding of the Order of the Arrow, a national Scout camping fraternity.[49]

Molly was not the only Wabanaki recruited by the directors of Maine's burgeoning camps. Her second cousin, Roland Nelson, eleven years older than she, worked at Pinewood Camps, a swanky resort on Anasagunticook Lake in Canton. Pinewood claimed to "offer greater attraction to lovers of camping, canoeing, fishing, swimming, tennis, golf, mountain climbing, horseback riding and recreation than any other camp resort in the state of Maine." On top of this, it had Roland as its Indian-in-residence. Known as Needabeh (friend), he offered a host of services: guiding fishing and hunting parties; giving fly casting exhibitions; demonstrating basketry, wood carving, leatherwork, and beadwork; and performing and annotating Penobscot songs and dances. For promotional purposes the camp published Needabeh's "The Unwritten Indian: A brief historical sketch of the Penobscot Tribe of Maine." The publishers added to the booklet a brief biography of Roland and descriptions of his programs, which were available during the rest of the year for schools, colleges, churches, sport clubs, hotels, and women's clubs. It praised his style: "Never do his talks and demonstrations become 'just another lecture,' for at the very start questions are invited and the witty and cheerful answers all go to make an educational, unusual and most entertaining program." Special note was made of the fact that when it came to bow and arrow shooting, Needabeh demonstrated "both white man's and Indian's methods, [challenging] any golfer to a game of archery golf, using his bows and arrows while the golfer uses his clubs."[50]

Camp Overlook, where Molly worked, was newly built. It was beautifully situated on Kennebec Point on the property of Mrs. B. L. Rich of Fitchburg, Massachusetts, one of Maine's many well-to-do summer residents. The camp's well-heeled dining and recreation halls, bath houses, and five "sleeping apartments" (housing six girls and one counselor each) had electricity and were built from timber felled and milled on Mrs. Rich's sweeping property.[51] When Molly arrived midseason, Mrs. Rich presented her to the campers at breakfast. Dorothy Crocker Reed remembers that morning: "Molly was introduced as the 'Indian girl,' and was supposed to instill in us the traditional Indian sense of nature . . . but we weren't too into that. . . . We were more interested in boys and lipstick."[52] Still, Molly took the girls out to collect sweet grass and taught them basketweaving. She also taught them how to canoe and how to do so-called "Indian diving," which she told them was a very deep dive accomplished by getting down on one knee, placing your hands above your head, and then pitching over into the water. At night she told them stories, giving each girl an Indian name, which was simply the Penobscot pronunciation of their Christian names: Dul-i-ty for Dorothy, Zabette for Elizabeth, and so forth.[53]

In addition to Molly's teachings, the girls did much hiking, had swimming lessons, and took many motor boat trips—to Bath, Reid State Park, Five Islands, Popham Beach, and neighboring camps which "didn't compare with ours." Evenings were devoted to storytelling, singing, and musical offerings by the camp's mandolin or ukulele clubs. Each Sunday night, dressed as usual in middies and bloomers, everyone gathered around the open fireplace in the recreation hall to read the "Log"—a collection of poems and narratives written by the campers. The topics of these musings ranged from descriptions of different outings to reflections on nature. After the readings, the girls voted on the "best" offering, awarding the author with the camp insignia. In the second week in August, the local newspaper, *The Sentinel*, reported that "after much debate the girls chose the [poem] written by Mollydello [sic] Nelson, the Indian girl." Molly's poem, an atypical Log offering, was a tribute to President Harding, whose sudden death had just rocked the nation.[54]

While Molly was included in all camp activities and it was clear the girls were fond of her, she was not fully at ease. A scholarship camper named Elizabeth, who slept in a tent with Molly and the camp's kitchen girls, remembers, "There was some prejudice and I'm sure Molly was conscious of it."[55] As cocamper Dorothy recalls, Molly "seemed like an exotic and distant presence, and kind of carried herself apart from us. . . . She may have felt a real social gap because we all knew each other and were from similar walks in life."[56]

Perhaps to narrow the gap, Molly frequently remarked to the girls that she was an Indian princess and that her father was a chief—no doubt basing this self-ascribed status on the fact that her father had just finished his two-year term as the Penobscot's representative to the state legislature. Unfortunately, the title of princess did not save her from suspicion when theft became a problem at the camp. One night a canoe disappeared and it was rumored that Molly had arranged for her brother to steal it. Soon thereafter, "little pieces of jewelry—nothing of any value" were reported missing and later found in Molly's trunk. Dorothy says, "We didn't believe Molly took those things. It was almost like a frame-up." Whatever the case, the "Indian girl" was promptly dismissed.[57]

This humiliating departure cast a dark shadow over Molly's summer. But dawn sat on the horizon. In the next few years she would blossom in many ways, gaining academic footing at the University of Pennsylvania, and making the leap from low to high end entertainment. If people would accuse her of anything in the days to come, it would be of artistry and intellect.

CHAPTER 6

ANTHROPOLOGISTS AND RANCHERS

*I found myself broke, at the end of a breakdown
caused by too much work at the University of Pennsylvania. [To pay for school,] I sang, danced, told
bedtime stories, entertained at big Eastern colleges
with a company of Indian dancers. I even washed
dishes.*

—Molly (Indian Island, 1927)[1]

In September 1923, Molly avoided road shows and returned to
Old Town High School, while Apid began nurse training classes
in Boston, sponsored by a wealthy couple named the Ashcrofts.
Thanks to Molly's connections, Apid had been hired by Mr.
Ashcroft, a stockbroker, and his wife to care for their only
child. Joining a household staff that included a cook and a
maid, Apid had worked for the family from the summer of 1921
through the summer of 1922. She had spent the following year
at home, attending school in Old Town, but returned to Boston
in the autumn of 1923 for training at Baystate Hospital. She
was eighteen years old, and recalls, "The Ashcrofts got me into
(the program), bought my books and uniforms, and helped me
get a place to live. I lived near Fenway Park next door to some
Harvard boys. I remember climbing out the window and shin-
nying down our sheets to meet them."[2]

Life was considerably less exciting for Molly, who continued
to have responsibility for a slew of homely chores, plus the
caretaking of her younger siblings. On weekdays, she crossed
the river with her sixteen-year-old brother Blun, who was also

in high school and thirteen-year-old Darly, who was experiencing her first year of school off the island. John, nine, and Eunice, eight, remained island-bound and under the tutelage of nuns. Pete was only two. Bunty, the youngest of Philomene and Horace's eight children, was in the womb.

As a twenty-year-old who had traveled throughout New England performing, Molly must have been somewhat at odds with her eleventh-grade classmates. Apparently, high school was as uninspiring as household duties, for Molly's grades dropped and her attendance waned as autumn succumbed to winter. She missed a half-day in September, a half-week in October, a full week in November, and nearly three weeks in December. The demise may have been caused by illness or the arrival of inclement weather, which always made river-crossing difficult. But surely Molly's yearning for a wider world and the stage also played a part. After fall term 1923, she never returned to Old Town High.[3]

That winter she embarked on a tour of large Eastern colleges with a company of Indian dancers. While at the University of Pennsylvania, she renewed an acquaintance with Dr. Frank Speck, chairman of the anthropology department, who had done field work among the Penobscots intermittently from 1907 to 1918.[4]

Speck, a sturdy, straightforward, and unimposing man born in 1881, was well-known and liked by many Penobscots. Invariably dressed in an old brown suit, crumpled felt hat, and well-worn shoes, he was at a loss in formal settings, but fully at ease with the downhome life of most Indian Island inhabitants. He hunted and played music with them, spoke their language, ate their food, laughed at their jokes, and told them his.[5] In particular, he felt a deep connection with traditionalists.[6] "Frank Speck, he's a good one," recalls Molly's Penobscot contemporary Gilbert Ketchum, whose adopted father Jim Lewis guided Speck on an artifact search along the coast. "He liked the Indians, and he could talk Indian as much as I could."[7] Speck's primary Penobscot informant was Newell Lion, a wizened old man who, until he froze to death in the woods in 1918, provided the anthropologist with a wealth of knowledge concerning myths, religious beliefs, shamanism, social organization, and decorative art. Speck also relied on the information and cultural insights of a host of other tribal members: "hunters, guides, fishermen, shantymen, idlers, basketmakers, housewives, the majestic forest patriarchs and the struggling derelicts of the swift age of transition." These included Molly's favorite storyteller Joe Hemlock and several of her relatives. Speck made special mention of her second cousin Roland Nelson (Needabeh) as a "friend" he "leaned on heavily for aid and encouragement" especially during his return visit to the island in the summer of 1936 and in the years he spent writing *Penobscot Man*.[8]

Perhaps during his 1924 winter reunion with Molly, Speck sensed that she, like Needabeh, might be a valuable informant.[9] Surely, she impressed him. In the seven years since they had last crossed paths on the island, she had blossomed from a thirteen-year-old, thin-hipped tomboy into a vibrant young woman on the lip of discovering her own intellectual and artistic prowess. When Molly responded enthusiastically to Speck's suggestion that she pursue a university education, he made arrangements for her to attend Swarthmore Preparatory School, located in his neighborhood. She quit the road show and accepted an invitation to live temporarily with Speck and his wife and their three young offspring. In between classes and studying, she worked for her room and board by taking care of the children and helping out with chores.[10] The Specks' fine stone home, set in an elegant neighborhood within walking distance of the commuter station, looked like the quintessential establishment abode from the outside, but within it was something else altogether. Here one found a cross-cultural array of people and artifacts such as baskets, hanging gourds, headdresses, beaded pouches and moccasins, Eskimo drums, Iroquois masks, and Plains Indian shields. Frank Speck was truly unique among his neighbors; it was hardly acceptable, let alone typical, for a member of the white community to invite Indians to reside in his home.[11]

In September 1924, Molly started taking courses at the University of Pennsylvania. Her university transcript shows that she took anthropology and English classes on an auditing basis during fall and spring semesters of the 1924–25 academic year. Her status as auditor may indicate that she did not acquire the necessary high school/preparatory school degree from Swarthmore before beginning at the University of Pennsylvania. The "Special Association" section of her records notes, "Family list—no tuition," implying that Speck claimed her as a dependent, thereby providing her with a special status that freed her of entry requirements and course fees.[12] Speck's oldest daughter says her father frequently went out of his way for his Indian friends. "He did a lot of things like that—getting Indian students into the university, helping them with the financial end of it."[13]

Welcoming Indian informants into his academic world was one way Speck expressed his genuine appreciation for the fact that they opened their world to him. He seems to have been especially gifted in avoiding one of the pitfalls of anthropology: turning one's informants into objects. Those who knew him best noticed that academic appointments and university functions never took precedence over the visits of Indian friends or an invitation to an Indian council or ceremony.[14]

Speck's priorities must have been due, at least in part, to the depth of his interest in American Indian cultures and to the fact that in many ways he felt more akin to native peoples than to members of academic and mainstream society. After all, among his peers, who else would ask Indian friends to make him deerskin pouches to hold the severed umbilical cords of his children, believing this would "make them less nebby" (timid)?[15] This was a man firmly attached to the natural world and to people whose traditions confirmed that connection.

According to his daughter, "My father wanted to be an Indian so badly. He and my mother were interested in genealogy, but they could never find any Indian ancestry." Her brother concurs: "I think my father was dying to be Indian, [and] lived his life imagining he was one. He was romantic [about his work]."[16]

But, while Speck's emotions inspired his research, they did not rule it. In his words, his work was "delicately leavened with sentiment"—not with sentimentality.[17] None of Molly's diaries from her time at Swarthmore and University of Pennsylvania have survived, but the story of Gladys Tantaquidgeon, a Mohegan classmate of Molly's, hints at the nature of Speck's outreach to Molly and reveals something of her university experience.

By the time Gladys was born in 1899, her family was well-acquainted with Frank Speck, who had spent much of his childhood in their small Indian community on "Mohegan Hill" beside the Thames River north of New London, Connecticut. In the summers between Speck's eighth and fifteenth year, his parents had sent him to live there with an old family friend, Fidelia Fielding, who was Gladys's great aunt. They shipped him off hoping that the rural environment and dry climate of Connecticut's rolling hills would undo illnesses thought to be caused by the marshy surroundings of their urban home in Brooklyn.[18] Young Speck gained much more than good health living with Mrs. Fielding. Keenly loyal to her Indian heritage, she shared with him her love for and traditional knowledge of nature. She planted questions in him about the ambitions and achievements of western civilization. And, as one of the last speakers of the Mohegan-Pequot dialect, she taught him her language. Speck's son says his father's interest in anthropology was born in this childhood association with Mohegans: "Over several years, he wrote a booklet of their language which was fairly comprehensive for a grade school boy."[19] Years later, after studying anthropology at Columbia University with Franz Boas (often referred to as "the father of American anthropology"), Speck began a "systematic attempt to investigate the long-neglected bands occupying territory in northern New England and eastern Canada."[20] Among these groups were Molly's Penobscot peoples and Gladys' Mohegan peoples.

Gladys, like Molly, had a precocious fascination with Native American tradition. She recalls that Speck nurtured this interest from the time she was a young girl, telling her, "Hurry and grow up, Gladys. When you get to be a big girl and I get married, my wife and I will come and take you home with us." Speck was true to this promise and took Gladys on as protégée. Beginning in 1910 (when she was just eleven) she often traveled with him and his wife on research trips, and frequently visited them at their summer home at Cape Ann, Massachusetts— known as "the camp" or "the wigwam." There, surrounded by an array of American Indian artifacts, she met a bevy of artists, academics, and members of other Algonkian tribes.[21]

Although Gladys never attended high school, in 1919 Speck arranged for her to study anthropology at the University of Pennsylvania. Like Molly, Gladys never officially matriculated, even though she attended the university for six years. Her last year overlapped with Molly's 1924–25 year. The two young women spent much time together in Speck's office at the top of College Hall—researching, typing, filing, and getting office supplies in order for Speck and his department.[22] Their professor's vast, cluttered, and busy workroom certainly reflected his fascination with natural history and American Indian cultures. Described by one colleague as an "eighteenth-century naturalist's cabinet," this long, narrow room, with ceilings high as a chapel, was a hybrid office-library-museum. A dust trap of the first order. Shelves, overflowing with books, journals, and Indian baskets, flanked the walls floor-to-ceiling. Indian artifacts and paraphernalia filled every nook and cranny: spears, gourds, snowshoes, crossbows, deerskin shields, feather headdresses, painted wooden masks, portraits of Indian chiefs. A battered seminar table stood in the room's center, and at the far end sagged Speck's desk. Ancient typewriters crowned spare tables tucked here and there. And then there were the animals—snakes and lizards in glass terrariums, turtles on the loose, even an uncaged white fox. Day after day, an ever-changing cast of colleagues, students, friends, Indian delegations, and strangers gathered here to work, visit, or participate in seminars. Here, unscheduled discussions could last for hours, and spontaneous "recitals" of traditional Indian songs were not uncommon. Bringing a sack lunch was a good idea.[23]

Gladys recalls that she focused fully on academics, while "Molly would go off and perform and give talks." For Molly, art and academic pursuits were inextricably intertwined: her studies deepened the content of her short stories, dances, and songs, and stirred her to enhance her performances with explanatory lectures when possible. Beyond performing Indian songs and dances as a member of the university's Women's Glee Club and giving Indian lecture-dance-song recitals for schools and social organizations in the area, she sometimes did theater and club performances. Speck's son, eight years old when Molly entered his world in 1924, remembers, "She was in and out of our house for years and kept her old beat-up trunk [of costumes] in our basement. She danced on stage with her long hair. I wasn't old enough to go, but [even offstage] she was effusive, pleasantly explosive, theatrical. Her vivacious spirit made her look more beautiful than she was."[24]

It seems that Molly, like Gladys, lived on campus in the International House, at least during part of her time at the university. Surely the irony of Native Americans being relegated to housing for foreigners was not lost on these bright young women. Yet, the setting offered a platform for enriching cultural exchanges. Gladys recalls that "different groups [of international students] entertained from time to time there, and I think Molly did too."[25]

While some of Speck's ethnographic and theoretical contributions—particularly his work on hunting territories—have been criticized by latter day anthropologists,[26] views on his character and genuineness of purpose are invariably positive. According to Speck's professional acquaintance Frank Siebert, who has done linguistic research among the Penobscots since the 1930s, the steady stream of visitors to Speck's office included "scholars, students, Indians and a miscellaneous assortment of peripatetic personages [who] were always hospitably received. There was no element of snobbery in Speck's character and he never 'acted out' his professorial rank. He was always prepared to listen to anyone and help everybody who sought his assistance."[27] Another colleague notes that "Though

qualified in every respect . . . Speck did not covet academic
honors; rather he valued the good opinion of his Indian friends
equally with the esteem of his colleagues among academi-
cians."[28] Correspondence filed among Speck's papers at the
Philadelphia Philosophical Society includes letters from Indian informants, acquaintances, and friends that reveal the easy
and trusting relationships he had with them. Clearly Penobscots passing through Philadelphia felt comfortable stopping by for a visit. Molly's lifelong friend Dorothy Ranco noted
in a letter to Speck, "I want to thank you for the luncheon at the
university and the wonderful time we had there. To you it may
not seem anything but to us 'injuns' eats means everything."
She ended her letter with a playful comment, "I hope when I
see you again I can borrow at least a thousand dollars." In this
same missive, Dorothy discussed Speck's agreement to have a
Passamaquoddy dress (apparently part of the university museum's collection) returned to its owner, Princess Pretty Woman.
Particularly in the 1930s and 1940s, Speck, who had collected
many American Indian artifacts for the museum (a means of
funding fieldwork in his day), was busy giving them back and
supporting native cultural preservation efforts.[29]

Gladys, the wholehearted academic, ultimately returned to
her reservation in Connecticut to manage and expand the
Tantaquidgeon Indian Museum built by her father John and
younger brother Harold in the family's backyard in 1931.
Before her homecoming, she did fieldwork and writing about
medicine and folklore among various New England tribes,
spent two years as a Bureau of Indian Affairs (BIA) community
worker among the Yankton Sioux in South Dakota, and worked
as a BIA arts and crafts field specialist. This last job included
arranging traditional crafts exhibits and helping various tribes
develop the economic potential of their crafts while passing
skills onto their children.[30]

Meanwhile, Molly strove to hold together her marriage of art
and academics, while supporting herself and sending money
home to her family. It was not easy. According to Speck's son,
club and theater dancing were more a necessity than a choice

for Molly: "She was hungry and she needed to [perform to survive]. Those [Penobscot] people were *poor* . . . struggling for an existence, trying to do something, anything, to get by."[31] At the end of winter semester in 1925, Molly yearned for a break. She decided to join Apid who had signed on with the 101 Ranch, a famous wild west show launched by Joseph, Zackary, and George Miller in 1906. The Miller boys had named the show after the ranch they had inherited from their father, Colonel George Washington Miller, who had started the outfit in 1893 on ground staked out in the second great Oklahoma land rush.[32] By the time the colonel died in 1903, he and his sons had turned their spread into the largest diversified farm in the world. Zack oversaw livestock trading, George handled fiscal matters, and Joe, following in his father's footsteps, coordinated all other aspects of the farm, including a wide variety of agricultural experiments.

It was Joe who came up with the idea of a traveling show or round up, aiming to preserve ranch and frontier life while developing yet another way to turn a profit. The show, which echoed Buffalo Bill's Wild West, included calf roping, bulldog-ging, trick riding, and other rodeo stunts, plus Indian dances and mock Indian massacres. While on the road from April through October, this extravaganza thrilled spectators through-out the United States and Europe. During the rest of the year, thousands saw the show at the ranch where the brothers had built a twelve-thousand-seat arena, the biggest and finest in the Southwest. At the peak of its success, the ranch drew one hundred thousand visitors a year.[33]

World War I brought performances to a halt for several years. But early in 1924, the Millers and their agents began scouring the United States, Mexico, Cuba, and the Far East looking for new talent to expand and relaunch the show. Joe Miller, the driving force behind the production, scouted talent in the eastern United States—and there, met Apid.[34] As she recalls, "After more than a year of nurse training in Boston, I went home for Easter break [in 1924] and never went back to Boston because that's when I hooked up with the 101 Ranch. They

were down in Bangor for three or four days. I went up to the
boss and asked for a job. He said, 'Can you ride a horse?' I never
had, but I said, 'Sure, I can ride anything!' So he took me on.
Went out to Oklahoma, the home base of the ranch. I stayed
right there on the ranch with all the other showpeople and
ranch hands. The ranch was like a regular little town with its
own store and restaurant. I waitressed, and trained to do
hurdles, high jumps, and ride dancing horses."[35]
The show did not travel during Apid's first year. Joe Miller
used that time to gather up more performers, refine the program, and test it out on visitors who streamed to the ranch to
witness a rodeo or two. Meanwhile, all other farm operations
continued: tending twenty-five thousand head of longhorns;
operating a packing plant and tannery; raising thousands of
hogs and chickens; growing, harvesting, and processing several thousand acres of mixed crops; running one of the largest
dairy herds in the country; and conducting a host of agricultural experiments, from raising lettuce beds for poultry
fodder, to producing a range of hybrids such as drought-
resistant corn, frost-proof cabbage, quick-growing hogs, and
bramolas — crossbred buffalo and Brahma bull valued for dis-
ease-resistant meat.[36]
It was not unusual for ranch hands to spend a couple of weeks
driving and roping cattle, and then hop into the arena to do trick
riding for public display. Among the best-known 101 cowboys
who mastered roping and riding stunts on the range and re-cre-
ated them in the show arena were Bill Pickett, Tom Mix, and
Buck Jones. Pickett, part Choctaw, part African-American,
was promoted by the Millers as the "first bulldogger." Crowds
went wild when he galloped into the stadium on horseback,
raced beside a wild steer, leaped from his saddle, grabbed the
bull by the horns, dug his heels into the ground, and sank his
teeth into the animal's nose, causing it to roll over prostrate.
Mix and Jones made it big as movie stars in early westerns, including those produced by the 101 Ranch. Initially, the Ranch
collaborated with Bison Films, a subsidiary of the New York
Motion Picture Company. Founded in 1911, Bison-101 pro-

duced dozens of westerns under the directorship of the determined and rugged Thomas Ince, who standardized the mass-production method of making movies. The Bison-101 "set" consisted of eighteen thousand acres of vast, undeveloped land abutting the mountains of Santa Monica in southern California. Most of the cowboy, cowgirl, and Indian actors, plus prairie schooners, stagecoaches, tepees, horses, oxen, and bison, were supplied by the Miller Brothers' 101 Ranch Wild West. Later, after Universal claimed control over the New York Motion Picture Company, 101 began producing and filming its own Westerns on the Miller ranch, with Marshall Farnum as chief director.[37]

Scores of Indians besides Apid lived at the 101 Ranch near Bliss (now Marland), Oklahoma. The ranch's vast acreage, sliced by the winding Salt Fork River, sprawled across a swath of the Great Plains where Cheyenne, Arapaho, Comanche, Pawnee, Sac and Fox, Ponca, Otoe, and Osage Indians ranged. When the Millers leased (and later purchased) land from the Ponca and Otoe, they encouraged the Indians to stay on the land. Many, lacking alternative subsistence options, hired on as farm hands and/or showpeople.[38] The Millers recruited other Indian workers and performers from neighboring and far-off reservations where the ranch sold meat and other goods.

All told, Indians from more than a dozen different tribes lived on the ranch. Some, like Apid, settled down at the "headquarters" near the Miller's spacious, seventeen-room home (known as the "White House"). Headquarters included lodging and a mess hall for employees, a school, general store, cafe, filling station, garage, and blacksmith shop, plus the cannery, tannery, dairy barn, other barns, and corrals.[39] Most of the more traditional Indians chose to live in tepees or rough houses in a nearby "Indian village." Visitors frequently "toured" this village, where women could be found fashioning pottery, doing beadwork, or weaving blankets and baskets, while men carved bows and arrows, young boys practiced shooting headless arrows, and little girls made and played with buckskin dolls. Infants were often seen nestled in cradleboards slung on their mothers' backs or suspended from poles.[40]

Since Indians from the federal reservations were considered wards of the United States government, the Millers were supposed to make formal arrangements with the local Indian agents for the care of Indians moving to their ranch. This care was to include schooling for children.[41] Such arrangements were often not made—and were not required for off-reservation Indians or Indians such as Apid who hailed from state reserves. Like Buffalo Bill's Wild West, the Miller Brothers' 101 Ranch recruited famous Indians to enhance its crowd appeal. Among these were three warriors who had played conspicuous parts in Custer's defeat: Geronimo's cousin Charlie-Owns-the-Dog, the aging but fleet-footed Standing Cloud, and Long Bull, who made several trips to Washington, D.C., to negotiate claims for his people. Some venerable Indian leaders were too old to perform but were hired to walk in the opening parade and to serve as "good influences" among the Ranch's Indian community—such as Flat Iron, an Oglala hereditary chief considered one of the Sioux Nation's greatest orators. Known to have harangued warriors before they went into the Battle of Little Big Horn against Custer, he was employed by the Millers to serve as a peace-keeper.[42]

Indians were called upon to perform a variety of traditional ceremonies, rituals, and dances—including war dances that the government had for years tried unsuccessfully to discourage and keep in check. (Federal law prohibited Indian children from watching these dances in which their elders all-too-convincingly feigned acts of war.) In addition, they were often asked to re-create battles from a history still vividly remembered, scenes which Indian onlookers observed in grim spirit.[43] While rooted in historic fact, these reconstructed conflicts typically presented Indians in sheer cliché as brute savages. A typical 1912 review of a Bison-101 film reveals the implications of these theatrical battles:

> The Indian . . . remains one of the most interesting and pictur-
> esque elements in our national history . . . a restless, dominat-
> ing, ever-struggling human creature, principally engaged in works
> of destruction. . . . He was essentially a man of physical action,

using only that part of his brain which enabled him to be crafty in the hunt for food . . . mentally he was far below the Egyptian of 6000 years ago, but he was the physical superior of any man on earth except the strong armed European who cultivated brain along with brawn.[44]

Many American Indians, economically tied to reservations but feeling utterly bored and purposeless due to the dreadful lack of work opportunities there, resorted to wild west shows and films for a livelihood and a diversion from their plight. But some spoke out against these productions as forms of entertainment that exploited native peoples and their traditions by reducing them to show pieces for the amusement of whites. Among the protestors stood hereditary Sioux chief Chauncey Yellow Robe, a man who would one day become an important figure in Molly's life. At the 1913 conference of the Society of the American Indians, he had this to say about three decades of wild west shows:

> Is there anyone here that will tell me that the Wild West Show is a good thing for the Indian? If this Society is in favorable accord with such a practice, I am willing to form a new Wild West Show right here among the members of this Society to take the place of the celebrated Buffalo Bill. . . . The Indian is not to be censured for the Wild West Show, for his condition and the present life which the Indian is forced to lead has drawn him into such shows. What benefit has the Indian derived from these Wild West Shows? None, but what are degrading, demoralizing and degenerating. . . . Tribal habits and customs are apt to be degraded for show purposes, because the Indian Bureau under our government is constantly encouraging the Indian to degenerate by permitting hundreds of them to leave their homes for fraudulent savage demonstrations before the world. All these Wild West Shows are exhibiting the Indian worse than he ever was and deprive him of his high manhood and individuality.[45]

Yellow Robe's words paled next to the ongoing and growing popularity of the shows he condemned. When Apid joined the 101 show in 1924, it was in the throes of expanding to become *The 101 Real Wild West and Great Far East Combined.* Cowboys, Indians, and rodeo fare were still the main attractions, but many new acts were being added. The Millers purchased the old Walter L. Main Circus, whose camels, elephants, tigers, lions, monkeys, ostriches, and other exotic animals were to form the background for the Far East segment of the new show, which would feature Slayman Ali's Arabian Troupe and the band of the former Russian Czar. In addition, they hired a Scottish highlander band, a minstrel band, a cowboy band, and a score of side shows.[46]

In April of the following year, the show, described by the press as "the most magnificent tented attraction ever put on wheels," was ready for the road.[47] "We went all over the United States," says Apid, "one little town after another." En route, they picked up Molly.

Molly, like Apid, did some horseback and elephant riding for the 101 crowds, but primarily she danced. Miller featured her as Princess *Neeburban*, the Penobscot word for Northern Lights. Molly had used this *nom de theatre* for at least a year when she joined 101[48] and probably took it from a Penobscot entertainer of her mother's generation. The earlier Neeburban appeared in a turn-of-the-century newspaper article that touted the virtues of four Penobscot "maidens" of remarkable beauty. The journalist noted that these "dusky fair ones" — Falling Star, Bright Star (Watawaso), Golden Rod, and Northern Lights — were such stunning "specimens of Western Indian women" that they would probably be invited to appear in the American exhibition of the 1900 Paris Exposition. Northern Lights is not identified by her real name, but it is likely Molly knew her and, being a lover of night skies, decided to assume the name.[49]

At the end of the road season in October, Molly and Apid traveled by train with the rest of the 101 gang to the show's winter headquarters at the Miller's ranch in Oklahoma. Soon after arriving, Molly danced at an enormous powwow, probably staged by the Miller Brothers to launch their season of home shows. Judges selected her as the best of some nine hundred dancers who hailed from Oklahoma's many Indian reservations as well as from the 101 cast. As she later told a journalist, beyond the engraved silver bracelet that was her prize, she had "the pleasure of being adopted by the Cheyenne" in honor of

Molly with Joe Miller of the Miller Brothers' 101 Ranch Wild West Show, 1925.

her fine performance.[50] Since adoption ceremonies typically included name bestowals, and Elk was a common name catagory among the Cheyenne (and other Plains Indians), it is likely that she gained her Spotted Elk appellation on this occasion. Certainly it did not come from the Penobscot, for the elk or wapiti did not inhabit her home region. When Molly returned east from Oklahoma, she billed herself as Spotted Elk, a more saleable name in the entertainment business. Years later, she would resurrect her first *nom de theatre*, Neeburban, as a private endearment, symbolizing a deep love.

That fall, both Molly and Apid had modest parts in *On With the Show,* a Miller Brothers' film about an American adventurer who returns from an expedition to Africa to find that his crooked brother has "defrauded him and his properties and become a [wild west] show groupie."[51] This experience hinted at film opportunities that would come later for both sisters. Apid relished working for the Millers and stayed with 101 for six years. "The pay was nothing," she recalls, "I did it mostly for the experience." As a featured performer, Molly probably earned more than Apid—perhaps thirty-five dollars a month.[51] This was not enough to build up her "school fund" and help out the family. Anxious to return to her university studies, and looking for more lucrative work to make that possible, Molly headed back east. In light of later diary entries in which she proclaimed her desire to do performances that were "authentic" and "true," it seems clear that it was more than low pay that drove her away from the 101's circus atmosphere.

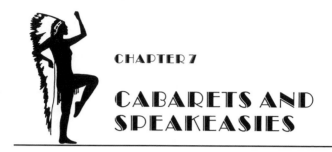

CHAPTER 7

CABARETS AND
SPEAKEASIES

*Once I become famous, mama will not have to make
any more Indian baskets.*

—*Molly (Indian Island, 1927)*[1]

Ill health foiled Molly's plans to pursue a rigorous performance
schedule and build up her school fund. Shortly after returning
east in December 1925, she came down with a serious case of
what she called the "grippe"—influenza with its miserable
combination of fever, muscle pain, and inflamation of the
respiratory system—exacerbated by her tubercular history.
She spent December and January in bed rather than on stage.
Molly battled her illness in the shelter of her parents' home on
Indian island. Although unable to dance during this time, she
did manage to write, penning short stories under the name of
Harold Van Dyke Smith and poems under the name of Anna May
Williams. She found publishers for some of her writings, includ-
ing a melancholy verse titled, "Musings of a Lonely Being."[2]

As soon as she was able, Molly got out of bed and went to
work. Her diary shows that in the winter of 1926 she ventured
to New York City "for the first time—alone and friendless, a
hungry innocent Injun girl."[3] The city was bigger, noisier, and
taller than any place she had seen—a stunning contrast to the
forest footpaths, ferry bateau, and little frame houses of Indian
Island. Here, masses of strangers from countless climes rushed
about in trams and taxis, while the fumes of garbage and
exhaust hung in the air, and the sun revealed itself only in
narrow shafts.

Molly entered this chaotic scene midway through the Roaring Twenties, a decade marked by virulent reactions to the 1919 Volstead Act that enforced Prohibition. Underfunded and understaffed, the Federal Prohibition Bureau had no chance of enforcing its wildly unpopular laws. With the public hell-bent on defying the law and having fun, the Volstead Act produced the opposite of its intended effect: a period of unparalleled frolic, drinking, and lawbreaking. Smuggling and illicit liquor manufacturing took place on a gargantuan scale, filling the purses of gangsters, from Al Capone in Chicago to Salvatore Luciano in New York. By the late 1920s, some 250,000 speakeasies and night clubs had cropped up across the nation, inviting people to imbibe beyond the walls of their homes—to enjoy a shot of social spirit along with liquid spirits. New York alone boasted thirty-two thousand establishments where one could get a drink. First class outfits in the city paid eighteen hundred dollars a year in graft to underpaid policemen, prohibition agents, and district attorneys—fees which slightly surpassed operation costs before Prohibition, when a state liquor license was fifteen hundred dollars and a federal license was twenty-five. Profit potential for liquor sales was stupendous on all levels. Women, barred from saloons pre-prohibition, eagerly ventured into speakeasies, where they argued that their presence was no more illegal than that of men. Both men and women, spinning in the moral chaos of the era, grabbed hold of a new sexual license, happily justifying it with a misinterpretation of Freud. Adding to the frolic were floor shows, offered by many speakeasies, and providing yet another forum for entertainers.[4]

If entertainment opportunities were plentiful during the 1920s, they were outnumbered by droves of young, would-be entertainers, combing the want-ads and lining up for auditions. Molly's first New York performance happened on an exceedingly tiny "stage"—the model stand in sculptor Bonnie MacLeary's Greenwich Village studio. Here she posed for a statue called "Flame"—the first of many pieces that would be fashioned after her firm, petite, and graceful figure by the

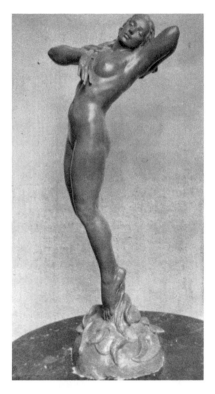

"The Moonflower," by
Bonnie MacLeary, 1929.
This life-size sculpture
is one of a half-dozen
MacLeary works for which
Molly posed. MacLeary was
one of many artists to hire
Molly as a model during the
1920s and 1930s. (Courtesy
of Sugar Glaspy.)

famous artist. Years later Molly would note in her diary that
MacLeary had sculpted her in "all stages . . . from the thin-
hipped, small breasted flame of girlhood on to womanhood."[5]
MacLeary, born in San Antonio, Texas in 1893, began studying
at the New York School of Art at the age of eleven, followed by
training at the Academie Julianne in Paris at age fourteen, and
New York's Art Students' League at nineteen. In 1921, the year
she opened her New York studio at 7 MacDougal Alley, she
exhibited at the National Academy of Art, and the Metropolitan Museum of Art purchased her bronze figure "Aspiration." She became known internationally for life-size and mon-
umental statues of children and historic figures, including two
Puerto Rico monuments for which Molly posed. In later years,
the Pathe and International News Films featured her at work in

educational reels demonstrating marble and bronze sculpting.[6] But modeling, even for a noted artist, was not Molly's goal; it was only something an aspiring dancer did between auditions to make sure she had bread on the table. Soon, as Molly told a journalist the following year, one of her auditions bore fruit: "I found a job in the Hippodrome with the famous Foster Girls. . . . I got into the chorus and that's how I happened to go to Texas for an [eight-month] engagement at the Aztec Theater in San Antonio."[7]

The Foster Girls, conceived and directed by one-time dancer Alan K. Foster in 1925, was the most innovative and acrobatically oriented chorus team of the three major precision dance choreographers of the period (which included Foster, Chester Hale at the Capitol Theater, and Albertina Rash working for Ziegfeld). The *New York Times* described Foster's team as sixteen extraordinary chorus girls "who appear as a unit in dancing, acrobatic and even in what might be termed circus numbers. They are skillfully trained and they move with a precision . . . which demands lithe bodies and firm nerves."[8]

Getting a job with Foster was no easy task. In his own words:

First, we gather girls together and select the likeliest. . . . The girls we choose are put through an eleven week's training in physical culture which aims to get them in condition to learn dancing. Then there is a five weeks' period of dance training, during which we teach them also swimming and horseback riding and other accomplishments which may be useful to them as a troupe. After that we sign them under a long-term contract which may be either five or three years. Then they are ready for work either as a vaudeville or production unit.[9]

The public and critics loved the results of Foster's rigor. When Molly began working with him, he had one of his several dance groups booked at New York's Hippodrome, a huge theater on the prestigious Keith Circuit. *Variety*, which consistently applauded Foster and his "girls," praised one of the many 1926 Hippodrome showbills that included the chorus: after gushing that the "Foster chicks, working more mellifluently than ever" were "always an eyeful," the critic saluted the other acts on the bill (including the Flying Erfords, the Disappearing Diving Girls, the equestrian Reiffenbach boys and girls, and Belle Baker singing "Yes Sir, That's My Baby"). In sum, wrote the critic, this was "a great show, with more youth and feminine skill and grace distributed through it . . . than ever came into one Hippodrome bill."[10]

At the end of May, Molly took a train to San Antonio, Texas for a long-term chorus engagement at the new, three-thousand-seat Aztec Theater, the biggest showplace in a city of 200,000.[11] By this time, the film-plus-stage-show combination had eclipsed straight vaudeville shows throughout the country. Ninety-seven percent of all theaters were film houses, and the other three were vaudeville, burlesque, or "legit" (including plays but excluding musical comedies, revues, and motion pictures).[12] The Aztec, following the new recipe, offered its audiences a mixture of live and on-screen entertainment. And it offered Molly consistency and a measure of financial security, rare luxuries in her life. She responded to the opportunity with determination. Show after show, day after day, she kicked her legs in precision with the other chorus girls, providing a lively prelude to whatever film was being featured at the theater. Eventually, she kicked her way out of the chorus into cameo performances of Indian dances as "Princess Spotted Elk."

Surely Molly welcomed the Aztec spotlight, even though it shone on stereotypic Indian dance forms favored by the director and the general public. But while she might have preferred to deliver a lecture-song-dance rooted in Penobscot tradition, a theater that regularly screened popular westerns full of clichés about Indians was hardly the place for authentic fare. That is clear in this billboard announcement of the Aztec's presentation of Metropolitan Pictures' melodrama, *The Last Frontier*:[13]

> NEVER BEFORE have we received so many flattering compliments from our patrons. They all say IT'S BIG! NEVER AGAIN will you be given an opportunity to spend two such delightful hours of unequaled entertainement. You'll join the rest and say

IT'S BIG! YOU'LL CHEER when the American troops under General Custer charge upon the savage redskins. When the hero rescues his sweetheart from the path of the 3000 stampeding buffalo in the world's greatest western drama. . . . Aztec presentation conceived and staged by Jack Mason: "The Round Up" featuring Princess Spotted Elk, Aztec Artists, Aztec Girls, Aztec Symphony Orchestra.[14]

During her eight-month stay in San Antonio, Molly at first shared a modest room in the Gunter Hotel with another Aztec dancer.[15] Still harboring hopes of affording a university education, she convinced her roommate to move with her when she found a "clean, spacious and comfy" room in an even cheaper hotel on Presa Street. With this move, she told her diary, "Maybe I will save faster to help the school fund."[16] Beyond adding to that fund and covering living expenses, she still felt obliged to send money to her mother.[17] To supplement her theater income, Molly gave dancing lessons and modeled footwear for Guaranteed Shoe Company—proudly displaying what she considered her best feature: elegant size five feet.[18]

The Aztec program usually changed weekly or biweekly, so dancers were always learning new routines as well as performing. The director typically demanded a rehearsal and three or four shows a day from the dancers—the last show ending after midnight.[19] In between this and other work obligations, Molly spent considerable time reading and writing, as usual. She made lists of writers and their characteristics: Flaubert—"believer of art for art's sake"; H.G. Wells—"stubbornly romantic notions of progress"; Proust—"master of dissociation"; Joyce—"master of synthesis" She also jotted down attributes she wanted to avoid in her own writing: "literary impropriety, incoherence, pedantry, elephantine grace, sentimentalism"[20] It is not clear if she produced any published poems or stories during her stay in San Antonio—although literary contacts noted in her 1926 diary and a 1927 reference to "poems published" imply that she did.[21]

Very often, Molly, along with her roommate or other dancer-friends, stepped out to Ebbings for sandwiches and to the Rio

Vista or Old South Cafe for dinner. When a new movie came to town, Molly invariably saw it—at the Palace, Rialto, Majestic, Princess, or one of the other seventeen theaters in San Antonio. As always, she reviewed films in her diary: "Went to the Princess to see Jack Holt in 'The Man of the Forest,' a virile picture but far from interesting . . ."[22] Sunday mornings were reserved for Mass at St. Mary's; late nights for outings with suitors who sent notes backstage asking to see her after the last show. The only one who warranted even a smidgen of diary space was a fellow named Ken Wendler, with whom she frequently spent the moonlit hours—dining, taking long sightseeing drives through "aristocratic neighborhoods," dancing at a rooftop club called St. Anthony's. But clearly Ken was not a significant romantic interest in her life. Nor was her old Yale friend Roy, with whom she continued to exchange letters and telegrams.[23] Although she relished being flattered and pursued by men, they paled in importance next to her career goals.

While living in San Antonio, Molly for the first time made it onto high society guest lists—as a performer: "About 8:30 the chauffeur came for us in Mr. Stern's car. Away we flew to Hillcrest Golf Club. The party consisted of jews in masquerade costumes. All Yiddish elite. Boring yet colorful."[24] As Molly began to receive these invitations, plus a measure of star treatment as a principal dancer, she noted in her diary hints of jealousy from some of her peers. For instance: "Mr. [William] Epstein [Managing Director] asked me this morning to do the Indian dance I did last night for the entire week. The audience liked it immensely. Used my brown costume. The other girls are sore because this is the only number I will be doing this week."[25]

But the petty arrows of jealousy that flew her way were inconsequential compared to the facts that she had found "true friends" and managed to put some money in the bank.[26] New Year's Day 1927 found her optimistic: "Well, little diary, I am hoping and praying this will be a lucky year for me. As well as prosperous. Anyway, there is one thing I have now, it is my health—something I did not have last New Years."

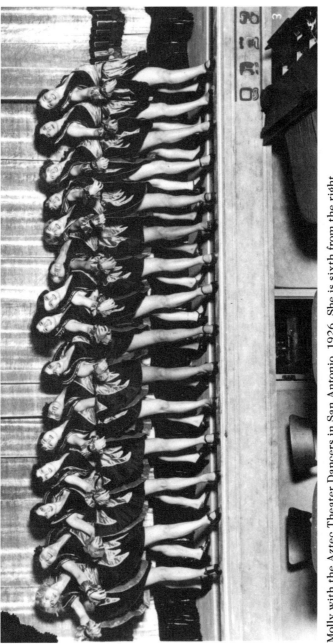

Molly with the Aztec Theater Dancers in San Antonio, 1926. She is sixth from the right.

A week later, the Aztec engagement concluded and soon thereafter Molly sat on a train heading northeast—reading Baudelaire and feeling apprehensive about returning to New York: "I'm going back to NY—to what? . . . [I] really hate to leave this place. I have been so happy, well and busy."[27]

In New York, Molly quickly found work with "Princess" Watawaso's Indian troupe. Watawaso, whose real name was Lucy Nicola, was the daughter of Joesph Nicola, former Penobscot Governor and Tribal Representative to the Maine State Legislature (and author of *Life and Traditions of the Red Man*—a remarkable book about the Penobscots). Intellectually and artistically, Lucy and Molly had much in common. Nearly twenty years older than Molly, Lucy was the first Penobscot girl to attend school in Old Town. In 1897, at age fifteen, she left home to work in Cambridge, Massachusetts for an independent accountant and Harvard University administrator named Montague Chamberlain.[28] By avocation a naturalist, and keenly interested in native traditions of northeast North America, Chamberlain had visited Indian Island on several occasions and written about the Penobscots. Although Lucy liked to joke that she was "faster at figuring than [Chamberlain] was," her real love was music, not numbers. It was probably through Chamberlain's associations that she linked up with the social elite of Massachusetts and New York. By 1900, the *Bangor [Maine] Weekly Commercial* reported:

> Wah-Ta-Waso, an educated and refined girl is often the pet of New York society. Being present at a woman's debating society recently, and it being resolved that immigration was dangerous and threatening to all true Americans, she arose to speak, her stately form commanding instant recognition.
>
> In a sweet but audible voice, she said: "I believe I am the only true American here. I think you have decided rightly. Of all my forefathers' country, from the St. John [River] to the Connecticut, we have now but a little island one-half mile square. There are only about 500 of us now. We are very happy on our island, but we are poor. . . . The railroad corporations, which did their share of robbing us of our land, are now begrudging us one half-rate fare.

"But we forgive you all."
There was a long silence, and the subject was laid on the table. The president said that the musical feature would have to be omitted as the pianist was sick, and "would someone please volunteer?" No one had the courage to try an impromptu before that large audience. When at last who should beg to be allowed to try but Wah-Ta-Waso, who played some selections from Chopin with the greatest ease and sang a plaintive air which touched the hearts of all those present and made them feel like doing anything in the world for her people.[29]

Eventually Lucy moved to Chicago to study voice and piano at the Music School of Chautauqua. In the summer of 1913, she toured the country giving recitals at Chautauqua "camps," where adults gathered to soak up secular and religious instruction that included lectures by well-known authors, scientists, explorers, and political leaders, plus "educational" musical offerings. Lucy usually performed songs by Thurlow Lieurance, a student of Indian music who based his work on the traditional melodies of various American Indian groups. Among the wide array of artists and literati she met on tour was Charles Wakefield Cadman, who, like Lieurance, wrote compositions based on Indian music.[30]

Cadman, better known than Lieurance, often performed with Cherokee-Creek singer Tsianina Blackstone. Their recitals, well chronicled in Blackstone's autobiography, hint at the fare preferred by the Chautauqua set and no doubt shed light on the nature of Lucy's showmanship. The lovely Tsianina usually performed standing erect between a grand piano and a pot of flowers. She wore long braids, a beaded headband, and a glamorized Plains Indian dress. The program combined Indian music and lore, usually opening with Tsianina singing several Cadman songs, first in Indian, then in English. Then Cadman gave his "Indian Music Talk"—a lecture about Indian music, illustrated by vocal and piano numbers, plus Indian percussion instruments and the flageolet (flute). In this segment, the composer typically played some "authentic Indian love songs" on the flageolet and presented a comparative selection of "primitive sacred music" (comparing, for instance, an Omaha tribal prayer with a seventh-century Gregorian chant sung in Latin). The program ended with "idealized Indian songs" played on the piano (such as Cadman's famous "The Land of Sky Blue Water," based on an Omaha melody), and several more songs sung by Tsianina. According to Tsianina, the "Canoe Song," an Ojibwa tune adapted by Cadman and Burton, was "the highlight of every program and always had to be repeated."[31]

Blackstone, acculturated into white society from the time she attended a mission school as a young girl, barely addressed in her book the obvious question of Cadman and Lieurance's wholesale appropriation (and romantization) of Indian melodies. She simply noted, "Cadman had trouble getting Indian cooperation in recording their music. . . . [Some complained that] after taking our land, whites now want to take our music. Then he won them over with 'The Land of Sky Blue Water.'"

Paradoxically, non-Indian musicians, even the well-meaning Cadman and Lieurance, simultaneously destroyed and preserved Indian music. In a kind of reverse reincarnation they picked up the bodies (notes) but not the souls of native songs, then adapted them for white audiences by replacing the original souls with white or generic ones. Some composers did this with such skill that the soul-switch went undetected, even to American Indians. Most native people of Molly's generation grew up surrounded by fractured traditions, unfamiliar with the seamless, integrated cultures of their own ancestors. This made it difficult to recognize the pure from the adulterated. In addition, those who chose entertainment as their livelihood were beholden to audiences who demanded the popularized versions of Indian artistry. So it was that many American Indians, including Molly who danced to Cadman's music, and Lucy who sang Lieurance's songs, adopted and promoted the corrupted artistic expressions of their ancestors.

After several years on the Chautauqua circuit, Lucy based herself in New York City, studying voice and recording Lieurance's songs for the Victor Talking Machine Company. The company sent her on promotional tours across the country, even to Mexico.[32]

Molly and Lucy were well-acquainted through entertainment circles and the fact that they both called Indian Island home. When Molly returned to New York from San Antonio in January 1927, Lucy introduced her to a beautiful Cherokee soprano known as Princess Wantura. Wantura, in turn, invited Molly and Lucy, along with an accompaniest named Tommie Little Chief, to join her in a booking at Keith-Albee's New Montauk Theater in Passaic, New Jersey. Molly accepted the offer, but apparently she had mixed feelings about working with an all-Indian troupe, for she told her diary: "Can't say I am so overjoyed. Indians are such a changeable lot."[33]

After the Montauk booking, Lucy organized a new Indian troupe. It included herself and Molly, plus five other performers—a Comanche, Onondaga, Pawnee, and two Kiowas. In March they set out on a two-month tour on the famous Keith-Albee-Orpheum Circuit, playing in major theatres in Ohio, Michigan, and New York State.[34] This was a significant booking. Although battered by competition in the 1920s (especially by Marcus Loew who was quicker to make the transition to film-plus-vaude programs), the much respected Keith-Albee Circuit had a new lease on life thanks to its 1926 merger with Martin Beck's Orpheum Theater Circuit, which dominated the entertainment scene west of Chicago.[35] No doubt Molly did her version of a corn dance, among others, and Lucy sang. Among Lucy's numbers was one with Kiowa "Chief" Bruce Poolaw, a former rodeo star from western Oklahoma. They sang their most popular duet, "Indian Love Call," in front of a painted backdrop of a tepee in a forest clearing. The duet proved to be providential; Lucy and Bruce became lovers and ultimately married one another, despite the fact that she was about twenty years his senior.[36]

In May, after the troupe's final performance at Shea's Hippodrome in Buffalo, Molly returned to New York City, found a room, and plunged back into the world of job hustling. She avoided the easy road of relying on Lucy or Wantura and began knocking on the doors of dozens of agents, directors, and producers, hoping to find her own niche. Doors opened one by one, and Molly found that her value in the theater world had grown considerably thanks to credits with Foster, the Aztec, and her latest Keith Circuit tour.

Sometimes with the Foster Girls, other times on her own, she landed slots in the well-touted revues of notable Flo Ziegfeld competitors Earl Carroll, Martin Beck, Harry Crull, and John Murray Anderson. Revues, beginning with the Ziegfeld Follies in 1907, were essentially glorified, glamorized, spiced-up vaude shows. Typically, New York revues were offered with films and included a variety of dance forms: tap and step, acrobatics, exhibition ballroom, musical comedy, and "art dancing." The last category embraced anything foreign or impressionistic, from interpretive numbers à la Martha Graham or Ruth St. Denis, to Spanish, Oriental, East Indian, and American Indian presentations.[37]

Very often, directors hired Molly to perform an American Indian dance. Her repertoire, drawn from the traditions of several tribal groups, included a Cheyenne warrior dance, Iroquois corn dance, the Penobscot snake dance and clown dance, a deer dance, and a whoop dance. Frequently, she did non-Indian numbers. As one journalist noted, "Molly Spotted Elk dances the difficult movements of her tribe, and 'The Charleston' and 'Black Bottom' of the pale-face with equal grace."[38] Describing a show directed by the much-respected Harry Crull at the "high-society," vaude-film Branford Theater in Newark, Molly wrote: "Four shows today, each one better than the last. First the Bachelor Four sings behind the screen, Mr. [Milton] Lewis comes out and Ruthie Hamilton plays; then the cornet trio, then Art [a female impersonator] as Camille. The boys play a selection, then my black bottom. Rushed upstairs to change. A song by Mr. Marshall—'Simply Ruthie,' Milton's dance, Alice Morely's blues song, Naomi the [East] Indian Butterfly, and last the corn dance—my specialty."[39] On another occasion she performed "a little Indian dance" in a revue called "Dancing Around," produced by vaudeville kingpin Martin Beck, builder of the Orpheum Theater Circuit.[40]

Molly danced, often as a principal, in revues at various other major vaude-film theaters: the delux 5300-seat Capitol Theater on Broadway,[41] the brand new, 4000-seat Academy of Music on Fourteenth Street (a Fox house reputed to be a "sellout any night"),[42] and the Audubon Theater (described by her as "one of the Fox houses . . . beautiful, the orchestra is fine and the stage large . . . [and the] audience is very appreciative being a high class type. . . . I have a separate dressing room"[43]).

Soon, she also stepped into cabarets (nightclub entertainment, offered along with food and drinks), beginning with Perry's at Coney Island.[44] Coney Island, known as the "poor playboy's paradise," was home to dozens of tiny hole-in-the-wall cabarets. But it also hosted a good number of spacious clubs that provided excellent entertainment (if no big names) at little cost. Perry's was the swankiest spot, with waiters in tuxedos, a captain on the floor, and a hat-check man in uniform. It always offered a splendid show and cheap drinks.[45]

Even though Molly was winning jobs in well-known show places, work came in fits and starts, only with great effort, and rarely with a decent salary. Her 1927 diary records day after day of pounding the pavement, trying to hit the moving target of theatrical opportunity:

To the Loew Office. . . .
    Jaunted to the [Earl] Carroll office and saw the producer. . . .
    . . . at the Columbia Building — saw Mr. Daley and was given an offer. . . .
    Down to the offices as usual — the same old stall. . . .
    Rushed down to the Capitol [Theater] with my costume for the tryout. . . .
    The regular mob gathered at 47th and Broadway — theatrical types are everywhere. . . .
    I hate waiting in these theatrical places — such elements as one finds there. . . .
    . . . down to the Hippodrome. . . . [They] told to come back. Over to see Mr. Grossman [an agent]. Waited three long hours, then up to the Roseland Building for a rehearsal. . . .
    Mr. Foster told me we were not working next week. Wonder if

my work pleased them? It seems the harder I try to do my best the less I get out of it. I realize I am not an artist, but I can try. And try I will until I'm satisfied!

Summing up a showgirl's struggle, she wrote, "Always running at random here and there to this agent and that one for something to do. This showbusiness is a heartbreaking one full of promises, trouble, glamor and rush."[46] Indeed, she lived an up and down life—one week buoyed by a job, applause, and a paycheck; the next week weighted down by exhaustion, false leads, and low pay: "What occupied my mind most was the business proposition set forth and the ridiculous salary offered. Yes, little diary, I am broke again. Being penniless has its unpleasantries, especially when one does not feel well."[47] Sometimes she sold her belongings to get by: "At last I pawned my ring to a Jew two streets below me for $10."[48] And sometimes it took valiant effort just to hold on to a measure of self-esteem and make the rounds: "When one is poor and struggling to get along, even respectability has its excuses. At times I'm so shabby it is a wonder I pass muster in the offices—and being such a homely girl."[49]

But if Molly's self-perception periodically plummeted, it is clear that others saw her as an exotic beauty. In April 1927 a portrait of her appeared on the cover of *Collier's Magazine*.[50] Her notoriety began to spread among artists, and many, in addition to Bonnie MacLeary, asked her to model for them. She sometimes noted them in her diary: "Posing for Mr. Huntington's fountain statue"; "Posing for Mr. Ward"; "Went to see Mr. Meyers on 54th Street. His studio is located on the top floor of church settlement house next to a synagogue. He is typically the artist in fashion, manner and ideas. For him I will be a gypsy maiden, not so bad after being painted and carved as many other nationalties."[51] One of the artists she posed for, Ben Ali Haggin, had garnered at least as much fame as Mac-Leary. Molly identified him as "the noted Italian society portrait painter," and described his painting of her as "a study in orange and feathers."[52] Haggin did more than society portraits.

He created elaborate stage tableaux in front of which Ziegfeld girls posed "like groupings in visual art."[53] Although he was the favorite in-town artist among the Broadway set, Molly found it frustrating to work for him: "Haggin told me to call him at 10—which I did and still he postponed the salary. These wealthy artists are the most negligent bosses to work for. Very tired."[54]

In July an opportunity Molly had barely dared to dream for came her way when an agent landed a momentous contract for her at the famous Casino in Paris, France. She rushed home to see her family and pack—taking the train to Old Town, then crossing from the mainland to the island on the ferry bateau, "captained" that year by her father. During her brief visit, H. J. Tewksbury, contributing editor for the *Portland Sunday Telegram*, the state's major newspaper, came to the island to interview the budding star. Tewksbury's long and laudatory article, complete with a large photo of "Princess Spotted Elk" in Indian garb, appeared on 10 July, under the title: "Indian Princess Will Paddle Own Canoe On Parisian Stage: Old Town Indian Maid Has Won Success On Stage As Well As In World Of Letters—Has Bright Future." Excerpts provide a peek into Molly's spirit and accomplishments:

> On Indian Island near Old Town, perched perilously near the edge of the mighty Penobscot in a little frame house with rickety steps lives the Princess Spotted Elk, a pretty Indian maiden. . . .
> Spotted Elk can do many things. . . . The princess is a dancer and . . . a mighty good one. She specializes in Indian dances, but can do anything . . . and she can write stories and poetry, and earn a bit of money posing for well-known artists. . . .
> Reared with the traditions of her people, the proud and haughty Penobscots, Princess Spotted Elk . . . amazed her kinsmen when she told them . . . she felt quite able to paddle her own canoe. "It is the Indian girl who is progressive," Princess Spotted Elk declared. For generations the Indian woman has been kept down. But now she and her sister outside the reservation are making their way into the world together. . . .
> "Do you intend to make dancing a profession?" this reporter timidly asked as he pushed one of the princess' little brothers off his knee.
> "Yes and no," she replied. "I have won some success as a short

story writer and in addition have had a number of poems published. . . . I am now at work on a story dealing with [Indian] Island. The publishers seem to think it has some merit and two of them, one a well known Boston firm and one a well known New York firm, have agreed to put it out and give me a royalty on each book sold. I have read some of it to my mother and she thinks it's pretty good. Once I become famous, mama will not have to make any more Indian baskets."[55]

The article would have been a grand send off—if the Paris engagement had not fallen through. It is not known why the booking was broken, but it left Molly back in New York, once again hunting for jobs—and deeply missing nature's solace. She always longed for nature when city-bound, but her all-too-brief visit home, coupled with the Paris cancellation, made this longing more acute. "Saw a bunch of oak leaves and brought them . . . to my room," she wrote that autumn. "I could see myself in the woods just by looking at the leaves." A few weeks later, she lamented, "It was beautiful outside—never have I seen the sun so bright . . . and never did I wish to be out in the woods so much as I did. City life and city scenes—oh how tired I am of them. God never intended the Indian to live always in the city . . . and see nothing but man-made things. Even the trees in the park are trained to grow to suit the mind of men."[56]

She also missed her family. One morning, just after her return to the city, she seized an opportunity to do something about that. Hearing that the 101 Ranch was coming to Connecticut, she hopped a train at Grand Central and made it to New Haven by 11:00 A.M.—too late to see the Ranch's promotional parade through town. In it, of course, were friends and family. Not only her sister Apid, who had just turned twenty-two, but seventeen-year-old Mildred Nelson, known in the family as "Darling" or "Darly." Having missed the parade, Molly "rode up to the grounds. Saw Darling in the cook house. In the dressing room met the girls. Saw the show, the Hopi Indians and the kids May and Flossie." At some point during the day, Molly and Darly decided Darly would join her big sister in New York: "After the show, called [old Yale friend] Roy. Rode down to meet him at the 'green.' Dinner. Roy was so lovely to us. [Drove us] to the cars for Darly's things. . . . Got trunk. To Station. Back to NY with Darling."[57] Darly moved into Molly's second-floor room in a boarding house called Mallery Hall. Molly described it as a "pokey room where one never knows whether the sun is shining or not."[58] Next door, she complained, lived "a vocalist trying to be a singer. I wish her vocal cords would break."[59] Darly's presence was a sweet distraction. She had stars in her eyes and loved to dance, and Molly delighted in having this little sister beside her on the entertainment roller coaster. She was agile and lovely to look at and with Molly's eager and remarkably non-competitive help, she began to audition for jobs.

During Darly's first weeks in the city, Molly took her on the auditions rounds. Among other bookings, they were hired for a week to perform various dances at the dubious Myrtle Theater in Brooklyn: "What a place! The smallest, dingiest and smelliest yet we've played. Two shows today. The first was terrible. . . . There are five acts—a trapeze, a singer, a skit, a coarse looking woman who does comedy and singing with her husband, and us."[60] Things improved when Molly, still working with Alan Foster, introduced Darly to the dance master, who hired her as a substitute Foster Girl.[61]

Three months after Darly came to New York, the sisters managed to move out of Mallery Hall into a sunlit room on Seventy-third Street—"a nice clean room . . . rather expensive, but . . . worth it. . . . Such a feeling to have sunlight again, fresh air, quiet, dignity and a spacious wigwam."[62]

Like most showgirls, Molly and Darly usually slept long after dawn. From late morning on they knocked on agents' doors, went to auditions, exercised, rehearsed, and arranged for costumes. When booked, they were usually obligated to do a matinee, followed by a string of shows that reached deep into the night. After a performance Molly sometimes found "stage-door johnnies" waiting for her, ready to woo. Typically, she paid them little heed, and only a handful achieved passing mention in her diary. In contrast, her old Yale University friend Roy, who now lived and worked as a lawyer in Manhattan, continued to appear in her life and, increasingly, in her diary pages. When free, Molly often spent evenings with "the three bachelors"— Roy, and his two apartment-mates, Charley and Ned. Sometimes Darly or Molly's Cherokee singer-friend Wantura went along: "Over to see the 'three bachelors' on 76th Street. We had nice music from the victrola and Roy played several pieces for us on the piano. We danced, played cards, ate nuts, poked fun. Darling told their fortunes and I read their palms." On another night: "Wantura and I went up to Roy's. A happy evening. . . . Wantura sang, Roy played the piano. Charley played the victrola. Ned and I danced. We all played 'pigs' [a card game]."63

On several occasions, Roy and his friends came to Molly's performances. After they saw her as principal dancer with the Foster Girls at the Academy of Music in October, Molly wrote: "It was sweet of the boys to come down to watch the Injun jump around and do a few meaningless steps. . . . Fate has been kind to give me such a friend as Roy has proven himself to be." Indeed, they were friends—frequently eating together, scolding each other for overworking, visiting one another when ill, and talking several times a week on the phone. There was one subject they rarely touched upon: "Miss Christophy—the singer," whose framed photo Roy kept in his apartment.64

Molly seemed determined to keep work as her priority and hold romance with Roy at bay. Perhaps she felt falling in love would interfere with her career, as this diary comment implies: "Surely the fire of ambition must be first. Would like to see it burn long."65 Or perhaps she felt just as fearful and ambivalent about an Indian-white romance as she did back in 1922 when Roy's weekend invitation to Yale prompted her to wonder whether "the gulf of difference" between them was not too broad."66 Now, when speaking of crossing this gulf she asked her diary: "What's the use? . . . As life stands now, I am happy with my friendships, tired of the city, yet interested in all that it holds. Still there is a missing factor. And that is what I am encouraging Darling to acquire—a softness toward the meaning of love and in being a regular sweet girl, to make love and be

loved, to kiss and to be kissed. But day dreams are not for me—
planning how to make a living and write is my pattern. And I
have been cut out so close along the outline that I fit like a
glove."[67]
Despite these bold determinations, Molly fought her feelings
for Roy. On 16 November, the night before her twenty-fourth
birthday, she wrote: "Felt the effect of another restless night.
Why does the face come to me so often? Whatever is the matter
with me? Before I add another year to my age tomorrow I will
have to adopt my former shell-like shield. . . . I must not forget
that I am merely a friend, no matter what it costs."
A month later, Roy helped solve her dilemna: "Rather a
strained feeling in Roy. . . . He mentioned a girl and of him
marrying. Very hurt about it. Tears and thoughts." The following week she wrote: "Called Roy—what a chat we had. One of
the most serious and heart to heart ones. [My] 'what's the use'
[comment] was referred to. . . . All I can say later to myself—
damn! and I mean it."[68] She wrestled through her feelings with
a poem, then never mentioned them again:

> We know not what love is
> until the hour
> When two souls meet,
> and each to each,
> In language unspoken, bind
> swiftly in the hearts
> A bond to last unto eternity—
>
> A hand clasp, an eye,
> a friendship long . . .[69]

About this time Molly auditioned for a Charles Cadman
program. The composer no longer worked with Cherokee-
Creek singer Tsianina Blackstone. After singing the lead in the
1926 Hollywood Bowl presentation of *Shanewis* (Cadman's
opera based on her life), Blackstone, a deeply religious woman,
had left show business to become a full-time Christian Science
practitioner. Molly was honored to work with Cadman. "Over to
Brooklyn to try out at the Mark Strand [Theater]," she wrote.

"Mr. Heyman . . . wants me for this next week with Mr. Cadman's program." Two days later: "Up early. Packed my costumes and rushed over to the Strand for rehearsal. Met Miss Eberhart, a Chicago opera singer with Charles Cadman. She is my roommate. Like her heaps." The show began the following day and seems to have been Molly's first and last opportunity with Cadman. "Did a brodie into the orchestra pit and was knocked out," she confessed. "The lights were bad and the stage so small that I did not see where I was going. Lots of excitement. My ribs were bent and I did the other three shows but could not do the fifth one. The doctor came, bandaged my arm and strapped me up in adhesive plaster." Despite her painful injury, she performed five more days, seeing the weeklong booking to completion.[70]

Although worn down by aching bones and muscles, financial stress, lost love, a Paris cancellation, and a humiliating onstage tumble, Molly kept going. Her tenacity reaped rewards. In mid-December, she signed on for a show at the classy but brassy Frivolity Night Club. "Down to the Frivolity for my first night's work," she announced in her diary. "Did my Indian number in the first show and the black bottom in the second. . . . Enjoyed it immensely."[71] She had been hired by Nils T. Granlund, known as "N. T. G.," "Grandy," or "Granny." A much-touted broadway character, Granlund worked as publicist and manager of Radio Station WHN. He also produced near-nude revues—for theaters (including the prestigious Palace), and especially for lively, chic nightclubs, such as the Frivolity, the Silver Slipper, and various places hosted by the city's long-favorite club hostess, Texas Guinan.[72] Through Granlund, Molly met "Tex," a former rodeo, vaudeville, and western film queen, who soon featured Molly draped in a head-to-toe eagle feather headdress—and little else.

Perhaps more than anyone else, Texas Guinan (born Mary Louise Cecilia Guinan in Waco, Texas, 1884) symbolized the playful spirit of the Prohibition era. Throughout the 1920s the flamboyant "Tex" ran a string of sophisticated night spots, famous for high prices and classy, yet rebellious entertain-

Molly as she appeared in Texas Guinan's clubs in 1928.

ment. Her clubs lured New York's wealthiest citizens, as well as visiting European aristocrats including the likes of Lord and Lady Louis Mountbatten, members of Britain's royal family — patrons who did not mind paying a three-to-five dollar cover charge and twenty-five dollars for a bottle of bootlegged "champagne" (carbonated cider with alcohol added).[73]

The New York press celebrated Tex as "the spirit of staying-up-late, the fairy Disobedience, patron of unruly children."[74]

Each night, this irresistable "fairy" happily welcomed a packed house of revelers with the greeting: "Hello Suckers!" She bantered with customers, sat down at their tables, and offered a floor show that featured an elite handful of girls renowned for their dancing and their beauty. She introduced a dancer by inviting the audience to "give the little girl a big hand!" Often she strolled table to table with the girls, encouraging them to visit with patrons. But she had one invariable rule: her dancers had to leave the club alone, and were not allowed to go on to "parties" under penalty of losing their jobs.[75] It is hard to imagine that these young women would want to do anything but go home and sleep after a night at Guinan's. The first floor show began at 11:00 p.m., the last ended at four or five in the morning. Some dancers, including Molly, frequently performed at Tex's on top of doing an evening revue at one of the nearby Broadway theaters.

Guinan's clubs were periodically raided on suspicion of liquor sales and sometimes padlocked by Prohibition authorities.[76] Prince Edward of Wales and Lord Mountbatten happened to be at Tex's on the night of a raid. Their hostess deposited Mountbatten behind the kettle drum and told him to play musician for a while, then rushed the prince into the kitchen, dressed him as a chef, handed him a frying pan, spatula, and carton of eggs, and instructed him to fry eggs until she returned.[77] Tex was as good at saving herself as she was at rescuing her patrons. She had a knack for slipping through the hands of the law, quickly opening a new place, and turning raids and arrests into promotional events. After one brush with the law, she greeted her customers wearing a heavy necklace of padlocks, led them in giving three cheers for prohibition, and playfully asked, "Where would I be without it?" On another occasion she appeared on Broadway in a Shubert revue titled, *Padlocks of 1927*.[78] As the *New York Times* put it, Tex always emerged from encounters with the authorities "unscathed and better advertised to boot."[79]

Indeed, raid after raid, year after year, New York's elite lined up to get into Texas Guinan's. And Molly, part of the alluring

receiving line, met them one by one. Among the many social-
ites in attendance was Bryan Cheedy, a good-natured, irre-
sponsible chap who enjoyed making and breaking marriage
proposals. Charmed by Molly, he, in turn, charmed her with
his curious mix of social finesse and recklessness. At one
moment he was "busy with the debs," and at the next "bored
with society's whirl" and seeking escape in some far-flung
forest in Honduras or Canada. His ambivalence toward the
trappings of high society New York echoed Molly's. She described him as a man who "loves injuns, children and the
woods . . . and always cheers me up," adding, "This means so
much since I get lonely so many times." In the habit of
proposing to the women he spent time with, Bryan asked Molly
for her hand. Apparently she said yes, although what they both
really wanted from each other was friendship.[80]

Wherever it was going, the Cheedy-Spotted Elk relationship
was put on hold when a dashing explorer-filmmaker named
Douglas Burden came into Tex's club looking for the "Indian
dancer." Seeing Molly perform and learning of her great love for
nature with all its rigors, Burden knew she was the perfect
female lead for the all-Indian film he was making in Canada's
north woods.[81]

CHAPTER 8

THE SILENT ENEMY

It was a great privilege to play the leading female role of Neewa [in The Silent Enemy*]. . . . I was not acting, but merely living and feeling the part of an Indian girl of long ago. It was as if I had lived fifty years ago on my own reservation, where my people were hunters. The mysteries of the woods, the handling of the canoes and the necessity of working hard and enduring hardships were not new to me. My interest in making an Indian film and the opportunity of being in the woods appealed to me more than anything.*

—Molly (New York, 1930)[1]

As a youngster in the North woods I learned how different it is to travel in the woods with an Indian as opposed to a white man. With an Indian you tend to be silent—you speak softly, if at all. You become increasingly sensitive to your surroundings and as a result you find yourself endlessly listening to what the forest has to say.

—W. Douglas Burden[2]

William Douglas Burden shared Molly's profound passion for wilderness, although he came to it by a very different road. His millionaire father, James Abercrombie Burden II, loved "rusticating"—stepping into nature to escape the pressures of his work as president of Burden Iron in Troy, New York. In particular, James Burden enjoyed fishing and hunting in the remote forests of Quebec. In the early 1900s, he built a camp near Bear Lake, and soon began taking his wife and three children there for a month's sojourn each year. Whereas Douglas's older brother James and younger sister Sheila simply enjoyed camp life, he adored it. Most of all, he relished venturing out with his father's ingenious hunting guide, Archie Miller, who was half-Indian, half-Scotch. Although tutored by an elite corps of educators at Groton and Harvard, Douglas's most influential teacher seems to have been Miller, who imparted to him a wealth of woods lore, camping skills, and hunting prowess. When he graduated from Harvard in 1922, Burden chose adventure in far-flung places over a job in his father's office. By this time he had summered in various hinterlands—trekking and hunting in Alaska and participating in an unprofitable but exciting diamond-mining expedition in Brazil. These credits, coupled with dozens of journeys into Quebec's frontier, won him a collection commission from the American Museum of Natural History in New York. If the commission failed to offer much in the way of financing, it lent considerable respectability to the young graduate's exotic pursuits. Over the next two years he hunted tigers in Indochina, honey bear in India, and markhor and ibex in the Himalyas. In 1924 he ventured off in search of a lost silver mine in Nicaragua.[3]

When Molly met Douglas at Texas Guinan's club in 1928, he was the toast of the town—a budding naturalist-explorer married to a beautiful New York stage actress, a new trustee of the Natural History Museum, a scion of wealth with a poetic yet virile handsomeness. His most recent expedition—to the tiny volcanic island of Komodo in the Dutch East Indies (now Indonesia)—had been much heralded in newspapers.[4] He had filmed the world's largest lizard, known as the Komodo "dragon." What's more, he had bagged fourteen of these giant reptiles, including two live specimens for the Bronx Zoo. Although the zoo lizards died, apparently because the keepers could not come up with the right diet for them, they helped awaken Burden's interest in living animals over trophies.[5]

Not long after returning from Komodo, Burden saw the

much-touted Merian Cooper film, *Chang* (1927), a docu-drama depicting a Thai family's struggle for survival among leopards, tigers, monkeys, and elephants in the jungles of Southeast Asia. The film, infused with spellbinding "natural drama"[6] that defied typical Hollywood fare, triggered in Burden a plan to make a "truthful picture of primitive Indian life." For years he had objected to the fact that nearly all "films about Indians projected not the aborigines, but the white man's notion of them."[7] He certainly did not invent this complaint. Back in 1911, American Indians in full tribal regalia gathered on the steps of the Capitol building in Washington, D.C., to demonstrate against the way films portrayed their people.[8] Sick of inaccurate and demeaning portrayals of Indians as wicked savages of the plains, Burden vowed to challenge the status quo by producing a realistic film record of traditional Ojibwa Indian life—before it and the wilderness vanished.

Looking for a coproducer, he presented the concept to his close friend and Harvard classmate, William Chanler, a junior parter at a prestigious New York law firm. Chanler, who shared Burden's blue-blood background as well as his enthusiasm for the north woods, fancied the idea and secured temporary leave from his job to work on it. Aiming to gain insight into sixteenth-century Ojibwa life, the two men studied and discussed portions of the *Jesuit Relations*—seventy-two volumes written between 1610 and 1791 by Jesuit missionaries, who had firsthand knowledge of the traditional cultures of the indigenous peoples of what was then New France.[9] When the young coproducers felt that they had reached "a mental state where we could interpret the psychology of the Indian mind under given conditions," Burden sat down and began writing.[10]

The storyline he wrote went like this: Arctic winter is pressing in on a hunting and gathering band of Ojibwa Indians in Northern Ontario during pre-colonial days. A "silent enemy"—hunger—lurks around the corner. Baluk, the great hunter of the band, is in love with Chief Chetoga's beautiful daughter, Neewa. So is Dagwan, the devious medicine man. Baluk saves Neewa from an angry she-bear with his bow and arrow and then skins the animal on the spot. Later, he tracks and spears a moose. But these kills only postpone the band's hunger. There is virtually no game left in the area. As snow blows harder and the threat of starvation increases, Baluk convinces the aging chief that the band must leave the sheltering forest and forge far into the barren lands of the north, where they will find food amongst vast herds of migrating caribou. The long, hazardous journey claims many lives, including Chetoga's. There are no caribou in sight, and the survivors are exhausted and afraid. Dagwan, who has tried repeatedly to discredit Baluk, capitalizes on the community's vulnerability. A flurry of snow whirls up as he does a medicine dance, and he tells the band that this is a sign that they must sacrifice Baluk, who has misguided them, to appease the Great Spirit. Baluk, ever noble, chooses to die by fire. A funeral pyre is erected, he climbs atop it, and the fire is lit. As the flames lick around him, Baluk pounds the drum and chants his death song with intensifying ferver. Suddenly, signal fires from the north proclaim the coming of the great herd. Baluk, lifted from the fire, survives and leads the hunt. A raging sea of caribou pours over the windswept plain—a feast on hooves. Baluk and his huntsmen return to camp with a plentiful kill. The tribe has been rescued from the silent enemy, and feasting and rejoicing abound around the camp fires. Baluk wins Neewa. And Dagwan, banished from the camp without food or weapons, walks into the frozen wilderness toward a sure death.[11]

Burden's epic tale included elements from *Chang* as well as three other landmark semi-documentaries. The caribou stampede echoed the thundering rush of elephants in *Chang*. The remarkable hunting scenes and the band's valiant battle against nature were reminiscent of Flaherty's *Nanook of the North* (1922). The Ojibwa's long and difficult food-seeking journey recalled another Cooper film, *Grass* (1925), which chronicled the tortuous, pasture-seeking migrations of Iran's Bakhtiari herders. And, similar to Curtis's Kwakuitl Indian film, *In the Land of the War Canoes* (1914), Burden's story required the reconstruction of a traditional culture among a people whose weapons, housing, clothing, and way of life had changed considerably under Euramerican influence. Also like Curtis's film, it featured an evil shaman, a beautiful maiden, a noble hero, and a huge cast of extras—plus a large investment in bad wigs for the men. Burden and Chanler hired H. P. Carver and his son Richard as director and script writer. H. P. had been general manager of Cosmopolitan Productions for William Randolf Hearst for five years and he had set up a studio in Florida. He and his son had worked on *Grass*.[12] Script in hand, the producers arranged financing with friends and private investors and approached Paramount's production director Jesse Lasky for a distribution contract. Lasky, who had handled the distribution of *Chang* and *Grass*, doubted Burden and his boys could get the shots that were scripted but was sufficiently impressed to draw up a contract.[13]

Then it was time to hunt for actors, with a commitment to hiring only Indians. Burden was by no means the first producer to cast Indians as Indians. But he was one of a handful concerned about tribal specificity and the ethnographic correctness of clothing and props. To portray Ojibwa, he wanted real Ojibwa dressed in authentic traditional Ojibwa clothing. Also unusual was the fact that his script included a love story between two Indians. This diverged significantly from the Hollywood recipe, which typically called for a white hero or heroine as one-half of the love interest.[14]

Burden began his casting effort by looking for actors to portray the principal characters. Hollywood producers, who packed their films with real Indian extras, commonly cast white actors to play leading Indian roles. While Burden did not do this, he did compromise somewhat by hiring Indians from other tribal groups to fill three of five star roles. One of them was Molly. Burden had heard about the Indian dancer at Texas Guinan's, and went to the club to witness one of Molly's impassioned performances. After giving her a screen test, he invited her to play Neewa. Molly ignored her doctor's dire warnings that roughing it through an icy winter in Canada

Molly with Ateek, a husky used in *The Silent Enemy.* After the film was shot, Molly took Ateek to Indian Island, and the dog spent the rest of his life in the Nelson household.

would overtax her lungs and might cost her life. She was so thrilled by the offer of a leading role in a "true" Indian movie that would be filmed on location in the great north woods, that she eagerly accepted Burden's offer, and signed a substantial contract for two hundred dollars a week.[15]

The film's director, H. P. Carver, found someone to play the role of Neewa's father, Chief Chetoga. As he strolled the halls of the Museum of Natural History one day, his attention was arrested by the striking and seasoned features of an Indian who was perusing the exhibits.[16] The wizened elder turned out to be Chauncey Yellow Robe, a hereditary chief of the Sioux and a grand nephew of Sitting Bull. Born in the last days of the buffalo hunt, Yellow Robe had spent his boyhood roaming the plains of the Dakotas, Montana, Wyoming, and Nebraska—fishing and hunting, and passing many hours listening to ancient Sioux stories in his grandparents' buffalo-hide tepee. At age fifteen, dressed in "full Indian costume, long hair . . . and painted face, [and] not knowing a word of English," Yellow Robe was entrusted to General R. H. Pratt, founder of the Carlisle Indian School in Pennsylvania. He was one of the first Sioux to be exposed to Carlisle's mandate to instill young Indians with the skills and values of Christian civilization. When he arrived at the school, the staff took his photograph "for curiosity's sake," cut his hair, and plunked him into a tub of warm water with plenty of soap. "Thus began my first process of civilization," Yellow Robe later wrote. "Never had I experienced such home-sickness. . . . How many times I . . . watched the Western sky and cried within my broken heart, wishing to see my father and mother again and be free on the plains." Despite this adverse beginning, Yellow Robe excelled as a student. By the time he graduated, with honors, the 1890 massacre of Wounded Knee in South Dakota had claimed the lives of three hundred Indian men, women and children. It was abundantly clear that he would have little opportunity to return to a traditional life. Surely, this fact, perhaps coupled with the hope of saving other young Indians from the trauma he experienced when he came to Carlisle, prompted Yellow Robe to accept a job as boys' advisor at the Federal Indian Residential School at Rapid City, South Dakota. He held the position for twenty-five years.[17]

Although the federal government provided Yellow Robe's paycheck for more than two decades, it never ruled his heart. As a true Indian patriot, he spoke out harshly against the injustices imposed upon native peoples. Among the exploitations he publicly condemned were wild west shows and other entertainments that "degraded, demoralized, and degenerated" Indians and their traditions.[18] When Carver approached him and described the plan to make a genuine film about Indians, Yellow Robe was intrigued, but skeptical. Soon Carver introduced him to Burden who felt certain he was the man they wanted for the part of the old chief. Bit by bit Burden convinced him that the film would be as accurate as possible and would not misrepresent Indians in any way. Yellow Robe agreed to participate, and ultimately he befriended Burden. In fact, they shared a tent throughout the on-location shooting, and Yellow Robe wrote and delivered the film's opening narrative.[19]

To portray the heroic Baluk, Burden and Chanler hired a Blackfoot Indian Chief named Buffalo Child Long Lance. From head to toe, Long Lance presented a captivating picture of chiseled manliness. His accomplishments matched his physical stature. He had graduated at the top of the class of 1912 at Carlisle Indian School, where he had run track and played football. (One of his teammates and friends was 1912 Olympic champion Jim Thorpe, who used him as his training partner.) After Carlisle, Long Lance won a scholarship to St. John's Military Academy near Syracuse, New York. In 1915, Woodrow Wilson selected him as one of his six presidential appointments to West Point, but Long Lance chose, instead, to enlist in the Canadian army for World War I service. He emerged from the war wounded but highly decorated. After his honorable discharge he settled in Alberta, Canada, and signed on as a reporter for the *Calgary Herald*. Over the next few years he worked mostly on investigative stories about the miserable living conditions of Indians on the reserves. Leaving the *Herald* in 1922, he expanded the circle of his publishing, winning credits in Canada's major papers and perios, and then in the United States. His 1927 *Cosmopolitan* story, "The Secret of the Sioux," presented a fanciful account of Custer's Last Stand that created a sensation and made Long Lance a celebrity overnight. It also won him a contract to write his autobiography,

Long Lance, published in New York by Farrar and Rinehart in
1928. It was the compelling, broad-shouldered portrait of Long
Lance in the book's frontispiece that convinced Burden and
Chanler that the author was made for movies, especially theirs.
What the producers did not know was that Long Lance was
not a Blackfoot Indian at all. In truth, he was Sylvester Long,
born in 1890 in North Carolina, into a tri-racial household
defined as "colored" by dominant mainstream society. His
father, Joe Long, was raised a slave, never knew his parents,
and took his name from his master, Reverend Miles Long. Joe's
ancestry was mixed—part-Indian (perhaps Catawba or Cherokee) and probably European and African as well. Sylvester's
mother, Sallie, was part white and part Lumbee (mixed Indian,
English, and African). Growing up in an era when racial
segregation and oppression were barely questioned, let alone
challenged, Sylvester soon discovered how limited his opportunities were as a "colored" boy. At age thirteen, he left home
and joined a wild west show. With his coppery skin and straight
black hair, he was able to pass and perform as an Indian—and
began to think of himself as one. After five years on the road,
he returned home in 1909. With his father's help, he applied to
Carlisle Indian School. Since Joe Long was uncertain of his
own particular Indian descent, he identified his son on the
application with the Indians best known in North Carolina—
the Cherokee. When Sylvester arrived at Carlisle, a sympathetic teacher added Lance to his name, apparently to "Indi-
anize" his identity among legitimate Cherokee students, who
taunted him as the "Cherokee nigger." For more than a decade,
Sylvester presented himself as Cherokee. Then, as a journalist
writing about the Canadian Blood (a division of the Blackfeet),
he was adopted by the tribe and given the name Buffalo Child.
Adding the title of chief, he henceforth identified himself as
Chief Buffalo Child Long Lance, Blackfoot Indian. In his
autobiography, he invented a new history to go with the name,
starting with a bold claim that he had been born in a Blackfoot
tepee on the Great Plains.[20]
    Burden, as obsessed with the "purity" of his film as domi-

Promotional poster for *The Silent Enemy* (1930), a docu-drama
about Ojibwa Indians struggling to survive wintertime. Three of the
male principles are pictured here: Yellow Robe (who played
Chetoga) in center, Buffalo Child Long Lance (Baluk) on his right,
and Paul Benoit (Dagwan) on his left.

nant society was with its racial categories, had no idea that
Long Lance was as much white and black as he was Indian.
Had he known, he would never have hired him to play the lead
role in his Indian epic.

With actors in place for three of the film's principal parts,
Burden headed to Northern Ontario to find a supporting cast of
one hundred Ojibwa Indians. He aimed to hire "pure blood
families" who still lived, at least seasonally, in the bush.[21] At
that time, a fair number of Ojibwa in the region spent the
winter months deep in the forest in scattered family groups
trapping fur-bearing animals, especially for Hudson's Bay Company. In the summer they gathered in lakeside villages where

they fished, picked wild berries, and tapped into incomes available for Indian guides and cooks at a modest number of tourist camps.[22]

Madeline Theriault, an Ojibwa born on Bear Island in Lake Temagami in 1908, was among the so-called "bush Indians" Burden encountered and hired to work on his film. What was life really like for her and her people at that time? Although Madeline never lived in a birchbark tepee, she remembers visiting elders on Bear Island who did. "We had log houses," she says, and "we made our own bark canoes, and snowshoes with moosehide. . . . We wore ordinary [cloth] clothes in real life, and [skin] costumes only for special occasions. I knew how to make traditional clothes because I lived with my great-grand-mother and she taught me." Madeline recollects a childhood intricately tied to the seasons: summers at the Ojibwa village on the island, setting fish nets and collecting berries; autumns and winters at the family's trapping grounds to the northwest—harvesting mink, fox, and muskrat for trade with Hudson's Bay. "We kept the meat, smoked it," she recalls. The pelts were delivered to the nearest trading post—a twenty-five mile walk. As a young girl, Madeline set snares, hoping to get the seventy-plus rabbit pelts needed to make a blanket. She remembers her great-grandmother making birchbark cups, and her great-grandfather using the cups to catch the sap dripping from the maple trees he tapped each spring. Although spring brought treats such as maple syrup, it also brought several weeks of trouble: "When the thaw comes, you cannot go anywhere to hunt. The snow is wet and the lakes are all water slush. . . . We would prepare . . . by stocking up food such as moose, rabbit, partridges, and beaver . . . [but] one year it came unexpected-ly and we were not ready. . . . I was barely able to walk, I was so hungry."[23]

The annual spring thaw was not the only threat to Ojibwa survival during Madeline's childhood. Ojibwa also faced the problem of encroachment on hunting grounds by white tour-ists, trappers, loggers, and farmers. Of these, tourism had the least negative impact, for it drew a manageable number of nature lovers who appreciated and paid for the bush know-how of Indians. Visitors who retreated to the area for a few weeks of hunting and fishing in the wilderness could hire Indian guides and rent canoes, tents, blankets, and other supplies from Hudson's Bay Company. Temagami was among the many tourist-drawing lakes in the region. According to Madeline, it "was a most beautiful lake. . . . very special with a lot of good fishing. There were only a few tourist camps with tents . . . [and] only one little motor launch. . . . [plus] the "Belle," a large steamboat [that] brought both passengers and supplies to Bear Island. . . . Everyone paddled to get around. . . . It was so quiet . . . [that] when the loons called the water would vibrate."[24] While tourism nibbled at the edges of Ojibwa culture, the other encroachments gobbled it. White trappers consumed the Indians' primary means of subsistence. Loggers, like farmers, destroyed their hunting grounds, plus nature's storehouse of traditional medicines.[25]

Undoubtedly, traditional Ojibwa life, based on nature's offerings, was on the way out when Burden decided to make his docu-drama. Yet, there remained a remnant population familiar with the old ways. To streamline his search for these semitraditional Indians, Burden decided to track down Father Evain, a Roman Catholic priest, and "trail along with [him] on his missions" at the various summer villages of the Ojibwa. Evain, a good-natured, roly-poly fellow with a forked white beard that draped over his chest, had traveled this vast territory by canoe in summer and dog team in the winter for over thirty years—visiting the Ojibwa's scattered villages to baptize their children, solemnize their marriages, and lead them in mass. His life echoed that of the seventeenth-century Jesuit missionaries, whose field reports had provided Burden with the basis for his script. As Burden made his way from village to village, tent to tent, he engaged the Ojibwa in conversations like this one, which took place at Low Bush on Abitibi Lake, near the Quebec border. In his words:

It was warm and sunny and I was sitting in the grass on the edge of a deep, slow-moving stream which a few hundred yards below entered the gray waters of Abitibi. The Indians were squatting on their haunches around me and I was conversing with them through an interpreter.

"There is no fur left on your trapping ground," I said.

"No, there is no fur left."

"Next winter, then, you and your family will be starving."

"Yes, we will be hungry."

"Well, if you come with me, you will have plenty of good food all winter and you will receive handsome wages besides."

Suspiciously, "What will we have to do?"

"You will simply have to lead your own life, hunting, fishing and pursuing game in the forest just as you and your forefathers have done for countless generations. But while you are doing this, you must let us taking moving pictures of you. It is easy. Will you come?"[26]

Come they did—more than one hundred Ojibwa from villages at lakes Temagami, Abitibi, Temiskaming, and Kipawa, from Timmins at Mattegami River west of Abitibi and from Mattawa on the Ottawa River to the south.[27] With fur at a low point, due to an influx of white trappers who gained easy access to the region on the recently expanded railway system, Ojibwa families were in great need of new economic opportunities.[28] Burden's offer of sixty dollars a month was too good to resist.[29] Two of the Ojibwa Burden met on his cast-gathering foray were hired as leading actors in the film. For the part of Dagwan the medicine man, Burden selected Chief Akawansh, better known by his Christian name, Paul Benoit. A trapper and guide from Golden Lake, Ontario, southeast of Temagami, Benoit happened to be in the north during Burden's casting expedition. He had the skills, enthusiasm, and appearance Burden was looking for, and proved to have a remarkable flare for acting.[30] A thirteen-year-old Ojibwa boy named Cheeka, whom Burden encountered at Abitibi, turned out to be another natural actor. Cheeka, whose Christian name was George McDougal, had lived all his life in the bush. The moment Burden saw the youngster, he recognized in him the wilderness savvy, courage, and playfulness needed to play Neewa's little brother. He hired Cheeka on the spot (adopting his name for the character he portrayed), along with his mother, Cassie, who worked as an extra in the film.[31]

By fall, Burden had lined up his cast, production team, and camp laborers. He brought the group together in Quebec at Fred Arnet's Tem-Kip Camp (short for Temiskaming-Kipawa). The site sat by the mouth of the Kipawa River at the lower end of Lake Temiskaming, which straddles the Ontario-Quebec border. With everyone on location, the *real* work began.

Molly arrived by train, traveling from the bustle of New York's Grand Central Station, through seven hundred miles of autumn-dressed forest, to the tiny station at Temiskaming. It was the same route her anthropology mentor Frank Speck took back in 1913 when he researched the myths and folklore of the Temiskaming Algonquin and Temagami Ojibwa. Molly's 1928 diary, chronicling this trip and her first months on location, is missing. But her 1929 journal survives, and contains daily entries about the picture's production during the on-location shooting from January through April. Molly also wrote a nine-page narrative for the film's publicist, detailing some of the harrowing events and typical daily doings that occurred on the set. She summed up the exceptional challenges of the production:

> Only someone who was on location can understand the hardships and the many difficulties that had to be overcome. The picture is not an ordinary one with all the facilities of a movie studio, personal comforts and experienced actors at command. It is a picture filmed as life among the Ojibways presented itself to the camera. . . . There were dangers encountered, delays of long duration, situations of all kinds to be met. . . . From the selection of leading characters and the assembling of the various [Ojibwa groups], to the erection of temporary camps, the [creation of traditional sets], the maintenance of staff, principals and extras, the transportation of supplies and mail, the uncertainty of weather conditions, and the hundred and odd duties and responsibilities of the movie camp, it was indeed a stupendous task.[32]

After several weeks of prop and costume preparation and filming fall scenes at Tem-Kip, Burden decided camp conditions and scenery options were inadequate and moved the entire production westward to Rabbit Chutes. Here, midway between Lake Temiskaming and Lake Temagami, Rabbit Lake emptied into the Matabitchuan River beneath long shadows of virgin red and white pines. Located more than twenty trail miles from the Temagami train station, the site posed logistical challenges, but these were more than compensated for by the pristine beauty of the place. A gently sloping, tree-studded ridge, bordered by the river's churning rapids on one side and the broad stillness of the lake on the other, provided a magnificent setting in which to film and camp from late fall through early spring.[33]

To build and run the camp, Burden hired twenty-seven-year-old Bob Hennessey of Haileybury—a tough, bush-wise scoundrel "full of Irish blarney." Hennessey, the son of a lumbering contractor, liked to say he picked his crew "by the way they walked." He ruled with an iron hand. Taking care of food, shelter, and fuel for well over one hundred people was no small task, since supplies had to be transported by dog team and canoe. It was particularly tough during transitional seasons of freeze-up and thaw. (On one run just after freeze-up, a dog driver, his tobaggan, and his entire dog team took a fatal fall through a stretch of unexpectedly thin ice.)[34]

The camp constructed by Hennessey and his crew filled several acres of forest. It consisted of nearly forty canvas tents set on platforms, encased by six-foot wood walls, and topped with a tarp to ward off moisture and cold. Heat came from small wood stoves, fueled by the harvest of the woods crew and its team of work horses. The spatial setup of the living quarters in this wilderness community reflected society's pattern of segregation. The Ojibwa lived four-to-eight family members per tent. Their shelters were set in a cluster about eighty feet away from the two-person staff tents that housed the film's executives and production crew, plus Molly, Long Lance, and Yellow Robe. Hennessey's workers lived near the film staff, three men to a tent. There was also a handful of wooden buildings—a small commissary, an office, and a forty-by-twenty-five-foot cookery/dining hall that doubled as a gym and dance hall. In the cookery, Hennessey's men ate at one of two

The on-location cabin where Molly lived during *The Silent Enemy*
filming (fall 1928–spring 1929). She shared living quarters with her
childhood Penobscot friend Dorothy "Dul" Ranco, who joined the
shoot as Molly's double and companion. (Photograph by Molly—
from her *Silent Enemy* photo album.)

long wooden tables, while the film staff dined at a smaller
table. The Ojibwa cooked and ate in their tents, with food-
stuffs supplied by Hennessey's team.[35]

With living quarters intact and inhabitants installed, work
began on reconstructing the traditional material culture of the
Ojibwa, including tools, weapons, snowshoes, toboggans, bark
canoes, and a village of conical birchbark wigwams. Snowshoe
frames and much of the animal skin clothing for the entire cast
had been made at Tem-Kip. Madeline Theriault, well-trained
by her great-grandmother, remembers being one of a handful
of women at the camp who "knew how to work with the leather
to make such items as moccasins and mitts, or how to fill the
snowshoes. . . . Don't think we . . . weren't busy! . . . [We] had
to make one hundred complete Indian outfits in one month for
use in the picture. This meant working all day and part of the
night."[36] While costumes and props were being made and the traditional village was under construction, the cinematographer,
Marcel Le Picard, worked on various closeups: Baluk talking with

Chetoga, Cheeka spearfishing, an Ojibwa elder constructing a bark canoe, a mountain lion battling a bear for a deer carcass. Molly's account provides a description of a typical day:

Each night, a schedule was issued . . . for the next day's activities, weather permitting. . . . With the beginning of daylight, and sometimes before . . . work would begin when Shorty, the night watchman, built our fires and awakened us if we were needed for the day on location. . . . We donned our costumes and packed any necessary props. . . . And after [we'd eaten] a well-cooked breakfast, the huskies were harnessed to our sleds, sandwiches and coffee packed on the lighter sleds and cameras on the heavier ones, and we were off. . . . Traveling was difficult and slow at times on snow shoes in winter, and on foot over unblazed trails in warm weather.

The scenes were shot according to the script, but when incidents arose which were not expected, they were filmed also. . . .

Work did not stop with the twi-light always, for many scenes were shot at night, sometimes at [temperatures] fifty [degrees] below zero. Between scenes, the groups would huddle about camp fires . . . [drinking] coffee to stimulate them into further action. When [these night shots] were done, it was a beautiful thing to see the Indians walking in single file and hear them singing as they moved in the moonlight or deep shadows of night.[37]

More often than not, scenes were rewritten just before shooting. Burden, anxious for accuracy, engaged in participatory cinema, reminiscent of Flaherty's approach in making *Nanook*. He and director Carver regularly summoned selected members of the cast for their input: "Every night we would gather with the leaders of the Indians and the older men of the company and talk over the events that were to be photographed the next day. Thus the story was essentially [re]written by the Indians themselves. One elderly chief would relate the traditions of his tribe as they bore on the incident we were preparing to film. 'My grandfather would say,' or 'I can remember hearing about just such a happening.' And so the picture grew out of the actual life experience of our players, the Indians."[38] From Molly's numerous notes about meetings with Carver each night before she was scheduled to be in a scene, it is clear that the director was always interested in her interpretation of a scene. She, in turn, welcomed every opportunity to collaborate with this "most generous, kind-hearted person in the company."[39] Although aiming for ethnographic accuracy, Burden and his cohorts made a classic documentation error: they focused on Ojibwa material culture (clothing, tools, housing, etc.) and failed to investigate thoroughly customs, associations, and attitudes. Plus, some of their Indian informants (Molly, Long Lance, and Yellow Robe) were hardly Ojibwa specialists. This led to significant errors, lost on the film critics and general public of his day: the cliché of an "evil" medicine man; the bizarre presentation of forty or more Ojibwa tramping about en masse during the winter (the actual strategy against hunger was to divide into small hunting groups); a funeral pyre scene unfounded among Canadian Ojibwa (perhaps based on Jesuit accounts of Iroquoian burnings and sacrifice). In addition, despite the authenticity of most artifacts and apparel in the film, Yellow Robe appears in Plains Indian regalia during Chief Chetoga's death scene.[40]

The truly rare wild animal scenes filmed by Burden's team were not all achieved without intervention. As Cooper had done in *Chang*, Burden captured several wild animal species and kept them in large fenced-in areas within their natural habitat until he needed them. For instance, to obtain the footage of a bear and mountain lion fighting over a deer, the animals were denied food for several days, then released with the deer.[41] In another scene, the moose speared by Long Lance was also a captive—but the man-to-moose encounter was nonetheless perilous for Long Lance, who was nearly taken onto the antlers.[42] Molly, too, faced life-threatening situations—among them, the shooting of this bear scene, which she later wrote about:

> There were times when my life was in danger [such as] . . . in the opening scenes of the picture when a she-bear and I were on a cliff shelf . . . [where] the men had found the lair of [this] bear and her cubs. . . . The shelf was reached by rope ladders from below [or by] a narrow passage of crumbling rocks from above.

Days were spent in shooting the scene, days of climbing rope ladders and my being left on shelf with the animal. After days of mere sniffing about, the bear became really angry. It was time to shoot. My directions were to move according to the movements of the bear. . . . When she suddenly chattered her teeth at me and charged, I ran as fast as I could, but she gained on me until I felt the warm moisture of her breath on my feet. There was no place to run to for safety, and had it not been for the arrow from Long Lance's bow in that moment, I probably would have leaped from the cliff to the rocks below. The arrow struck home and the bear fell . . . with a thud.[43]

According to Long Lance's biographer, Donald Smith, it was actually Chanler, an expert archer, who shot the arrow that killed the bear, but the footage was later edited to make it appear that the saving arrow came from Long Lance's bow.[44] However, David McLaren, a fourteen-year-old camp worker whose mother served as schoolteacher on the set, asserts that the bear actually died from a gunshot wound: "The bear was eight feet away from Molly with a crevice between them and they thought it wouldn't jump, but it did. . . . A fellow named Bob Miller was hanging by a rope outside of camera range with a gun and fired. The arrow didn't kill it at all."[45] Even with two superb marksmen, one poised with a gun, the other with a bow, it was a hair-raising event for everyone on the set. Burden witnessed it, and later wrote, "I personally was present when the scene of the girl and the bear on the cliff was photographed, and I may say that I spent a very unpleasant half hour wondering whether or not we would have a heroine to complete the picture with."[46]

To shoot the film's spectacular climax, a massive caribou stampede, Burden sent his friend Ilia Tolstoy (grandson of the famous Russian novelist) on an expedition some one thousand miles northward into the Barren Lands. His harrowing mission matched that of Baluk in the film: to find a vast herd of migrating caribou. Tolstoy traveled by canoe with a party of Indians and two cameramen. They paddled tremendous distances, trekked terrific portages, and braved months of hardship—only to miss the migration, perhaps by as much as five

Head cameraman Marcel Picard and assistants shooting *The Silent Enemy* in Northern Ontario, 1929. Douglas Burden's young cousin, Shirley Burden, whose mother helped finance the film, is third from the left. (Photograph by Molly—from her *Silent Enemy* photo album.)

hundred miles. A second expedition had to be sent. With no time to spare, Burden went for the sure thing. While Carver continued filming at Rabbit Chutes, he sent Assistant Director Earl Welch by air to Alaska's North Slope, near Point Barrow— a quicker, but nonetheless perilous journey. Here, the Loman brothers, known as "the reindeer kings of Alaska," could guarantee footage of enormous herds of reindeer (domesticated caribou). Welch traveled with costumes, a camera-man, and several cast members, including Cheeka. In addition to capturing on film the thundrous maelstrom of thousands of hooves pounding over the tundra, Welch staged a chilling stunt: he instructed Cheeka to shelter himself behind a dead reindeer, and then he drove the rest of the herd over the boy and the carcass. Cheeka emerged unscathed, and Welch obtained extraordinary footage.[47]

Everyone involved in the film endured physical hardships, not the least of which were long hours of filming in bitter cold temperatures that took a toll on the health of many. Like Molly, Paul Benoit (Dagwan, the medicine man) had a history of tuberculosis. Burden, although he didn't know it during the shoot, was battling amoebic dysentary—contracted during his 1924 travels in Nicaragua.[48] From January through March, Molly's diary includes entry after entry about illness: "Burden sick—also Paul, both colds." "Paul Benoit taken to hospital for pneumonia. Not feeling good myself." "George [Cheeka] froze his big toe." "My good knee is worse than my bad one." "Mr. Burden is very sick in his tepee." "My spine ached. Trust vertebrae has not slipped again." "Boss not well." "Mr. Burden not well." "Sick all night with a cold. The hot tody did me no good. Chilled and sweated at intervals. Slept all morning. Lungs sore. Hot water bottles and more hot todys." "Stayed in bed. Bones ache all over. Doctor in to see me." "Took some aspirin and glass of gin for my chills." "[co-producer] Willie Chanler not well." "Willie Chanler is sick and fevered." "Willie—he is very sick."

When not feeling under the weather or involved in shooting a scene, Molly worked to maintain her dance figure and strength by keeping up a rigorous daily exercise program that included long snowshoe hikes and workouts in the gym. She often hiked alone, although Paul Benoit and Yellow Robe were frequent partners. Typical among diary notes are these: "28-mile hike . . . [with] Paul . . . to Sunrise [Lake and] on to Temagami [Lake]. It was cold and windy." "Out snowshoeing this afternoon. I found a new little lake and many ermine, fox and deer tracks. Glorious afternoon through the bush." "Yellow Robe and I walked. We had a slippery but interesting one . . . [to] Bass Lake. The old chief is a marvelous hiker." "In gym to sweat out with Paul." "Up to gym to exercise, stretch and dance. Made crude trapeze. Did some Foster [Girl] stunts on it. Tired out." "Exercized in gym on trapeze, jumping rope, and stretching." "Worked out all afternoon." Occasionally, the five-foot actress "worked up a sweat boxing," gingerly, with muscleman Long Lance, who also kept to a daily exercise regimen. Long Lance's real sparring partners were the robust Hennessey boys—Bob, his brother Alex, and their cousin Ted. He typically boxed nine rounds in a row, three with each Hennessey.[49]

But life on the set was by no means all work and hardship. There in the north woods, where there were "no luxuries" and "no need of money," Molly enjoyed many simple pleasures. Sometimes she and Yellow Robe went tobogganing together.[50] Other times she and Long Lance would break a hole in the ice and go swimming with Shirley Burden—Douglas' twenty-one-year-old cousin who received on-the-job-training in film production in exchange for his mother's major capital investment in the film. Shirley remembers well the first time Molly coerced him into taking an icy dip: "She came to my tent very early in the morning [the day after I arrived on the set], and said, 'Let's go Shirley—swimming!' I said, 'My god, it's thirty degrees!' But I went. She was warm and friendly and I got along beautifully with her."[51]

In addition to relishing what she called "one of the greatest events of the day" (mail delivery by dog sled), Molly made notes about traditional Ojibwa life, read voraciously, helped sew costumes, and took great pleasure in typical "evenings of merry-making, quaint songs, friendly visits and chatter, cards, dominoes, and checkers."[52] There were also occasional dances and special events in the dining hall, such as this one described by Burden's sister, Sheila Lawrence, who visited the set for two weeks:

The night before I left, the leading characters in the camp gave me a party. It remains the best party I have ever been to. After dinner and speeches, in the cook house, a lantern was placed on the floor, its flickering light making long shadows on the rafters and the moving figures. Andy and Antoine [Ojibwa guides and extras] did their mountain lion and bear pantomine. . . . Paul Benoit did a convincing medicine man dance. Shorty, a tiny East End Londoner, sang cockney songs with gusto. . . . Molly and "Dul" [her Penobscot companion] sang a song for us. . . . Ilia, with his guitar, sang some of his gypsy songs. Douglas stepped into a tepee with a large squaw and somehow stepped out with a young beauty. Long Lance, stripped to the waist, with his full feather headdress streaming behind him, did a superb Indian dance to the beat of Ilia's tom-tom. With sweat gleaming on his powerful torso, Long Lance was a thrilling sight. . . . The climax of the evening was a speech by Yellow Robe, also in full regalia, delivered with his usual dignity and simplicity.[53]

On several occasions, Father Evain came to Rabbit Chutes. According to Burden, the priest always arrived with cash in his pocket and "a twinkle in his eye." Madeline Theriault recalls, "Father Evain brought money so we could cash our [pay] cheques and give our . . . donation to the church."[54] Beyond conducting mass and fundraising for the church, the priest sanctified common-law marriages that took place on the set and baptized babies born during the filming expedition— some of whom received curious names such as Shirley Burden Batiste or Douglas Burden Benoit.[55]

When children were not needed in a shoot, they attended a one-tent schoolhouse set up by Burden. Their thirty-five-year-old teacher, Elizabeth McLaren, had an eigth grade education. She had worked as an itinerant teacher for Indian children for nearly two decades under the auspices of the Department of Indian Affairs. She herself was one-eighth Ojibwa, and many, including Molly, referred to her as a "half-breed." During the production's stay at Rabbit Chutes, Elizabeth lived in a nearby log cabin with her husband, Donald (a commercial fisher and woodsman), and their teenage son, David—both of whom helped out at the camp. As she had done in every Indian community where she had taught, Elizabeth also served as midwife.[56]

According to Burden, Molly almost needed a midwife herself: "When problems arose in our camp that called for something extra special, as when our leading lady, Princess Spotted Elk became pregnant in a starvation theme picture, I told Bob [Hennessey] he would have to handle this delicate matter in such a way that not a word got out. And he succeeded. I never asked any questions but it was all expertly managed so that, after a brief visit 'outside,' our Princess returned in full health."[57] The story may have been a ruse, fabricated by Bob Hennessey, who resented the fact that his romantic interest, Dorothy Ranco ("Dul"), had to play second fiddle to Molly as her companion, assistant, and double. Hennessey was infamous for his tall tales and Molly repeatedly complained about his rumor mongering. There is no hint of an abortion in her diary, which shows that she left Rabbit Chutes for the "outside" only once during the entire shoot. Eager to have a break and wishing to get herself "fixed up" for close-up interior shots, she asked Burden for a two-day leave in February. Burden agreed. The overnight trip—one hundred miles round trip by sled, train, and taxi to Cobalt and Haileybury—took less than forty hours. It included a hair dye, facial, massage, dentist appointment, professional ice hockey game, and a bit of relatively fancy dining. If Molly had had an abortion in addition to (or instead of) these activities, surely she would have needed some time to recuperate before making the rather strenuous journey back to camp.[58]

Yet, at the beginning of 1929, it is clear from Molly's diary that she was romantically involved with Ted Hennessey, Bob's happy-go-lucky cousin and crew member, who frequently broke the camp's no drinking rules. In the wee hours of the first morning of the new year, he glued a small photo of himself in her diary and beside it wrote this message: "January the First, 1 A.M. The most eventful night of my life. [Signed] Ted Hennessey." On 3 January Molly confided to her diary: "Here I am supposedly engaged to the [New York] scion [Bryan Cheedy] and friendly with the bush man." Burden, probably anxious to prevent undue complications on his set, explicit instructed Bob Hennessey to put a stop to Molly's rendevous with his cousin. Molly made note of this: "Slipped over to [Ted's]. . . . Learned we are not to see each other again. If we do, he loses his position." They continued to meet secretly, and Molly's diary begins to read like the script for a bad soap opera. On Valentine's day, she learned that a young woman in Toronto had become pregnant with Ted's child. After hearing the news, she told her diary, "My God! The whole thing is awful." The next day she wrote, "What more is there to misery?" A week later: "At first, knowing Ted I thought I was deeply in love with him, but lonely as I was, I can understand—gradually that feeling is fading." Then, at the end of February: "At dinner Bob told me Ted was 'hooked.' My God! Married. I thought he was joking. Saw Ted accidently in the cookery. Our stolen moments. . . . From his lips I heard everything. He says he loves me. Am so heart and soul sick that I am moving about like an automaton." Her diary entry the next day shows that her concern about her relationship with Ted went beyond heartbreak and included a possible pregnancy: "Saw the [camp] doc and had examination. Let the others say what they wish—for it was not true. How happy I was." Then, one week later: "Ted fired and gone."[59]

At first glance, Molly's romance with Ted the woodsman does not make sense. Although she craved flattery and did her share of flirting, she was a woman who focused on work and guarded her heart. If she pursued men at all, it was usually as friends, and the men she was drawn to typically exhibited a certain refinement born of intellect and, occasionally, wealth. For the most part, this leaning continued at Rabbit Chutes. She greatly enjoyed discussing and solving conceptual problems in the film's script with director H. P. Carver. She treasured her long walks with Yellow Robe, punctuated by his philosophical musings, which she believed were "wonderful and deep." When Bill Laurance, a noted film critic and journalist for the New York *World*, came to Rabbit Chutes for nearly two weeks, she spent many evenings talking with him about writing—and later supplied him with descriptive narratives to use as background for his articles about the film. Frequently she and Tolstoy talked over the ethnographic and aesthetic requirements of the film's interior scenes, and dressed the sets together.[60]

In particular, Molly was fond of William Douglas Burden, whom she referred to as WB in her diary. In fact, she fell in love with him. She could barely admit this, even to herself, but here and there in her diary it comes through: "Talked to WB. Just to see him is heaven enough." "Unbelievably happy to see WB . . . someone whom I think is the most wonderful person alive."[61] Sometimes, Molly cleaned Burden's tent. It may have been during one of her cleaning sessions that she came across a letter of caution sent to Burden by some member of the film's staff. Part of the epistle seized her attention and haunted her long afterwards with its demeaning implications. She quoted it in her diary: "Don't forget your reputation and what your friends would think. For you are human and that Indian girl is attractive. . . . To think we eat at the same table with her."[62] After reading this, she wrote, "What am I? Only an Indian girl—with an illusion of love for someone far beyond me."[63] Unlike Burden, Ted Hennessey stood well within reach. And, although Molly was the film's star, she, like this roughhewn white man, held a social status somewhere between Burden and his batch of "bush Indians."

So it was that while Burden strove to create images on film of Ojibwa life before contact with whites, life at the camp reflected social divisions that grew out of that contact. Long Lance, writing from Rabbit Chutes, said this in a letter: "The white fellows on this trip. . . . are not used to being out of the world for so long, and their remedy is to herd together all of the time: the very worst thing that they could do."[64] McLaren recalls "a clear social division" between the Ojibwa extras and the "staff," which included the film's executives, production crew, Hennessy's men, and the leading actors. As he tells it, "Molly and the other stars weren't allowed to associate with rank and file Indians. It was a rule of the company."[65] There is no other indication that Burden had a rule against these associations, but they seemed to rarely occur. According to Theriault, Burden and his inner circle were "distant." She describes Burden as "hard to get to know," Long Lance as "unfriendly and full of himself," and Molly as a "proud" person who "kind of kept herself apart."[66]

While it is true that Molly socialized primarily with the production's elite corps, plus Hennessey and his crew, her dearest friend on the set was an old Ojibwa fortune-teller who portrayed a medicine woman in the film. Molly described her as one of "the finest examples of bush women" in the group, and affectionately referred to her as "Mother" Nelson—noting that the old woman had adopted the name Nelson years before

Millionaire explorer-naturalist William Douglas Burden (in parka
and mukluks), producer of *The Silent Enemy,* on the set in the
Temagami Forest of Northern Ontario in 1929. Behind him, in the
black hat, is the film's director H. P. "Daddy" Carver. (Photograph
by Molly—from her *Silent Enemy* photo album.)

because she thought it "sounded good." Molly spent many
evenings visiting with Mrs. Nelson—listening to her childhood
stories, confiding in her, basking in her "sympathetic understanding," and holding out her palm for the old woman to
read.[67]

Although a few friendships were forged between the "bush" and
"civilization" folks involved in the film, a line of demarcation,
emphasized by salaries and separate living quarters, certainly
held great sway. For Molly, it must have been a confusing line. It is
evident that she felt a deep sense of kinship with Mother Nelson. Yet, when writing about the Ojibwa overall, she repeatedly
took the stance of an anthropologist writing about "the other."
In contrast to earlier diaries when she referred to "us injuns,"
in her 1929 journal she wrote about "the Indians." Ironically,
during the months she portrayed the prototypical Indian maid-
en before film cameras, she seems to have felt less Indian than
ever. Before coming to Canada, her social position had been
less ambiguous. In New York she was the "Indian dancer." In
Maine, the Penobscot River drew a vivid and highly symbolic
line between her people and the white community at Old

Town. At Rabbit Chutes, it was as if she had crossed the river. She felt mixed about this. The power, intellectual breadth, worldly experience, and wide social respectability enjoyed by a man like Burden attracted her. At the same time she admired and often yearned for what she saw as the uncluttered, close-to-nature lifeway of the Ojibwa who had come to Rabbit Chutes. For her, Mother Nelson's life, still so tied to the forest, struck a deeply familiar chord. It echoed the lives of her Indian Island childhood heros, such as old Joe Hemlock. Yet hers were bittersweet memories, for as much as she had cherished the simple ways of a man like Joe, she had struggled with the poverty and humiliation born of living such a life in the shadow of a growing and prospering white community. Here, on this set in the remote wilds of Northern Ontario, Molly saw two parts of herself at once and could not figure out how to put them together. To choose one over the other was unthinkable, for she was not wholly at home in either. In truth, she needed both.

In April, as the snow melted and the river ice began to break, Carver directed his last scenes, and everyone prepared to break camp. At the end of the month, the Ojibwa abandoned their caribou costumes, climbed into their canoes, and paddled to their summer villages. Molly boarded a train in Temagami and headed back to New York's vast cultural arena, where she would once again become "Indian dancer." Surely, as the train swept past a blur of emerging spring green, she contemplated her shifting position. Upon arrival, she jotted in her diary, "To return to civilization is such a disappointment."

During the next year, Burden and Carver cut and edited 250,000 feet of film down to eight thousand.[68] Concerned about the fact that "talkies" were eclipsing silent films, Burden decided to add a sound-synched prologue and to hire Paramount's Music Department to compose, record, and synchronize a musical score for the film. Hoping to strengthen the film's authenticity, Burden had Paramount work with Messard Kurzhene, who assembled Ojibwa musical motifs on which to base the score.[69] Yellow Robe wrote and delivered the prologue, speaking as if he were Chetoga, the Ojibwa chief. In an ironic

verbal twist, he endorsed the film as a "real" portrayal of Indian
life, created by the "White Man" who had "destroyed" that life
and now tried to "preserve" it on film:

> This is the story of my people. In the beginning, the Great Spirit
> gave us the land. The forests were ours and the prairies; the wild
> game was ours to hunt. We were happy when the game was plenty;
> in the years of famine we suffered. We loved our country and our
> homes. Now the white man has come; his civilization has de-
> stroyed my people. Soon we would have been forgotten. But now
> this same civilization has preserved our traditions before it was
> too late; now you will know us as we really are.[70]

Sadly, Yellow Robe died of pneumonia six weeks before the
film's debut. Molly, who saw him often in the months after they
left Canada, made this entry in her diary on 7 April: "Awakened
by the news that the Chief died last night. I felt badly — more so
than at [my own grandfather's] death. He was like a father to
me." On 10 April, she attended his funeral at St. Marks with
Long Lance, and that night told her diary, "Both of us guilty of
tears. . . . I've lost a dear old friend and will miss him."

The Silent Enemy opened on 19 May 1930 at Broadway's
Criterion Theater in front of an enthusiastic crowd that belonged to the filmmakers' social standing and included names
like Morgan, Roosevelt, Vanderbilt, and Whitney. The invita-
tion-only audience paid five dollars each to see the one-hour
and twenty-minute film. Molly, attending the debut in "the first
full evening outfit I ever had," admitted to the Maine *Sunday
Telegram* that for a little while she had "a stroke of inferiority":

> [O]n the evening the young heroine of the cinema had to shake
> hands with and hear the comments of her admirers, she was as
> frightened, she said, "as a rabbit looking for a hole." However, her
> moment of fear soon passed and she began to enjoy her first
> presentation at the court of moving picture "First Nighters."
> Casually she mentioned a few of the personages in the audiences,
> names known in every phase of life. . . . "But," she continued
> more soberly, "The only one that really mattered," her "little
> mother" away up in Old Town, was unable to be present.[71]

Darly, performing down south, was also absent. Molly could

have used a familiar face from home that night. It was an awkward evening for her, apparently fraught with conflicting emotions about her identity and place. Did this strictly upper-crust audience confuse her with Neewa? How was it that people from a social group that normally shunned Indians were praising her? Was she, hobnobbing in a lace evening gown, pretending to be someone she was not? Where was her own reality in this reel presentation? In her words, "Am I civilized only on the surface and still just a savage underneath?"[72] Apparently Long Lance had similar wrestlings, and the two of them escaped the film's glittering coming-out party early. Describing the event in her diary the next day, Molly wrote: "panicky meeting so many people. . . . Texas sat with me. Enjoyed the picture. Sad when Yellow Robe's death scene was shown. After the show the audience kept clapping. What a select audience too. . . . Had to listen to compliments and meet more people. Ran away from the mob. Long Lance and I ate at Sardi's, joined by Tex later."[73]

Not only did the social register set applaud the film with gusto; so did the dozens of critics who reviewed it during its opening week. The *New Republic* ranked it as "the only significant film to be produced in this country for a long time."[74] George Gerhard of the *Evening World* called it "a thing of wondrous beauty" and concluded that "as an historical and educational document, few pictures ever made carry the import of *The Silent Enemy*."[75] After describing the film as "beautiful," "superbly acted," and "tremendously exciting," Robert Sherwood, a widely syndicated critic, declared, "The production of pictures like *Nanook, Grass,* and *The Silent Enemy* is one of the cinema's most important functions. Such pictures will continue to be of intense value. . . . [as] permanent eloquent records of races and customs that are vanishing from the earth."[76] A *New York Evening Post* editorial topped all praise, proclaiming that *The Silent Enemy* deserved a "Pulitzer Prize as the best American dramatic creation for the year 1930."[77]

Despite invariably stellar reviews, *The Silent Enemy* failed at the box office. Ironically, silence was its downfall: the public, smitten by talkies that were sweeping the market,

The Indian Island home Molly purchased for her family
with money she made starring in *The Silent Enemy*. The
house which was the largest on the Penobscot reservation,
remained in the family until her death.

expected to hear, not read, what screen heros had to say. Betty
Shannon, the film's publicist, resorted to sensational ads such
as this one in an effort to win the public over: "Splendid mating.
Adventure and love to inspire every red-blooded human being!
A hero with the most beautiful body God ever gave a man!
. . . It's real! It's true!"[78] But the film continued to suffer
silently. On top of this, it fell victim to a block-booking system,
with Paramount failing to promote it as a unique, indepen-
dently produced picture.[79]

In the year end "memorandum" of her 1930 diary, Molly summed up her feelings about the film's release: "Reviews— some publicity—then oblivion again." No doubt, Burden had similar thoughts.

But, if the film failed to woo the public and make money for its producers, it provided its leading actress access to new career doors, plus enough money to buy her family a new place to live—the largest home on Indian Island.

CHAPTER 9

NEW YORK TO PARIS

*How I wish I could always have the proper atmo-
sphere to do my work as it should be. . . . The more I
dance, the more I want to interpret my emotions
without limitation, to create a freedom of primitive-
ness and abandon. If only one could dance solely for
art! Maybe someday I will have that chance. If not in
America, then in Europe.*

—Molly (New York, 1929)[1]

When Molly emerged from the Canadian woods and re-entered
New York in the spring of 1929, work opportunities awaited her.
Never mind that the Great Depression lurked in the wings like a
villain waiting to make his entrance. Texas Guinan wooed her
back to club life with an offer lucrative enough to prompt Molly
to tell her diary: "Over at Texas' home. The contract—whee!"[2]
Molly also signed a new contract with Douglas Burden, obligat-
ing herself to be available for retakes and promotional work for
The Silent Enemy, giving Burden Pictures first right to employ
her within a year of the film's release, and agreeing not to write
an article or book about the film.[3] Since she had already begun
work on a manuscript she referred to as her "bush story," she
must have hesitated before signing off on the last item. She
managed at least a measure of writing satisfaction related to
The Silent Enemy by penning a first-person narrative solicited
by the film's publicist, Betty Shannon.[4] In addition to these
new contracts with Tex and Burden, by the end of 1929 Molly
had signed on with the prestigious Provincetown Players and

big-time showman J. J. Shubert. In 1930, after the release of *The Silent Enemy*, several film and radio show producers knocked on her door. So did a wide variety of famous dance directors, ranging from Ruth St. Denis (master interpretor of metaphysical dance) to Nils T. Granlund (grand creator of underclad but classy dance revues).

During this time, Molly shared an apartment with Darly in Greenwich Village, the city's Bohemian enclave. At times they made room for Apid. While genuinely fond of both sisters, Molly adored Darly, describing her as "the other half of me," whose "brightness is like a tonic in my lonely moods."[5] Apid, in contrast, was "big hearted, brutally frank, gruff, humorous." The two younger sisters frequently clashed, and Molly acted as arbiter.[6]

Apid took a waitress job in the village,[7] while Darly pursued her show career. Molly was the major (and often only) breadwinner in this Penobscot trio. Typically, she worked more than one job at a time, driven by dreams even more than by dollars: "Someday, with patience, hard work will be the means of reaching that hilltop I want to reach so badly—not fame but realization."[8]

Halfway through her summer 1929 contract at Tex's posh Valley Stream Roadhouse on Long Island, Molly successfully auditioned for the Provincetown Players—a highly respected theater group, credited with introducing the plays of Eugene O'Neill and Edna St. Vincent Millay, among others. The group opened its fall season with *Fiesta*. In this lively musical comedy, a girl returns to her father's hacienda from Mexico City for a fiesta held in her honor. To everyone's surprise, she arrives with a fiancé—a famous, rather effeminate radio star, utterly citified, and quite out of place in the village. Her hometown *muchacho*, who had anticipated proposing to her midfiesta, is heartbroken. But Lupe, the fiery maid, devises a plan to scare away the fiancé with a local *bandido*. The plot develops amid a whirl of Mexican folk tunes and dances. Director Jimmy Light cast Molly as a featured dancer and as understudy to one of the leads—Lupe, the maid. According to Molly, "Jimmy Light wished I had gotten the role, but I was too late for it."[9] Nonetheless, she was thrilled to be associated with the "refined Provincetowners." The production was all the sweeter because Darly also danced in it, and shared a dressing table with Molly.[10]

During the month leading up to the play's opening, Molly continued to work for Texas, squeezing in *Fiesta* rehearsals between morning-time slumber and late-night club performances.[11] She completed her summer contract with Tex two nights before the play's September seventeenth debut at Garrick Theater—the company's new location on Thirty-fifth Street and Fifth Avenue. The audience gave Molly a "marvelous hand" for her "wild dance" solo,[12] and reviewers made special note of the dancing:

> In the third act . . . five girls [including Molly and Darly] come upon the scene and dash into the fiery sort of dance that one likes to believe belongs to a Mexican fiesta. At that moment the play flares into new life. . . . The warp and woof of the play are in the dancing . . . [performed with] a delightful freedom as of spontaneous merry-making, almost impromptu in its informality. Yet the dances have been carefully designed and are accurately performed.[13]

Molly clearly took great pleasure in her part in the play, describing it as a welcome opportunity for "true expression" and "passionate outburst."[14] Unfortunately, at the end of *Fiesta's* scheduled five-week run, Provincetown Players faced a deep deficit. The company's recent move from Greenwich Village uptown to the Garrick had sapped its resources. The timing of this shortage was abysmal. The week after *Fiesta* closed, Wall Street crashed, and rich patrons, crucial to the group's survival, began reneging on their pledges. Drowning in debt, with no lifeline in sight, the drama group disbanded.[15]

Molly, ever the two-timer when it came to work, had anticipated this turn of events, and by the final Provinctown performance was well into rehearsals for J. J. Shubert's latest road show, *Broadway Nights*. Starring none other than Texas Guinan, the production featured a tidal wave of 130 performers:

singers, comedians, impersonators, ensembles, an orchestra, concert dancers, plus three dance troupes—the Guinan Girls, Foster Girls, and Hale Girls.[16] Molly, who had danced with all three groups at one time or another, was a Guinan Girl this time around. In addition to soloing, she performed en masse with Tex's batch of blonds. "How funny I must look in the line-up of fair-skinned girls," she jotted in her diary.[17] Although annoyed by the "fresh Broadwayite stagehands so different from the Fiesta boys," Molly was fascinated by the scope of this "mob production." She found Shubert "very likeable," and appreciated his high, if exhausting, standards. Rehearsals were grueling but rewarding, all-day events, with "each troupe dancing over and over again until perfection is gained."[18]

After three weeks of intensive rehearsals, the show hit the road. Molly said a reluctant goodbye to Darly ("the only one I hate to leave behind"),[19] and traveled by train with the rest of the cast to Pittsburg, their first booking in a two-month tour that included Chicago, Cleveland, and Detroit. The engagements lasted a week each, except for Chicago where the show ran for six weeks. While in the windy city, Texas went moonlighting after each show, working from midnight until dawn as entertainment hostess at Club Royale.[20] She took a few of her "girls" with her, including Molly, who, as always, wanted to earn a few extra dollars to send home.[21] Molly noted that this double-billing was "enough to drain any amazon's energy,"[22] but kept it up throughout the *Broadway Nights* Chicago run.

Back in New York, sick of the milieu, repetoire, and hours of club work, Molly vowed to avoid it and "do something worthwhile with dancing."[23] She complained to her diary: "More than ever the club atmosphere bears the appearance of a joint. A drunken brawl, a young major dragging his girl partner over the floor. The petty squabble of waiters and a singer. The heat, perspiration, blah of music. Am bored to death with it. . . . Only sheer need of work will ever make me [return]."[24]

On the following page: Molly. A promotional photograph taken circa 1930, when she was twenty-seven.

Molly's hiatus from nightclubs lasted only three months. The "sheer need of work," coupled with an open offer from Tex, lured her back to club work, a financial mainstay. But her string of stints with Tex were punctuated with more meaningful pursuits and possibilities—and much running about to meet with agents, directors, and producers.

Right after *The Silent Enemy*'s May 1930 debut in New York, Molly gleefully noted in her diary a call from her agent announcing that an MGM executive "saw the picture, liked [her] work and the way [she] photographed," and wanted to "do something" for her. A meeting was arranged, ending with a promise that the studio would find a suitable part for her.[25] A followup came in early July, when the studio approached her to play the lead in Cecil B. De Mille's talking remake of his first film, *The Squaw Man*—the story of an English nobleman who falls in love with an Indian princess. "Terrific news of MGM," Molly jotted in her diary, adding, "'Squaw man'—what an ugly term. I have heard it [in my own life] and will never forget it."[26] About the same time, Molly noted an invitation from *Silent Enemy* director Richard Carver to "go to Morocco and southern France on a picture." She promised to accept the offer "if the Squaw Man thing falls through."[27]

It did. Several months later, on 14 January 1930 she penned this cryptic journal entry: "Letter from Cecil De Mille that Lupe Velez has been signed for *The Squaw Man*."[28] Molly's disappointment would later be echoed by De Mille himself, for the film flopped and critics attributed a large measure of its failure to the "mighty miscasting" of Lupe Velez.[29] Meanwhile, Carver's overseas film project was delayed, and Molly met with Broadway producer David Belasco about a role in his latest stage production—an adaptation of the 1929 Pulitzer prize-winning Indian romance novel, *Laughing Boy*. Unfortunately, Belasco, who was in his late seventies, fell ill and died before getting the production off the ground.[30]

While dramatic roles fell through, Molly remained busy—writing, performing, posing for many artists, making promotional appearances for *The Silent Enemy*, advising choreographers on Indian dances, teaching and taking dance lessons, and studying voice. Apparently her singing was good enough to warrant several New York radio performances, including WHN's the *Children's Hour*.[31]

In February 1930, Molly told her diary: "I have made a great resolution, and that is to write something worthwhile in the coming year . . . no matter how many rejection slips I might get."[32] Throughout the year she worked diligently on a set of Indian legends: "Water Boy," "Mud Turtle and Deer," "Long Haired One," "The Singing Maiden," "Upside Down," and "Froth."[33] She wrote whenever and wherever possible—in her apartment, in libraries, in club dressing rooms. To spur herself on she read voraciously—"I must have books to read. They are the best stimulant in the world."[34] In particular, to "give sparkle to [her] spirit,"[35] she spent much of 1930 reading fairy tales and harking back to her childhood days with old Joe Hemlock: "Wrote one legend [today]. I can hear Joe Hemlock telling me in his funny voice, in Indian, those tales in which he always figured as the hero. Bedridden soul he was! Wooden carved dolls he made me. Checkers we played. The faraway look he used to have when he talked of long ago days."[36]

These literary endeavors gave Molly enormous pleasure: "Over the typewriter all afternoon. . . . It's so good to be able to travel away from reality and feel that the characters are my little friends. . . . To write and dance is happiness enough!"[37] In the spring, a newspaper article about Molly claimed, "She has had many of her legends and poetry published and during the past year sold a short story to Collier's. At present she is working on another set of Indian legends which are to be taken by a large publishing house when they are complete."[38] But there is no other evidence that she succeeded in finding a publisher for these legends. In her diary she mentioned taking them to a publisher and getting "good advice," but nothing more substantial.[39] Still, she continued to write, and after years of wishing for "someone to criticize my things before I submit them," she found a willing critic in Betty Shannon, publicist for *The Silent Enemy*. To Molly, Shannon, credited in a variety of publications, including the *New York Times*, was a "woman with depth." She turned to her often for encouragement—and friendship.[40]

Dancing remained Molly's principal and most salable talent. It also remained her primary passion, "a part of me, like my arms."[41] Increasingly she filled the "specialty dancer" slot on programs, almost exclusively doing solo Indian dances, making them as authentic as the glittery bounds of Broadway clubs would permit. Once in a while a relatively serious production came her way, such as Chester Hale's Indian ballet at the Capitol Theater, which Molly helped to choreograph. She noted in her diary: "Chester used some of my dance movements in groups and they looked lovely—the head shake, the rigid arm and body bend, and the bell stamp."[42] On several occasions, Ruth St. Denis (the "mother of modern dance")[43] and her husband/dance colleague Ted Shawn invited Molly to come to their Denishawn dance school in the Bronx. These paragons of interpretive dance, dedicated to the idea that pure dancing was a reflection of the true spiritual state of being, apparently recognized a rare quality in Molly's dancing, and at different times each came to see her perform.[44] Although Molly did study briefly with St. Denis, the association did not last—apparently because of Molly's income needs and other work commitments and pursuits.[45]

St. Denis and Shawn were not the only notable dancers to look seriously at Molly's work. In January 1931 she received a bid from the elite Dancer's Club. The nomination came from Yeichi Nimura, founder of the Ballet Arts Studio at Carnegie Hall. Nimura, who came from Japan to New York after World War I to study math at Columbia University, soon left the halls of academe for dance studios where he studied with renowned teachers of ballet, interpretive dance, and ballroom. To this training Nimura brought a profound mental and physical discipline developed through years of martial arts instruction. This discipline, along with his utter grace, artfulness, and distinct Oriental dance technique lifted him out of cabarets and into the more highbrow world of experimental theater productions and concerts. Molly admired his work immensely, and when she received the Dancer's Club bid, she confided to her diary, "Feel I'm not good enough for such a group." According to Nimura's dance partner and wife, Lisan Kay, this was sheer nonsense, for "Molly was a true artist [who] moved exquisitely—in a way that was practially non-human." Nonetheless, perhaps fearing failure, Molly cancelled her Dancer's Club performance, noting in her diary that she felt sick and "hated to dress up."[46]

Club life continued—often with double billing between one of Tex's clubs and Granlund's cabarets at the Silver Slipper or the Hollywood. Time and again Molly recorded her dismay at working in nightclubs, where, in her words, "money is spent like a silly girl's tears," and young female performers "fill the dressing room with meaningless prattle."[47] Often, she brought her typewriter to work, placed it atop her dressing table, and wrote in between shows.[48] What a dichotomy there was between this berobed, backstage writer and the (often) barely dressed dancer seen by audiences. Granlund was fond of saying that his dancers' costumes were so tiny that he had them flown in by humming birds.[49] Molly, while not prudish, clearly felt that the scanty outfits chosen by her directors undermined her would-be authenticity as an American Indian dancer. Among many comments in her journal, are these:

> My costume made me embarassed. Looked like a loin cloth affair of satin and beads instead of leather and fringe. Not natural for my Indian dance. . . .[50]
> Something new once in a while . . . but mostly nude parades. I am an injun in the flesh parade. Feel terrible about being bare and walking around, but I must work. . . .[51]
> Bashful about my two parade costumes . . . the nudest I've had to hang on me. . . . Thias is Eve with long blond hair, bare breasts and an apple.[52]

But club work paid Molly's bills—and her family's. It also gave her exposure, in every sense of the word. Tex's Argonaut Club and Granlund's Hollywood attracted not only the wealthy leisure class, but other show business people (from Tom Mix to

Charlie Chaplin), plus newpaper columnists who relied on both groups for fodder.[53] Louis Sobol of the *New York Evening Journal* frequented these establishments, and on several occasions devoted a portion of his popular "Voice of Broadway" column to Molly. He enjoyed speculating on her romantic interests but usually missed the mark.[54] This is not surprising given Molly's endless string of suitors and the air of confusion that increasingly surrounded her relationships with men She was highly skeptical about their intentions and equally leery of her own feelings. Unsure of her social standing among the moneyed white men she associated with, she toyed with them, testing her allure, drawing them near, then pulling back warily. Afraid of being hurt, and cautious about being distracted from her professional goals, she constructed so many detours and road blocks on the route to her heart that even she had trouble getting there. Her diary entries on the subject during this time are revealing. She referred to her romantic liaisons as "experiments, all!" and commented, "What a creature I am to test out friendships to determine exactly what true love is."[55] After enticing men into romance, she claimed to have been misunderstood, and cajoled them back toward friendship. Among others, this was the case with Bryan Cheedy, the "scion" who became her fiancé just before she went on location to shoot *The Silent Enemy*. By the time Molly returned to New York, their engagement had metamorphosed into friendship, and, with apparent relief, she referred to herself as his "good ole standby."[56]

At one point, Molly confessed to her diary, "In friendship I am at a better advantage."[57] Indeed, this was the relationship realm where she felt safe and self-assured. "I mean only friendship. Who am I to long for anything else?" she asked.[58] Again and again she tripped over the ambiguity of her social position as a noted American Indian entertainer. This comment about one of her genteel admirers is typical: "Wen at the club to see me. Said he'd wait three years for me. . . . His mother has high hopes for her son—her pride in love with a poor Indian girl. . . . Wen is 'somebody's son' while I am merely nobody's daughter, and things would become complicated. . . . His interest in me is mere fascination—a novelty to see if I am human."[59]

Molly was aware that men in the audience pinned their romantic dreams of ideal primitive life on the exotic "sexy savage" dancing for their pleasure. And she was frequently frustrated by grossly stereotyped, external definitions of who she was. Periodically, waves of insecurity washed over her. Yet, she seems to have felt that her shore, reinforced by native roots, was a moral high ground; deep within, she knew full well that she was much more than high society's narrow image of her. Sometimes this made her so indignant that she turned her critical aim away from herself and onto her carefree, upper crust suitors:

> Rod says I'm like a wild horse and have to be made tame. . . . I'm tired of hearing all this rubbish about sex appeal—it makes me sick. . . .[60]
>
> George Kent the polo-playing playboy in [the club] again, sixth time, with . . . Rockefeller's grandson. . . . What would Louis Sobol say if he knew this millionaire radio heir was giving me the rush instead of those he put in the paper? I pity George as he is so helpless and miserable with all his wealth. . . .[61]
>
> Van is a neurotic weakling, like a big ship without ballast, a young, blond giant with a large frame—all the makings of a steel-rigged man, but instead he's covered with indolent fat. He was to marry Chickadee once, just another white-Indian romance.[62]

When these and other men declared their love for her, Molly usually "said nothing," or "teased [them] out of such a thing."[63] In part, this stemmed from the fact that she remained in love with Douglas Burden, even though she seems to have had little, if any, encouragement from him. After *The Silent Enemy's* New York debut, she saw or spoke with him rarely, and soon noted wryly, "It's always those we want to see that pass without being seen, and those we don't care to see are those who are seen."[64] Still, she kept track of his whereabouts through mutual friends, and mentioned him frequently and fondly in her diary. Often, she referred to their "supremely happy" evening together in a log cabin at the film's first on-location camp.[65] Occasionally

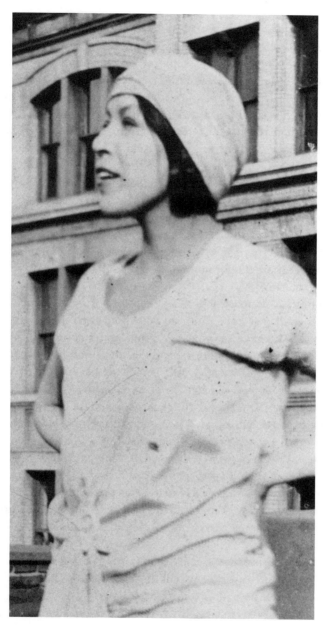

Molly in street clothes, circa 1930.

she chastised herself for these romantic ruminations, which could be triggered by a whiff of cool autumn night air, the mention of his name, or some other incidental happening: "Phoned office. WB answered. . . . I've been on air since that phone call. But it is in vain to harbor a vision that is only a mirage. It's reaching for the impossible." Paradoxically, if Burden had responded to Molly's pining, she may well have retreated or coaxed him to the safe zone of friendship. By holding him in her imagination rather than in her arms, she brought him to her world and shielded herself from the judgement of his. Conscious of this, she wrote: "Is my beautiful inspiration like Pygmalion's marble statue of Galatea? What would I do if ever the first significance dawned that it were alive? Would there be madness, sorrow, or happiness? There is a sort of ethereal light now for me in the illusion—reality may be too glaring."[66]

For Molly, security, joy, and a sense of self worth came from family and work. She affirmed this often with diary jottings such as "My great happiness is in my work and home," or "In the joy of one's work there lies the secret of all happiness."[67] Devotion to family and work merged in her efforts to help Darly's career. She led her little sister on the entertainment rounds, introduced her to the right people in the business, and helped her get auditions. When journalists interviewed Molly, they often got a story that included Darly. As one reporter wrote in 1930, the year Darly turned twenty and Molly twenty-seven: "It is with great pride that Spotted Elk speaks of her little sister who is known as Little Elk, who has [danced] in the same company with her. 'Darly,' she says, 'has made rapid strides and has received many favorable comments on her work.'"[68]

When Molly's *Silent Enemy* costar, Long Lance, began wooing Darly, who was exactly half his age, Molly felt responsible and nervous. She had introduced her sister to this full-fledged man-about-town—this celebrity, "social lion," and "Beau Brummell of Broadway."[69] Darly, far less cautious about romance than her big sister, tumbled into Long Lance's arms like a ripe peach from a tree. The next thing Molly knew, the "lovers" (as she called them) were engaged: "Darly plans to marry him. My God! He is too old for her." Molly, incredulous about the famous philanderer's commitment to Darly, and equally wary of her flirtatious little sister's ability to resist the lure of younger men in the future, thought they were a terrible match. She pressed Darly to wait a year "to see if she really loves Long Lance," and made similar appeals to him. But the lovers continued to see each other, and on one occasion Molly and Apid walked in on the pair in the throes of passion.[70] Ten months into the affair, Molly's mother visited her in New York and implored her to help end the romance. "Talked [with mama] about Darly and Long Lance," Molly wrote in her diary. "It's up to me to try to solve the problem for the happiness of all. Will write to LL." Nine days later, he responded, agreeing to step out of Darly's life at least for awhile: "Letter from Long Lance. It is a fine one. He promised to do his part and let time decide for him and Darly. Like the way he took the situation. I pity the both of them, but what can I do? Only to advise wisely and understand. How well I know what it is to love someone."[71] Darly, crushed by the breakup, spent two months nursing her broken heart on Indian Island.[72] Then she joined a four-month show tour in Florida and Havana. Upon her return to New York in the spring of 1931, Long Lance left the city and moved to Los Angeles. A year later, haunted by the hardship of the struggling family he had abandoned as a youth and increasingly fearful that his true tri-racial identity would become public, he put a pistol to his head and ended his life. We can only speculate as to whether the failed romance with Darly contributed to his suicide. Although Darly married several months after his death, family members say that Long Lance owned her heart throughout her life.[73]

Unlike her role in this crisis of the heart, Molly found helping the family through financial struggles a satisfying task. According to her second cousin Ernestine Tomer:

Molly was always working and sharing her earnings. . . . I don't think she enjoyed luxury. Didn't feel comfortable with it. But she didn't want her family to live SO poor. So she bought them two houses [with her *Silent Enemy* earnings]. . . . The first one they didn't live in too long. Philomene rented it out after Molly bought them the bigger house across from the graveyard. Whenever Molly came home, she brought boxes and boxes of stuff—shoes, coats, dresses. That's how we got clothed.

Molly's diaries are filled with brief but revealing references to the assistance she provided. For instance, 1930 and 1931 entries include:

Giving my heart and soul to my dancing and my career to help my folks is my task now. . . .
Must work hard to get mama a cow and pigs this spring. . . .
I'd be content to live another life and devote it to mama. As it is I have not done half of what I would like to do for her. . . .
With Ap[id] to shop. Some things to send home for Mama. Bought clothes for Ap. . . .
[Brother] Blun in again. Gave him money to get a room for himself. . . .
Wish I could have given more this week to the folks. . . .
To accomplish what I have begun . . . means I can help others—the folks. . . .
Got [sister] Eunice three dresses. Poor thing, she needs school clothes. . . .
Telegram from mama: "[baby brother] Bunty is dead." I want to go home but no one in the family is working and I can't stop. Got club salary and bought Darly's [train] ticket home.[74]

While Molly's family appreciated her generosity, it was, to a degree, taken for granted. The communal ethos of the Penobscot's traditional hunting and gathering society still pervaded Indian Island. Those who abandoned egalitariansim and hoarded their prosperity risked social exclusion—and surrendered their rights to an "insurance policy" of reciprocity. Yet, Molly's extensive family caretaking often came at the cost of her own health and comfort. As the Great Depression deepened and more and more people lost their jobs, she felt fortunate to be working at all. But employment competition grew, salaries shrank, and her family needed more help than usual. Making ends meet became increasingly difficult. Describing the chal-

lenge, Molly wrote, "I must slave to keep my head above want."
Soon thereafter she noted, "Wanted to go uptown but am so
shabby that any casting director would throw me out—just
enough to pay rent."[75] She continued working regularly for
Texas and periodically for Granlund. When other jobs came
her way, she did them too—sometimes doing six shows a day.
Her performance schedule, coupled with continual efforts to
find new work, led to exhaustion, weight loss, and illness—
especially problems with her lungs. The many notes Molly
made in her diary about her physical struggles are summed up
in this one: "Nerves. Restlessness. Tired physically and mentally. I am honestly worn down like a threadbare coat with little
possibility of being patched up. From theater to club, from the
Hollywood to the club—shows shows. Nervous about time.
Trying to get a few minutes sleep. It's awful. Patience is the only
thing that keeps me up."[76] In desperation, she asked Granlund
for a break—not a week, but a day: "Asked Granny to let me off
tomorrow. Can't triple like this in the condition I'm in. After
all, my health means something, and I'm afraid to snap suddenly like the last breakdown."[77] Granlund, recognizing Molly's tendency to overwork, sometimes invited her to his country home for a rest. But on the rare occasions when Molly
surrendered work efforts for a few days, she preferred going
home where there were no hints of Broadway. Just thinking
about Indian Island brought her a measure of peace. As she
told one journalist during this period, "I often close my eyes
and imagine that I am back home. It is a source of joy to think
that I am walking around the island, sitting at the table
enjoying a real old-fashioned meal, or getting into a canoe and
paddling up the river to the quiet places I used to love."[78]

Usually Molly made it home several times a year. "Molliedell
was always so glad to come home," recalls Ernestine. "She
would grab us all with a huge hug and say, 'Oh Auntie!' or 'Oh
Ernestine!'"[79] These were truly homey visits, filled with the
solace of ordinary doings—a bit of housework, basketmaking
with "Mama," chopping wood with "Pops," shaking apples out
of the trees with "the kids", strolling along the river under a

moonlit sky, writing letters, reading. This diary entry is typical of many made during days back home: "The kids did not go
to school today. Started to clean up . . . played the piano.
. . . Had some cod fish for dinner and beans for supper. Quiet
evening listening to the victrola and stories. Out for a walk to
fill my soul with the silence and beauty of winter. It is lovely
outside—dark night with snow on the housetops and piled on
the branches of apple trees in the yard. To bed early."[80]

Holiday visits usually included some special event at the
tribal hall, which Molly invariably attended and made note of.
For instance: "Down to the Christmas tree in the hall. The
youngsters were cute in their playlets. . . . After the entertainment the missionary gave a speech, then the presents were
given out." When she stayed on the island more than a couple of
days, she and Philomene would give a party for relatives and
friends. There was always plenty of food, card games, and
checkers, plus a dance by Molly. Ernestine remembers these
occasions fondly: "Molliedell would dance for our amusement.
She'd get [someone] to play the piano. Her dancing was just
beautiful. She responded to the music. And she danced in her
regular clothes at the parties. One time she went down too hard
and hit her nose on a stool and that was the end of that
party!"[81]

Although never home long enough to get seriously involved in
tribal politics, poverty conditions on the island coupled with
the patronizing and often inequitable actions of the state-
appointed Indian Agent, disturbed her. It was not uncommon
for her to take protest action with her pen, writing letters to
state authorities or the local newspaper. Sometimes she made
note of her protests, which reflected the emergence of Indian
women into public political forums, in her diary:

> Long letter to [journalist] Tewksbury at the [Portland] Telegram
> on tribal matters—the [criminal] result of the cash basis system
> of [state] appropriations [to the tribe], the [tribe's] protest
> against excuses made by the agent, the [unfair] wood situation
> [re. fees paid by lumber companies for cutting rights on Pe-
> nobscot land], [low] salaries [for Indians]. "We want our rights

[they tell me]—we are human like the rest of mankind. We want action not promises." Fair play is an all compelling creed and my people certainly need it.[82]

In New York, Molly's social and political activism was eclipsed by her work. However, she often gave benefit performances, using her talents to support various causes. Beyond frequent charity events presented by Tex and Granlund,[83] she participated in activities sponsored by the Aboriginal Council, the Indian Confederation of America, and the Society of the First Sons and Daughters of America. The latter organization, founded in 1922 by "Princess" Atalie Unkalunt, a Cherokee soprano, was open to "blood" members ("authentic Indians who can prove their tribal affiliation") and "associate" members ("pale-faces who are sympathetic to our cause"). Its primary goals were to foster "understanding with pale-face brothers and sisters," to provide "authentic Amerinds with fine and dignified opportunities for artistic expression," and "to influence legislation" on behalf of American Indians.[84]

Indian entertainers receive mention throughout Molly's diaries during her New York years.[85] These individuals, belonging to disparate tribal groups, were bound, not by a shared cultural heritage, but by the history of colonization which was responsible for the fact that they were performing their traditions on stage rather than in life. In truth, their performances barely matched their traditions, for most modified their acts to please audiences that responded only to archetypical Indian models—the romantic stuff of James Fennimore Cooper's novels or wildly dramatized Plains scenarios à la Buffalo Bill's Wild West. To succeed as an Indian entertainer, one could not be rigid about cultural authenticity. As Molly observed, "Penobscots—everyone thinks we are from Oklahoma. There is no romantic appeal to the modern white in an eastern tribe of Indians. . . . When they want a Sioux, oop, I'm one—the universal Indian."[86]

As off-reservation Indians marketing themselves to dominant society, Molly and her cohorts lived in a liminal zone between two cultures. Their cultural exile paralleled that of "Hollywood Indians" chronicled in a New York newspaper:

> Hollywood has acquired a permanent colony of representatives of almost all tribes still extant. With the cinema as their melting pot, these expatriates are taking on the semblance of a tribe all their own. . . . One among them, a stalwart of Cherokee blood, known professionally as Chief Thunder Cloud . . . has taken the initiative . . . [in] applying to the Bureau of Indian Affairs for recognition of the "De Mille Indians" as a new tribe composed only of Indians who work in films. . . . A Hollywood tribe is not beyond the imagination, for, sadly enough for most of us, the only real Indian is a Hollywood Indian.[86]

Of course, for Molly and her Indian friends and associates, the "real Indian" was not the one they presented on stage or in front of a camera. It was the ineffable and often elusive inner self, inextricably linked to the independent and viable lifeways of their pre-colonial ancestors. It was the self Molly longed to articulate. Instead, she found herself half naked on a stage, doing dances that only hinted at the content of her soul.

In the spring of 1931, Molly was offered an opportunity to place an ocean between herself and Broadway. It is not surprising that she seized it.

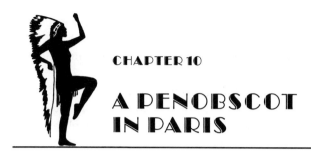

CHAPTER 10

A PENOBSCOT IN PARIS

So my life begins anew in Paris.

—Molly (Paris 1931)[1]

Molly's Paris invitation arrived between shows at Nils Granlund's Hollywood Restaurant in early spring, 1931. It came from the lips of Thomas O'Brien, a shrewd and enthusiastic talent agent.[2] O'Brien managed an Indian jazz band made famous by its performance at the 1929 inauguration of President Herbert Hoover and Vice President Charles Curtis, who was part Kaw Indian. Now, after two years of solid bookings at major theaters across the country, O'Brien had won a place for the band at the International Colonial Exposition opening in Paris in May.[3] After seeing Molly dance, he quickly concluded she would make an ideal addition to the all-male band, especially in a city known for its appreciation of feminine beauty and grace. She could play the tom-tom and expand the band's repertoire with her dancing. Weary of American audiences, which she felt had little interest in authentic Indian dancing,[4] Molly jumped at this chance to take her talents to another corner of the world.

Some members of the band were already part of Molly's social circle. In particular, she was acquainted with the band's Pawnee-Otoe leader, Joe Shunatona from Oklahoma. After meeting Joe during her stint with the 101 Ranch, their paths continued to cross on the vaudeville circuit. Joe performed as a member of a male quartette known as the Four American Indians and as a master of ceremonies for Publix Theatres.

Sometime during the latter 1920s, New York City became his professional home base, and he moved there with his wife Gwen and their two children. Molly was a frequent visitor at their apartment.[5]

In Paris, the Indian Band would form part of the United States' exhibition, which featured a faithful reproduction of George Washington's Mount Vernon home, plus displays of the nation's "empire"—Alaska, Hawaii, Puerto Rico, the Philippines, and the Virgin Islands. Since the United States was in the throes of a depression, its Colonial Exposition commissioner Bascom Slemp held firmly to the $250,000 budget allocated by Congress for the event. Although willing to endorse the musicians and grant them permission to use the title "United States Indian Band," Slemp required that the band finance its own participation in the fair. O'Brien accepted these terms, certain that publicity spawned by the band's expo performances would win valuable European bookings. Through France's Ambassador to the United States, he won free passage for his group on a French oceanliner—agreeing that, in exchange, the band would entertain ship passengers en route.[6]

At noon on 25 April, accompanied by an entourage of family and friends who came to wish her bon voyage, Molly boarded the Ile de France. Even her mother, traveling by train from Old Town for the occasion, was there to kiss her. Although Douglas Burden did not join her farewell wishers that day, he had called to say good-bye and was very much in her thoughts as the ship pulled out of New York's harbor.[7]

Eight days, several performances, and a few suitors later, Molly stood on the ship's deck and watched the port of Le Havre glide into view.[8] As she disembarked, her eagle-feather headdress bobbing and swaying above her gleeful face, she waved to a cheering, welcoming crowd. Photographers seized the moment. The caption under her picture in the European edition of the *Chicago Tribune* the following day announced: "American Princess. 'Hello palefaces.' Princess Spotted Elk, member of the U.S. Indian Band which is taking part in the Colonial

Molly and band leader Chief Shunatona, dancing to the music of the United States Indian Band, aboard Ile de France, headed for the 1931 Colonial Exposition in Paris. (From the U.S. National Archives, RG43, Records of the Commission Representing the United States at the International Colonial and Overseas Exposition at Paris, 1930–32.)

Exposition is shown on the French liner Ile de France on her way to Paris. The princess is considered one of the most beautiful members of her tribe." Like most major French dailies, *Le Petite Journal* ran a front page photograph of the Indian Band the next day, and reported that the "picturesque jazz band . . . played the Marseillaise in a somewhat unexpected rhythm. Everyone applauded the fantastic band leader, Shunatona. For his young partner, Princess Spotted Elk, which translates approximately 'Speckled Deer,' there was an ovation."[9]

From Le Havre, the troupe traveled by train three hours to Paris, where they found another press crew waiting for them. One paper described the scene like this: "Hurried travelers in St. Lazare Station were treated to an unusual sight this morning when the boat train . . . pulled in. Wearing picturesque feathered headdresses and costumes of American Indians, a fairly large jazz band descended from the train and struck up a lively tune as it marched into the street and boarded a motor bus bound for the French Colonial Exposition."[10]

After a brief tour of the exposition grounds in the sweeping Bois de Vincennes at the southeastern edge of Paris, band members were taken to their hotels. Molly settled in at the modern high-rise Hotel Rovaro on Rue Brunel, a stone's throw from the Arc de Triomphe on the Right Bank of the Seine River. The next day, she stepped out on her own to stroll the Champs Elysées and drink in her wondrous new surroundings.[11] What did she find? An enormously cosmopolitan city bursting with energy, elegance, and creative spirit—and a stunningly deep history that reached back more than a millenium before the first European landed on her continent's shore. On the Right Bank of the Seine, broad, tree-lined avenues connected scores of stately edifices, elegant shops, and grand-scaled monuments. On the Left Bank, the narrow, cobblestone alleyways of the old *Quartier Latin* snaked between small, low-slung buildings where students and Bohemians lived above street-level shops. Paris had a profound pulse, an almost mystical appeal. It hosted a "moveable feast" of maverick artists and literati whose combined expressions were shaking and shaping the

course of the arts around the world. Here one might encounter
Miro, Matisse, Ernst, and Picasso, who were all painting mas-
terpieces. Or Calder and Brancusi, who were sculpting them.
Or Hemingway, Fitzgerald, Miller, Joyce, Colette, Malraux, and
Celine, who were writing them. Daily, these and lesser-known
artists emerged from their studios and garrets to gather in
crowded cafés—especially along the boulevards Montparnasse
or Saint-Germain-des-Près—to drink, dance, and talk about
each other's work.

Beyond the cafés was a flourish of literary salons, music
halls, nightclubs, and lavish costume balls. An aura of pride
and self-satisfaction glowed around Parisians as they prolonged
celebrations of the post-war economic and social revival.
France's job market was shrinking, but no one seemed to
notice that the Great Depression was about to crash every
party in the nation.[12]

And now, in a stupendous tribute to creativity, progress, and
itself, France was hosting the grandest world's fair to date. The
event built on a tradition of western chauvinism evident in the
first world's fair—Britain's 1851 Great Exhibition of the Works
of Industry of all Nations, held in London in a nineteen-acre
glass pavilion known as the Crystal Palace. This pioneering
event gave birth to a long string of international fairs in Europe
and America, all proclaiming the power and virtue of western
civilization, and aiming to illustrate worldwide progress born
of western colonial influence and intervention in industry,
trade, transportation, science, and culture.[13]

As colonialism approached its heyday at the turn of the
century, world's fairs became inextricably intertwined with
racism, nationalism, and imperialism. This was particularly
evident in exotic "human showcases," which became of central
importance to international exhibitions.[14] Presentations of so-
called primitive peoples were interspersed with product displays of industry and technology (cameras, elevators, lawn
mowers, steam machines, et cetera), all serving to edify western claims of "progress." To create these showcases, indigenous
peoples from colonized corners of the world were brought to

the fairgrounds and placed in settings that to a degree replicated their home habitats. They were instructed to go about what was thought to be their daily business (headhunting, performing religious rituals at set times, feigning cannibalism, pantomiming hunting activities, dancing, singing, and doing various arts and crafts) while a stream of onlookers strolled by gaping, giggling, sometimes sneering.[15] Colonial powers produced brochures interpreting these exhibits to make sure onlookers got the message that colonization was more than justified; it was a blessing to all concerned. For instance, literature connected with a West African village display at the Imperial International Exhibit of 1909 stressed the violent brutality of Dahomey's "bloodthirsty potentates . . . [and] amazons," and hailed France's 1892 intervention, which brought "order, decency, trade and civilization" to the region. The text concluded, "France has placed its hand on the blackest spot in West Africa . . . [and] days of savagery are passing away."[16]

Such commentary echoed the ruling social paradigm of the day: evolutionism, which held that humans developed along a straight line from savage, animal-like creatures ruled by nature into civilized (citified and industrialized) beings that rise above nature and gain control over it. In this social-Darwinian model, which maintained a tenacious hold deep into the twentieth century, progress equalled technological and material advancement. Those who mastered nature with technology and accumulated material wealth were higher creatures. Those who lived simply in partnership with nature rather than as lords over it were lower in the human hierarchy—living fossils articulating the conquered limits of western man's past. The road of evolutionism was straight, narrow, and one way; western society forged the route and drafted the rest of humanity to march in its footsteps. This linear notion of progress left no room for mutual cultural influence. On the contrary, it gave ample room for cultural domination, justifying the actions of western imperialists as they dismissed and destroyed the cultures of their colonies without ever understanding them or tapping into their wisdom and knowledge.[17]

People presented in human showcases faced psychological and physical hardships. Beyond homesickness, public ridicule, and being used as objects to demean their own cultures by presenting them out of context, they struggled with alien foods, climate, and viruses. Some ran away once they realized what it meant to be on display. Many became sick, and some died.[18] For instance, when Filipinos were brought to the 1904 St. Louis fair, several perished en route and three lost their lives to pneumonia while camped in the fairgrounds.[19] Pygmies displayed at the same fair were required to remain in their scant native outfits when temperatures sank to levels unimaginable in equatorial Africa. When they huddled together in their leaf huts to stay warm, some fairgoers threw stones to get them to come out and pose for pictures.[20]

In addition to human showcases, dance and music concerts by indigenous performers were common features at international exhibitions.[21] This is where Molly and the Indian Band fit in in the 1931 Colonial Exposition in Paris. Unbeknown to them, they, too, were being used to reinforce colonial notions of progress. Letters between their manager O'Brien and U.S. government officials involved in the Mount Vernon exhibit make this clear. For instance, C. J. Rhoads, then Commissioner of Indian Affairs, wrote to U.S. Expo Commissioner Slemp: "I understand that the band will be made up largely of college graduates; and that this is intended to exemplify the cultural progress of the Indians." O'Brien, in a communication to Slemp, made this suggestion: "Don't you think it would be quite fitting to have an old buck and his squaw accompany the band, thereby showing the true type of the first early American just before you show the present highly talented and educated Indian that comprises this band?" And Slemp, writing to O'Brien, explained that the State Department was willing to let the band use the name of the United States in its title "because you are endeavoring to exhibit the cultural development of the Indians, which idea the Indian Office here desires to promulgate."[22]

So it seems that Molly's position was an ambiguous one,

somewhere between the people from western cultures who visited the expo, and those natives from colonized countries who were displayed more or less as primitive objects. Of course, the "objects" were also observers, no doubt musing and marveling among themselves about the curious habits of their onlookers. Certainly Molly noticed and mulled over what she saw as "strange customs" among the French. Often she mentioned them in her diary. They included such things as using street toilets, paying for baths, being excessively frugal, marketing for food daily, drinking coffee that was "foul and strong," having no credit system in neighborhood shops, and allowing prostitutes to display themselves openly in doorways "like fat nuts ready to burst."[23] One day, after listing a series of French oddities, she concluded, "Each race of people has as many different customs as even us Injuns. But we do not think of marrying for money"—or, she also mentioned, eating snails or tongue.[24]

The 1931 International Colonial Exposition, outdoing its predecessors in scope, introduced Molly to dozens of cultures in addition to the French—not only those on display, but those of visitors from all around the world. More than thirty-three million people streamed through Vincennes Park during the fair's May to November run.[25] Besides France, exhibits were presented by Belgium, Denmark, The Netherlands, Portugal, Italy, and the United States. (Great Britain, having staged a huge exhibition of its own empire six years earlier at Wembley, did not participate in the Paris extravaganza.) France's exhibits rivaled all of the others combined. A walk down the expo's long Grande Avenue des Colonies Francaises revealed a stunning variety of pavilions representing France's vast colonial holdings. These included replicas of extraordinary buildings such as Cambodia's Temple of Angkor, Madagascar's Ambohimanga Royal Palace, and West Africa's Djenne Mosque. Beyond this, the expo featured a sprawling zoological park, hosting an array of animals from the far away plains and forests of colonized lands: elephants, lions, baboons, ostriches, flamingos.[26] One journalist aptly described the fair as "a brilliant spectacle, vividly summing up the glory and diverse conquests of a colonial effort extending over centuries."[27]

The official opening of the 1931 Expo took place on a sunstruck spring day. On 6 May, fifteen hundred invited guests crowded into the Exposition Theater in the Musée des Colonies[28] to hear speeches by President Gaston Doumergue, Marshal Hubert Lyautey, and Minister of Colonies Paul Reynaud, among others. The addresses, printed in newspapers around the world and broadcast throughout Europe and America, were grandiose and self-laudatory. (No doubt Molly's family listened to the speeches on the radio that Molly had given her mother—the first on Indian Island.) Each speaker, in his own words, touted the fair as "a great testimonial to the onward march of civilization."[29] Marshal Lyautey, described by one journalist as "a conquerer whose name has been associated with colonial history for half a century," proclaimed: "Our concern during the [exposition's] six months is to bear witness not only of the material things achieved in our colonies, but of the intellectual, social and moral progress realized, demonstrating that our colonial activities have been essentially constructive and beneficent." Reynaud explained that the French colonial enterprise consisted of the "instructive organization and education of native peoples" in which the French had "destroyed in order to construct," working for the "advancement of . . . humanity and civilization." Following Reynaud's speech, President Doumergue "rose and, in a single solemn statement, declared the exposition open."[30]

Notably missing in this ceremony were the voices of the colonized peoples—a fact that gives a hollow ring to Lyautey's statement that the expo's primary purpose was to "teach the lesson of union between all the races of the world."[31] But, if absent in word, native people were present in deeds orchestrated by their colonizers. According to journalists, as Doumergue and Lyautey rode in an open car leading a procession through Vincennes, "wild overtones of the jungle [were] apparent in every rhythmic gesture of the marching columns" of accompanying colonial troops made up of "fierce, gay children

of the desert"[32] and "fierce and magnificent looking [Algerian]
spahis on their Arabian horses." The procession passed by
exhibits—"tropical civilizations with costumed natives moving about them." At the French West Africa pavillion, "blue-
black Senegalese infantrymen, their cheeks slashed in the
savage designs favored by their ancestors, stood at attention as
the President's car passed."[33]

Although not invited to speak, some native people attended
the ceremonial proceedings in the Musée des Colonies. For
instance, one newspaper reported that "a hush fell over the
throng" as the Emperor of Annam (Vietnam), dressed in a
yellow gown and turban, jewelled tunic, and broad red sash,
"advanced slowly to take his seat" next to President Doumergue.[34] Molly danced for the illustrious crowd. The *New
York Herald* (European edition) report on the inaugural included her photograph with this caption: "Princess Spotted
Elk, the full-blooded American Indian princess who added a
picturesque note to the proceedings."[35] Another newspaper
offered more detail:

> On the opening day . . . Princess Spotted Elk interpreted in her
> dances . . . centuries of joys and sorrows of the Red Man. The
> little princess is a university girl, but she loves the century-old
> traditions and lore of her people, and by the intensity of her
> feeling she made them live again. . . . She showed the dances that
> the Indian along the St. Lawrence River displayed for Cartier and
> Champlain, the gorgeous sun dance of the far Northwest, the
> fierce firelight rituals which impressed La Salle upon the shores
> of Michigan, and the Thanksgiving rites which the Jesuits saw
> offered up to Manitou on Huron's beaches.[36]

Molly's diary entry on inaugural day was terse but full of
delight: "International Colonial Exposition by the French Government. It was wonderful. All the pomp, color, beauty of the
foreign buildings, people and things awed me. It was colossal
and impressive. I danced. Reporter from NY Herald visited me
for an interview. . . . A memorable day." Several days later she
noted, "Went out to the Exposition . . . took pictures, walked
for hours, saw everything—the mobs, the voices, the smells."

Perhaps following the lead of American writer Janet Flanner whose "Letters from Paris" had become a popular bimonthly feature in *The New Yorker*, Molly wrote up a vivid account of her expo tour in a letter to the *Portland Telegram*. A portion of her published description, perhaps the only native account of the fair, follows:

"The rich variety of the exposition is overwhelmingly striking," Princess Spotted Elk declares. . . . "Forest, plain, farm and factory, primitive arts and people unite in a tribute to the power of the French. It is for this that the pageant glitters. One sees the wonders of the world unfolded before him, dazzling, crude, bizarre, fantastic, grotesque, stately, modern and primitive. . . . "No two pavilions are alike, and each has an interest all its own. The Dutch East Indian exhibits are sheltered in a pagoda of collosal proportions. Belgium shows her colonial wares in a huge shed which takes one into the depths of the Congo jungle. Madagascar is housed in a stupendous model of the royal palace of the Hova Dynasty approached by a hundred steps. . . .

"Against the white of the African villages, the mellowed yellows of the distant Oriental buildings, the verdant green of spring and the brilliant flowers, color rolls up like the tones of a symphony barbaric in its splendor. It glints from the sabres and tips of bayonets, from gay robes and gowns, from black inscrutable men from North Africa, from little yellow men from the Orient, the brown faces of the desert, and the copperish tints of the American Indians. Besides such people, the pale faced man and woman seems colorless. . . .

"On a byway near the temple of Angkor-Vat, one finds a small piece of Tanis [the ancient Egyptian city]. Its chipped white walls, dusty with age, conceal dungeon-like streets. Every corner has a shop keeper's window from which the brown-faced owner leans to plead, 'Sentez le parfum de jasmin, la rose,' as with a graceful gesture he lifts the stopper from the bottle and wafts the delicate fragrance of the Orient through the air. In the next shop is the rata-rat-rat made by a Mohammedan boy creating a plate of hammered brass.

"More patient and less noisy is the dark-skinned girl in a Tunisian shop, weaving on a loom . . . surrounded by completed rugs which whole families have helped to weave. And in the courtyard of Tunis are low bamboo stools where visitors may sit to drink thick Turkish coffee.[37]

In the weeks following the inauguration, each country staged its own official opening. For the United States, this event took place on 26 May. United States Exposition Commissioner-General Slemp presided over an internationally broadcast ceremony that included addresses by Ambassador Edge, General Pershing, Marshal Hubert Lyautey, former Premier Tardieu, and Minister of Colonies Paul Reynaud. The *Chicago Tribune* reported:

> a galaxy of French and American military, political and social notables gathered in the banqueting hall of Mt. Vernon yesterday for the inauguration of the American section of the . . . Exposition. . . .
>
> The American Indian Band, in full war paint, played the Marseillaise and the Star Spangled Banner. . . . Miss Anne Madison Washington, great great grandniece of General Washington, was a gracious hostess to . . . thousands. . . . Ambassador Edge, declaring Mt. Vernon open, paid tribute to the constructive civilizing force which France has exercised in her colonies.[38]

Mount Vernon, with its adjoining buildings displaying the United States' colonial possessions, proved to be an enormous attraction from day one of the expo's general opening in early May, averaging twenty-five thousand visitors a day. (In the two days following the official inauguration of the U.S. site, over 750,000 people strolled across the broad green lawn and entered the mansion.)[39] Molly and the band, performing outside the house almost daily from 6 May onwards, were a major part of the exhibit's public appeal—its "most appreciated feature," according to the European edition of the *Chicago Tribune*.[40] A journalist reporting on the Mount Vernon inaugural for another newspaper wrote: "The U.S. Indian Band attracted much attention, not only because of their costumes, but because of their splendid music. Particularly causing much comment was the pretty Indian girl playing the tom tom. She is also a dancer of great talent."[41]

In addition to afternoon performances at Mount Vernon with the band, Molly danced with the Expo's International Ballet

Molly and the U.S. Indian Band at the 1931 Colonial Exposition in Paris. They are standing in front of the United States Exhibit (a replica of George Washington's Mount Vernon Home), where their performances drew great crowds. (From the U.S. National Archives, RG43, Records of the Commission Representing the United States at the International Colonial and Overseas Exposition at Paris, 1930–32.)

Corps at the Exposition Theater. She and the band had several bookings beyond the fair gates. They performed for two weeks at the Empire Music Hall beginning mid-May—for a fraction of their usual fee. They offered a program of sophisticated jazz, which had become wildly popular in Paris during the 1920s, topped by Indian songs and dances. They also gave concerts for American Ambassador Edge and the Franco-American Society, plus benefit performances at various hospitals.[42] But anticipated engagements in London, Berlin, and Rome fell through because the musicians had been issued special passports through the U.S. Department of State, and these were valid only in France.[43] Before finding a solution to this problem, band manager O'Brien hit another stumbling block: England and Germany had just passed new labor laws curtailing foreign entertainers.[44] After five weeks abroad, the band had earned less than eighteen hundred dollars.[45] O'Brien barely had enough money to feed and lodge the sixteen musicians, let alone pay them. He sent several written pleas to Commissioner Slemp for funds to cover the band's basic expenses so it could continue to perform at the exposition. But Slemp, budget bound, refused.[46] In contrast to the rest of the band, Molly had come to France with a small savings and, after arriving, had managed to get an unrestricted passport. She also had various job prospects, including film roles, and a European tour with other dancers performing at the expo. Plus, as a soloist, she was less cumbersome and costly to hire than the band and had already given several paid performances.[47] Toward the end of May, she began subsidizing the band members' income, frequently buying cigarettes and food for the whole lot. On 5 June she told her diary: "Talked with Joe [Shunatona] about the condition of the band and the boys—poor things. . . . O'Brien is to blame. At the [Chicago] Tribune—want to write about it. . . . The poor Injuns are more or less hungry. Gave them money."

The *Tribune*, and just about every other paper in the city, did, indeed, run articles about the band's fiscal dilemma. By 8 June, it was clear that no solution would be found. That day the *Tribune* ran a front page swan song about the band:

The band has proven a most popular attraction, particularly with the French to whom the American Indian has always been a romantic figure. . . . The redskin band has been so popular with French visitors at the exposition that it was believed possible that the French commission at Vincennes might make arrangements to keep it there . . . but the French commission will refrain because it might seem to be a slight to the United States which finds itself unable to support the redskins.[48]

The next day the band headed home. Molly, deciding to "gamble for a stake," did not go with them. In her diary she wrote: "The U.S. Indian Band left Paris for the States. . . . Up early to see them off at Gare Saint Lazare on the boat train to Havre. Felt so lonely. . . . Weepy when train pulled out." Then, resolute, she added, "So my life begins anew in Paris. Am so eager to learn, to grasp the best . . . and to really know myself as a woman. I am not afraid, for I know what fight means—and I want to return home with some satisfaction in my work. It means so much to me."[49]

CHAPTER 11

CITY OF LIGHTS

*Some serious success with my dance; seriously in
love with a real man; serious start on my first
novel—an Indian novel.*

—*Molly (Paris 1932)*[1]

Remarkably, during the Indian Band's last week in Paris, a
different French-American drama was taking place at the port
of Le Havre with yet another entertainment troupe very familiar to Molly: Texas Guinan and her girls. Tex, planning to open
a nightclub in Montmartre for the summer, had arrived on
France's shore with her girls and a band on 25 May—only to be
denied entry because they had tourist visas rather than work
visas. Officials could have resolved this. But they were deterred
by speculations that Tex had mafia connections and by heavy
protests from French entertainers who claimed it was unfair to
welcome a foreign troupe into the country when show-business
people already outnumbered available jobs. According to one
paper: "It is understood . . . that the night club queen had
contracted to work in France contrary to statute. . . . There
are hundreds of jobless French cabaret entertainers in Montmartre and the Labor Minister has refused ninety percent of
recent applications for permission for foreigners to work in
Paris."[2]

Guinan and her gang were held at a third-class hotel in Le
Havre to await deportation. Tex called it "Hotel Hoosegow."[3]
While they waited, she campaigned for the right to stay. Jour-
nalists flocked to interview the nightclub queen, and news-

papers peppered their pages with Tex's tantilizing commentary:

> I have only one desire, that's to ride Waco [my white horse] down the Champs-Elysées. If they'll let me land long enough to do that, I'll be happy and promise never to come back again. . . . Now I understand why the French shipped the Statue of Liberty to New York. They didn't need her anymore. . . .[4] The French said my auto was equipped with machine guns, but they ought to know that the only guns I use are wisecracks. . . . I sure was a sucker to come 3000 miles to go to jail.[5]

Molly, it seems, visited Tex "in jail," and with her fledgling media contacts, helped to wage the battle to keep her old patron in the country.[6] One journalist, who discovered that Molly was somehow linked to Guinan, reported that a young woman who sang and danced at the Colonial Exposition Restaurant and then disappeared was rumored to be a truant from the Guinan entourage.[7]

Ultimately, after ten days in limbo, Tex and her girls were shipped home—in the wake of the Indian Band, which had left the day before. Molly declined Tex's invitation to go along and rejoin the troupe. Paris' entertainment community was glad to see the competition go, declaring that France was "the original home of nightclubs and gayety and didn't need lessons from America." Many, however, regretted their departure. Paul Reboux, a well-known columnist for *Paris Soir*, the city's most-read newspaper, filled his 3 June column with a public letter to Texas. In it he criticized France's "laughable" protectionism and called Tex a "poor innocent" for believing "the word of 'liberty' written on the arches of France's public monuments." He concluded his long epistle with "an apology for the treatment you were forced to endure," and "the hope that one day France will again become a world-wide meeting place of good will, no longer ruled by Javert and Tartuffe."[8]

Back home, Tex told the *New York Times* that scores of Paris nightclub owners had petitioned the government to exclude her because she would take away their business. She vowed to sue "someone" for the French fiasco. Instead, in true Tex form, within a week of her return, she capitalized on publicity and turned the rebuff into a satirical revue called "Too Hot for Paris."[9]

With the band and Tex gone, Molly told her diary: "Sorry to be alone here. Maybe I am foolish, with no money, but hopes galore. But I DO want to do something with my Indian dancing here in a serious artistic way. And I'm willing to take a great chance to accomplish it."

Even with the departure of these friends, Molly was not without familiar faces in Paris. While walking along the Champs Elysées on her very first day in the "City of Lights," she had run into her old friend and associate Earl Welch, who had been assistant director for *The Silent Enemy*. Earl and the film's director, H. P. Carver, had just arrived in Paris to shoot *Little Occident* for Pathe-Natan Films. Two days later they took Molly to the studio, gave her a tour, and introduced her around. Back at her hotel after the tour, she noted in her diary "the marvelous offer given me"—probably referring to the chance to audition for a role in *Gitane* [Gypsy].[10]

Other opportunities quickly came her way, for French fascination with the exotic stretched well beyond the gates of the Colonial Exposition. Curiously, outside those gates, Molly ceased to be seen as a colonial subject. Instead, she was a dancer whose obvious "otherness" had enormous appeal, especially to the artistic and aristocratic elite of Paris. Like black American performers, including the sinuously playful Josephine Baker who had come to Paris six years earlier, Molly was struck by the relative lack of color prejudice in France. What prejudice there was did not result in social exclusion. It manifested itself as intrigue rather than insult and seemed to work in an artist's favor.[11] According to Molly's friend Lisan Kay, who gave concerts throughout Europe with her renowned Japanese dance partner and husband, Yeichi Nimura, the fact that Molly "stood out" helped her get work. "After all, she was an American Indian and looked that way every inch. She wore an Indian coat and braided her long black hair into muffs. . . . [On top of this,] she moved exquisitely."

Lisan recalls that "being a performing artist in Paris during the thirties was marvelous. When new artists arrived in the city, patrons, impressarios, and the press all flocked to their shows." Often an artist's first "shows" were at soirées held by titled patrons who relished discovering (and sharing the spotlight with) new talent. For Lisan, Nimura, and Molly, patrons included the Marquis d'Armaille, Comtesse de Moltens-Villermont, Comtesse d'Andigne, Madame Yolande, and Madame Lorel de La Tour. Typically, patrons hosted soirées in their ample homes. For instance, Mme. de La Tour's spacious apartment on Rue d'Algiers, a block from Tuileries Gardens, included a thirty-by-forty-foot ballroom. "Molly danced for her and her guests there, as did I," says Lisan. "Also, when Madame's friends wanted to study dance, we taught them there." Performances for patrons were usually gratis. But they opened the door to paid bookings, for impressarios and art critics were often among the invited guests.[12]

Patrons also held luncheon parties to honor and introduce new talent. On Molly's third day in Paris, Madame Yolande gave a luncheon for her and introduced her to Charlie Oskomon, a Yakima Indian dancer-singer. Although Molly doubted Oskomon's Indian and artistic authenticity almost immediately, he appealed to Parisians. In fact, he garnered enough income from his performances and patrons to live very comfortably in an apartment Molly described as "big enough for a soirée." In particular Oskomon was the protégé of Madame Clement, a French composer who was enamored of "things Indian," and managed Oskomon's career. Mme. Clement, who also attended Mme. Yolande's luncheon for Molly, suggested that Molly and Oskomon perform together.[13]

They did. Their first shared bill was at the American Conservatory of Music at Fountainbleau (where Aaron Copland and other esteemed American composers had studied).[14] According to one newspaper, "celebrities of both America and France" attended the Fountainbleau recital by "noted Indian artists, Chief Oskomon and Princess Spotted Elk."[15] Although Molly felt Oskomon's dance fell short, she enjoyed performing in the venerable palace, and made special note of meeting philanthropist Anne Morgan and Indian music composer Thurlow Lieurance.[16]

During her first few months in Paris, Molly launched into a new kind of career that included concerts, cabarets, and lecture-recitals. Although Paris was famous for its nude revues, Molly decided she had done her share of flesh parades in New York. After a successful audition at the Folies Bergères, she rejected the contract because "they want me to dance with less clothes on!"[17] In addition to performances at the Mount Vernon exhibit, the Exposition Theater, and private soirées, she danced in some of the most renowned and upscale places in the city, including the Ritz, Lido, Ambassadeurs, and even in the gilded salons of the Ministry of Justice. According to one journalist of the day, Les Ambassadeurs attracted "the world's most brilliant social, professional, political, and artistic persons. . . . [plus] gorgeously clad women bedecked in sparkling jewels." (Molly described it as "very snooty.")[18] The Ritz, Paris' most expensive hotel, offered garden dining to its utterly chic guests. After Molly's performance, the audience (including several princesses) gave her a standing ovation and a bundle of roses, and shouted, "Bis Bis!" (Molly, whose high school French was rusty, thought they were calling her a beast, until someone told her they were were crying, "Encore!")[19] Before the year ended, her French became quite proficient, and she became known in France's literary and art circles. She danced in Versailles and Vittel and also traveled beyond France's borders for performance tours in Spain and Italy.[20] Adding to her public exposure, *The Silent Enemy*, which had received a plethora of press coverage from September 1930 through its first month at French box offices in January 1931,[21] continued showing at some Paris movie houses. In fact, Molly went to see it at the Crystal Palace Theatre with several new French friends.[22]

How did Molly feel about her newfound work atmosphere? According to one newspaper:

Princess Spotted Elk says, "I am very happy over the wonderful opportunities given me, and by hard work I hope to bring out all the artistic feeling I possess . . . I have found already that [Europeans] appreciate real expression and Indian art." The princess is emphatic in her desire for nothing but genuineness. . . . and she tells of the struggle she had in the States for a true appreciation of Indian dances. The average American, the princess declares, "is satisfied with a dancer bedecked in feathers, making war-whoops and leaping aimlessly about with savage gestures to the beat of a tom-tom."[23]

Among the many journalists who wrote about Molly during her early months abroad was a young man named Jean Archambaud. He worked for *Paris Soir*, which, with its two million readers, boasted the largest circulation among Paris dailies.[24] As an *envoyé special* Archambaud spent a lot of time outside the office, gathering up material for a wide variety of feature stories. His interests, gravitating toward natural history, philosophy, and the arts, were decidedly cross-cultural. For example, in the months before Molly's arrival he covered topics such as Marcel Griaule's anthropological expedition to Africa, a lecture by Hindu philosopher Krishnamurti, the development of the Trocadero Museum of Man, and the avant garde film *Golden Age*, directed by Spanish surrealist Louis Bunel.[25] It is not surprising that this reporter was interested in writing about American Indians in Paris.

The day before the inauguration of the American exhibit at the Colonial Exposition, Archambaud knocked on the door of Oskomon's apartment, introduced himself, and invited the Indian entertainer out for a walk. Oskomon, apparently testing Archambaud, declared, "I am not a circus animal or curiosity." After a bit of talking, the journalist won him over, and Oskomon suggested, "Perhaps you'd like as well the company of a charming squaw [Molly]?" "And thus it was," wrote Archambaud in an article that appeared in *Paris Soir* two days later,

that there appeared on Bois-De-Boulonge Ave. [now Ave. Foch] a strange trio: a huge Indian with eagle feathers on his black hair, a young Indian woman with a beaded band around her forehead, and a wretched pale-face.

Curiosity was widespread. The noble carriage of the chief and the beauty of his companion attracted the looks of Parisians and countryfolk visiting the capital. . . .
Emotions rose with our passage and went through the roof when we went into a big café on the Champs-Elysées.
When we were seated, I asked the chief what his plans were.

Archambaud went on to chronicle Oskomon's plans to settle down in France, where he had a sense of freedom about his artistry—in contrast to the United States, where he felt confined. The journalist described the chief's desire to found an "'Institute of Sacred Indian Dance'" in Paris, and to "'make known the rich folklore of my people. . . . the true redskin, so different from those you read about in adventure novels.'"

After dinner, wrote Archambaud, he showed his Indian interviewees around Montparnasse. The trio created yet another stir when they stopped for a glass of wine on the terrace of Café de la Rotonde,[26] a favorite hangout for artists and writers. Archambaud asked Molly what she thought of Montparnasse, and included her reply in his story: "'It is too loud,' the young Indian woman says simply; 'I prefer the woods.'"[27]

Although this was the only direct quotation from Molly in Archambaud's long article, what she said struck a major chord with him, for he was an outdoor enthusiast, who, like Molly, felt uneasy if he spent too much time away from nature.

In her diaries, Molly rarely mentioned by name the many journalists who interviewed her. She made an exception with Archambaud. In fact, she noted more than his name: "Rendezvous at Oskomon's apartment. . . . Met a young journalist. Gave him a picture for Paris Soir. . . . We talked like old friends. . . . Does love come like this? Jean is his name."[28] She did not offer a physical description. But photographs show that Jean was a fit, broad-shouldered fellow of average height. He had a mass of wavy brown hair, high cheeks, a strong nose, wide-set blue eyes, and a generous mouth. His smile was sheer magic—a burst of lively warmth that engaged every feature of his handsome face.

Molly's French lover-husband Jean Archambaud, a journalist with *Paris Soir*. Circa 1938.

Smitten by Molly, Jean went to see her perform at the expo's American inaugural the day after their interview. The day after that he stopped by her hotel to return the photograph of her that appeared with his article, and to invite her out for coffee. The following day he showed up yet again, and she took him to meet some of the Indian Band members. And so it went, day upon day.[29] During long walks and even longer café talks over the next few weeks, he discovered that Molly loved art, literature, and history as much he did. She spoke with a captivating blend of passion and knowledge about about an American Indian culture that intrigued him profoundly. She even sang, just for him, Indian songs. Unlike previous suitors, Jean pursued Molly not as an exotic curio, but as a reflection of something deep within himself.

Despite her initial romantic reaction to Jean, Molly restrained her feelings about him, even in the intimate confines of her diary. When the Indian Band sailed home without her two weeks after she met Jean, she wrote: "I am staying only for my work and purpose. My newspaper admirer is certainly insistant and anxious to prove his case. He's a nice chap, clean."[30] The next day she noted: "Johnny—he dropped around to see me. He's really in love with me. . . . Like him, but [have reservations]—We both read. What a visit, a silent one, but it was good." Then, his first love letter arrived. Written in English, it was a perfectly graceful, if not perfectly grammatical, epistle:

Dear little one,
The sun is in my heart. It seems our happiness even affects the weather. This morning the sky was blue and a mysterious thing was in the air. I am so happy, dear brown little daughter of the forest. At last it seems to me I have reached all that I have craved for. You opened the door and here in the entrance I stand, marvelling. It is all I wanted and more. I want to pray and kneel, and at the same moment I could jump and give some joy whoop.
    You are the guide, a delicious guide for my clumsy footsteps. You take me by the arm and you show me the path. And the road is lovely, splendid. I bathe in an ether so beautiful. I breathe it and my heart is filled with awe and love. Your tongue, who will be

mine, is poetic and musical. Your voice takes a different tune and modulation. And far, far back, years and years, it seems familiar. I feel that the life of the "Old Time" must have been mine too. The simple songs you sing to me pleased me more than I will be able to write or tell you. In them there is a reflect of rushing water, winds in tree tops, and cool shadows of blazing camp fires. Through a single modulation you detect the pulsation of life, of a vibrant beautiful soul.

And as I was there, picking in that beautiful garden, our souls were united and flyed like two colorful birds on the flowers and trees. Thousands of tiny musicians played for us, but none could be seen. It was the music of the Red gods and I was united to you in the simple and sacred ways of your people—of my people. It was the simplest thing and yet the meaning of it was great and more awing than any beautiful ceremonies with people around. . . . It was the uniting of two loving hearts.

I can hardly write. It is impossible to express all that is in my heart. I worship you silently.

Your devoted Wawagosh [next to a tiny drawing of a wolf's head][31]

After reading this, Molly told her diary: "Sweet love letter from Johnny. . . . He baffles me and what it is I don't know. . . . I admire his frank simple honesty . . . even though his English amuses me. Maybe he is only interested [in me as a passing fancy]—it would be better for his heart. I wouldn't want to hurt him."[32]

By this time, having helped the Indian Band financially, and having paid a costly by-the-week rate for her hotel room, Molly found herself nearly out of money. Jean suggested she board with his parents, renting a spare room in their town apartment on rue Quincampaix. After visiting the place, located in an old, "quite ordinary" neighborhood near the huge, open air city market in the fourth *arrondisement*,[33] Molly wrote: "Strange to understand how such a fine family would live here. J said that during the war, building stopped and it was hard to find any kind of apartment afterwards. So his folks moved here. The best places were taken by strangers at the old rate of exchange."[34] Not caring whether she lived in a chic or ordinary neighborhood, Molly decided to accept Jean's offer. Surely she made the move, at least in part, out of romantic curiosity, although she told her diary it was for economical and anthropological reasons. Her explanation for moving in with the Archambauds reads like a paragraph from one of Professor Speck's lectures on fieldwork: "To classify a group of people, justice must be given them by understanding the how, what, when and why of things. . . . One must, to absorb thoroughly the Gallic mind, the Parisian culture (shall we call it that?), and to understand the economical, moderate life of the people, live with and among them. Afterall, I want to learn and absorb all I can while here."[34]

So Molly settled in with the Archambauds, where she was warmly welcomed. She described a typical day in the household:

> Mme A works every day in the Paris Soir. Her husband is chief of the race course dept. [Each morning] they leave here . . . for the same paper. For breakfast they have cocoa, half-toasted bread and butter. So I am alone quite a bit of the day. At noon Mme markets and gets [lunch] for the three of us, and dinner in the evening. Must help her—she is sweet to me. . . .
>
> Typical French dinner—hors d'oeuvres, potage, entrée, légume, fromage, fruit, salad, and café & small glass of kirsch. Monsieur is so fond of fine cooking, wines and his pipe. He is a dear old man, quiet and sweet. . . . After dinner [he] reads the journals, smokes, sits near the fire in his favorite chair . . . [while] Mme sews or reads.[36]

Even sweeter than Mme. and M. Archambaud was Jean, who proposed to Molly two weeks after she joined his family. Apparently he tried to ask her face-to-face, then resorted to a letter:

> Dear Molly,
> Ye who love the haunt of nature,
> Love the sunshine of the meadow,
> Love the shadow of the forest,
> Love the wind among the branches,
> And the rain-shower and the snow-storm,
> And the rushing of great rivers
>   through their palisades of pine trees,
> And the thunder in the mountains,

Listen:

I know you for a very short time, but it seems to me I have always known you. And we take a very serious subject as in laughing tonight. . . . I love you very much—and I am asking you, will you be my wife, dear Molly? Of course I don't [dare] hope you will simply answer yes. But if you are willing, if I am not for you only an amusing chap from France, we can examine the matter.

Jean illustrated this letter with a series of little drawings: an elk on a boat, a wolf coming to the elk's tepee, the wolf and the elk hand in hand, the wolf approaching the reclining elk, and a circle of hearts. "That is a very poor immitation of the '[Indian] Love Song,' he wrote. "Forgive me. Anyway, I will be at 8 PM in your hotel tonight. Your Johnny, chief of the Love Clan."[37]

A hint of Molly's response is in her diary: "It seems strange that Johnny should want to marry me—he knows me so little. Learned that a woman becomes French if she marries a Frenchman—and that the man is 'boss.' It's complicated, and I don't want to marry yet, to anyone."[38]

If not willing to marry Jean, she was more than pleased to take a three-week camping and hiking trip with him and his friend John Scotchman.[39] They went in July, a month when Paris stood still as its urban-weary citizens made their annual retreats to coastal beaches, mountain trails, or the rolling countryside. Toting backpacks stuffed with tents, sleeping bags, and other camp gear, the threesome headed for Basque country. They traveled southwest by train to Bordeaux, then on to the coastal town of Arcachon. Unlike most visitors arriving at this resort, Molly and her travelmates ignored its casinos and beach *cabines*. They took a boat to Cape Ferret, camped there for the night, then returned to the mainland and headed for Arcachon Forest Station. After filling their canteens at the station water pump, they hiked fifteen miles across the forest and camped at its southern edge. The following day they walked to the coast, and with hot sun pouring down on them, followed the shoreline twenty-five miles south to Mimizan. They camped where beach met woods, not far from an encampment of gypsies. After a day of sightseeing, they traveled another sixty miles southward by train to Bayonne in the province of Bearn. Jean, an avid hiker who usually trekked only with male friends, must have delighted in Molly's sturdy legs, stalwart spirit, and enthusiasm for the outdoors—uncommon among French women of the day.

Molly felt an almost mystical connection to this land—to its dramatic geography and its history. She knew that Basque fishermen from the coastal towns of Bearn Province had crossed the Atlantic to fish and whale in the Gulf of Maine beginning in the early sixteenth century. Well before European traders, settlers, and colonizers moved into Wabanaki territory, these fishers had spied it from the sea. Some had ventured close enough to anchor near shore and trade with Molly's Wabanaki ancestors, who approached the fishing boats by canoe.⁴⁰ Bearn was also the homeland of Jean Vincent de St. Castin, a seventeenth-century French baron who figured significantly in the history of Molly's people. In 1665, thirteen-year-old St. Castin went to Canada as an ensign with France's famed Carignan Salières regiment to subdue Iroquois warriors challenging French colonization. After succeeding in its mission, the regiment was disbanded, and many of its members chose to stay in New France. By 1670, St. Castin had settled at Pentagoet (now Castine, Maine), a French fort at Penobscot Bay. He traded with, befriended, and often lived with Wabanaki Indian bands in the region. Eventually, he married Mathilde, daughter of a notorious Penobscot River sagamore named Madockawando, and became a chief.⁴¹ Molly, familiar with this story, must have marveled at the historic coincidence of a Penobscot woman exploring St. Castin's homeland with a Frenchman who wished to marry her. Certainly she told the story to her companions.

After a full day of sightseeing in Bayonne, the trio of intrepid hikers succumbed to its magnificent mountainous backdrop, trekking six miles toward the profile of peaks into Biarritz. They set up camp at midnight. The following day they moved on to St. Jean de Luz, walking into evermore picturesque and hilly country. After a good night's sleep with the stars above them and a brook beside them, they ambled into the village

Molly and Jean Archambaud (on her left), on one of their many mountain treks in France. (One of Jean's hiking friends and fellow scouts, John Scotchman, is on Molly's right.)

and boarded a cable car that carried them to the seaside town of Hendaye. Here, the great spine of the sky-high Pyrenees rises up from the Atlantic to divide France from Spain. And here, writing in her diary by the campfire's dancing light, Molly noted: "Serious hiking now."

They set out the following morning on a trail that took them past lush alpine meadows strewn with wildflowers, glacier-fed waterfalls and streams, crumbling Basque churches and grave-yards, an ancient fortress, wee mountain villages—and breath-taking views of snow-crowned peaks. One night they camped in a pasture grazed by sheep; another night streamside under trees; another on a mountain lip that jutted out over a deep valley. Each day they hiked for about eight hours. Their third day on the trail, they reached Bidarray, where they boarded a train that took them to Mauleon and then on to Lourdes, nestled deep in a valley. Here, in a grotto, the Virgin Mary is said to have appeared to Saint Bernadette in 1858. Thereafter, some who visited the site experienced miraculous cures, and it became a Roman Catholic shrine and a pilgrimage destination for sufferers. Molly and her companions spent several days in this place of miracles, watching veiled women making no-venas, bathing in the mineral springs tucked in a hillside, hiking out to the Lac de Lourdes. They met an old poet-prospector, and a sculptor who owned a religious trinket shop and invited them to camp between the flower beds in his back yard. On the last day of their vacation, they took a long bus ride back up into the highlands to Gavarnie. Driving through "beautiful country—deep ravines, lofty mountains," they reached Gavarnie in time to see the famous Pyrenee Circus. After the show they walked up to the snow line, leaping over summer streams, watching other tourists travel the route on the backs of mules or horses. Then, "back to Lourdes. Rush through dinner. Took train to Paris. Tired but happy."

Molly did not mention love once in her diary during the trip to Basque country, except in regard to nature's glory. But an entry written upon her return to Paris shows that she did notice more than the scenery: "Beautiful vacation—my first.

Woods, mountains, sea, camping life, freedom. It [was] wonderful. Would that I always remain close to nature—as it gives
me all. . . . My health is improving and I am finding new real
friends. New sights, new things, newness of everything that is
interesting. A friend who loves me—a companion who believes
in me—what a friend he is."[42]

This was not an admission of love, but it hinted at a transition taking place in her heart—as does this note, penned
several weeks after their trip: "I'll write Douglas [Burden]
. . . [for] I still do think of him. I do not think seriously of
anyone [else] yet—but I wonder about Johnny."[43] In September, over tea, Mme. Archambaud told Molly about Jean's former
fiancé "whom he loved for five years and who nearly broke his
heart. Then he just drifted from one girl to another." Mme.
Archambaud, unaware that Jean was seriously courting her
Indian boarder, sadly concluded that her son was "finished
with women."[44] How wrong she was. By the end of October,
Jean's love had finally melted Molly's heart, and she admitted to
her diary: "A realization that I really am in love for the first
time—the other [was] idealistic illusion . . . [This is] companionship, honesty, honor, understanding and confidence. A faint
idea of someday being married dawns on me—when my work
is done."[45]

Her work. It tugged. She followed its pull, signing a six month
contract with an impressario who booked her in Italy and
Spain, as well as in France. With full-page profiles in *Pour Vous*
and *Danse* magazines[46] and scores of shorter articles about
her, publicity was plentiful. So was loneliness. Her first Christmas abroad found her among strangers, performing in Madrid
at the "very chic and exlusive" Club Lido and living alone in a
pension that was over twelve hours (by train) from Paris. On
Christmas Eve she wrote: "Walked around the little alleys
again. . . . Felt blue and lonely. Got a telegram from Johnny—
bless him—saying 'Happy Christmas, love.' And how it cheered
me up. I certainly miss him and honestly love him with all my
heart and soul. And he loves me." Five days later, she wrote:
"One of the happiest surprises—Johnny dropped in to see

me. . . . He is traveling on a political campaign with another journalist. . . . With him alone for a few hours. . . . At the club. They saw me [dance]."[47] As the months rolled on, it was often this way: Molly performing outside of Paris, Jean away on assignment, both of them doing whatever they could to make their paths cross.

During her second year abroad Molly barely left Paris. Work outside the city included only several engagements in Versailles and a week-long booking at the Biarritz Casino in Basque country (which she squeezed in midway through another three-week camping trek with Jean).[48] She continued to live with Mme. and M. Archambaud, who had moved from their rue Quincampaix apartment to a home in Sevres at the city's southwest edge, near the St. Cloud woods. "There are three stories and much room," Molly wrote in her diary. "I am on the top floor—in a sort of studio room. . . . I have space, light, a fine floor and am left entirely alone. In fact, no one comes upstairs but Johnny to visit and chat!"[49] She performed often in the city, sometimes solo, sometimes with Oskomon, other times with Anita Patel, a dancer from India whom she met through the exposition. Bookings included private soirées, La Boîte à Jou Joux (a nightclub for children),[50] L'Aéroport night-club and Gaite-Rochechouart theater in Montparnasse, and the Empire Music Hall and various other cinema-music halls.[51] At the small and highly exclusive Left Bank theater Vieux Colombier, Molly danced in Yeichi Nimura's "Life Perpetual" with Lisan Kay and American ballet dancer Margaret O'Brien. In this avant-garde production, one of Nimura's "cosmic poems," the women depicted the cycle of life with all its joys and sorrows, while Nimura sat in a corner, played a drum, and gave an expressive commentary.[52] Molly also performed at Salle Pleyel,[53] the Carnegie Hall of Paris. Long associated with the best music making in France, the Pleyel was founded by and named for a piano-manufacturing friend of Wolfgang Mozart's in the eighteenth century. During Molly's stay in France, its stage hosted a wide spectrum of remarkable musicians, from Duke Ellington to composer-conductor Maurice Ravel.[54] At the end of her second year abroad, she accepted an engagement at the elegant Ranch de California coastal resort in Ostend, Belgium.[55]

Despite many significant bookings, impassioned performances, and consistent newspaper coverage, Molly did not become *truly* famous. Certainly she was not a sensation comparable to the inimitable Josephine Baker, with whom all of Paris had a love affair. Why? Much of it had to do with personality and audience. Josephine reached out to a wider public and gave them shows both onstage and off. She danced naked. She painted her fingernails gold, draped herself in furs and jewels, and sashayed down the avenues with her pet leopard Chiquita (whose jeweled collar usually matched his mistress' outfit).[56] She seemed to know instinctively how to woo her onlookers. "If I'm going to be a success," she said, "I must be scandalous. I must amuse people."[57] And so she did— with abandon, talent, and bigness of heart, creating a stir wherever she went. Even Molly made note of this in her diary: "Luncheon with J[ohnny] at the Village de la Fol Butte (Silly Hill) Mairie in the XIX arrondissement. Josephine Baker there, the press and other notables. Miss Baker is charming with oodles of personality. . . ."[58] Utterly enchanted by "La Baker," Parisians placed her on a pedestal, and from that lofty vantage point she proclaimed, "Paris is the dance. I am the dancer."[59]

Molly, in contrast, felt uneasy when the spotlight followed her offstage. She was charming and forthcoming when interviewers asked her about American Indian cultures and dance, but shy and tight-lipped about her personal life. When a writer for the popular French magazine *Pour Vous* commented at the end of a lengthy interview, "You talk little about yourself, Spotted Elk," Molly responded: "What could I say about myself? I am of the Mongolian type. I have studied two years at the University of Pennsylvania—journalism. I adore ethnography, music, and dance. Above all dance." The journalist pressed for more, asking "But what are your tastes, what do you like?" Molly answered, "You can add that I love snakes, very strong tea, crossword puzzles . . . canoeing, camping, and some corners of France where nature is splendid. And I hate journalists who talk about my private life."[60] To a degree, Molly's reticence to put herself forward stemmed from the sense of inferiority that sometimes cropped up within her. More than this, it came from her roots in an egalitarian culture that frowned on excessive praise (or ridicule) and never erected pedestals (or dug pits) for its members. According to her dancer-friend Lisan Kay, "Molly didn't have enough ego to be truly famous. She wasn't into puffing herself up."[61] Which is not to say she did not care about applause; she absolutely relished an audience's appreciation—especially when *she* felt she'd performed well.

It mattered little to Josephine or her fans that she never read books and had no idea who Albert Einstein was; she was spirited, sexy, and well-equipped to give the public exactly what it wanted: sheer entertainment.[62] But books and intellectual expression were as crucial to the well-being of Molly's soul as dance and song. She attended Marcel Mauss's anthropology lectures at the Sorbonne. She sought (and found) opportunities to give lecture-recitals—at private soirées, the Trocadero Museum, the Sorbonne, the Archives de Danse, the Cercle Internationale des Arts, and the Salle Adyar.[63] At these headier occasions, Jean often participated, playing the tom-tom as she danced and translating as she talked. Molly found him "marvelous to work with as he understands everything."[64] Such programs were hardly crowd-drawing Music Hall fare. Audiences were relatively small, exclusive, and very polite. They offered modest fame and respect. Just what Molly wanted.

Both Molly and Jean gravitated toward exhibit and recital events at the Trocadero Museum of Natural History in the immense, oriental-style palace erected for the 1878 Paris Exhibition. In 1930 Professor Paul Rivet, who founded the Sorbonne's Institut d'Ethnologie (with Marcel Mauss and Lévy-Bruhl in 1925), set out to reorganize the museum's ethnographic exhibits. To help with the task, he hired Georges-Henri Rivière, a jazz amateur with a keen publicity sense and many high society connections. With Rivière's help, funds were raised to refurbish interior museum space and to finance an

Molly and her French lover Jean Archambaud. Paris 1934.

ambitious collections expedition to Africa. Known as the Dakar-Djibouti Mission, this much-publicized expedition, headed by ethnologist Marcel Griaule, traversed the width of Africa along the southern rim of the Sahara. Between the summer of 1931 and the spring of 1933, its members gathered ethnographic photos, recordings, and documents, plus some 3500 objects for the museum.[65] From 1930 through 1933, Jean reported regularly on the Trocadero's transformation and the Dakar-Djibouti Mission.[65]

When Molly landed in France on 2 May 1931, the mission was just getting underway, and the museum's new Galerie d'Amerique was nearly complete. The first exhibit scheduled for the new space was "Les Peau Rouges d'hier et d'aujourd-hui" ("Redskins yesterday and today")—a display of American Indian artifacts and clothing collected in Canada by a Franco-American painter-writer-illustrator named Paul Coze ("Dabija"). The exhibit also featured Coze's paintings of American Indians.[67] Molly, who apparently had met Coze before coming to Paris, ran into him at a reception on her very first day in the city. He asked for her input on his exhibit, and she made several trips to the Trocadero before the show's opening. Through Coze, she became acquainted with Rivet and Rivière.[68] By the end of the May when Molly met Jean, the Trocadero was one more thing they had in common. For Molly, the ethnographic collections of the museum had great meaning: "Even the sight of primitive things and real pictures of natives does me good. It always makes me feel that [Western] civilization does not mean so much after all—that there are still some people who can live without it or even knowing about it, and they are happier, healthier, more genuine as far as human nature is concerned. . . . At least they are hospitable and can laugh with laughing eyes and souls."[69]

Over the next few years, Molly mentioned the museum frequently in her diary—noting Jean's articles about it, her lecture-recital performances there, and her participation in various exhibits:

> At Trocadero to see Paul Coze. Helped with work. . . .
> With Charlie [Oskomon] at Trocadero. Met [with] Riviere, Paul Coze and the producer [about Coze's exhibit]. . . .
> At Trocadero to see books. Saw Riviere, spoke of [showing] the picture [The Silent Enemy] there. . . .
> J[ohnny] writing on Dakar-Djibouti expedition. . . .
> Injuns [from a rodeo] at apartment, gave them watermelon and drinks. Chatted. J[ohnny] and I took them to see Riviere at Trocadero. . . .
> At Trocadero to help for the Dakar-Djibouti exposition. Worked with Mr. Richard, the South American explorer. Lots of fun. All of [the expedition] bunch there—[Marcel] Griaule, [Michel] Leiris, and that funny jewess Miss [Deborah] Lifchitz. . . .
> At Trocadero—helped [with Dakar-Djibouti]. Busy. . . . Dinner given us by Mr. Riviere and Rivet. . . .
> J at work on Dakar-Djibouti [article]. [I] am to write it in English for the London Illustrated News. . . .
> Am to dance next month at the Theater Trocadero for benefit. . . .
> J[ohnny] phoned. Said the Trocadero may close due to lack of money. Riviere is sick about it. What a calamity, and the government can't keep it up. J is to write about it in the paper. He's always helping someone.[70]

Ultimately, efforts to patch up and modernize the old Trocadero Museum were abandoned. In 1937 the palace was torn
down to make room for a new, modern-style Trocadero Musée
de l'Homme (Museum of Man).[71]
After Molly helped Paul Coze with his Trocadero exhibit, she
posed for him several times in his studio on Premier Com-
pagne. Among other works, she modeled for his painting of
Kateri Tekakwitha, a seventeenth-century Mohawk Indian,
long considered a saint by Catholic Iroquois and other Indians.[72] In 1667, when Kateri was eleven years old, French Jesuit
missionaries came to her village (in present-day Auriesville,
New York). After conversion and baptism, Kateri refused to
marry, and chose a life of chastity, prayer, and service. It is said
that she worked miracles during her holy but brief life. At age
twenty-four, several years after moving to a mission village at
Kahnawake, Quebec, she died. The Catholic church had not
canonized Kateri at the time Coze used Molly's likeness to
paint her "portrait." Nonetheless, she was a cherished subject
among artists. In fact, Molly posed for several other artists'
renderings of Kateri. (In 1943, Rome recognized Kateri as
"venerable," and in 1980 Pope John Paul II beatified her.)

Beyond dancing, and posing for artists like Coze, Molly
continued to pursue writing. Periodically she sent letters
about her life in Paris to the *Portland Telegram* and collaborated with Jean on articles about their hiking trips for an
outdoor French magazine called *Au Camping*. She continued
refining the Penobscot legends she had worked on in New York,
and Jean set to work translating them in hopes of having them
published in France. Whenever Molly could find time, she
researched the Baron de St. Castin story, which she planned to
coauthor with Jean one day.[73] According to the *Portland
Telegram*, during her sojourn in France,

[Spotted Elk has done] much research work at the National
Library where there are many old manuscripts, documents, and
even Indian histories of the early French voyagers who went to
Maine. Among those who married Indian girls was Baron de [St.]
Castin, and descendants of this union are on [Indian] island

today. A French publisher is interested in the idea of a novel centering on the romance of the baron and the chief's daughter, and it is Princess Spotted Elk's hope to collaborate some day with a French writer in developing this theme.[74]

Molly often wrote in the apartment of her friend Mary Knight, a vivaciously bold American jounalist who arrived in Paris about nine months before she did. Sick of her job as shopping columnist for the New York *American*, Mary boarded a cattle boat in New York and headed for Europe with $378 in her pocket and a borrowed Ford roadster in the ship's cattle hold. After two months of solo travel in England, The Netherlands, Belgium, Germany, Austria, Switzerland, and France, she decided to ship the car back to the States, settle in Paris, and find a writing job. Several weeks of door knocking at every English and American newspaper and advertising firm in the city yielded no job and left her with only forty cents to her name. Desperate, she returned to the United Press Paris Bureau where, in her eyes, director Ralph Heinzen had left the door open a crack: instead of an absolute no, he had said hiring a woman would be a "dubious experiment." Her determination won him over, and he hired her on as a reporter. "In the years that followed," Mary later wrote, "I discovered that the role of Woman Foreign Correspondent was of comparatively recent development. . . . There was but one before the war, May Birkhead of the New York *Herald* staff in Paris, who entered her job with the sinking of the Titanic. That strange accident in mid-Atlantic gave Europe its first American woman correspondent." Mary Knight did her job well, covering a wide spectrum of stories, from political events to beauty pageants to murders. Several months after Molly met her, Mary disguised herself in men's clothes in order to witness the beheading of Pavel Gorgouloff, the crazed Russian refugee who assassinated President Paul Doumer. On another occasion, she outwitted a horde of journalists who were trying to get a peek at Anne and Charles Lindbergh at their hotel in Le Bourget, just outside the city; sneaking up the back steps of the luxurious hotel and marshalling two garbage collectors to stand guard while she knocked on the Lindbergh's door, Mary won an exclusive interview with Anne.[75]

Molly noted that she met Mary while having tea in a café with her old pal Texas Guinan, who returned to Paris as a tourist for several weeks in the spring of 1932 (and once again tried unsuccessfully to woo Molly back to the States). It is not clear whether Molly joined Tex and Mary in the middle of an interview or whether Mary recognized the two show women at the café and introduced herself.[76] Whichever is the case, Molly and Mary hit it off and several days later met for dinner at the University Club in Montparnasse. Henceforth, they got together often to gab, brainstorm about writing, and critique each other's work. And after Molly moved from the Archambaud's Sevres house to a "small cheery room" on Rue l'Arcade near Notre Dame Cathedral in September 1932,[77] she often went to Mary's apartment to write. There she had more light and space, plus a stove to cook on and a view of the Seine. A strong friendship evolved between these two ambitious young women. They respected, relied upon, and drew inspiration from one another throughout Molly's stay in France.

Mary was part of Molly's café circle—one of the people with whom she rendezvoused regularly in Montparnasse, which she described as: "the Greenwich Village of Paris . . . student district, popular bohemian center of night life, art colonies, studios, orgies, and bums."[78] For those who lived in small hotel rooms, the cafés of Montparnasse were annex salons. Certainly this was the case for Molly. Among her frequent haunts was the Dome Café, not far from the American Express office where she often stopped to check for mail from home. The Dome (along with the Coupole, Select, and Rotonde) was one of the most popular Latin Quarter cafés for American artists, writers, journalists, students, and tourists during the 1920s and 1930s. Here Molly regularly met up with Jean, Mary, and others central to her life abroad. Crowded around a tiny table (surrounded by many other crowded tiny tables), they drank café, gossiped, talked about the arts and politics, and watched the intriguing diversity of Paris stroll by. Among her friends and

café mates were dancers Yeichi Nimura and Lisan Kay who
from 1932 to 1937 used Paris as home base for their European
concert tours. Her closest dance friends were three women
who, like her, had remained in Paris after performing at the
Colonial Exposition. She described them as "ambitious" dancers
"interested in other things than being on the stage." Aloma
from Malaysia studied tropical medicine, Tchai from Indonesia
took drama classes, and Anita from India studied political
science. "All of us *must* have something to strive for," Molly
noted about these friends and herself.[79] Dearest to Molly
among these three was Anita Patel, described by Lisan as "a
tiny East Indian dancer with a round head; a wonderful performer who had her own troupe."[80] Anita's father was Vallabhbhai Patel, longtime leader in the Indian National Congress that spearheaded India's move toward independence.
(When the colonial bond was broken in 1947, Patel served as
deputy prime minister.) Like Lisan and Nimura, Anita was
often away on tour, but Paris was her harbor, and whenever she
was in town, she and Molly spent much time together. They
taught one another some of their traditional dances, and quite
often performed together. Jean's friends were also part of
Molly's circle, especially John Scotchman (his hiking friend),
Alex Aunanoff (a Russian prince who fled to France with his
family after World War I), Raymond Gast (another journalist),
and Jean Bushman (a political activist).[81]

Cafés were also informal offices, gathering points for agents,
art critics, and magazine editors who had their eyes out for
talent. In all likelihood, it was at the Dome that Molly met
literary agent William Aspenwall Bradley. Described in one of
Janet Flanner's 1929 *New Yorker* letters as the "leading agent
and prophet here on trans-Atlantic affairs,"[82] Bradley repre-
sented a host of noteworthy writers: Stephen Vincent Benét,
Ezra Pound, Edith Wharton, Thornton Wilder. He negotiated
the sale of Gertrude Stein's *Autobiography of Alice B. Toklas* to
Harcourt, Brace, and he connected Henry Miller with Obelisk
Press for the publishing of *Tropic of Cancer*.[83] It is not known
when Molly first met Bradley, but in autumn 1932 he began to

Molly in East Indian costume, Paris, circa 1933. She sometimes performed East Indian dances with her dancer-friend, Anita Patel (daughter of Vallabhbhai Patel, long-time leader in the Indian National Congress, which spearheaded India's move toward independence).

pop up frequently in her diary, sometimes in descriptions of social gatherings:

> Read Savage Paradise. Enjoyed it. It's one of the books Bradley gave me from his "heaven, purgatory and hell" pile of books. The heaven group are the latest out, the purgatory to be either thrown to hell or left for special special use, and the hell are ready to be given away to friends. . . .
> Christmas. . . . Up to Mr. Bradley's. Had marvelous dinner. Got a present from his wife. Met a charming Persian woman, a Mr. Murphy, a young writer and Mr. B's neice. . . . Danced for them. Murphy did too. Lovely evening. Murphy walked home with me. He used to be [Ford] Maddox Ford's secretary.[84]

But most of Molly's entries about Bradley centered around writing. It was he who pressed her to get going on her long-intended "Indian novel." Early on in their association, she gave him a verbal sketch of this would-be novel, set on Indian Island. Afterward, she noted his encouragement: "Thought of what Mr. Bradley told me about [my] novel and the help he could get for me. Am dying to start."[85]

She did start, cutting back dance engagements in order to concentrate on the task. A *Portland Telegram* article published about two years later provides an overview of Molly's story and hints at the verbal sketch she presented to Bradley:

Not all of Molly Spotted Elk's activities were bounded by the stage and camera during her stay in Europe. Much of her time . ·. . was devoted to writing a novel with Indian Island in former days as a setting.

Of it she says, "It is a simple tale of the people at home as they were about 30 years ago with their life, the changes and the present day. I have brought in the life of the river drivers, the lumber camps, Old Town and Bangor, tribal matters, the [Indian] agents and the few evils that were in evidence when I was a mite. Basketry, the intimate home life, ceremonies, salt water trips, education, and so many true incidents of the tribe impressed themselves upon my mind so that I can now write about them even to the smallest detail. Most of the characters are real, though some are dead and the rest partly fiction. The family, referring back to the time of my parents and their romance, is my own with minor changes. The heroine who belongs to it is partly fictitious and partly one of my sisters. The hero is a young half-breed with a mother who returned from the outside [off the reservation] when he was a small chap. This brings in the contrast that is found on the island. The bad men of the story are [the government-appointed Indian] agent and an Indian who would sell his soul for favors received from the white man.

"For once, the Indian heroine will not die, nor will anything happen to the hero at the end, as I hate to kill off Indians for the sake of a few prejudiced readers who cannot understand why an Indian can win the heart of the young white hero or heroine. . . .

"As I wrote, I felt I was not so far away from the island. Often I imagined I could hear the distant pounding of an ash log [by a basketmaker preparing splints] or smell the damp, cool, water-soaked pine logs [in the river drives]. The people I described seemed to be in the room with me.

"In the pages I set down, one can recognize old Clara Neptune; blind Liz, the braider of sweetgrass and the very soul of all that was Indian; Andrew Sockalexis, the marathon runner who won fame in the Olympics in Sweden; Peter Glossian, the ferryman; Watawaso [the singer] who has returned to the [reservation]; my old pal Hemlock Joe, the bedridden wood carver and a book of all the early life of my people; Piel Sockus, a fiery orator and champion of the old order of things; and a few others that pass through the story.

"Incidents, too, will awake recollections—the flood of some years ago and tribal claims after it, the visit of Governor Percival P. Baxter to the island when I was in high school; the serious matters of Indian funds, the agent, and the appeal for a square deal by the different Indians; and a trial at which an Indian hunter defended himself on the charge of shooting out of season."[86]

While writing this novel, Molly made frequent references in her diary to the work, her struggles with it, and Bradley's input. The following entries were penned between October 1932 and April 1933:

Mr. Bradley phoned me. Told me of the Harper Prize competition. But what can a poor thing like me do in a thing like that? Anyway, I'll try to get the novel finished before the end of February. He is a marvelous friend. . . .
Busy writing. Some inspiration. . . .
Sometimes I feel so incapable of producing a thing—and feel my brain child [book] which Bradley says is so large should be left to mature at a future time. . . .
Marketing, writing. At Bradley's—long talk. . . .
Worked all night . . . [on the section about] Bunty's death. . . . Sad and depressing as it was, that chapter is complete [and] I love to write as well as to dance. . . .
Busy at work night and day. But not as rapid as I had planned. Guess I can't make it for Harper's prize. . . .
Worked feverishly on the clambed and Madasun episode. . . .
Worked all night. . . . Wonder how I can get my Piel to land in jail? Ah, to knock the hell out of the [Indian] agent and the doctor. That's what I'd do if they were around and I was at home. . . .
One cannot become a machine for writing—it is cold-blooded to try to write a thing in so many days. . . .
. . . to Mary's. Worked hard . . . wrote rather well. Mary read me the manuscript. Am not satisfied with it. Johnny around, ate, read while I wrote. . . .
At Mary's. Worked like a machine.[87]

By spring, the book was falling into shape and several chapters were more or less complete. Bradley asked to see a sample. Although reticent, Molly agreed. It was time to find out if her written pages verified his hunch that Paris could offer her literary blessings on top of dance opportunities and love. On 11 April she told her diary: "Mary and I at Mr. Bradley's with manuscript. He is to read the chapter tonight. Am nervous."[88]

CHAPTER 12

PARIS NOIR

*Wonder who the snake is, of green and yellow, which
appears in my dreams—is it a warning?*
—Molly (Paris 1934)[1]

Molly had reason to be nervous in the spring of 1933—not only
about William Bradley's response to her writing, but about
France's increasing economic and political strife. By this time
the Great Depression cloaked the country, including the City
of Lights. Germany had reneged on war reparation payments
vital to the French treasury. President Roosevelt had devalued
the dollar, boosting in effect France's export prices twenty-five
percent and contributing to a decline in production. Unemployment and the national deficit were rising; agricultural
prices and civil servant salaries were falling. An unstable and
uninspired government offered no hope of reversing the decline, and frustration among French citizens threatened to
erupt into violence. Plus, the nation next door had a new and
disquieting regime: Hitler and his Nazi party had come into
power.[2] A storm was brewing.

Bradley, who had pressed Molly to slip him a sample chapter
before she felt it was really finished, read the work immediately. The following day Molly told her diary: "Called Mr. B.
Sorry I did as he criticized that chapter mercilessly—too
much religious thought, too drawn out, quick change for Piel,
not enough conversation. . . . He said, 'The pulse of your writing is there, Molly, but the actual feeling seems hazy.' . . . So I
told him to wait, wait until I had it down the way I wanted it. He

likes the style . . . etc., but he is so critical!"³ The haziness
Bradley pointed out reflected Molly's reticence to display emotion and reveal her deep sentiments—in writing, as in relationships. Even her diaries, written for her eyes alone, tended to be
discreet. Beyond her personal psychological makeup, this guard-
edness hearkened back to Penobscot tradition, which valued
masking one's feelings for the sake of group harmony. It was a
remnant trait from the era of small hunting communities when
people relied on each other for survival and had little tolerance
for emotional displays that might lead to conflict.⁴ Dancing
and music provided rare acceptable outlets for impassioned
expression among Penobscots. Molly, a passionate woman,
seized upon dance and surrendered herself to it. In the words
of her sister, Eunice, Molly's dancing was like "fire, real and
elemental."⁵

In writing, free expression came less easily for Molly. When
she encountered Bradley's critique of her zealous effort, she felt
as if she had turned her canoe against the current after a
rousing downstream paddle. She had to struggle for inspiration. Challenging the tide of disappointment, she announced
in her diary: "Dickens with criticism. Will finish my book, cut
it down, fix it up."⁶ Still, notes about writing during the next
months were unusally downbeat: "Rather little work on story
this week. In a way discouraged. . . . [Worked] at Mary's. . . .
Watched the boats move along the river. The leaves are bursting out, life is glowing. . . . I try to write, and move slowly,
slowly, slowly."⁷

Molly stayed in touch with Bradley and continued to work on
her novel, albeit at a less fervid pace. She had spent several
months devoting her work life almost exclusively to writing and
now needed to begin accepting dance engagements again—for
both financial and emotional reasons. Dancing not only paid
her bills, it gave her a needed break from her typewriter and
reassurance that she excelled at something. Mid-April she
signed on for three weeks at the Empire Theater, and after the
first show told her diary, "It was so good to dance again. A
breathing space on my book . . . " But there was a downside to

this booking. She appeared with Charlie Oskomon, with whom she felt increasingly uncomfortable sharing a stage. From the outset of their association, his Indian heritage and performances had struck her as dubious. After rehearsals for their first joint appearance at Fountainbleau in 1931, she had noted in her diary, "Oskomon strikes me as a good showman, but ignorant of real Indian art, music, dances and mythology. ... Studied him, saw picture of his father—typical negro type. Must be from the Carolinas or the southern Atlantic seaboard. . . . He's no more a chief than he is a Yakima . . . but I won't disturb him."[8] Molly's suspicions, if correct, might explain Oskomon's jealousy toward her, an emotion that sullied their relationship and that Molly frequently mentioned in her diary:

> Oskomon disturbed—he couldn't followup after my warrior dance. . . .
> Oskomon insulted because I said Nimura is one of the best dance artists. Hope Osk doesn't think *he* is the best! . . .
> Oskomon made such a fuss about my dances—the old jealous cat. Even the manager said he was jealous and difficult. . . .
> Oskomon fighting and nagging at the theater. . . . his temperment isn't Indian—and if he gets too mouthy, I'll tell him [I know] what he really is. . . .
> Oskomon—I cannot tolerate the partnership.[9]

After their spring 1933 run at the Empire, they did not share another billing. Her next engagements—including the Gaite-Rochechouart theatre, the Salle Pleyel, and the Trocadero in Paris, and the upscale coastal resort "Ranch de California" in Ostende, Belgium—were all solo.

Molly faced another social conflict far more disturbing than a final falling out with Oskomon. Her move from the Archambaud's Sevres home in the fall of 1932 had not been graceful. Apparently Mme. Archambaud had gradually come to disapprove of Molly—her sense of independence, her casual use of hot water and gas, the occasional tardiness of her rent payments, and the fact that she had become a serious love interest for Jean. Madame's bourgeois values of orderliness, protocol, and responsibility had bumped up against Molly's Penobscot and Bohemian values of flexibility and freedom. These diary entries tell the story:

> Mme. cannot understand the freedom of Americans. She thinks I am, well—unique. I go and come as I please. This does not conform to the French idea. Maybe she is afraid for her J, as he is her favorite son. . . .
>
> [Mme. A. wants to know] do i feel grateful? Yes and no—yes because she was sweet once, no because I pay for what I get. . . .
>
> Am rather lonely now since there is misunderstanding where I live. I can't stand that woman much longer. If I had money enough, I'd have left long ago. The idea of her telling me what she does! When I have money, she is sweet. When I don't she's unreasonable. Johnny's father is wonderful. . . .
>
> Awakened rudely by Mme. A. Packed all my things. Had to hurry or I would have poked a fist at her. Boy, I got enough of that miserly Swiss-French women. She dislikes me because she realizes J loves me. Moved . . . to Anita's in Montparnasse. Sad. But happy to do as I wish. . . .
>
> Slept the sleep of a free bird. Washed, bathed, shopped, cooked and used all the hot water, gas, soap and anything I wished. . . . Anita and I cooked a big dinner. Johnny slept in the salon. Said he didn't want any more words with his old woman. Poor John. He's in a quandrum.[10]

Interestingly, while Mme. Archambaud tried to convince her son that an attractive, well-to-do young woman named "Nadia— or any real French girl—would be better for his life,"[11] Molly's mother sent similar messages from across the ocean: "Mama thinks my friendship with J is not good," Molly told her diary. "She prefers an American. All I can say is at least men I know here have no race prejudice, and when [Johnny] loves a woman, it's regardless of color or creed. He is devoted and respects her as a woman, a friend, and is honest about all.[12]

There were other letdowns. Although she did not dwell on it in her diary, Molly must have been disappointed that the half dozen or so film propositions that came her way in Paris between 1931 and 1934 ultimately fell through, including one with her old director H. P. Carver, whom she saw frequently.[13] In Baroncelli's *Gitane*, for which she had been approached to play the lead, she appeared as an extra. For this modest role, she donned a gypsy outfit, spent a day on the set, and earned a paltry sixty francs.[14]

As the Depression deepened, payment for club and theater bookings dropped, as did remuneration for concerts and benefits sponsored by patrons of the arts.[15] Sometimes, Molly felt that the elite of Paris were excessively miserly toward artists: "The Beaux Arts asked me to dance. . . . They should offer to pay something," she told her diary.[16] On another occasion, she wrote, "Mme. Lorel called to ask if I would dance at some thing. . . . She always says how poor the group is—when only wealthy women belong." Molly gave this performance the following week and received one hundred francs (about four dollars) from Mme. de la Tour. Given the social status of her audience and her own stature as a dancer, she considered this rather stingy compensation—although it was more than twice as much as principal dancers at the Folies Bergères earned for a day's work at the time.[17] Lisan Kay recalls that she and Nimura faced similar problems: "As concert artists, we were treasured, but poorly paid." Molly noted regretfully that with the ten-dollar-a-day salary Texas Guinan paid her chorus girls, "one could live like a queen" in Paris.[18]

Jean, like Molly, faced financial misfortune born of France's growing economic and political turmoil. For years, French newspapers, costly to run and rarely profitable, had slanted their editorial content to reflect the views of those who could afford to support it—the conservative right. Certainly this was true for the nation's major dailies during the twenties and early thirties. For instance, textile magnate Jean Prouvost owned *Paris Soir*, while a consortium of industrialists and insurance tycoons owned *Le Temps*. Additional incentive for papers to tow the party line came from the government's *fond secret*. Part of this discretionary fund, available without accounting requirements to the prime minister and his cabinet, paid for subventions to papers and journalists who cast the government in a positive light.[19] The mercurial political and economic climate of the thirties made journalism a shaky profession. As the nation's economy faltered and the old guard faced growing opposition, favorable media coverage was all the more vital to those in power. Jean, at that time a centrist tending toward socialism, did not fit the leading political line in 1931. This may account for his sudden dismissal from *Paris Soir* in early autumn that year. As Molly put it in her diary, "J has no work— he got his notice from the Paris Soir—political strings . . . "[20] After his dismissal, Jean freelanced for a year. Making considerably less money than a staff writer, he penned pieces for various newspapers and magazines, including *Voila*, *Le Petite Parisian*, *Blanc et Noir*, and *Au Camping*. He also began an in-depth comparative study of the world's navies, intending to write a book on the subject. In fall 1932 he secured a job at another major daily, *Le Petit Journal*, where the father of his friend Raymond Gast worked as editor. In November 1933, a victim of staff cutbacks caused by the Depression, he lost this job. A month later he began work at *Nouveau Soir*, only to have the paper close within nine days due to financial problems. After being out of work again for two months, he landed a part-time job in February at *L'Ami du Peuple*, owned by François Coty, wealthy perfumer and principal financier of the far-right ex-servicemen's league, Croix de Feu.[21] Jean's association with this paper hints at his own shift toward the political right, a common bourgeois response to the nation's troubles at the time.

During these years, it seems that Jean sometimes lived with his parents in Sevres, although he spent most of his time wherever Molly lived—first in her Rue l'Arcade hotel on the Left Bank, then at her new place near Parc Des Buttes Chaumont at the city's northeast edge. She noted in her diary, "So many people living together. . . . I don't disapprove. If two people can be happy together and, when they can afford to, marry . . . it is better than a hasty marriage and an unhappy union afterward. Mama of course gets shocked at the idea, but long ago our people never needed a ring, a ceremony or a paper to be united."[22]

Molly described her Rue l'Arcade place as a "cheap but

respectable" hotel that offered new lessons on "poverty struggles." Here, she wrote, lived a "conglomeration of people of old and new regimes, nobility and bums—everything from the survivors of the Russian revolution and the riots of Nuremburg, to the idealists of Cubism and Freudianism. . . . Above me is an impoverished count, some nobles on the roof, an Irishwoman translater, a blond girl, an old crank, a Russian jewess dressmaker, and a kid cook. What a group, and all have stories strange and different."[23] In June 1933, Molly moved to equally inexpensive, yet nicer, accomodations a short walk from Buttes Chaumont. Her new room had "blue wallpaper with . . . white apple blossoms, a sink with running water, gas stove in a closet, a clothes closet, divan, dresser with mirror on door, 3 chairs, 2 tables and commode."[24]

Living near a large park in a less congested (if less convenient) location had great appeal to Molly, for the natural world continued to play a vital role in her life. Given her countless references to nature in the context of her being an "injun," she seems to have been drawn to it not only as an aesthetic pleasure, but as a deep identification point with her heritage, a challenge to assimilation into industrialized western society. Just before moving to Buttes Chaumont, she wrote: "Am anxious to . . . breathe fresh air and see the sky and trees. The city stifles me and makes me feel like a caged animal. Peace: air, sun, trees and friends. Life is then full of golden promise for any Indian. And I'm more injun than ever."[25]

At Buttes Chaumont, Molly encountered more poverty-stricken neighbors: "Heard from the concierge that my neighbors had not a sou to buy milk for their little baby. Poor things— they were wealthy a few months ago in Germany. Being jews they had to get out and leave their money behind."[26]

By November 1933 Molly was faring as poorly as her neighbors. Jean was out of work, and she had become ill to the point that working was all but impossible. Her muscles ached, breathing was sometimes difficult, nausea and cramps gripped her belly, and large, inflamed boils cropped up on her backside. In addition to her usual tubercular problems, she had contracted anthrax, perhaps during the late summer camping trip she and Jean took through the mountains and valleys of France's Mediterranean coast—a region replete with sheep, which carried the disease. Jean tried nursing Molly himself, then finally convinced her to go to a doctor, taking her there by taxi. That night Molly wrote in her diary: "Doc gave me medicine. Bawled me out for staying over here in this [damp cold] weather. Advised me to go to California for my lungs. Suggested the Aid Society [for financial help with fare.] Not me. I am proud enough to help myself!"²⁷ The illness was tenacious, and Molly's diary entries over the next few months were unusually emotional. Reminiscent of Puccini's tragic opera, *La Boeheme*, they include a rare admission of tears:

> Nothing to eat but bread and tea. . . . Wish I felt better for must get out or I'll starve. . . .
> J is blue and discouraged. No luck either for him. Work is so hard to find. And to borrow money at this time is worse. Am discouraged myself and almost heart broken. Couldn't help but cry tonight. It's so hard, *so hard*, to smile when one has done it so long. It seems my smile is a mask now. Somehow the spirit has gone from it. . . .
> It's almost a waste of lead pencil to put anything down anymore diary. I'm just helpless. I can't dance very well because of my anthrax and new boils. My health is shot to pieces. Blood comes from me everyday. I'm undernourished. No work. It's all so discouraging. . . .
> J took me to the American Hospital. [Found out] I must pay first—50 frs a day, before I could be admitted. . . . Decided it was better to remain in my apartment . . . and help myself as I have been. . . .
> Maggi soup again. . . . J and I teased each other about a roast chicken, with peas, a real dinner. . . . If I were home I'd take a snare [and] get a rabbit. . . .
> J—poor thing, runs around all day looking for work. . . .
> Coincerge said if the gas wasn't paid by tonight, it would be closed off . . . must borrow money from somewhere. . . . *Nit-tam-swew! Wen-ooch-uk!! Ski-gin-uk ma-we-ah-sin! Biskit-poor kat* [That's the end! White people! Indian people, work together! There is no light].
> Stayed in bed—no heat today . . . situation on my nerves.²⁸

Molly escaped these "dogged difficulties" with "a somewhat forced pretense of indifference," which she attributed to her Indian upbringing: "Indifference, yes, I am injun."[29] She also turned to nature for comfort. But, given her ill health, she walked less often in the nearby park than she would have normally. When unable to seek nature's refuge, she found a measure of solace in the view from her room. Her window looked up at Montmartre, crowned by the dome and bell tower of Sacre-Coeur. Molly called the basilica her "church of dreams," and mentioned it often in her diary: "The mirage-like pinnacle of the Sacre-Coeur [is] like a goal one wants to attain—at times so near and clear in the sunlight and then so far away in the misty atmosphere."[30]

Molly took turns helping and being helped by her dance friends, including Anita, Aloma, Lisan, and Nimura. Diary notes like this one were common: "Lisan and [her manager] Virgina around. They are broke again. . . . Borrowed money for Nimura to eat tonight."[31] Lisan recalls, "I know there were times when Molly didn't have anything to eat. We were all on the very ends financially . . . but we were young and loved what we did. I never saw Molly depressed; she had great inner strength and faith."[32]

In truth, Molly was depressed but was too guarded and too proud to reveal her struggles to anyone—except Jean. Her diary gives testimony of the depth of her dolor at this time and shows that the difficulties she faced compounded an already intense homesickness:

Have been terribly homesick. . . . tired of civilization, white people and the city. Despite this, the thought of J not being around if I should return [home] frightens me. For I love him dearly. . . . Only my work gives some comfort. . . .

With injuns again in my imagination. . . .

If I could only be [back home] in the woods to fill my eye, heart, mind and lungs with just pure air, trees and contentment—and in the mystery of nature find inspiration. . . .

Restless . . . this is getting to be a daily thing. Lonely. J and I out to play Russian billiards at our favorite cafe [Straitbourg].

Bless his heart. He does anything to keep me from being blue.
This mood is awful—stays for days. . . .
   Rainy again, cold and morbid. Watched the leaves falling
. . . thought of home. . . .
   Tired of white people. Want to see my own kind. . . .
   No heart for anything. . . . J for dinner, he cheered me up.
. . . [I] am restless, terrible. . . .
   Watched the sky for a long time. Oh god, to be back in the
wilderness. Am so tired of noises and white people—everyone
but Johnny. . . .
   At [American] Express. No mail. Wrote half of that dancing
article [for Archives de Danse[33]]. . . .
   This feeling, god what is it—its grip almost scares me. . . .
   Oh, to hear injun voices speak and the sound of someone
pounding the ash log somewhere in the distance . . .[34]

While Molly longed for home, Jean longed for some sign of his
nation's recovery. Like most French citizens, he had become
exasperated with the inertia of a backward-looking government so bound by party conflicts and outdated notions of
economics that it failed again and again to halt France's
downward spiral. Instability was the rule. Members of parliament proved unable to form a truly viable coalition between
their parties. The legislative and executive branches were in
perpetual conflict, resulting in short-lived presidencies and
revolving-door cabinets.[35] One of the main challenges to forming a workable coalition was the abstentionism of the Socialist
party headed by a brilliant yet stubbornly doctrinaire man
named Leon Blum. As long as the Socialists refused to throw
their hats in with the Radicals (centrists), it seemed the
government would be stuck in uninspired neutral. Month by
month, economic conditions worsened and distrust and disunity grew—between officials and the public, between classes,
between parties.[36]

   Infuriated by the apparent inability of the principal parties
to take action, citizens splintered off and formed a plethora of
new parties. Considerable numbers of people, representing
every corner of the political spectrum, looked enviously at
dictatorial regimes that seemed to be striding forward while

their parliamentarian government stagnated. A group of leading Socialists, weary of Blum's immobility and starved for
national authority, broke away and founded a neo-Socialist
party with Fascist leanings. Some deputies from the left passed
directly into new authoritarian parties that drew their numbers from disaffected Radicals as well as from conservatives.[37]
In a similar vein, Jean, up until this point professionally
informed but personally inactive concerning politics, joined
up with the new National Socialist Party—described by Molly
as "neither right nor left but inbetween," a mix of "Socialism
and near Fascism."[38] Jean attended his first party meeting on
New Year's Eve 1933, and was officially presented as a party
member one month later. In the months that followed, he
became increasingly active—penning articles for the party
paper and recruiting new members.

Meanwhile, disorder and disunity grew. Taxpayers refused to
pay increased taxes, veterans demonstrated against reduced
pensions, and Communists found ready listeners among an
evermore downcast peasantry. In January 1934 a financial
scandal known as the Stavisky Affair drove the disorder to a
pivotal clash. Serge Alexandre Stavisky, a crooked financier
with strong political connections, was found dead just before
he was to have been investigated for bond fraud. His mysterious
death fueled suspicion that political leaders had ordered him
killed to prevent the exposure of their cooperation in his
nefarious dealings. The scandal seemed to demonstrate that
parliament was not only incompetent but corrupt.[39] Extre-
mists of the Left and Right launched demonstrations against
"Republican corruption," culminating in the great riots of 6
February. Forty thousand demonstrators converged on the
Place de la Concorde and tried to force their way across the
river to the chamber where President Daladier was presenting
his cabinet to parliament. After five hours of fierce fighting
and several police gunshots into the crowd, fifteen people were
dead and about one thousand injured. This marked the beginning of what some call "The French Civil War"—three years of
violent interparty threats, conflicts, espionage, and vigilian-

tism.[40] It was by no means a safe time to participate in party politics, and Molly frequently noted her concern for Jean's safety: "J's political work is risky. . . . In these days of political parties and jealousies and recent attacks, it's not safe for any man who is working for a party. After J[ohn] Scotchman's rumpus, his friend's attack in the subway, and M. E.[Escautier] being biffed at the entrance of his apartment, anything is possible. Spies, agitators. . . . And J's articles are rather strong."[41]

In the throes of personal and political tribulations that pervaded Molly's life in the early months of 1934, she turned down most dance opportunities. "Hard luck to get so many [performance] chances now—with my not feeling at all well," she wrote after declining another invitation.[42] However, she did accept an offer for a month-long tour in the Baltic States since it came with a much-needed six-thousand-franc paycheck. To her great regret, the contract for this job did not arrive in time for her to make the booking. She blamed the costly holdup on postal strikes initiated by Communists: "The poste closed and many stores. . . . Communists could put a city out of commission by their organizations and propaganda. They have done well in the postes—no wonder few people get their mail now and I lost my contract."[43] On the heels of this disappointment, she accepted two engagements at the prestigious Salons du Cercle Internationale des Arts, which sponsored concerts for the city's leading art patrons and critics. Jean helped her with these recitals by painting costumes and playing the tom-tom. She gave her first 1934 Cercle performance right after a trip to the hospital:

Saw doctor F. . . . Rather dangerous, he told me. . . . In no mood for dancing tonight. [At the] Cercle to dance for the jury. Many there—Nimura with Mme. Lorel [de la Tour]. Divoire [and] all the [other] dance, music, art critics there & many famous people, dancers etc. I did the corn dance, variation of step dances and warrior. . . . J played tom tom. Audience liked it, but I fell short of my own force—[felt] miserable, but got thru it. Complimented . . . on my "rhythm, finesse and artistry."[44]

Two days later, *Volonte* gave Molly a write-up for her performance,[45] and two months later, at the end of March, the Cercle
jury invited her to perform again. This time they initiated her
as a life member:

> J there to help me with my things. M. Fabre of Le Temps, critic,
> Mme. Rabette, Mme. Lorel de la Tour and others. . . . M. Divoire
> spoke and I sang some songs [with piano accompaniment].
> Danced the corn, fat man, variations, and my warriors. Kind
> audience . . . artists, reporters, admirers etc. Everyone liked it,
> at least they said so. Met Canadian girl who knew Long Lance.
> . . . [Received] 150 francs, did not expect it. . . . The Cercle
> initiated me as a life member. . . . It's so good.[46]

Remarkably, for both of these performances Molly was not
only ill, but *pregnant*—nearly five months into term for the
second concert. She had discovered her condition in February,
during a week-long stay at Hospital de Cochin for tests and
treatment for her anthrax and ailing lungs. Given her small-
ness, malnutrition, and the fact that her menstrual cycles had
never been regular, the news came as a surprise. It troubled her
deeply—not only because it compounded her already serious
health and financial difficulties, but because it would be seen
as scandalous by Jean's family. "Angry at myself for being
where and in the condition I am," she told her diary. Throughout her years in Paris, Molly had stayed as close as possible to
her family with letters and telegrams. Now she wrote to Apid,
telling her that she was pregnant and considering an abortion,
even though this was anathema to her strict Catholic upbringing. Apid, who had married and moved to California with her
husband, responded immediately, imploring her sister to come
stay with her and have the baby—adding that she would care
for it if necessary.[47] Going one step further, Apid sent Molly
money:

> Ap sent me my fare home. Bet she borrowed it. Bless her heart. . . .
> She made me feel things could be much worse. . . . I suppose it is
> risky to try to force things and probably regret them afterward,
> and if the thing has to come out then I should accept it as it is—
> but it makes me feel so helpless. But then, after all, I may be

happy for it, which I am in a way and in a way not. Will plan to go out and stay with Ap for my health, peace of mind, and write. Later everything will be okay.[48]

The possibility of motherhood cast a new light on Molly's relationship with Jean, who had often asked her to marry him, beginning with his first proposal two months after they met. Even though she adored him, she remained wary of marriage, believing she would lose her identity in the institution. Early in 1934, shortly after her thirtieth birthday, she had written in her diary, "J wants to me to marry him soon. I love him dearly, but do not want to marry yet. I want to [accomplish] something [first]. He understands, but insists I can continue my own life and says he's willing to wait for me all of his life. . . . Sooner or later, I, as a woman, will have to make a choice between two things. . . . I will be happy in my work and lonely . . . or happy with someone and discontented with myself and my work."[49] But now, she held their child within her, as surely as she held Jean in her heart. In truth, union had already taken place on every level. More than this, her love for Jean somehow transcended her lifelong struggle to choose between Indian and white society. Aware how wedded she felt to this Frenchman who "never seems alien or a white man,"[50] she agreed to marry him. "I will never again find such unity with any being," she wrote.[51] Then she prepared to leave.

Her friends rallied to help. Mary Knight, an old hand at bargain travel, arranged for Molly to travel on the Fruit Express Line, a small cargo boat: "To the United Press. Saw Mary and [Dir.] Heinzen—their news about a boat and their friend who is willing to take me back for a cheap price—21 or 24-day trip thru the Panama Canal. It sails [in ten days] from Havre."[52] Molly broke the bittersweet news to Jean, and told her diary, "J almost sick at the thought of my going so soon, but said it was up to me."[53] They decided to marry immediately—but could not: "What a complication for marriage here," Molly wrote. "A foreigner must provide his birth certificate and write here and there and wait, then to the foreign ministry, wait 15 days for the [*dispense de*] *bans* [marriage license] to be posted. All sorts of red tape. Will be better for J to come over later and we can marry [in the States]."[54] At some point in their final days together, perhaps during their last moonlit walk along the Seine,[55] Molly gave Jean a Penobscot name: *Neebowset*, a name for the moon, which literally translates as "Night Walker." And she told him her first stage name, *Neeburban* ("Northern Lights"). This gesture honored the "Indianness" she recognized in him: "At times," she wrote, "I would swear Jean had injun feeling—for he understands so well. As it is, the arms of the forest enveloped him in his childhood, and its warmth and mysteries . . . saturated his white skin and soul."[56] Later, when the miles between them seemed endless, they would look to the night sky for these signs of light and find solace.

On Molly's last night in Paris, the weather wept: "Rainy. Packed all night with J. Had to sleep an hour or so—in his arms."[57] Among the items packed was a Cree cradleboard that Jean had bought for their baby from an Indian artifact collector.[58] The next morning, 24 April, they took the train to the harbor at Le Havre. Jean escorted Molly onto the ship. As they sat on the deck in their last moments together, he reached for her diary and wrote this message:

> Dearest Molly, almost three years! 1095 days. But, in reality, I hope that, like me, you have the feeling we have been together always. . . . We suddenly realize, cruelly, what it means to be truly and deeply in love. . . . Our hearts are in our mouths. . . . We wish we could be alone, kissing each other. The sudden cry of the boat whistle will cut like a knife. Alas, civilization is around, we must behave. But I read in your face, in your sad brown eyes, what you really think, and I know you know that I am the same.[59]

Then the whistle blew, forcing their parting. That night, traveling the dark sea between two worlds, Molly wrote:

> [We] sat on deck, wanting to be alone. . . . J wrote some things [in my diary] and when I had to bid him goodbye, god! it was the hardest thing in my life. Walked to the drawbridge with him, and

Molly's love, Jean Archambaud, bewigged and bedecked—no doubt to assist Molly (as translator or drummer) in one of her performances.

he walked back with me. Then he had to tear himself away. I fell to pieces and nearly rushed after him to return to Paris with him. And after he had gone, I was merely a numb thing, so alone, so heartsick and torn between staying on the boat and returning to him. . . . Had to fight myself to stay on, even as I watched the shore disappear in the night. I have only one heart and that I have left behind—in the care of someone whose great love has been an inspiration itself. The cool green forest [of home] will be shadowed until Neebowset fills its depth with light. And there under the largest pine, this tired lone traveler will not be alone—for unseen its mate will whisper and caress the traveler's brow.[60]

CHAPTER 13

BIRTH

*Yes, I am human—fully cognizant of its meaning,
without conflicts and complexes, without racial standards. . . . Human to the degree where I can feel the
pulse of throbbing life and understand in a simple
way my purpose as a woman.*
—*Molly (Los Angeles, 1934)*[1]

After pulling away from Le Havre, Molly's ship plowed the
English Channel northward, through the Strait of Dover and
into the North Sea. It stopped in Rotterdam, chugged up the
Elbe River to Hamburg, then on to the Baltic Sea and up to
Goteborg, Sweden. During a week-long Goteborg harboring,
Molly walked into town each day. There, as in the other ports of
call, she mailed letters to Jean and seriously considered going
back to France. "The temptation to return to Paris is so strong
that I have to curb myself and keep on—on—on," she wrote.[2]
Leaving Goteborg, the ship doubled back through the North
Sea and English Channel, skirting France, as if to taunt Molly's
decision to leave. Finally, two weeks after she bid Jean goodbye, her ship entered the rolling open waters of the Atlantic.[3]
Midway across the vast ocean she concluded that she had made
a horrible mistake. The sea churned as much as her thoughts:
" . . . spasms of *mal de mer.* . . . Nauseated until I thot my
insides would come out and harm the [baby]. . . . No woman
should tear herself from the man who loves her and whom she
loves at such a critical time in her life. . . . I [will be] an alien in
my own native land. . . . I am not happy to be returning alone."[4]

As Molly made her way across the Atlantic, Jean traveled through southern France on what she called a "propaganda trip" for the Party. It seems he was also gathering more information for his naval research project. From a hotel in Bordeaux, he wrote to Molly:

Dearest,

. . . . After your silhouette walked in the distance with your red coat and the glow of the sunset on your face, my heart went jumpy. I am very proud . . . and don't like people to see my sadness. I have always concealed or tried to conceal from others my inner self. Well, going on that bridge, I almost burst into tears. I fought and grounded my teeth and kept hurrying, trying not to think. But two or three times I had to stop and look back, so much was my desire to run back to my beloved. . . . [On the train back to Paris,] everything was dull and dead. I had no desire, no pain. It was as if I was already dead. No interest of any kind. Just a body. For three days I was like that. I did not want to see anybody. . . . Then I had to go traveling [for work]. . . . I went to the American Express [hoping for mail from you], but nothing was there. I asked the concierge to send any letters to Niort, my first stop . . . and had a big joy receiving a packet of letters from you. There was a big fiesta under my window at the hotel, but alone in my room, I forgot everything and breaked down. For three hours I read your lovely letters and cried. . . . It did me good and restored my own self. I kissed your pictures (I travel with a full set of them) and felt a little better. And went peacefully to sleep for the first time. . . .
    I am a savage. I hate people trying to get close to me. I have closed myself. When you went you took the key of my heart and soul. You are the only one that knows the secret and the way to open it. So don't lose it or I will be a strange case. Kisses and kisses and kisses again, on your head, the back of your neck, and all the nice little places that I love so much. Kiss for me that place near your elbow—where your skin is so soft.
Your Johnny.[5]

Each night Molly strolled the ship's deck, seeking air, exercise, peace of mind. Often, she paused to sit on the bench where she and Jean had spent their last moments together. As she sat or walked, her eyes sought the moon: "Around the moon tonight, as always, I see Nebowset, his eyes, his heart sending out a message to me—only through nature can one fully pattern the inner thoughts of our souls."6 Jean, like Molly, often slipped into reverie. On his way back to Paris after more than a month on the road, he wrote to her from Figeac, where the hilly countryside reminded him of one of their hiking trips:

My Love,
I have a fire burning inside of me. . . . It is always there, and familiar scenes like this make it burn almost violently. I picture you here. I remember all the little happenings of our trip in those narrow prehistoric gorges. You remember that bunch of [gypsies] in their carriage when we were hiking? I remember mostly you, your skirt flying around your strong brown legs, your pack on your shoulders, and a happy, free, wild look on your face. If I am right, we left Quesac that same day after seeing the procession of the Black Virgin. We had walked and passed a few old castles, and on the road we . . . found some red earth. We [smeared] it on our arms and faces and it added I am sure to our strange and wild appearance. On the road under the sun, after we had passed that hotellerie-castle where high hat people looked at us like they were being confronted with an unknown species, we saw the caravan of covered wagons coming. Men and women, brown, pointing at us and watching you, my love. It was such a lovey day. . . . Then I could read your eyes, watch your lips moving, touch you, adore you. Now I miss you. I am alone with my sorrow.
Sorrow is not such a bad thing. . . . It makes things more serious, more sacred. More solid. To laugh together is alright. To speak together is good. But to endure hardship and sorrow with or for somebody, that is much better—if you can stand it. It is like silence. Few people can be silent and in harmony together. As says Carlisle—the souls then talk to each other directly without the masks of the words. I love you dear. I love you terribly. I worship you and I can't live without my Mollydell, my mate. So we will be reunited soon.
Always yours, Nee-bow-set.7

On Sunday morning, 27 May, a full month after leaving France, Molly's boat pulled into Los Angeles' San Pedro Harbor. She disembarked, cleared her baggage through customs, and telephoned Apid—only to find that her sister's phone had been disconnected. Since it was Sunday, she could not change the few francs she had into dollars. Borrowing a dollar from a fellow passenger, she rode the trolley to town, taking only her most important possessions (her typewriter and novel manuscript). From the trolley station, she took a taxi to Apid and her husband's address: "To Apid's. No one home, so called on neighbor. Learned they had moved—frantic. Found landlord who had a letter from Ap—she is in New York!"[8] Indeed, Apid was waiting for Molly at the wrong port on the wrong coast.[9] Fortunately, Molly knew a few people in Los Angeles. Persuading the cab driver to accept her typewriter as collatoral, she taxied to Bunny Weldon's, Texas Guinan's old chorus director. Bunny offered her a place for the night, but after visiting several other acquaintances during the day, Molly decided to stay with Apid's friend Ann Ross, a Cherokee actress from Oklahoma.[10] Ann was a direct descendent of the famous Cherokee chief John Ross who, after a vigorous but failed resistance against the forced removal of his people from ancestral Tennessee lands, led them on the arduous 1838 "Trail of Tears" to Oklahoma, where he became chief of the united Cherokee nation. Ann had come to Hollywood after a photograph of her won a national movie contest. She had a broad, radiant smile, dimples, full cheeks, and big brown eyes. Soon after coming to California, she had received a contract with First Consolidated Pictures. By the time Molly arrived in Los Angeles, Ann knew nearly every Indian in the movie business. She was president of the city's Cherokee Woman's Club and a key player in the efforts of Jim Thorpe, the great Olympian-turned-actor, to get film studios to cast real Indians for Indian roles.[11]

Although seven months pregnant, Molly was still quite small, and noted in her diary that certain clothes "hide the temporary deformity of my body." Bunny, unaware of her pregnancy, threw a slew of impossible work opportunities her way. But Ann, in whom Molly confided, offered more practical help. She took her in, arranged to have her trunks picked up at the harbor, and phoned a doctor for a housecall: "Ann's doctor, a kind person, came to see me," wrote Molly. "Said the unborn seemed to be all right. . . . Advised me not to travel right away, but I do want to get home so my baby will be born among [family]."¹²

Penniless, thrown by Apid's absence, distressed over her separation from Jean, and anxious about the well-being of her child, Molly felt like a "mental wreck." Truly stranded, she surrendered her sizeable pride and did something she had never done before; she asked her mother for help: "Telegram to mama for money; it's the first time in my life I've asked her for such a favor."¹³

By Molly's fourth day in Los Angeles, word of her arrival had spread, and she noted in her diary, "Photographer from LA Times came to take pictures of me and for an interview—in costume." Before the film made it to the darkroom, and well before Molly could make travel arrangements back to Maine, she became a mother. As she told her diary, soon after the photographer left, she "began to feel sickish."

> Had to call Doctor Richley, he took me to the hospital about 9 [P.M.]. . . . The hypo did not ease the pain. On the bed a little while and what agony. To the delivery table—if only Johnny were near. . . . My little baby girl born—10 minutes past 11 o'clock [P.M.], 5 lbs, 12 oz.¹⁴

The next day, she wrote a more detailed description in her diary:

> Sylvan Lodge Hospital. . . . I awoke to consciousness, my body as tho it had been twisted inside and torn into rough jagged edges. . . . Remembered everything—the suffering of labor pains, my mental acceptance of life/death, the nurses, the agonizing wait, the suddenness of it all, my need for Johnny. . . . Gradually, the significance of the ordeal . . . soaked into my inner being. . . . The new role of mother will temper me to some hardy steel and influence my life from now on. . . . [She is] injun looking, long black straight hair, with hands like her father's, and something in her face like him. . . . Thru her one of the fulfillments of a woman's life has been made, and the full estate of man given to Johnny. . . . Ann to see me, said she sent telegrams to mama and Johnny.¹⁵

Jean, like Molly, never expected their child to arrive two months early. In fact, while Molly was facing the inescapable

challenges of birthing and motherhood, Jean was trying to
escape his sorrow. During much of June, he didn't pick up his
mail because he had found that reading Molly's letters magni-
fied his sadness. He tried to dull his feelings by drinking and
"going to the cafés"—Molly's euphemism for a quick and purely
sexual fling. When these efforts failed, he finally picked up his
mail, including Ann's telegram announcing that he had become a father. After reading the news, he wrote a letter that
typified the love and candor he and Molly shared:

Dearest Molly,
I did not seem right since you have been away darling, and
everything goes wrong. I miss you terribly. I just can't stand it. I
can't stay alone in a room and I hate people. I am sorry to admit
that I tried to drink and go to cafés but I am over it and none the
better for it. . . . You can imagine I kept not reading your letters
because I was after too sad and felt like jumping in the river. Well,
the wire from Ann Ross reached me at last and that was too much
for me. I am so glad darling that you went through it without
anything happening to you. I am glad and proud of the baby, my
baby—I should say ours. I can't look at a little girl without tears
coming to my eyes. I would like so much to be near you and her. I
am wondering how she looks like and so on. . . . What is the name
you gave our little darling? It is too bad I can't walk to California—I would have gone hiking.
I have seen father and mother. They are not so good. When I
told them about me being a father they almost dropped, but they
don't quite believe me. Well I can't help it.
Of course lots of girls are giving me the rush . . . but I hate
white women. I am as they say, "going native." Just as well. I am a
squaw man and proud of it. And believe me I am a white man who
will not desert his woman. I don't care what people think or say.
You are the best woman on earth for me and now you are the
mother of my child. . . . Rest yourself dear, and kiss my daughter
for me many times. As for you, I can't tell you how many times I
feel like holding you and kissing you again and again. . . . I kiss
your eyes, your forehead . . . your cheeks, your lips. I am longing
for their warmth, and certain little places you know.[16]

The name Molly gave their "little darling" was Jean. She
welcomed this child with profound joy, as a "link" to her love in
France and as a "symbol of strength, courage, and everything

that is good."[17] Her initial ambiguity about becoming a mother had vanished on the delivery table. In contrast, her own mother's response to the baby's birth was anything but celebratory. Philomene wrote Molly a letter that reached her in the hospital and dampened her spirits. She made note of it in her diary:

> Like the rain that falls from the sunny sky, the letter . . . from mama drenched me with a cold penetrating touch. She was shocked and grieved over the news of my baby. . . . She rented the Oak Hill house [the first house of two houses Molly bought for her family] for a year for the money she sent me—Eunice had to go without her graduation dress, and she sent me a dollar. The irony of the Mother's Day stamp on the envelope. Oh why can't she wait for an explanation before thinking the worst? . . . Whatever Power watches over me, help me to be an understanding woman and mother.[18]

Molly also received a letter from Apid, writing from New York and revealing that she, too, had troubles. "Ap's letter was sad," wrote Molly. "She and [her husband] Alf have been separated a month. She is looking for work, and can't see her way about helping me—but is worried about me."[19] Given Molly's own health problems and the prematurity of little Jean, they both stayed in the hosptial for nine days. The bill consumed all the money her mother sent, plus a small, rather ironic loan Ann secured using Molly's cradleboard as collateral. "Like an angel," wrote Molly, "Ann brought lovely baby clothes" to the hospital, then took her and the infant back to the apartment that she shared with her mother. "They had a bassinet fixed for the baby," Molly added, with gratitude.[20] Two weeks later, Apid showed up, thanks to Molly's old friend Bryan Cheedy who gave her the money to take the train back to California from New York.[21] After spending one night at the Rosses, Apid found a short-term, live-in housekeeping job. Two weeks later, the job ended, and she, Molly, and the baby moved into a little house on Fountain Avenue.[22]

The next few months were difficult emotionally and financially for the two sisters. Both of them had aching hearts.

Apid's sorrow was rooted in her marriage to Alf Heiberg, a tall, blond, and handsome musician from Minneapolis. Although dashing, he was abusive when he drank, and he was unfaithful. Apid was no mouse, and his actions stirred her wrath. She retaliated, and after Molly's arrival, she filed for a divorce.[23] But she still loved the man, and periodically visited him, prompting Molly to comment, "Ap didn't come home last night—she stayed with her husband. They are peculiar—getting a divorce and hurting each other, and now this!"[24] When Alf cut Apid off financially, Molly yelled in her diary, "Ap saw Alf tonight—returned nearly heartbroken; he gave her $5 and told her not to bother him again—the cad!"[25] It is not surprising that Molly found Apid "so hard to live with . . . so emotional."[26] Still, Apid did all she could for her sister, from daily job hunting, to pawning her possessions, to seeking charity. Molly recorded these efforts: "Ap pawned her jewelry to Homer for ten dollars [to] buy some things for Jean." "Ap out to try to sell stamps and coins." "Again Ap went out to look for work, but prospects are discouraging . . . so many pretty girls with an eye to the movies." "Ap to the County Relief Bureau. The list [of foodstuffs] available for unemployed is rather poor . . . " Molly's pride made it tough for her to accept charity from Apid or anyone. "Poor Ap," she wrote, "with her heartache and her added troubles with Jean and I. If only I could work. I hate to depend on or ask help from anyone. . . . Miss Miller [from the Relief Bureau] came this morning. She regarded everything in the room, I suppose to see if we were in actual need. All this charity process of asking questions, of being helped, is awful."[27]

Apid landed occasional one-day jobs as an extra with RKO or MGM studios, but this was hardly enough to sustain the trio. When the sisters exhausted their stipend from the Relief Bureau toward the end of August, Molly turned to another local charity: "Ann drove me down to Angeles Temple—got an order for food and other things. Many people there, also needy. I never realized I would be on the receiving end someday. Were it not for Jean I would never have considered even a thing from anyone." On one especially trying day, when Molly had no money to pay the milkman, she reflected, "One can almost understand why some poor mothers, who are broke, sick and desperate have just forsaken morals to give life and food to their babies."[28]

Sometimes the sisters tried to cheer one another on with singing and story telling, but these efforts could backfire: "Ap sang tonight," wrote Molly, "But tears were in her eyes and a choking sound in her voice. Together we sang songs of our childhood—so far back it seemed. Songs we sang in those days even were not carefree, for ours was a hard, working life."[29] It seemed that motherhood and memories were Molly's only solace during this period: "Jean is my little star and the brilliance of her being gives me a warmth of peace and love," she wrote, "while the filling moon gives me memories and sometimes a message—courage—for it is a symbol that her daddy and I know well."[30]

Clearly, California was not the haven Molly had hoped for, and Apid was in no position to give all she wished to give. At the end of October, the sisters parted. Apid, still in a quandary over her marriage, stayed in California. Molly, apparently using money provided by Angeles Temple, boarded a train with her five-month-old child, and headed home.

CHAPTER 14

A FAR CRY

Out of the whole of existence, the most paramount of
my life is bound up in two people.
—Molly (Indian Island 1935)[1]

The train carrying Molly and little Jean to Maine in the fall of 1934 passed through Chicago where the Exposition of Progress was in full swing. As with the Colonial Exposition in Paris, Molly had been invited to dance at this international fair, but this time did not feel up to it.[2] However, her photograph and biography appeared in the exposition's Indian Hall of Fame, organized by Marion Gridley of the Indian Council Fire, a national organization devoted to Indian interests and welfare.[3] Gridley, a white woman married to Winnebago Chief Whirling Thunder, often lectured and wrote about American Indians. The exhibit she organized led in 1936, to a book, *Indians of Today*, with a foreword by former United States Vice President Charles Curtis, who was part Kaw Indian. Among the fifty Indians profiled in the book, appeared Molly, along with a fair number of her friends and associates—including Ann Ross, Penobscot singer Watawaso, Indian Band leader Shunatona, and her University of Pennsylvania classmate, Gladys Tantaquidgeon.

Arriving in Old Town, Molly crossed the river and climbed the slope to the Nelson home. For the first time since buying and furnishing the house for her family five years earlier, she would live here—she and her child from another world. After months of hardship, stepping into a comfortable, eight-room

This postcard photograph, taken circa 1938, provides a view of Indian Island from Indian Landing at Old Town. Molly's father, Horace Nelson, worked as ferry master in 1928, rowing folks to and from the island in a bateau. Molly's childhood house, frequently flooded by the river, had been demolished by the time this photograph was taken.

dwelling that embraced an utterly familiar way of life made Molly sigh with relief. The home offered no luxury—no electricity, no indoor toilet, and no running water except in the kitchen—but it did provide the security of knowing that basic needs would be met, even as the national Depression dragged on. The root cellar burgeoned with potatoes, apples, and garden goods preserved by Philomene after the fall harvest. In the parlor stood the old upright piano and the well-worn Victorian horsehair couch. On the walls hung family photos and a massive moosehead crowned with antlers shaped like the hands of a giant. Philomene's basketmaking materials spilled out of one backroom corner. Horace's rocking chair held its kitchen position between the wood cookstove and a bay window. One of the four upstairs bedrooms had been cleared out for Molly and little Jean, whom she often called *Gee-gis* (baby).[4]

This was a home that she and her mother, in long distance consort, had created—Molly providing the nest and Philomene filling it. Philomene appeared as industrious as ever, weaving baskets, transforming muskrats into tasty stews, baking cookies and doughnuts to sell, playing cards with her lady friends, working on the tribal census committee, and practicing traditional medicine. When Gee-gis fell victim to a whooping cough and influenza epidemic two months after arriving on the island, Molly noted, "Mama resorted to Indian medicine. . . . applied onions and pork on her chest and head." Philomene gave this treatment on top of modern medical care provided by a white doctor from Old Town.[5] This mixing of methods was not unusual on the reservation; most figured it increased the chances of healing. It worked for Gee-gis.

Unlike many of the islanders, Horace had surrendered little to mainstream society during Molly's sojourn in France. He remained as unassimilated and unambitious as ever. Not that he was unconnected to the white world—he corresponded with state legislators in Augusta about political affairs, he listened to the radio, loved a good book and the daily paper, and sometimes walked thirteen miles to Bangor to see a movie. But he continued to resist full-time work that would wrest him entirely from traditional life and rob him of sacred flexibility. Like a fair number of other Wabanaki Indians in the region, he believed in flowing with life's current, ever-ready to respond to unexpected offerings from nature and social life. While others signed on with the railroad, the post office, a mill, or the canoe factory across the river, Horace and his cohorts leaned toward seasonal, part-time, or short-term jobs. His underemployment was intentional. It left him time to hunt, fish, and chop wood, to work in the vegetable garden and pick berries and fiddleheads, to gather sweet grass or cut brown ash for Philomene's baskets—and to maintain the tight social network that kept the traditional reciprocity insurance system intact.[6] What Horace enjoyed most about paid jobs was quitting, which often made Philomene furious—so much so that she had kicked him out of the house more than once over the past few years, telling him to come back when he had a paycheck. He was away when Molly came home with his granddaughter. Referring to her father around this time, and revealing a bit of her own ambiguity about his irregular work habits, Molly wrote: "Pops—it is sad, his life, but who is there to say he prefers it another way? With all his brilliancy, education and energy, he should have been an independent man now—but that one characteristic of his has made it quite impossible. . . . I can understand him and his submission to things—it's so injun in a way. And he is injun to the core of his pagan heart and I love him all the more for it."[7]

Except for Apid, all of Molly's brothers and sisters were on the island when Molly arrived. Blun, John, Eunice, and Pete lived at home, and Darly in a nearby house with her husband and their two children. Molly, looking anew at these siblings, who now ranged in age from thirteen to twenty-seven, described them as "a family grown—[with] problems, fears, extreme personalities, dreams."[8]

Darly, whom she had once described as "the other half of me," was now twenty-four, and no longer a kindred spirit for Molly. After Long Lance's death, she had married Watie Akins, a Cherokee musician from Oklahoma, who performed at the Paris Exposition with Molly in Shunatona's Indian Band. The couple had settled down on the island and Watie had taken a job as a postman in Old Town, keeping a small orchestra going on the side. Although he possessed none of the charisma of Long Lance, this pleasant-looking, kind-hearted fellow shared Darly's delight in music and performing. Their union had held promise, if not passion. But the night their first child, Mary, was born, something happened that changed Darly forever: while in labor, she had a vivid and terrifying vision of Satan. By all family accounts, this event transformed Darly into a religious fanatic, appalled by the promiscuity of her past, and desperate to find a way to heaven.[9] This shift in her psyche seems have had a negative affect on her closest relationships. It robbed Molly of a soulmate. In her words: "Darly is becoming small-town minded about things. Unbelieveable. . . . Her religious conversion is akin to fanatic obsession—and poor me, there seems no hope for her understanding. Only Johnny can know that the principle of 'man and nature—man and man—man with self' can teach us as much as any doctrine."[10] If distanced by Darly's character change, Molly felt drawn to the growing intellect and determination of her youngest sister, Eunice. After graduating from high school in June, Eunice had gone job hunting, only to end up in Portland housecleaning. One day, lying on the floor and dusting under a bed, she had touched an electrical wire, getting a shock that knocked her still. At that very moment, stunned and looking up at a sky of bedsprings, she had resolved, "If housework is all I'm prepared to do, I better go home and get more education." Shortly before Molly's return, Eunice had hitchhiked home, signed up for a Latin class in order to qualify for something other than a Home Economics major, and started pursuing odd jobs to build up a school fund. She found inspiration in her oldest sister. "Molly was my role model," she later stated. "She had gone to college, so I had to go."[11] Molly, who described Eunice as "a silent creature [with] unspoken ambitions," recognized and encouraged her little sister's yearnings.

Of the boys in the family, Molly felt closest to "brother Johnny," who, at twenty, was a year older than Eunice. Like Eunice, who had called Molly "Mama" as a child, much of the mothering John received during the first ten years of his life had come from Molly. Also like Eunice, he had finished high school, although he had not yet figured out what he wanted to do next. His regional reputation as a superb high school baseball player had not translated into a professional team opportunity. He loved working with his hands, and made beautiful moccasins for the tourist trade. He was kind, fun-loving, and popular, but undirected. Alcohol binges kept him from getting his life on a steady course. But Molly loved being with him, and they always stood ready to help each other.[12]

While Molly found John endearingly uncomplicated, she described twenty-seven-year-old Blun (Francis) as that "silent, brusque, skeptical brother of mine—an enigma!"[13] He was, indeed, introspective, and more interested in intellectual pursuits than sports. He was a sinewy, handsome fellow, with heavy black hair, dark skin, full lips, and penetrating eyes like his father's. After graduating from high school, he had ventured off, eventually entering Haskill Indian College in Kansas, where he studied to become a teacher. From there he roamed hither and yon, hitchhiking and riding the rails, stopping wherever he found a place to stay, a short-term job, and a woman he liked. When wanderlust struck, he moved on. Because he loved roaming as much as reading and learning, family members called him "the educated hobo."[14] Periodically, he returned to the island. At the time of Molly's homecoming, he had recently come back to the family nest to attend the University of Maine in Orono. Molly referred to him as "a roamer back home, intent on his studies, a peculiar mixture of character."[15] If at times puzzled by Blun, Molly was no less fond of him. Most of all, she treasured the care and sweetness he showed toward Gee-gis.

With the childhood death of Bunty in 1930, Pete had become the youngest Nelson. Now he was thirteen, at the height of "mischievous boyhood," according to Molly. He was also on the verge of emerging into the handsomest member of a good-looking family.

As with Lucy Nicola (Watawaso) who had moved back to the island about the time Molly went to Europe, little was made of Molly's celebrity status by the folks at home. She was simply another tribal member who went away and came back. As one family friend said, "Whatever happened 'out there' people here weren't too impressed with. It was the white people that were impressed."

Molly's return conincided with tribal elections. She noted with pleasure the enthusiastic political involvement of women, and with regret the intense factionalism overall:

> Women around to visit and *booda-wa-zin* [have a political meeting]. They seem as eager as the menfolk in tribal politics. . . . Down to caucus at the Hall, peered in window, heard nominations thru a crack. . . . Tension among factions—sad when life brings all of them so close together here. . . .
> Mama down to the committee meeting—census and tribal committee elected. The opposing faction and the small represen-

tation of the majority club—the 'real Penobscot' remark. It is all so silly this trouble . . . Injuns, the way they fight among themselves. Will my Johnny's idea of them totter when he comes here someday?[16]

Molly found the familiar scenes and faces surrounding her simultaneously comforting and disconcerting. Her roots, the sense of place and home she had longed for, thrived on this small island of five hundred inhabitants. But what about her branches and leaves, the new views of companionship and creativity that had been nurtured abroad? It was one thing to live in Paris and long for the simple reservation life she idealized in her mind. It was quite another to abide on a rural island day after day. Indian Island was like an old pair of mocassins that one dreamed of during years of high-heeled city life—only to find, upon slipping into them, that they felt less comfortable than remembered because the shape of one's feet had changed. "I try so hard to adjust myself to the old ways of things here," Molly wrote, "but somehow I can't."[17] On one melancholy day, even the forest disappointed her: "Went for a walk in the woods . . . gathered some evergreens. . . . It was all the same, but somehow the full beauty was gone."[18]

The weeks passed with mothering, housework, sewing, and basketmaking, punctuated by snowstorms, long walks, and letters from Jean. His pages contained testaments of love for Molly and the daughter he longed to see, as well as reports on France's ever-tenuous political-economic scene. Once in a while, he sent a five or ten-dollar money order to Molly, but his own financial situation was abysmal. He lived on a subsistance salary from the Parti Social National, supplemented by occasional payments for freelance articles. He hoped that his vigorous work on behalf of the party would eventually translate into a job that paid well. As he wrote Molly in November: "I am gambling on the party. Things are going fast here. . . . Prime Minister Doumergue is hanging on his hind legs and few people know what will happen. . . . I think I will know in 6 months what we have in store. If, as I think, we will be in power it means at least for me a job of about 10,000 dollars a year in France."[19]

But this was a long shot. In truth, it did not look promising that either Jean or Molly would soon secure enough money to finance their reunion.

As winter deepened, Molly grew more anxious to work—not only to earn money to get back to Jean, but to free herself from dependency on her family. "It hurts to have to depend on others," she wrote after being home for just two months, "and the thought makes me want to get out and work—work hard and help them."[20] Mid-January, she received a telegram from Peter Joseph Engels, a German composer, who needed a dance director for his three-act Indian opera, *Minnehaha*. If Molly would come to New York immediately, the job would be hers. Except for the fact that this work required her to leave her daughter, it seemed an answer to her prayers. She wired a "yes" to Engels, pawned her typewriter for the $8.50 bus fare, and hurriedly packed costumes and a few personal belongings. "Felt happy to go to work," she wrote, "but at the last moment would rather remain at home [for I'm] leaving what is left of my heart and soul. I would take Gee-gis with me, but at this time I can't. Mama promised to take good care of her for me. So the woman leaves—another parting from a loved one."[21]

Arriving in New York the night after receiving Engel's telegram, Molly went to see her Paris Expo cohort, Joe Shunatona, assistant director for the opera. Joe and his wife Gwen invited her to stay at their apartment. The following morning she and her old publicist-pal Betty Shannon went out for breakfast, caught up on each other's lives, and brainstormed about a press release for Molly. After eating, they strolled to Radio City, stopping at a new Indian shop where Molly admired a little buckskin doll that brought her daughter to mind. Walking on, they reached the Manhattan Opera House at Thirty-fourth Street and Eighth Avenue. Here Molly bid Betty goodbye and stepped inside to find the producer of the opera she had come to work on.

Immediately Molly set to work with the dance ensemble, comprised of non-Indian Weidman Dancers who she felt were "too immature to do well real Indian work."[22] Regrettably, she did not have the opportunity to prove herself wrong. Eight days after she began rehearsals, funding for the opera fell through, and her job ended abruptly. So she started making the rounds—stopping by agent offices, going to auditions, visiting artists for whom she had modeled. Sculptress Bonnie MacLeary, more prominent than ever, hired her at first knock to pose for a monument titled "Memory." "Bonnie said my figure was all right," Molly jotted in her diary, "'richer,' whatever that may mean, and 'more character' in my face. It seemed like old times to pose for her. There was 'Victory,' 'Spirit of Puerto Rico' ([which replicates] even my hair and face), 'Moon Flower,' 'The Flame,' and 'Pioneer Woman'—statues, mostly monuments."[23]

Molly also found modeling work with an accomplished painter named Carl Link, the Academy of Rome in the RKO building, City College, and the Phoenix Arts School. But these jobs barely covered her living costs, so she continued to search for dance engagements. As a thirty-one-year-old mother, who had not danced professionally for a year, she felt a bit out of her element. The nation's ongoing economic depression and the absence of Texas Guinan, who had died more than a year earlier, made the work hunt all the more difficult. "Making the rounds becomes tiresome," she wrote. "[There is so much] critical scrutiny. One starts at the first stairway with courage and strength. Then come the same questions and usual answers . . . until the last [office] is reached and the assumed freshness falls off. Then a tired face, heart and body follow the exit down out to the street, where, again, the actress resumes her dignity."[24]

Betty Shannon's news release about Molly prompted the *New York Post* to run a sizable article about her, accompanied by a photograph, noting, "Molly Spotted Elk, that full-blooded Indian from Old Town, Maine . . . is just back from a four-year tour of Europe where, to put it very mildly, she wowed them." After recapping Molly's career, the *Post* commented: "[Spotted Elk] expects to be back in Europe in the fall. . . . She likes Europe better because over there they pay more attention to the original Americans."[25]

The article no doubt helped Molly win an engagement at Jimmy Kelly's Rendezvous Club in Greenwich Village, just off Washington Square south. "Hate the place, but am happy to get the work and money," she wrote. "It's a bohemian spot, rather ribald—they like nude dancers and the like. Not a cheap place but not sophisticated like Tex's club. Hope to last a week or two to break even and get enough to return home to be with Gee-gis."[26] Usually the dance number at Kelly's changed weekly, but the manager renewed Molly's contract three times, keeping her on the bill a full month. She gave three performances nightly, getting off work about four in the morning. In between sets she and the other female entertainers were required to hobnob with customers. Sometimes the company was interesting, such as songwriter Ernie Burnett who composed "Melancholy Baby." But more often she felt bored by the clients. As usual, men were intrigued by her, whispering in her ear as she danced with them between shows, calling her a "sphinx," a "novelty," or a "beautiful brown one," and telling her they could fall in love with her if she would let them.[27] It was all in a night's work.

In contrast, she truly enjoyed her visits with Carl Link, a German artist known for stage designs and portraits of famous actors. Periodically Carl lived Germany, but he spent most of his time in New York. He and Molly had met in 1930, shortly after he returned to Manhattan to exhibit his newly completed portraits of the Passion Play actors of Oberammergau. In addition to posing for him in his East Fifty-seventh Street studio, she took drawing lessons from him, and they occasionally shared long conversations over dinner.[28]

Molly also delighted in seeing her old blueblood chum and former fiancé Bryan Cheedy, who popped up in New York in May after several months of flying lessons and a sojourn in Tahiti. Since her departure for France, they had written each other a few times, but Molly had typically refrained from giving details about her personal life. In fact, even though Bryan had done her a favor by paying Apid's New York-Los Angeles train fare the previous year, Molly never told him why she had needed her sister so much at that time. "That is my private secret," she had noted in her diary, "and I don't like to advertise my personal life."[29] Apparently, Bryan had written her in California, proclaiming she remained first among the women in his life and announcing that he would wait as long as five years for her to return his affection. She took this as playful puffery but seems to have appreciated the flattery. When they saw each other in New York for the first time in four years, she wrote: "At Bill P's penthouse. Bry met me at the door, greeting warm. . . . Saw the Tahitian pictures—the natives and Bry. Bry rather inquisitive, the marriage bit . . . accused me of being non-commital. He's healthy, developed, older, and more dignified. He kissed me at the door and held me so close. The way he kissed me surprised me—not a casual kiss for him. Gave me a picture of himself."[30]

Several days later, Bryan phoned Molly to say he was going to a Western ranch for a few weeks, but she was very much on his mind, and he was anxious to see her when he got back.[31] If his intentions were amorous, they were in vain. His overtures only reminded her of Jean's absence. After mentioning Bryan briefly in her diary, she added, "If only my J could travel at will [like Bry] and come over here. It's hard to be poor."[32] She wrote to Jean about this encounter, apparently saying she had decided to refuse to see Bryan at all, and asking for Jean's thoughts on her decision. His response suggests that he was not the sort to harbor jealousy: "I pity poor old Bry in a way, but I understand you and I can feel in your letter that he is not great enough to be just a friend. I think he is an honorable man, but he can't help himself. He is hoping against everything and everybody [that you will care for him]. It sounds cruel for you to be the way you are, but I think it is for the best for him and you, and you know better than I do what to do in those matters. You can feel. I can only imagine."[33]

By the time Bryan returned to the city, Molly had gone home to Maine: "May 23. Home about 10:30. Walked on back street to surprise the folks. Heard Jean making noise. She was out doors in a pen, dirty, healthy and standing about hanging on to

Molly and her daughter Jean ("Gee-gis") sitting on the stoop
back home on Indian Island, circa 1937.

things. Shy of me, almost afraid. . . . Hurt me to realize she
had forgotten me. . . . The image of her father when he was a
baby. Seeing her was almost like seeing the two I love—one in

person, the other an ever alive presence."[34] This time she
stayed six months. Her father was home, and so were all other
family members except Apid. Summer days were filled with
gardening, basketry, and playing in the yard with Gee-gis and
Darly's children. Molly's diary entries provide an overview of
family life on the island at that time:

> Mama swapped her dandelion wine for deer meat. . . .
> Pops dug a hole to prepare for baking beans. He lined it with
> rocks, and Pete got some hard wood [for the fire]. . . .
> Took pails and baskets to the canoe at the Paul shore. Helped
> Howard [Ranco] paddle up via Joe Pease's to Eva's Point. Began
> picking raspberries. Other pickers appeared. Enjoyed it. Sweet-
> est berries grow among the ferns and saplings. . . .
> Ma out picking berries. She and pops in the garden afterwards.
> Darly down with her babies. Jean slept and while she did we went
> swimming in the river. . . . Garden thriving, tomatoes, radishes,
> lettuce, and beet greens and flowers coming along. . . .
> Pete sleeps in the French scout tent under one of the apple
> trees—[to make sure] kids [don't] steal apples. . . .
> To the lower garden to find a few things for soup—carrots,
> turnips, beets, corn, cucumbers for Eunice, and a few ripe
> tomatoes. Opened a can of government roast beef. . . .
> Pops returned from his [sweet] grass gathering trip [in Rock-
> land at the coast]. Brought about 200 lbs or more. Worked his way
> [there and back] on the boat. . . .
> Mama swapped grass for a log of ash with Mamie. . . .
> Boys came to pound ash [for baskets]. Ma cut and split it.
> Roland [Needabeh] was here—had asked me to make him some
> dolls. Paid me. He's on his way to New York in a week [where he
> will sell them]. . . .
> Mama busy making baskets. Many peddlers here to buy bas-
> kets for the summer season. Even the gypsies sell them. At least
> it's a means for a living. The island seems deserted with so many
> away for the summer. Business [in baskets and other crafts] must
> be good [at the coast]. Ma and pops went out for a stroll tonight.
> As usual, I thot of my J and the moon. . . .
> Braided grass until my fingers got too worn and hurt. . . .
> Mama had a braiding party. Twelve women came. I took Jean
> upstairs so she wouldn't disturb them—and to work on cra-
> dleboard babies (dolls) and to be alone. . . .
> Finished my buckskin cradleboard and doll—Ma got 35 cents
> for it. No mail. Buddy came for a dance lesson—50 cents. . . .

Philomene Nelson selling her baskets, circa 1945.

Darly brought her babies down again. Sewed and ma scraped [ash splints]. Finished half my basket. Ma said Darly and I would starve if we tried to make a living as basketmakers. Listened to Watie's orchestra [playing on the green]. . . .
Jean attended to, and then did my usual share of housework, etc. and basketry. . . .
Mama preserved most of the day — mincemeat, beans, cranberry jelly, and greens. Very few Indian women here preserve or plan for the winter — two or three, that's all. They say they are too busy making baskets, which requires so much time and pays so little. But it is the only means for some money, and to most a livelihood."[35]

Just about everyone on the island agreed that the high point of the summer was the week the circus came to town, complete with an Indian act. "The Sioux Indians in regalia from the Ringling Circus in Bangor paid the island a visit," wrote Molly. "They danced, sang and had a pow wow. Could see them from the house. All the tribe there. Onions [Eunice] with one [of the Sioux performers]. Sent some deer meat down for their dinner." The next day, almost everyone on the island, including Philomene, went to see the circus' last performance in Bangor. When the show left town, Molly noted in her diary, "People

gossip that Onions ran away with the circus. She left early this
morning for Eastport with Madaline, looking for work, hitchhiking—the usual way for folks to travel about here. . . . She is
so anxious to save money for tuition."[36]
All summer long Molly barely left her daughter's side. Each
night, in the sanctuary of their room, Gee-gis lay beside her as
she read letters or books, or mused in her diary. One night, by
the light of an oil lamp, she wrote: "My Jean is cuddled close to
my back as I write this. I can hear her breathing."[37]

In the deep of each night, with the light extinguished and
darkness wrapping her in infinite space, Molly wrestled with
her separation from Jean. On one hand, as she put it, "Money
seems to be the obstacle." But there was more to it than that.
Although Jean's letters frequently discussed the possibility of
his leaving France and moving to the States, he could not seem
to bring himself to make the bold move. He wanted assurances
that he would be able to make a living there. "We have to plan
on the worst," he said, noting that French newspapers had
agreed to consider the stories he would write in America, but
would give him no advance pay and no guarantees. "What
chance have I to sell some articles to American newspapers?"
he asked her.[38] Unable to assure him of a market for his
writing, Molly seemed to favor returning to France with Gee-
gis over having Jean immigrate to the States. She felt increasingly confined by reservation life. Yet, the "apprehension of
war" in Europe and the fact that Jean wanted "to do his duty if
called to arms," made both of them cautious about uprooting
their child from the relative haven of Indian Island. "I couldn't
think of remaining here, but where Gee-gis is concerned,"
Molly wrote. "It is best to think things out for her future.[38]

Jean, meanwhile, had become deeply enmeshed in the Parti
Social National. In a long letter to Molly he described how his
journalism skills had catapulted him from being a mere member to associating with Party leaders and helping to shape the
political platform. Soon after Molly's departure, he had started
contributing regularly to the Party newspaper, writing under a
pseudonym. "I always wrote what I wanted," he told Molly with

pleasure, "and they never changed a word." Then, time and again, "a few weeks or days after [my article appeared] the Party adopted officially what I had written." Jean relished this new forum, telling Molly, "you seldom in France have [such] power to treat subjects as you [truly] see them." Early in 1935 he penned an article that exposed unfair and unlawful treatment of actors by agencies. He hoped his report would "get a few new members" for the Party. Indeed, by March 1935, the Party had signed on six hundred "movie people" and established a film corporation to lobby on their behalf."[40]

Jean's work made Molly uneasy. "Everything political is a tangle," she commented in her diary.[41] How true this became for Jean. While it is often unclear exactly who was allied with whom in France's confused and volatile political arena at this time, it appears that there was a strong faction within Jean's Parti Social National seeking linkage with its German counterpart. Jean seems to have been vehemently opposed to this, but no doubt had to play his cards close to the chest in order to build his position within the Party. His influential articles and successful recruitment of entertainers heightened his political profile so much that he became a target for people outside the Party, and for emerging factions within it. Also, the fact that his articles included reportage based on his long-term research of foreign and domestic naval capacities and strategies stirred suspicions among some Party members that he might be a secret government agent. Someone decided he needed to be watched.

In the suspense-laden political climate of Europe at this time, female spies, posing as love interests, were common. In spring 1935 Molly wrote Jean that she had dreamed of him in the company of "a fair woman." Jean responded to her uncanny insight, confirming that he had had an affair with one Gisele Morhange, an "intelligent femme fatal," who had been "sent to spy on me." Beyond this jolting news, his letter revealed direct ties between some of his Party members and the National Socialist Party that now controlled Germany. This, in part, is what he said:

When I wrote certain articles on foreign politics I happened to
write of some little known facts . . . and important people began
to be interested to know who I was. . . . [Some] thought I was an
officer in the secret service or a diplomat writing under a
supposed name. . . . I think that is the real reason Miss Morhange
came to the Party. Now, no matter what she is, she is a strong
game. Foreign officers, Poles, etc. were put out of the way because
of her. She was quite a while in Germany. She can talk German,
French, Italian and a little English. . . . She is in good with [Nazi
foreign minister] von Ribbentrop and a few other important
Germans . . . [who] got interested in [our] Party . . . and tried to
[take over] it. I know for sure that [three of our Party leaders] met
secretly in Paris a German envoy of [Nazi propaganda minister
Paul Joseph] Goebbels.

Anyway, they or some others decided to [watch me and] sent
Morhange to do it. . . . She came [to my office] one afternoon to
register as [an actress in our] Corporation Francaise of the
Movies. . . . If people had thought I was going to fall for her, they
were disappointed. . . . About a month later, I was called by [my
boss] into his bureau. He told me "I want you to meet an
interesting woman who might be useful to the Party. When I came
in I immediately recognized the girl and said, "Well is not that
Miss Morhange . . . ?"

She became a member of the Party and I had to work with her a
lot. . . . Living near me, she [took the same bus] home with
me. . . . My intuitions [told me she was] dangerous. . . . But you
know I love to fight and I like danger so I did not dodge her. She
became very friendly, a little too much. . . . I talked of you and
Jean. She told me many times she was very fond of me. . . . Then
she said "I wish we had an affair. . . . Why not try it once
[without] romance or sentiment?"42

So it happened. As Jean elaborated, Gisele soon fell in love
with him, told him the Party had hired her to spy on him, and
offered to betray her allegiances to help him. Jean claimed that
he told Morhange that a love relationship was impossible, given
his bond with Molly. Yet he agreed to continue seeing her
occasionally, and offered Molly this ironic explanation: "You
know I don't like to hurt anyone." After assuring Molly, "I love
only you," he reminded her of their parting agreement: "When
you left you were wise. You said, 'You are a man, you need to
step out once in a while.' I said no, but being sincere I was a

fool. Well I did step out. Less, much less than people imagine and nothing more. I was true to you the way you wanted me to be. . . . My nature needs you. I belong to you. There is nothing else. . . . I am more injun than ever. I hate the white world and civilization."[43]

Jean's news stirred Molly's anger in all directions. She felt angry with him for betraying a sacred trust, with herself for leaving France, with a mysterious woman for her manipulative interference, and with the fact that Jean's affair presented yet another obstacle to their struggles to reunite. To her, the idea of taking her child to live in the precarious economic and political arena of France seemed shaky enough without the additional challenge of a husband and father who might be unreliable. Venting her fury and frustration in a letter to Jean, she accused him of betrayal and chastised him for equating this affair with the casual and occasional one-night forays she had sanctioned. And she vowed she would not return to him without verification from friends that "[Miss Morhange] is out of our lives completely!"[44]

In the months that followed, it became evident that Jean was in over his head. He wrote Molly voluminous letters apologizing to her and agonizing over the political swamp that increasingly engulfed him. He revealed to Molly that he was being "watched" perpetually. He did not know whom to trust. He had been "poisoned [and] almost died." He now carried a gun. French military officers had courted him and tried unsuccessfully to make him drunk to elicit information they thought he had: "People think I must have been an agent in the Orient or Asia [because I have become an expert in naval affairs there]. Yet they can't trace me because there is no track."

Gisele Morhange, in particular, seemed determined to unveil the secret political link she assumed Jean had. She certainly kept him on his toes. As he confessed to Molly with a mix of defensiveness and relief: "When she was around, I was in earnest and felt I was in danger. She was never to me what you think she was. . . . For her to have no illusion, I told her, 'You know there is Molly. I love her. There is Jean. I love her . . . but even if I had been free I could never have married you or lived with you. I don't trust you.' . . . She is nothing to me, and anyway she is out of my life for good." Then, giving his actions a romantic, perhaps self-serving twist, he responded to a comment Molly apparently made about men being hunters who played with danger:

> You are right about the hunter in man. . . . I know that deep at heart I am a hunter, but I don't like the kill. . . . I am glad when I have cornered the foe, when I feel I could have it my way . . . but after it loses all interest to me. I was like that toward women. In a way I was not interested in having them, but in having the possibility. The more great the odds, the better. [Except with you—] you were not hunted by me. I recognized you the minute I saw you as my missing half. I acted as a hunter in the case of Morhange but it was a case when the prey hunted also the hunter. For a real hunter, that is a real hunt, full of danger. But I always knew the prey had no chance. When you have a clever adversary you might admire their tactics intellectually and like to fool them, but the more cleverness they show, the less you trust them. . . . You have always the consciousness of danger that keeps you on the alert. . . . How I can understand Indian customs that seem strange to whites—the young brave on the war path [who "counted coup" by] touching the central tent pole of his adversary's leader.⁴⁵

With an ocean between them, Molly and Jean struggled to sort out the Morhange affair and other issues, ever hampered by erratic, unrealiable mail service. Many letters arrived months after they were written, and some never at all, compounding misunderstandings and hurt feelings on both sides of the Atlantic.⁴⁶ "When there is no news [from Jean] for a time," wrote Molly in her diary, "I become restless and wish so much to be able to take Gee-gis and get a boat to return abroad. It's such a far cry, Paris—the reservation."⁴⁷ Her old insecurities surfaced when she didn't hear from Jean for months on end, prompting her to write bitter reprimands—only to subsequently receive from him several cards, letters, or newsclips within days of each other. Jean, in turn, was baffled when Molly failed to respond to important letters. On one occasion he wrote enthusiastically that his parents would provide boat fare for her and little Jean if they would come in time to spend the summer of 1935 at their family home on the coast of France. Why did you "keep mysteriously away?" he asked, not realizing the letter never reached her.[48] Mixed in with bungled efforts to sort out their conflicts were two-way messages of love, remarkably tender. And diary notes like this remained common: "Thot of my big Jean and wondered what he could be doing— while my little Jean played before she fell asleep. I love them both."[49] In large measure, the strength of Molly's love came from a conviction that it was destined, something that she believed "had always been, even [before] we met."[50] Still, she wrestled mightily with the fact that Jean had tempted fate, and the issue of Gisele Morhange alone took more than a year to resolve.

In the meantime, Molly yearned to dance, for sheer joy of expression as well as to get over the financial hurdles that continued to play a role in her separation from Jean. She also longed to write. These creative desires were repeatedly thwarted by motherhood, family, visitors, daily chores, and her own distracted mental state. Occasionally she found her situation amusing, as when she wrote this: "The usual house cleaning— artistic aspiration over a dust pan and mop. More or less I have to become adjusted to dishes, dust and the washboard, even tho I feel like dancing, writing or doing something else. [So I imagine] a dance motif in the soap suds . . . or live with a story character mentally over a tub of soiled clothes."[51] But, as the months rolled by, her frustration grew, and she confessed, "I'm rather tired of it here. . . . This sense of retirement does not suit me. It brings a certain restlessness that is partly mental, partly physical. . . . Can't be inactive, idle, broke and tied down so. I don't mind losing my freedom because of [little] Jean, but to be bound down in a way to a state of helplessness financially is a different story."[52]

In August, Molly accepted a one-day engagement at the intimate Abbe Indian Museum, situated on a knoll in a forest clearing at the edge of the coastal tourist town of Bar Harbor. Tribal governor Howard Ranco drove her there in the priest's

car, taking a load of baskets to sell to vacationers. She gave her
concert under the open sky. As she told her diary: "Sang and
danced on [the] green, the audience sat under shady trees.
Howard sold some baskets."[53]
In October, the Atlantic Casino on Exchange Street in
Bangor booked Molly for a week, which turned into three. She
noted that the meager salary made her "heartsick," yet it was
"better than nothing."[54] During this time the local paper ran
her photograph day after day in promotional advertisements
and published a feature story about her. It read, in part:

> Manager George Petrikas has presented many American dancers
> since the Atlantic Casino opened, but last night his program was
> headed by a REAL American dancer, one whose people roamed
> the trackless forests of the Penobscot before Columbus even was
> introduced at the court of Queen Isabella.
>
> In fewer words, this dancer is an Indian—Princess Molly
> Spotted Elk of the Penobscots. Born on Indian Island at Old
> Town, she has been really prominent in professional life. . . . Last
> night she appeared in a rhumba rhythm dance followed by an
> Indian dance typical of her people. She is lithe, sinuous and
> graceful. . . . Beginning tonight, [she] will present a new and
> sensational nautch dance in addition to the two she gave yester-
> day.[55]

Here, Eunice first saw her oldest sister dance professionally.
The show took her by surprise: "When Molly performed at the
Bangor Casino, everyone was silent. Her dance inspired awe
. . . a recognition of something true and strong. . . . When she
finished, I [had] tears coming down my cheeks. It just stirred
me. I can't explain. It struck me as something so honest, so
down to earth, primitive, pure."[56]
When her Casino engagement ended, Molly went to New
York. After two weeks with Wahletka's Indian Revue, she spent
a month dancing at the Grove Hut in Greenwich Village, and
then signed on to dance in a Philadelphia revue produced by
her old boss Nils T. Granlund for seventy-five dollars a week. At
last, a decent salary, a chance to earn real money toward her
trip back to France. After a quick jaunt home for Christmas
with her family, she took a train to Philadelphia for the show.[57]

Molly's 1936 diary is missing, but Jean's letters, family memories, and various newspaper articles about Molly show that when Granlund's revue closed, she did not go to France. Instead, leaving Gee-gis on Indian Island with Philomene, she took the train to California, moved in with Apid, and worked as an extra on several films. She chalked up a list of modest credits in big-time movies, including *Lost Horizon*, *The Good Earth*, *Charge of the Light Brigade*, *Ramona*, and *Last of the Mohicans*. *Los Angeles Times* columnist Lee Shippey wrote about Molly that year, providing a peek into her various west coast activities:

> When an American Indian girl calls on a Hollywood picture studio to get material for an article to be written in French, that is something to make even a Hollywood publicity man wonder if he is all there.
>
> Molly Spotted Elk did that the other day. Molly is a Penobscot Indian who has learned all the Indian dances of America. Six years ago she was chosen to present those dances at the Colonial Exposition in Paris, and made such a hit that she toured Europe. Then she married Jean Archambaud, newspaper man on the staff of Paris Soir. A French magazine wished an article on Indian dances, which she wrote with her husband's help. Eventually she learned French well enough to write in that language herself. Recently she came to Hollywood, where she has worked in a few pictures and dances at night clubs, writing for French newspapers between times.[58]

Although grossly inaccurate about Molly's dance repertoire, wrong about her marital status, and overly generous about her fluency in French (she could speak and read it well, but never penned anything publishable in the language without Jean's help), Mr. Shippey was correct on all other counts. Molly and Jean were, indeed, writing together over the miles. By January 1936 Jean had quit the Parti Social National out of fear and utter frustration, so he was once again fully dependent on freelance writing. Usually their collaboration consisted of Molly providing information on American Indian topics, sometimes roughing out an article in English, and Jean transforming her information and prose into a French article. This is evident in

Molly and her younger sister Apid on location in California as extras during the filming of *Ramona*, 1936.

Jean's correspondence and Molly's 1935 and 1937 diaries. For instance, one of Jean's letters instructed: "Send article, 400 lines, on Indian women, like our lecture, and one on Indian dancing."[59] Sometimes he drafted stories in English for her to "fix up" and try to sell: "Dearest Mug: I am enclosing a legend of Britany. . . . Please fix it (change part of it if you want). As is it is the real form of an ancient legend of low Britany. Try to sell it for Christmas to a magazine. . . . Keep half the money and please send me the rest as I need it."[60] Their ongoing project was the story of the seventeenth-century Baron de St. Castin and his love for Mathilde, daughter of Penobscot River Chief Madokawondo: "Will send you some information on those early French explorers. I am still waiting your notes on Baron St. Castin," wrote Jean.[61]

Beyond story concepts, Jean's letters during this time were full of love, hopes for their reunion, and ideas about how to manage it. His pages also included detailed answers to Molly's ongoing questions about his involvement with Gisele Morhange. This response is typical of many: "I may not have been physically true, and you gave me that right . . . but I did not fall in love. I am dying for you."[62]

Although working on schemes to get Molly and Gee-gis to France, Jean continued to feel that, given France's political instability, it might be wiser for him to go to the States. In his words: "I feel conditions are much better over there. . . . Please Mug, consider I have no work, little prospect, conditions are really bad. . . . The government wants to reorganise the press. Many papers might go down for good. . . . Nobody can say that we will not have . . . war or revolution. What about you and Jean then? I don't think it is wise to plan to come here for good. For a short stay it might be o.k., but not for long. I think it is easier for me to go to you."[63] He pursued several work possibilities to make this possible, from working on a French ocean liner to being press agent for a French mission traveling to the States to celebrate early French explorers. One after the other, his schemes fell through.

Just when Molly finally felt convinced that Gisele was out of the picture, two rumors arrived via friends in France that set her reeling: Jean was seeing yet another woman, perhaps two, and he questioned whether he was Gee-gis's father. Troubled by the allegations and anxious for the comfort of being near her child, she quit California and returned to Indian Island in late autumn 1936. The first entry in her 1937 diary shows the depth of her disappointment: "Something killed in the soul of me," she wrote. "This is the most critical time of my life." Certainly it was a time of deep contemplation as she tried to reason through conflicted feelings: her love for Jean; her dismay over his infidelity, which not only hurt her, but marred the much-cherished respect she held for him; her yearning to return to France; her determination to do what was best for her daughter; and her fear that France and the man she loved would forsake her and Gee-gis. Diary entries during this period included many metaphysical musings, such as this one concerning the relationship between truth and happiness: "Happiness must be a pleasure of the mind and one can trust it only when it comes from the pursuit of truth. Right means correct, fit . . . and mental excellence. [It depends] on clear judgement, self control, symmetry of desire, artistry of means — the achievement of experiences [through] giving with consideration and acquiring with selfless gain."[64] These wrestlings of the mind did not deliver swift answers. "Once the life of reason was so just, so fair to me," she wrote, "and now, God, what a mental and physical wreck I've become — a shadow of myself.[65]

When friends in France wrote to Molly of Jean's unfaithfulness, she seems to have written back in his defense, attributing his affairs to "human deficiencies" that afflict everyone. In her diary Molly transcribed part of a letter from two unidentified friends who sized up Jean. In their estimation, Jean's commitment lacked stamina and depended upon Molly's presence: "[He] played a role as your devoted husband as long as you were near him, [but in your absence, he has shown] cruel treatment [and] we feel we are not unjust in [this] condemnation." They felt Molly should sever ties with Jean, and told her: "Snap out of it — pull yourself together, go back to work and forget a husband who has shown unworthy of your devotion. . . . You are far from through. The world is still open for you to conquer. You have allowed a man unworthy of a moment's thought to dissuade you from a glorious conquest and worthwhile career. . . . You have too noble a mind to allow it to be clouded by any 'human deficiency.'"66 Mary Knight, no doubt influenced by her own broken romance with a Frenchman, expressed her opinion more succinctly, telling Molly, "Forget that damn Frenchman!"67

The final blow came in April when Molly received a packet of photographs from Mme. Pascal, a well-known Parisian sculptress. According to Lisan Kay, Pascal had sleek dark hair, cut short and worn close to the head. "She was not a beauty but she was very alluring and exhibited great pursuing qualities"— toward Nimura and Jean, among others.68 The photos showed Pascal, her two children, and Jean, at St. Martin de Ré, where Jean had spent the previous summer at his parents' home. In an accompanying letter, Pascal implied that Jean had fathered the youngsters. "So it is Pascal!" Molly exclaimed in her diary. "God, what is all this cruelty, all this mess J [has] got into over there?"69

Meanwhile, Jean's letters, full of love and longing, continued to make their way across the ocean. Molly did not know what to believe, but she realized she could not yet return to France confident that her daughter's well-being would be secured.

So, yet again, she went to New York, this time accepting an offer from Carl Link to work as his studio assistant: "Carl, he is a fine friend. He paid me for the bus fare. . . . [He's] willing to help me with a job—filing . . . doing research on some pictures to be sketched on the Civil War. I shall be paid so much for the work and have some time to run around to the theatrical and employment agencies."70

During the next few months she spent considerable time at Link's spacious studio as both assistant and model. Her friend Lisan, who had just returned with Nimura from their European tour, knew Carl well and describes him as a "marvelous, darling, and lively person, whose eyes were alight and who always spoke as if he were excited." Molly described him like this: "Carl is a bachelor of talent . . . a brilliant conversationalist. . . . [He] has many women friends—many of them of

wealth, beauty, position, with husbands lost or discarded.
. . . The front and back entrances of his studio offer an amusing bit of masculine intrigue—Carl can have one woman visitor
in the front room and another in the back. . . . [Our] friendship—platonic."[71]

Watching women pursue Carl, Molly noted: "As his secretary,
I'm learning tricks of the female and . . . the superficialities of
their emotions. . . . God, women make me sick where a man is
concerned. [They] make me think of [Gisele] who got J mixed
up in such a horrid mess."[72]

When Louis Sobol of the *New York Evening Journal* stopped
by Carl's for a visit, Molly caught his attention—as she had
years before as one of Texas Guinan's dancers. The next edition
of his weekly "Voice of Broadway" column included this bit on
her: "Dropped over to inspect Carl Link's amazing pencil
sketches of town's characters and Manhattan scenes. . . . Introduced me to his secretary—Molly. Full-blooded Indian beauty.
Looked familiar. No wonder—this is Molly who used to do that
sensational dance at Texas Guinan's and then went to Europe.
Now she plans to be a writer and is studying art on the side."[73]

As agreed, Carl gave Molly as much time off as she needed for
auditions. The thirty-three-year-old dancer performed about
three weeks out of the ten she spent in the city this time.
Among the various theaters, clubs, and hotels that booked her,
some were less reputable than others: "Appearing uptown in
the Bronx," she wrote. "Hurt to dance [on the] tile floor—and
such a small stage. . . . A blond singer, a dance girl duet,
myself and singing waiters make up the bill at this 161st Street
place. No name written here as it does not mean anything, only
a few dollars."[74] When asked to perform topless, Molly who had
refused to join the "flesh parade" in Paris now commented,
"Dislike it, but if it brings money then money it will be."[75]

In mid-May, she went home for a week to see her child,
celebrate Philomene's birthday, and dance at Keith's in Portland. As usual, she went bearing gifts: "Bought a set of forks
and knives for mama's birthday, cloth for Jean's dresses. . . .
Got extravagant and bought a doll with curls, paid $2.95. So

excited that I will see my little one tomorrow. . . . Never tire of watching her, praying so many times that I may be a worthy mother. . . . Sometimes I get chokey, thinking of her and her father who hasn't seen her."[76]

For her performances at Keith's, Molly received considerable publicity, including profiles and photographs in the *Portland Evening News* and *Portland Press Herald*. The last paragraph of the *Herald* article showed that despite her disappointment in Jean, she still planned to go to him: "Miss Nelson hopes to make her home in France where she lived for four years. When asked if there was some special reason for her 'yen' for France she merely smiled and replied, 'I believe an actress' private life should be her own.'"[77]

Back in New York, Molly continued working for Carl, who now introduced her to visitors as "my Indian, Molly." Soon rumors of a romance between them reached her. Their falsity may have made her rethink claims that Jean had engaged in multiple affairs. "God it is funny, all twisted up," she commented in her diary. "There is nothing to it. Carl has been kind to me. He did things that he never did before for any woman . . . and he asked nothing."[78] Except for modeling services. Molly posed for him regularly, including for his painting of Kateri Tekawitha, the Mohawk Indian whose sanctification everyone felt was imminent: "At Carl's. Posed for hours," she wrote. "It was hard, but the 'saint' is finished. 'You're the first woman I'd do this for,' he said about waiting on me and doing things for me. He wants me, yes, I know it, but it can't be. He loves me—for how long, he can't say. . . . He forgets my situation and talks as tho there may be hope for him."[79]

Soon after Carl's professions of love, Molly went back to Indian Island for three months, arriving on the Fourth of July. Apid had come home for the summer, and at Molly's initiation the Nelsons took in a New York artist named Wilson Harold Ellsworth, who paid forty dollars for a month's room and board. Molly described Wilson as "a young painter, a thin, pale, delicate sort of chap, but with something muscular about him."[80] Among other works, he painted an oil portrait of Gee-

gis that summer, and gave it to Molly as a gift. His stay on Indian
Island, and especially the time spent with Molly, seem to have
been precious to him. As he wrote Molly after leaving: "You
gave a new interest, a new enthusiasm and a new joy in life
[when] all had appeared so futile. You and the island changed
all that. Something has come into my life that had been
lacking. . . . You say that you did nothing for me to feel kindly
about . . . but if anytime you feel I could help out a little, I shall
consider it a privilege."[81] It seems that Wilson, like Carl, had
romantic feelings for Molly. There is no evidence that she
returned them.

During the summer, Molly received a long letter from Jean
answering more questions about his alleged affair with Mme.
Pascal and rumors that he did not think he was Gee-gis' father.
An excerpt follows:

Dearest Molly,
I have seen Pascal as you said, but only casually. She sees the
same people that I do, so when she appears I can't run away. But
you have, Molly, no reason to worry about her or anybody. I belong
to you and you to me. . . . I met that woman in St. Martin. She
knows mother and father. We were friendly, that is all. But later,
she thought it would be nice to marry again and tried me out, but
I stuck to you and Jean. She had no chance. She was always
getting on my nerves. . . . After I told her very plainly that I loved
you and Jean and always would, she turned nasty. . . .
   I sometimes wonder if [you and I] understand each other. . . . Here I am fighting to live, get some money, with only one
goal, to go to you or get you back and Jean. Loving you, admiring
you, believing in you like I always did. In your letter you love me
but you seem to get wild ideas. You seem to think that I doubted
you, which I never did and never will do. You get ideas from what I
wonder that [I think] Jean is not my daughter. I am sure Jean is
Jean Archambaud's daughter, as I am sure you are the most
perfect wife that can be found under the sun. If people have been
talking, they are big liars and should be blown apart. . . . What
you wrote on page 3 about belonging to each other is beautiful
and true. Others don't count and never did.[82]

Jean's statement, "We were friendly, that is all," excluded
emotional attachment to Pascal, but not sexual involvement.

The fog between Molly and Jean diminished, but did not entirely dissipate.

Returning to New York in October 1937, Molly assumed a lighter work schedule with Carl and began working part-time at Dance International on East Fifty-fifth Street. According to one New York paper:

> Molly Spotted Elk is a dancer . . . but she also knows how to punch a typewriter, so Dance International is letting her help out with the correspondence until it comes time for her to perform at the Rainbow Room.
>
> She sits in the organization's headquarters . . . wearing a buckskin dress with fringe and beadwork, her hair shining black as anthracite. Sometimes she has to answer the telephone. She doesn't say, "Miss Elk speaking." She insists upon informing callers that she is "Molly Spotted Elk." Most of them think its some sort of gag, but Molly Spotted Elk is used to that. She encounters it everywhere. She goes to the bank and spends a half hour quibbling with the tellers over her name.[83]

Molly frequently socialized with Wilson Ellsworth, as well Lisan and Nimura, and Carl, who was painting Nimura's portrait at this time. She also saw much of her friend and confidante Mary Knight, who had moved back to New York. Mary had come home to considerable notoriety as the only woman in a new and much publicized book by fifteen foreign correspondents, titled *We Cover the World*.

Toward the end of the year, a letter came to Molly from Jean's parents. She had stayed in touch with them since leaving Paris, occasionally sending them pictures of Gee-gis. Their letter bascially verified Jean's explanation of Mme. Pascal, making it clear that she was now out of the picture, while leaving open the possibility that Jean may have succumbed briefly to her pursual of him. Also, it implied that Molly, as the mother of their grandchild, had gained a measure of acceptance in the family. It said, in part:

> Dear Molly:
> Your French letters are . . . difficult for us to understand. But what we do understand is that you are in great despair and life for

you very hard. Yet there is something we want to explain to you and that is why we ask a friend to write to you an English letter. . . .
Never have we, and John too, put into doubt the legitimacy of little Jean's birth. She is the daughter of John and Molly and nobody else. Nevermore trouble your head with Gisele Morhange and Madame Pascal. There is over a year ago now since John saw Gisele Morhange last, and six months have passed since John broke away definitely with Mme. Pascal. This last one did all she could to marry John, but he always said: I have a small daughter and my duty is to abide by her and her mother. Mme. Pascal is mother to two children but I swear to you that no one is John's. . . . The letters Mme. Pascal sent you were in order to compel you to accept to break away from John who never had such a thing in mind.
In his last letter John wrote to us: "Molly's letters are down-hearted, but what can I do without money?" Now, here is the real situation: If one day we are able to do it, can you manage to send us little Jean? We are far from being wealthy, but our granddaughter will partake our bread.

The Archambauds made no presumptions that Molly, providing she accepted their offer to take Jean, would be willing come herself, but their invitation did include her:

In your distress, do remember one thing. We are whole-heartedly with you and it is a great pain for us not to have you here, both of you, for you are our two girlies.
Papa Archambaud
L. Archambaud[84]

This one-page epistle seems to have been a turning point. In December, Jean went to the American Embassy to apply for an immigration visa. After learning that he needed to have "an affadavit from someone in the States about money or a job," he wrote Molly to ask if she would take care of this immediately. When he didn't hear from her, he assumed his letter had been lost or stolen, and set out to pull together the two hundred dollars needed for a tourist visa. After going to Saint Martin de Ré to say goodbye to his parents, he returned to Paris "to fix everything," planning to sail to the States on 19 January.
Then, suddenly, he fell ill with septicemia, "a deadly kind of

blood poisoning." He asked his friend Raymond Gast to wire Molly several weeks into his illness, without disclosing to her the seriousness of his condition. He did not write her himself until late February, but apparently this and two subsequent letters never arrived. Baffled by Jean's silence, Molly vacillated between anger and worry. She received no clear word on his situation until June, when he recapped his illness in the following letter. By this time she had written to tell him she would soon be on her way to Paris.

At first, I thought it was just a cold or flu and did not [take] care of myself. But friends noticed I was in a very bad shape. My fingernails were already getting blue. They took fright and sent a doctor to see me. They really saved my life. The doctor told me after that if I had waited two or three days more without care that would have been the end of me. Can you imagine!

Well, I was for almost two months in bed. I was so feeble that I could not speak and fell alseep in the middle of a phrase. . . . Friends were marvelous for me, taking care of me, cooking, fixing things and pretty soon paying the bills—mostly [Raymond] Gast and Roger Chanteau. I owe them my life. When Gast sent you the wire I was pretty bad but I did not want you to worry too much.

When it was over the doctor sent me in the mountains. He was afraid of Paris for me. . . . Knowing that I was expecting to go to the States, [he] told me that they [would] not [give] me my sanitary papers for at least three months.

It is all over now. . . . I am working a little, just enough to live on and pay some little debts . . . but God it is a slow start. I am in a cheap little hotel, 16 rue Fermat, Paris XIV. I pay 320 francs a month [and earn] around 600. . . .

Please do forgive me for all your trouble. . . . You are a marvelous girl mug. . . . We will be reunited soon. I will kiss all your scars with my loving lips. . . .

Of course I am glad to hear that you are coming. Bring your papers so that we can marry soon . . .[85]

CHAPTER 15

PARIS REVISITED

*I pray that God will be good [and] bring my family
together where there might be tranquility.*
—*Molly (Royan 1940)*[1]

The departure from Indian Island was not easy. When Molly told Philomene she had decided to return to France with Gee-gis, a "horrible fight" ensued. Philomene did not trust France or Jean Archambaud—certainly not with the grandchild she had sheltered since infancy. Molly's daughter recalls, "My mother and grandmother ("Meme") had me between them. Meme pulled on one arm and screamed at Mama, 'You gave up all rights to her!' And Mama pulled on the other and yelled, 'She's mine!'"[2]

Wounded by Philomene's disapproval, but no less determined, Molly took her child and left home. On 6 June 1938 she secured their passport and within a month they boarded a ship bound for France without a final goodbye to Philomene. There is no indication of how Molly financed the voyage. Help could have come from a number of friends—Bryan Cheedy, Carl Link, or painter Wilson Ellsworth.

In contrast to Molly's first trip to France, no press corps awaited her arrival in the harbor of Le Havre. Only one lone journalist named Jean. What a multitude of emotions must have welled up in his and Molly's hearts when they saw one another for the first time in four years. They stood before each other profoundly familiar, yet strange. Surely, joy danced in their eyes among spectres of doubt. Could they gather up the lost years and heal the wounds of separation? Would France, with all her troubles, be kind to them? And what of the four-year-old French-Penobscot girl who now stood with them? "My memory of my first encounter with my father is vague," she says today. "I remember my mother saying, 'This is your father,' and that he had a little French sailor doll for me."[3]

Within days of reaching France, Molly wrote to Philomene to reveal her whereabouts and to make peace. Distinguishing between her "two Jeans," who were finally side-by-side, she now referred to big Jean as "Johnny."

> Paris, July 15, 1938
> Dearest Mother—
> The envelope will tell you much, and even tho you may feel sad and worried, I am sure you will all feel glad to know that everything will come out all right and that I feel there is a God, somewhere. Johnny and I will be married soon, as soon as possible. And Johnny loves the both of us and he is already devoted to Jean as she is with him.
>
> I realize how you all feel about things—but it is right and best that Johnny and I, being the parents of Jean, should both assume our responsibility about her. And of your kindness and love in caring for her as you did, I will never let her forget it, nor will I ever forget it. And someday, I am sure, Johnny too will tell you. We are all together and Jean is very happy, and Johnny is making up to her all that is possible.
>
> He may spoil her with so much affection, but it is good. Yesterday we had our second picnic and . . . he carried her back from the parc [sic] and she loved it. . . . It is her "daddy" this and "daddy" that, and I know he will always be kind to her. He is happy—Jean is too, and so am I.
>
> All those things which were hard to understand have been cleared up and I should not have been so miserable about them, as they really didn't mean much of anything. I have seen many old friends, Johnny has told me everything—so it has made things and the future much better.
>
> [Brother] Blun wrote to a Mme. Pascal, a woman with two children who wanted to marry Johnny—and why Blun should have done that I don't know, but he wrote that he would see that Johnny couldn't land in the States and that Johnny could never have Jean. It made me mad. Things were hard enough without Blun writing around even over here and talking around as he has done.

I will retain my American citizenship after marriage. So there will never be any red tape about things in the States.

I hope you will not feel badly—about the three of us being together. But it will also help you to just consider your own things now, as it is about time. You need a new set of teeth, and less to worry about. With Jean and I away and happy, you will be able to help yourself, mama. And I hope the rest of the family feels kindly about things.

I had not planned to come to France so soon, but I had some luck—and someday we will see you all, surely, when we return to the States.

Jean is singing. I'll let her scratch a line to you all—

[Here, in childish scrawl, little Jean wrote:] Dear meme—kiss from Jean.

[Johnny also added some words:] Dear Mother, You will forgive me I am sure if I call you that, but after all, Molly's mother and nanny of Jean is also in some way a mother for me. Molly's family and friends are my friends. I only regret not to know them really—only from all the good Molly is telling about them. I hope some day we will all be together and that all the misunderstanding that could have happened will be finally cleared.

Don't feel too sad about not having Jean around. I understand how you can miss her, but she will never forget you—and think that she is also my daughter and that I love her.[4]

No diaries are available from this second sojourn in France except for one written in the month of June 1940. Still, we can piece together this part of Molly's life from letters, various other documents, and the recollections of her daughter Jean, who retained numerous keen memories from this period despite her young age.

Soon after Molly and Jean arrived, the newly united threesome traveled to see Johnny's parents at their home on St. Martin, an island just off France's central west coast. Etienne and Louise Archambaud were eager to have the trio stay with them, but Molly and Johnny prefered to live on their own. As he wrote to Molly before her return to France:

Father and mother . . . are kind, generous in some ways, but hard to live with. Even now I know deep in my heart you could not get along well for long with mother. . . . She has her habits, you have yours. They are different. And you know how mother, without

knowing it, is bossing everyone. . . . I know there will be a climax
some day if we live together. . . . With Father, it is different
. . . [although] he is despaired because [Jean] will not be typically French (thank God). . . .
    You can understand them. Getting old, they would like to have
us nearby. But . . . they forget a little that we have our life to do.
Of course they have some nice plan—I will work in Paris. You will
live with them and Jean. . . . But I want the both of you around
me, close to me, not out of reach.[5]

At first, it seems, they managed to be independent, moving
into a Paris apartment and plunging into shared writing projects. Their work included coauthoring fictional adventure
stories for *Junior* (a kind of French *Weekly Reader* for boys),
drawing heavily on the American wild west and Molly's intimate knowledge of American Indians.[6] No doubt Johnny also
wrote and sold some free-lance newspaper articles on his own.
Together, they finished revising and translating Molly's collection of Penobscot legends, and began seriously seeking a
publisher for the work. There is no sure evidence that Molly
performed as a dancer during this stay in France. However, she
did maintain her association with the Cercle Internationale des
Arts, so it is likely she gave an occasional recital there, as well
as at the homes of various patrons.[7] Artful events continued in
Paris despite the Depression and the threat of war. In fact, for
the nation's elite, soirées and theatrical productions were
much-sought diversions from the painful reality of France's
economic and political chaos.
    Molly and Johnny made sure their daughter shared in their
cultural and social lives, introducing her to the other half of her
heritage—an urban cosmopolitan world so different from that of
Indian Island. Jean recalls going with them "to [puppet] shows in
the park, to concerts, theater, ballet . . . " And she remembers
well Johnny reading to her from Rudyard Kipling's *Jungle Book*
day after day. Her father reiterated what she already knew from
her mother: "Toys were not that important, but books were."[8]
    More vivid than memories of cultural events are Jean's
recollections of the affection her parents showed toward her

and each other. Johnny, it seems, knew how to awaken Molly's tenderness. In their daughter's words, "Mama was not [naturally] affectionate . . . [and] at times seemed to be off in her own world. . . . Moments when she would hold and hug me [increased] when my father was around. . . . He was a loving man. He always kissed mama when he left and returned, and other times too. . . . I was a jealous little bugger and [when I saw them kissing I] would grab a chair, pull it up to them and say, 'Me too, me too!'" At night they often brought Jean into their bed and held her sweetly between them. "We called it spooning," she recollects fondly. "I was the little spoon, Mama the medium, and Daddy the big one." Looking back on her childhood, Jean concludes, "What learning I got of love was from what I saw between my father and mother."9

These happy scenes offered bright contrast to the economic struggles that plagued this little family in particular and France as a whole. After several months, financial strains forced Molly and Johnny to accept his parents' offer to live with them. They did this on a rotation basis, going back and forth between Paris and the Archambaud's new apartment home in the coastal city of Royan at the mouth of the Gironde River, nearly three hundred miles southwest of Paris. A popular seaside resort, this ancient and picturesque city hosted a year-round population of about five thousand inhabitants. To maintain work connections in Paris, Molly or Johnny usually remained in the capital city while the other kept Jean company at the Archambaud's. In Jean's words, "Sometimes I was sent to my grandparents, or my mother and I would go there while my father did the best he could in Paris to get ahold of some money to keep us together. Other times my father would go and stay with his parents and Mama and I would stay in Paris, or I would go with him and leave Mama."10

That first autumn, it was Molly and Jean who went to Royan, leaving Johnny in the capital. While apart, the couple continued to collaborate on stories by mail. And, as always when separated, they penned letters to each other. Soon after reaching Royan, Molly received these words from Johnny:

It was sad to see you go with Jean in that train. . . . Since [you left] it is always the same old routine—going to bed rather late, getting up at 8, . . . breakfast. Then sitting at the [work] table. I am not in a writing mood since you left. I am missing you. . . . Even Jean's noise that used to make me mad sometimes. Everything is so quiet. Dead it seems.

Darling, when we are separated, it is no use, I am lost. As you can read in "De Profundis," "When wisdom has been profitless to me, philosophy barren and the proverbs and phrases of those who have sought to give me consolation as dust and ashes in my mouth," only the souvenirs powerful and real of our mutual love . . . can make me feel better.

I am glad in a way to know you are safe over there because Paris might not be so safe if something happens in this troubled Europe. . . .

I have my secret garden . . . [and] you are there, my blessed little wife, smiling lovingly to me. The world can be black outside, [yet] I am happy in the shrine of my soul where you are queen.

. . . Yes, there is a magical holy contact between our souls. . . . It is not an ordinary mortal love, sweet. It is holy, sacred in a way I feel but can't explain. . . .

I am going to save money. . . . So that when you come again to me, I will at last have a decent place for you to live in. And then we will be married. You want it so badly darling, and me too.

I press you strongly over my half broken heart and cover your face with kisses. Give some to our Gee-gis.

Your husband that misses you terribly,
Johnny"

About two months later, Molly and Jean rejoined Johnny in Paris. By this time it was evident that Molly, now thirty-five, was pregnant. They moved into a large one-room apartment on rue Cels near Montparnasse Station. Late in the spring of 1939, Molly gave birth to their second child. Her old dancer-friend Anita Patel watched over little Jean on this occasion, which turned out to be a sad event. As Jean recalls, "The only time I remember being placed in someone else's care [in Paris] was when my mother had my sister. . . . My mother went to the hospital and had the baby—but she never brought it home. Something went wrong and it only lived two weeks."[12]

Molly (back row, left) and her daughter (front row, right) with Jean Archambaud's parents, his brother Jacques, and Jacques' daughter Claudine. The photograph was taken by Jean in his parents' Royan apartment, 1940.

Pulling herself together after this tragedy, Molly continued living in Paris during the summer of 1939, while Johnny took Jean to live in Royan. His parents helped out with child care, giving him time to write. Typical among his letters to Molly about shared story projects is this, written in late July:

Darling,
I have received your letter this morning. I hope you have received the end of the story . . . for Robert at the Societé Parisienne . . . to be paid [for on] the 29. We need, darling, money at the end of the month, so that is important. . . . What was his complaint about "La Voix Puissante" ["The Mighty Voice"]? Did you send

"Wild Justice"? . . . I will send you another story in a few days
and the navy [manuscript or article?]. . . .
   Please don't worry about Jean. She is a darling bug, full of live
[sic] and love for her daddy and mother. She is our treasure. This
morning I went to church and prayed again for you and all of us.
This afternoon Roger will take us out in his car.
   Thousand kisses from your loving and true husband . . . and
loving arms around your neck from Jean.
   Johnny[13]

Following the grievous loss of her second child, Molly must
have taken heart that summer when she learned that something else she had given birth to had a chance to come to full
fruition: Paul Geuthner Publishers accepted her treasured
Penobscot legends for publication. This major Parisian house
published primarily academic works (for Musée du Louvre,
Institut Francais de Damas, and American Schools of Oriental
Research, among others). A two-page missive from the editor
announced:

Madame:
We've studied carefully the possibility of publishing your work
entitled Katah-din: Wigwam's Tales of the Abnaki Tribes. We find
the work very interesting and to us it gives every indication of
belonging in our collection "Les Joyaux de l'Orient," whose
announcement we're enclosing with this letter.
   We've never before published stories of North American Indians and it will be necessary to prepare in advance a press release,
a lively promotion to rally as many subscribers as possible. . . .
   We will begin publicity during the month of September. Toward this purpose, we ask you to prepare a notice of 20–25 lines
revealing the interest and novelty of your work. . . .
   We will be able to begin printing when we have gathered 150
subscriptions. . . . [and] the print run will be set according to
the number of subscriptions received. . . . We will pay you an
author's fee of 10% on the cover price of all copies sold.[14]

Apparently, Molly accepted these terms, for a month after
she received the offer, Johnny asked in a letter, "Did you write
the [notice] for Geuthner [yet]?"[15] No doubt she did—but to
no avail. On 1 September, just before the promotional campaign
for her book was to begin, Hitler's army invaded Poland. Two

days later, France and England declared war on Germany, and Molly's book became one of the casualties of war.

For years the French had been too busy fighting each other to pay attention to the growing momentum in Hitler's drive to restore (and expand) the property and power Germany had lost in World War I. In fact, French authorities had been so preoccupied with domestic troubles that they had barely blinked in 1936 when Hitler broke the Treaty of Versailles by occupying and remilitarizing Rhineland, or in 1938 when Germany annexed Austria and Sudetenland (Czechoslovakia's ethnically German region).[16]

France and Britain's military response to Hitler's invasion of Poland failed. By the end of September, Warsaw surrendered. Germany and the Soviet Union, who had entered into a pact the previous month, split the country in two. Two months later the Soviet government imposed a mutual defense agreement on Finland. When the Finns challenged this, the Soviets invaded and Germany supported the attack. Despite Finland's heroic resistance, the Soviet Union emerged victorious in mid-March. Over the next two months, the war would seethe its way southward from Norway and Denmark, to the Netherlands and Belgium, and then into France.

Soon after Poland's surrender, Johnny and Molly finally married in a ceremony their daughter remembers as "very private." Then they quit Paris and moved to a two-room bungalow in Royan, several blocks from the Archambaud's apartment. Johnny, who had long been associated with the Boy Scouts, became the regional Scout master in Royan. He, with the help of his teenage charges, managed the city's growing war refugee center and assisted the Red Cross. They attended to the needs of evacuees (the majority of whom were Jewish) from Germany, Austria, Poland, and Czechoslovakia, plus wounded soldiers from the Front. For their work, they received room and board, but no additional income.[17]

Anticipating the need to get out of France, and concerned about financing the trip and securing the necessary papers for Johnny, Molly contacted philanthropist Anne Morgan (banker

J. P. Morgan's daughter) for help in late October. She had met
Anne, thirty years her senior, in 1931 at her Fontainbleau
dance concert. They had taken an immediate liking to each
other and had stayed in touch ever since. Anne, like Molly,
lived a life that spanned the ocean. Although New York City
was Anne's home, she had been a Francophile since her first
trip to Europe with her father at age sixteen. During World War
I and World War II her philanthropic concerns embraced
France. A few days after Hitler's 1939 march into Poland, she
reactiviated her Paris-based American Committee for Civil
Assitance that had helped France during the First World War.
Among other things, she raised money to establish a volunteer
ambulance force and urged women to serve as ambulance
drivers.[18] In early November, she responded to Molly's request
for assistance:

> My dear Mollie,
> It was good to hear from you again, and I am of course delighted
> to know what your proper [married] name is now.
>   I am a little at a loss to know what would be the best way to help
> you both. Do you feel a visit in Paris for a week would bring you in
> touch with somebody that would help either of you or both [in
> securing the necessary papers]? If so, is there any way you could
> leave your child down there? . . . I would be perfectly delighted
> in your having a chance to come here. . . . If you would like to do
> that, please give me a general idea how much you think it would
> cost to come.
>   . . . Let me hear from you, my dear, and believe me,
>   Affectionately yours,
>   Anne Morgan[19]

Molly accepted Anne's offer, confirmed by this note from Anne:

> My dear Mollie,
> What good news that it really would be a help for you to come here.
> Then we can see what plans can open out for you. Anyway, I think
> the change will probably be a help, as the atmosphere of evacuees is
> pretty heart-breaking, as I know from my own experience. I am
> delighted to have you, and am enclosing the check. . . .
>   Looking forward to seeing you and your husband,
>   Affectionately yours,
>   Anne Morgan[20]

They traveled by train to Paris the first week in December, and spent several days investigating the possibility and requirements of going to the States as a family. Residency visas were tough to win, given America's ongoing economic depression, its attendant job shortage, and increased security measures prompted by the war.[21] Skilled writers were hardly in demand. And Johnny's work as a journalist, coupled with his former role as an officer and propagandist for a party that once flirted with Germany's Nazi party made his case all the more troublesome. Plus his authenticity as Jean's father was difficult to verify since she had been born in the States and he and Molly had only recently married. They returned to Royan with no guarantee beyond Anne Morgan's promise to pay for their transportation once the proper documents were in order.

Johnny, apparently torn between serving his country and escaping with his loved ones to the States, took a military physical exam in February. Tests showed him unfit for service due to "heart trouble."[22] While waiting for some indication that he was eligible for a U.S. visa, he continued his work with the Scouts. It was his task to meet trainloads of disconsolate civilian and military evacuees and bring them to Royan's refugee center. There he coordinated the distribution of food, clothing, and other supplies. Sometimes he and the Scouts assisted in minor operations on wounded soldiers. With each month, the war gained momentum and his work intensified. The Netherlands surrendered to Hitler 15 May, the same day German tanks broke into France at Sedan. Belgium waved the white flag 28 May. Dutch and Belgians joined Royan's refugee ranks. On their heels came thousands of uprooted civilians from northern France, including Paris, while Nazi troops made a hard drive toward the capital city.

Now air raids interrupted life several times a day in Royan. Quiet moments were haunted by the uneasy sense that they were only pauses between the wail of sirens. "There is something electric in the air," Molly told her diary, "a grim atmosphere of suspense, nervousness."[23] To Jean the recollection of these howling warnings is still vivid: "I'd wake up in the night and find my father putting my shoes on, my mother pulling a top over my head. Daddy would put me over his shoulder and we'd . . . go to the empty beach and sit there in the dark because it was the safest place to be."[24]

By 1 June, Molly seems to have received some indication that she and her two Jeans would be allowed to travel together to the States. That day she sent a letter to the American Consulate at Bordeaux (temporarily elevated to the status of embassy) asking for confirmation that all was in order. The Consul responded within days:

> In answer to your letter of June 1 . . . I have received from Miss Morgan a telegram and a letter . . . in which she states that she assumes responsibility for your transportation to the United States. I am willing to accept this as evidence that you will not become a public charge.
>
> You may complete your application for a visa whenever it is convenient for you.[25]

Immediately Molly and Johnny made the sixty-mile journey to Bordeaux, only to be told that Johnny's visa request remained problematic after all. In addition, officials informed Molly that the Consulate would not be responsible for her and young Jean's safety if they did not go back to the States on the last American refugee boat (the Washington), scheduled to depart in several days. Explanations for the delay or denial of Johnny's visa were vague at best. After two days of talking, waiting, and filling out forms without success, they returned to Royan. Molly refused to claim a place on the boat without Johnny. It left without her.[26]

The next week, Nazi troops marched into an unrecognizably silent and deserted Paris. Of nearly five million inhabitants in the metropolitan area, less than a million remained.[27] Even the government had fled. Based on General Weygand's adamant argument that a modern aerial attack would reduce the city to rubble in a week, the nation's top officials had declared the capital an open city and transferred their operations to Tours and then on to Bordeaux.[28] A tauntingly polished procession of German foot soldiers, tanks, and infantry trucks poured through the city's empty streets, led by a broadcast truck shouting instructions from the German high command. Here and there knots of grim-faced French citizens stood watching silently. Within hours, German flags draped the city's official buildings and monuments, and huge propaganda posters plastered the walls, proclaiming, "Abandoned people, put your trust in the German soldiers."[29] Few who had fled the city in the days before occupation had a specific destination in mind. Driven only by a primal urge to escape the clutch of the pursuing enemy, Parisians merged with a wild scramble of some four million other refugees, choking every French road leading south. Some traveled by car, only to surrender their vehicles when they could find no gasoline. Most made their way on foot, carrying a few belongings in peddler's carts, wheelbarrows, baby carriages. By day they trudged mile after mile and scrounged for food. By night they slept in their cars or fields. Again and again, hearing the terrifying drone of German planes over head, they plunged into ditches or tried to hide under trees. For many, such efforts were in vain, for over large areas of France, the Luftwaffe mercilessly dive-bombed or machine-gunned refugees on roads.[30]

Those who tried to escape by train faced other challenges, equally traumatic. As Molly noted in her diary, few trains were running and "the rush at the stations has been maddening [with] people fighting to get on [board]."[31] Doggedly refusing to surrender a hard won place on a platform, citizens waited for nonexistent trains in stations filled with stench, filth, and grief. Babies were suffocated in the senseless crush of frantic humanity. Families lost each other. Children, exhausted, hungry, thirsty, and afraid, cried relentlessly.[32]

Hearing this news and fearing the spread of German occupation to Royan, Molly now felt impelled to get out of the country, without Johnny if necessary, to ensure her daughter's safety. She drafted a letter to the American Consulate in Bordeaux, the country's new provisional capital: "Dear Mr. Taylor—If there is a fourth American boat to take back the remaining Americans, I would wish to return to the States with my young daughter at this time." After penning this brief opening query, Molly seems to have lost any sense of resignation she may have had about going home without Johnny. She launched into a lengthy and vigorous challenge of the authorities' decision to

• deny her husband a visa. How could they claim "that his heart trouble would make him incapable of earning a living in the States" when Anne Morgan had assured her that "venereal disease was the only malady" that could prevent entry? Why had the clerk refused to call Anne Morgan to "confirm that she would bear the expenses [for visas and travel] for the three of us"? Why had the clerk said "that J would never be allowed to go to the States and that even all the money of Anne Morgan would not help him"? In the last paragraphs of this letter, Molly tried to identify and dispel possible suspicions that could have caused the consul to reject Johnny's visa application:

> My husband and myself have never been in the [secret] service or even employees of any country. If there were such ideas or suspicions about this, it is ridiculous. Our purpose in going to the States is to have a normal family life . . . nothing more. I am interested only in my family, my writing, and my tribe. . . . I am a real American Indian and adhere to no foreign isms, [even] Americanism. My tribal creeds are far better than anything I have heard about. . . .
>
> I have received a bulletin "Indians at Work" for a long time, even at the American Express in Paris. This bulletin is with the new [Indian] Reorganization Act and the progress of its work among many tribes. It is an Indian Office publication—as you know Indians are dealt with by the Department of the Interior. Since my brother . . . has been employed in the Indian Service and I have friends who work under John Collier, Commissioner of Indian Affairs, all this has possibly given rise to suspicion [among] those who do not know or understand.
>
> My husband is a writer and a translator, a former newspaper man, but his work has been chiefly in writing boys stories, adventure and cowboy stories, for "Junior," a weekly sheet for boys. If his being a former journalist has been one of the reasons [for denying him a visa] . . . it would have been better understood than what was told him.
>
> [The] why and what of so many delays past the last boat train last week has been fully incomprehensible.[33]

Actually, the delays were understandable, given the multi-tude of people seeking a haven. On the day Molly penned this letter, frantic Americans, French, and other foreign visa appli-cants anxious to get out of the country jammed the hallways and offices of the U.S. Consulate in Bordeaux. Desperate to secure exit visas, transport, money, shelter, food, advice, they pushed and shoved at one another. Outside the nearby Por-tuguese consulate, evacuees, frazzled by endless lines, rioted and stormed the building.[34]

As the war and its miserable effects escalated, so did the demands on Johnny, taking a toll on his health and diminishing the time he could spend with family. Often he worked around the clock, and time and again did not make it home for dinner, let alone for a night's sleep beside his wife. Sometimes Molly went looking for him: "Stopped at the refugees' haven to see Johnny," she wrote in her diary. "He slept in the kitchen [last night] . . . to prevent stealing, as there had been theft of food by some of the refugees the night before. . . . Things don't seem to function right when J is not at hand. . . . He is ex-hausted physically and mentally. . . . He has a bad carbuncle on his right hand which I fixed up yesterday with salt pork . . . and he took some pills for his blood and against sep-ticimia.[35] Consumed by the needs of the masses, Johnny had little time or energy to consider the fate of his own family. Fueled by apprehension, Molly's response to this sometimes erupted as jealous despair: "Jean's ear bothered her last night but that did not concern her father so much as the refugees, scouts or this or that meeting," she wrote. "He said that a train of refugees were coming in . . . and it was necessary that he be there to meet it . . . to which I answered that he should have the same responsibility about his family as he has for them."[36]

Beyond these aggravations, on several occasions Molly re-turned to the bungalow and found it totally ransacked. She was convinced that Communist agents, looking for Johnny's naval research to help undermine France's marine capabilities, had done the damage.[37] This seemingly far-fetched explanation has a measure of plausibility, for Communist agents did take steps to sabotage France's war industries.[38] Whether Molly was correct or not, she firmly believed that the underlying cause of France's weakness and downfall was the steady infiltration during the 1930s into every layer of French society by Communists intent on destablizing the nation. As the war progressed, she declared, "France should have rid herself of the Communists long ago. Everything that has happened is due to [their] internal machinery working to ruin the country."[39] Johnny and much of the French citizenry shared this view. But for Molly, it became an obsession that later turned into paranoia.[40]

On 22 June, French authorities signed an armistice with Germany, choosing a middle ground between total capitulation and a prolonged and destructive battle for which there were inadequate military resources and national will to win. Armistice terms obliged the French to finance German occupation of more than half of their country—the territory north of Tours from the west coast to the east, plus a broad strip down the west coast to the border of Spain, giving Germany control over the Atlantic seaboard. Unoccupied southern France would remain independent—emasculated but preserved as an entity with its own government administration.[41]

Right up until the signing of the armistice, fighting within France had continued, slowing the German advance and giving hope to all who abhored surrender. But once the agreement was sealed, there was nothing to retard German troops as they marched southwestward to secure the French coast. With the Nazis less than a day's march from Royan, now declared an open city, French soldiers who were based there hastily prepared to leave. Those who stayed behind were highly likely to be taken as prisoners of war. Johnny, as a journalist known for political articles and extensive naval research, also faced the danger of arrest. Or, as an able-bodied man whose refugee center job would end under occupation, he could well be forced into German labor service—along with his Scouts. Having no safe alternative, Johnny arranged to flee with the scouts on a boat up the gaping Gironde estuary toward the remnant of free French territory.[42]

He expected to take Molly and Jean with him but soon discovered that no women were permitted on the boat. Since his departure was imperative to his well-being as well as to that of the Boy Scouts in his charge, Molly urged him on without her. As Jean recalls, "We went up to . . . the docks in a car, my mother and father and I. There was a boat waiting for him and his Boy Scouts. . . . My father told me to be a good girl and told my mother he loved her. Those were his last words. Then he walked away. We stood by the car and watched him get on the boat, and watched the boat leave. I don't know if my mother cried. She didn't cry easily . . . "43

Molly's diary entry after Johnny's departure reveals the grief she hid from her daughter. Her sole reason for being in France had left, and the sight of his boat disappearing at the river's bend created an ache so profound that life itself seemed unbearable.

After a sleepless night haunted by thoughts, tears, memories and by the vivid face of J with tears in his eyes . . . I felt desperately alone with Jean. To be alone with her at this time under these circumstances has been a hard blow. I feel mechanical. . . . It is as if all of my being . . . were numbed to lethargy. Part of myself is gone, . . . abruptly, broken by the cruel hands of circumstances. "No women allowed!" Those words sealed this page of our life, our second separation. How long will it endure? Will God bring us together soon, all of us? . . . Had I been absolutely alone last night . . . [after] those sad moments of farewell, I would not have wanted to live much longer. But there was and is Jean.44

On the heels of Johnny's departure, Hitler's orderly troops streamed into Royan without a hitch. "Their peaceful entry was such a contrast to stories that one was at a loss to understand," Molly wrote. "Many heavy guns passed by on the street toward the coast, and they have already occupied the station, post office, marie [town hall] and other public places. . . . With many inhabitants perplexed [yet] resigned to circumstances, it is all so strange. What the heavy cost of peace will bring, no one knows."45 Jean, six years old at the time, remembers the event like this:

Jean Archambaud with his and Molly's daughter, Jean, 1940.

The day the Germans took over we were at my grandparent's apartment. They had a balcony that looked out on the street. Everyone was ordered to present [themselves] to watch the soldiers come in, [and we watched from the balcony]. We were warned that if anyone laughed . . . or took pictures they would be shot. Of course Mama was behind the curtains taking pictures like crazy. . . . I remember she whispered to me, "Come with me," and I went with her through the apartment to the back balcony and she said, "Look up at the sky," and there were paratroopers parachuting in. She didn't share this with my grandparents.[46]

Over the next few days, Molly worked on a plan to leave France with Jean, aware that "if war continues between the English and the Germans along the French coast, it would be horrible for the civilian population. If we had known what would eventually come, it would have been better that Jean and I returned home sometime before, for her sake. She has become nervous, cried in her sleep to have Daddy near. . . . He loves her dearly and she loves him too. It is good, so good, that we love each other."[47] Within a week, "some definite idea of a plan for things" fell into place. Molly determined to put a safe distance between her and the tumult of France, to travel to Portugal and find a way home from there. On 30 June, an American offered to drive her and Jean as far as Bordeaux the next day. With this sixty-mile promise, she gathered up her child and a few belongings, and began the long journey home.[48]

CHAPTER 16

HOME

The beautiful things live and heal the wounds of sorrow.

—*Molly (New York 1929)*[1]

Molly's escape from German-occupied France echoed the Trail of Tears: an Indian mother, child clasped to her breast, forced by strangers from a land replete with reminders of love, achievement, self-realization. As she pressed her way south along the French coast—by foot, ambulance, and horse-drawn cart—German planes roared overhead, surveying the Atlantic and backing up troops moving in to claim the country's coastal strip. Each night Molly cradled Jean in her arms and comforted her with old Penobscot legends until, exhausted, they both fell asleep by the roadside. And each day she passed places kissed with sweet memories that now seemed like elusive dreams. Near Bordeaux, she had hiked with Johnny through the sheltering shadows of Arcachon Forest, then mile after mile along sun-hot shores to Mimizan. In Biarritz she had stepped out of her hiking boots and into her moccasins to dance at a chic casino, where Parisian vacationers had cried for encores. In the Basque fishing village of St. Jean de Luz, she had watched the setting sun spill fire across the sea, while telling Johnny the prescient story of a seventeenth-century French baron and his love for the daughter of a Penobscot River chief. In Hendaye, where the great spine of the Pyrenees rises to divide France from Spain, they had set out on a glorious and tortuous trail between snow-crowned peaks, past glacier-fed waterfalls and streams, through lush alpine meadows strewn with wildflowers, and into Lourdes with its cave of miracles.

But now, this dramatic geography only slowed Molly's progress in the burdensome seven-hundred-mile journey to Lisbon. During the first week of exodus, she and Jean barely covered 150 miles, more than half by foot. On day seven, they finally stepped out of occupied France into Spain, then made their way another fifty miles to Bilbao. There, at an American Consulate office established to meet the special needs of wartime, Molly obtained a $154 promissory note (backed by Anne Morgan's organization) to cover third class fare home on the S.S. Manhattan. To board the steamship in time for its 12 July departure, she and Jean would have to travel the remaining five hundred miles in five days. On foot, this was impossible, so the Consulate provided a second promissory note to pay for railroad transportation "from Bilbao to the Portuguese frontier." It is not known to which "frontier" station the train took her, but from there she and Jean managed to reach Lisbon in time to board a boat burgeoning with weary refugees.[2]

For eight days they sailed the sea, while grief and relief went to battle in Molly. She had brought her daughter to safety, but at significant personal cost. Unlike her last westward sail across the Atlantic, this time she left no artistic triumph in her wake. France, broken and ever more distant, could no longer offer her promise or hope, and she had no assurance of Johnny's well-being or of their future together. Surely, she walked the ship's deck in the vault of night and sought Neebowset—the moon—for solace. But now, the stars surrounding that beacon had arranged themselves into question marks.

Arriving in New York, mother and daughter did not tarry. Within hours, they boarded a bus bound for Old Town, and knocked on Darly's door. Word of their return spread quickly, and several newspaper and radio reporters promptly approached Molly for interviews. Excerpts from one interview, in particular, reveal something of the shock she suffered:

Perhaps one who has come in close touch with war reaches the place where they can discuss it calmly. They must, for Mrs. Archambaud showed no emotion. . . . Viewing the past year with an analytical mind, this woman . . . pictures a war more horrible than depicted in the current news releases. . . . The dreadful experiences of refugees were told her by many of those who escaped from the area of the Battle of France. Soldiers, dead soldiers, were piled so high that people fleeing had to crawl over the bodies. . . . She told of the dreadful confusion as Paris was evacuated, of the mad scramble on foot, by motor car, and of the people who were killed or wounded in the confusion. . . . She substantiates claims that Red Cross hospitals and trains have been bombed. . . . Her home on the coast of Royan was the first place the Germans occupied as they came toward Bordeaux [from Paris]. . . . It had many aerial attacks and in the harbor were numerous naval battles. Mrs. Archambaud . . . said that the sound of oncoming planes was not as bad as the dreadful sirens which gave the warning—a wailing sound . . . that brought terror to the heart. . . .

She does not know where [her own husband] is . . . or whether she will ever see him again. "He knows that I would try to get here and if he is alive will contact me when he can," is her quiet philosophy regarding her future. "[Many] wives in France don't know where their husbands are—many were taken away by the Germans and are probably working in Germany on the land or in the munition plants."

The memories stirred up by Molly's robot-like recounting troubled Jean, who sat on her mother's lap throughout this interview. As the journalist noted:

When one sees this little six-years-old Jean, hears her excited nervous sobbing, they have some idea of the mark which war has left on the minds of little children. Too small to appreciate its dreadfulness, yet in many ways realizing the awfulness of weary trudging over roads, of sleeping where and how they could, always forging ahead to that place from which a ship would carry them to America and safety.[3]

Jean was not convinced she was in America until she crossed the river from Old Town to Indian Island. "In New York, on the bus, and at [Darly's], I kept saying, 'We're not in America.' Finally, when my grandmother and Uncle Pete came over to get us in the canoe and we started plying across the river, I stood up, pointed to the island and said, 'There's America!'"[4]

Little had changed on the island during their two-year absence, beyond the addition of a new sewage and water system and the completion of some twelve miles of graded roads (despite the lack of cars).[5] Jean and Molly moved back into their second-floor room in the family's Victorian home—now the house of Penobscot *Governor* Horace Nelson. Undoubtedly, Molly regretted missing her father's inauguration ceremony in the tribal hall the year after she took Jean to France. It was an occasion when she might have danced in his honor. For Horace, serving as chief did not mean surrendering tradition-oriented activities he enjoyed. In fact, when a reporter from one of the state's major newspapers came to do an extensive profile on him and island life several months prior to Molly's return, Horace skipped the fellow's visit to go sweetgrass gathering at the coast. The journalist found plenty of other informants, and noted in his two-page article: "On the occasion of the Lewiston Journal representative's visit, Governor Nelson was in Rockland procuring sweet grass for the basketmaking season."

Horace was, of course, collecting grass primarily for Philomene's handiwork—but also to sell to other basketmakers on the island. Many sold their work to Lucy ("Princess Watawaso") and Bruce Poolaw, who now owned a basket store next to their home by the landing. Madeline Shay, a decade younger than Molly, remembers sitting on the front porch of the store, weaving baskets with Philomene: "We were like demonstrators. I got three dollars a day. Philomene probably got more because she was older and more experienced. She was a terrific basket-maker—and a woman who spoke her mind. One time a tourist asked her, 'So this is your hobby?,' and she said, 'Hobby, hell! This is my bread and butter!'"[6] Philomene's house remained a nexus for women on the island, who gathered there regularly to play cards, braid sweet grass, exchange social and political gossip, smoke their pipes, and tip a few glasses of choke cherry wine.

Of Molly's siblings, only Pete, now a nineteen-year-old student at the University of Maine, still lived at home. He would soon interrupt his studies to join the army when the United States stepped forward to help the Allied Forces in Europe. Eunice, nearly twenty-five, had completed her undergraduate studies in 1939—a year after secretly marrying a young zoologist named Ralph Palmer. With her degree in hand, she left Maine to join her husband, who was finishing up his doctorate at Cornell in upstate New York. (Eventually she earned her own Ph.D. in anthropology from New York University, and later received an honorary doctorate from the University of Maine.) Apid, after being divorced from Alf for five years, had recently remarried. Still in California, she worked occasionally as an extra in movies and had a war-time job with Adel Precision, making engine parts for warplanes. Darly and Watie and their two children had moved across the river to Old Town, where Watie continued to work at the post office and to direct his own orchestra. Darly, busy with church and children, also played a major role in the annual Penobscot pageant and other special events that included dance. Twenty-six-year-old Johnny, still an endearing fellow struggling with alcohol and dreams of being a professional ball player, had married a young white woman named Clara MacKay. He, like Pete, would soon go overseas to join the war effort. The life of Blun, now thirty-three, had taken a tragic turn in Molly's absence. His "enigmatic personality," aggravated by several debilitating head injuries, had become increasingly troubled, depressed, and aggressive, resulting in a complete breakdown and institutionalization at the Bangor State Mental Hospital.

Molly, too, faced a mighty mental struggle—not knowing if Johnny had made it out of occupied France safely. By this time, Marshal Petain and a host of other defeatist leaders of the Third Republic had established the Vichy government in southern France. Sanctioned by the Franco-German armistice, Vichy now controlled the nation's free zone and its colonies. Unlike General de Gaulle and other French exiles who continued to fight the Germans on distant fronts, Vichy officials believed judicious collaboration was the way to survive military occupation, safeguard French traditions, and secure an independent place for France in what they saw as the inevitable German New Order.[7] They would be proven wrong, but for the time being, Vichy France seemed to be a safe place. Molly prayed Johnny was there.

He was. His first letter reached her at summer's end. After a long, arduous, and hungry journey by boat and foot, he and the Scouts had made it beyond German lines to a refugee center in the town of Pau, "beautifully situated on the first range of the Pyrenees." In late September, another letter came, reporting that he and the boys had left Pau after hearing "rumors that the Germans would come there also." After several more weeks of moving from place to place, they had settled at a refugee camp in Toulouse in southern, unoccupied France. Here, he wrote, as in Royan, they tended, nursed, fed, and entertained wounded and weary civilians and soldiers, receiving "room and board but no money":

It is better not to write now about what the French are thinking about the war. . . . The number of incidents with the German are growing from day to day and we are still quite a number feeling that some way or some other we will be victorious yet. But we have no news. Only those that the German allows to be published . . . [but] somehow we do learn things. . . .

Life is not . . . so easy here. Work is scarce, food rare (ration cards) and the spirit of the people somewhat broken. Yet if war was going to start again there will be lots of volunteers. But the awakening of France will be slow and painful too. Many people don't realise that we have been vanquished. . . .

What about you . . . and our Jean. Please do write, my love. In spite of all the movement and peoples, of 28 boys for which I am everything, even father, I feel terribly sad and lonely without you and Jean Jean. News from you would be a godsend. . . . [Yet] Sweet, in a way I am glad that you are away with Jean. A country in war is not a pleasant place for those you love. One of us [here] is enough. . . .

Neebowset is tired, deadly tired of roaming, and will be happy to be "at home" with you and Jean anywhere. . . .

I will close now this little loving chat. I am in a room with two [Scouts] . . . and they want to put the light out.

Good night darling. Many kisses for the both of you. Pray for
me, and many happy dreams.

Your loving JSF Archambaud Neebowset[8]

Once again Molly and Johnny entered a long season of
meeting one another on paper while yearning for a touch, a
glance, a whisper in the ear. If Molly kept diaries in the early
1940s, they are now missing, so Johnny's letters at this time,
along with various newsclips about Molly, are particularly
important in shedding light on their lives. Much of their mail
passed through German controls and took months to meet its
mark—and much of it never arrived at all. In January Molly
wrote, "I have not heard from you since last September's card
and pray that this may reach you and find you well—have
scarcely slept, wondering, praying and thinking of you. . . . I
have written you many many times." About the same time,
Johnny began a letter with these words: "Dearest wife, Still no
news from you." Two months later he wrote, "Outside of the
short notice [via] the American Red Cross, I am absolutely
without any news from you since your letters of November 17
and December 2nd. And I am worried, deeply worried about
you and Jean. Do you get the many letters I am sending?"[9]

The Franco-German armistice allowed unoccupied France a
limited degree of rearmament,[10] and by January 1941, Johnny
and his Scouts had relocated to an armistice army base and
medical center at Bagneres de Luchon, some fifty miles south
of Toulouse:

Here we are still working for . . . our food, which is something in
our days. We are also playing [Indian] theater and get some
success. . . . We are very busy. From 8am to 8pm I have to be
there and the boys too. Lately there was an epidemic here and the
sick soldiers and officers were kept isolated in the hospital and
we had to take charge of almost everything, starting from the
cooking for 300 men. . . . And after hours of work we managed to
rehearse and play theater 4 times in three weeks. . . . I beat the
tom-tom and think of you. . . .
    Jacques [my brother] is in Germany [at a POW Camp near the
Danish border]. Maybe you can send him a card and have the Red
Cross send him parcels. I've few, very few news of father and

mother. And it is hard, sweet, to be separated from you and Jean. One feels so sad and lonely. . . . But the wheel will turn someday.[11]

Molly, and everyone else living in the United States, where the Great Depression dragged on and on, also yearned for the wheel of fortune to take a positive turn. Jobs remained frightfully scarce. Nevertheless, Molly went looking for one in New York, and found a brief respite from unemployment. Maria Gambarelli, premiere danseuse of the Metropolitan Opera Company, hired her as "dancer and wardrobe mistress" for a small, select troupe making a forty-four engagement tour of Canada and the United States from 1 February through 1 May. Although Molly, now thirty-seven, had to mend and clean costumes, she did have a supporting dance role in the program.[12]

When the tour ended, Molly had trouble finding another job. Weeks of making the rounds without success left her footworn, discouraged, and willing to take just about any paid position available. Toward the end of May, she ran into Louis Sobol, still a columnist with the *New York Journal-American*, and still highly intrigued by her. After hearing about her job-hunting problems, he wrote this in one of his May 1941 columns:

A talented young woman, not unknown to the Broadway paragraphers, is desperately in need of employment. Once an interpretive dancer, she writes in French as fluently as she does in English. . . . She is an expert cook, a skilled seamstress. Graduate of the University of Pennsylvania, she worked her way through by doing housework. Now, because of certain circumstances, she is completely without funds—and rather than appeal to friends, she has been looking for a job doing, as she says, "anything." So the other day she went over to a certain night club owner who shall be nameless here and pleaded that he put her in charge of the powder room, having heard that he needed someone. "I'd be glad to," he said, "but these days you gotta be careful. I can't give a job to a foreigner—it's got to be an American or nothing. The "foreigner" he refused to hire is Molly Spotted Elk, full-blooded American Indian.[13]

Sobol's words may have helped, for Molly secured a summer job as "leader-consultant" on Indian lore and woodcrafts at a

National Girl Scout camp on the outskirts of New York City. At summer's end she returned to Indian Island, where letters from Johnny continued to reach her, however fitfully. He and she now numbered each letter they sent one another in order to keep track of missed messages. Typical among Johnny's missives is "letter no. 43":

Darling Sweet:
After a long time without any news from you, I finally got a post card and the day after a letter. They were a godsend. I miss you terribly sweet, and my Jean Jean also. . . . If only I could cross over and be with my loved ones. . . .

I went lately to Toulouse and met a few friends from Paris Soir. . . . [The Germans] wanted to send the staff back to Paris, promising two full years of wages in advance—but none wanted to leave from here. . . .

I have started to write again short stories, but I have not sold any yet. Anyway it is real good for the mind. Too bad Offerstadt [Publishing] is closed by German orders.

I have just finished an interesting book, "The Great Passage" by Kenneth Roberts. It is about the "Roger's Scouts" and the massacre of the St. Francis [Abenaki] Indians in 1759. Try to get hold of it. It is worth reading and might be valuable for our projected book on Baron de St. Castin. . . .

What are you doing sweet? . . . How is our Jean Jean? Tell her her daddy is proud of her and is waiting for her letter. How is her mind and imagination? Does she tell many stories to her mother? Daddy is jealous. How he would like to watch over her, help her with her study, read to her, be a real daddy to her . . . and how I would love to have mama and Jean's arms around my neck. Have a walk together, meals, reading, studying, working together. Instead, the both of you have lonely lives and daddy is a proscrit [exile] and all alone. . . .

Some of the [Scouts] have left for "youth camp" or contracted enlistment in the "Army of the Armistice." In a way it is good for them and for me. Less responsibility.

I am assistant to the commandant of the two centers now.
Receive a thousand kisses from your loving Johnny.[14]

Almost all of Johnny's letters, in one way or another, pleaded with Molly to "do what you can about my coming over."[15] More than once, apparently prompted by her, he considered leaving

Members of the Nelson family sitting in front of their Indian Island home, circa 1946 (left to right: Jean Archambaud, Molly Nelson Archambaud, Mary Akins (Darly's daughter, named for Molly), Philomene Nelson, Peter Nelson, Eunice Nelson Palmer [Bauman]).

the country illegally. "I often tried what you asked me," he wrote, "but the odds were too great, and being a father and a husband I decided to stay put. It is easy to leave [the center], but after is the complete unknown. Lots of betrayals."[16] By the end of September 1941, his desire had turned to desperation: "I wish to God I will be over there with the both of you," he wrote. "This life is breaking. Abnormal conditions, shortage of many things. . . . But what is killing is no news from the dear ones. . . . My health is not so good and I have lost part of my sleep, but I am fighting. By hook or by crook I will try to reach you."[17]

He never did. In December, just after the United States entered the war, this letter from a French poet-friend of Johnny's reached Molly on Indian Island:

Dear Madame:
The present war caused many sorrowful losses. Your beloved husband, M. Jean Archambaud, also belonged to these losses. He died October 23-rd 1941 in the Hospital St. Gaudens at St. Gaudens.

The long captivity and the following disease weakened his heart, and after twelve days in the medical treatment there was — alas — no remedy more for his poor, completely exhausted physical organism.

All his friends supported him. He was never alone in his last days. We profoundly adored him as a good French[man], good soldier, good fellow. Above all, he was a very good husband and father. He spoke always of you and his daughter. This conversation was his recomfort. He did never [lose] hope to join you again. He died, Madame, with your name on his lips.[18]

It was a message impossible to absorb. Perhaps it was false? Perhaps Johnny had somehow been taken captive and this was a cover. Molly wrote a flurry of queries to the Red Cross, the French Consulate in Boston, and the U.S. State Department, among others. One by one, they confirmed the awful news. The Red Cross sent her a letter from Johnny's parents telling her they had learned of their son's death from the same source as she and that they were "weeping" with her and little Jean. The French Consulate obtained for her a copy of Johnny's death certificate. The State Department acquired a copy of the

Jean Archambaud (holding the flag), receiving a commendation from the commandant of the armistice army base and medical center at Bagnères de Luchon, 1941, a month before his death.

hospital report affirming that Johnny had been admitted to St. Gaudens Hospital 12 Oct. 1941 and died 24 Oct., "quite peacefully and without pain." The report went on to note that "during his last days Mr. Archambaud enjoyed the solicitude of his numerous friends and scouts. As he did not consider his condition serious, he entertained hopes of being able to join in the near future his family. The deceased was buried in the cemetary of St. Gaudens."[19] A second letter from Johnny's poet-friend told Molly:

> The dark evergreen cypresses watch [his] grave. . . . The cemetary is situated on a hill. There is plenty of air and sunshine. The fresh wind from the western hemisphere can bring your words of love to your beloved husband every moment.[20]

Numb, still only half believing, Molly reached out to Johnny in halting verse. Her unfinished poem commemorating his death reads, in part:

> Hushed is thy voice and laughter,
> Still as the lonely midnight air,
> Tucked beneath the dark green cypress
> That stands so stalwart, sentinel—watching
> The sacred spot where you, my beloved, rest.
> I wait the distant day when I reach
> My place beside thee lying there,
> And all I pray is that
> *Mes chers amis, quand je mourrai*
> [My dear friends, when I die]
> *Plantez au pin au cimetiere,*
> [Plant a pine in the cemetary]
> And let it stand beside that cypress
> So that both will evergreen remain.[21]

Friends and family on Indian Island say Molly was never the same after escaping from France and losing her husband. "She was a different person," recalls Ernestine Tomer:

> She was friendly to us, but her smile was just so little from then on. When she came back, she didn't sleep well. I used to stay with her sometimes and she walked around a lot of the night. I think she was nervous after what she'd been through. But she never

complained. She suffered so silently and kept her hurts to herself. She was so kind and timid. In a way, Molly died when she came back. People began to ignore her and say she wasn't all there. Her mother started to notice, and said we might as well feel she's not alive anymore.[22]

During the next decade, age swept across Molly's face like an autumn squall flashing acorss the Penobscot River. Still, she followed an old pattern of dividing her time between Indian Island and New York. Surviving diaries from this period show that the city had little kindness for an aging dancer who had lost her radiance. She waitressed in a coffee shop, worked briefly in a shoe factory and in the *Daily News* library. Often she had no employment at all. On and off, from 1943 to 1947, she served as mail clerk at Sloan House YMCA.[23] There, in 1945, she met an American soldier named Lon Jones who stayed at the Y several times a year during weekend leaves in the city. Inch by inch, Lon maneuvered his way through the fortress surrounding Molly's heart. He talked to her at the desk, took her out for coffee, then dinner. He bought her simple gifts, which she accepted as treasures. Then, time and again, after pulling her close, he pushed her away. When out of town, he sent her letters—confusing, hot-cold pages that toyed with her feelings. Lonely, she clutched at his kindnesses and only momentarily puzzled over his sudden rejections. After knowing him nearly two years, she learned that he had a wife and children. Yet their relationship continued.[24]

In 1948 the army transferred Lon to California. Moving there with his family, he abruptly cut off all communication with Molly. The break left her desperately confused. With clouded head and heavy heart, she boarded a bus bound for Sacramento. It seems that every fear, loss, ambiguity, self-doubt, disappointment, and battle of her life roared into her consciousness to be relived all at once during the long ride west. Painful memories tore through her head and twisted her thoughts: she was a hostage, the other passengers were armed enemies, the bus was a mighty hearse. By the time Molly checked into the YWCA nearest Lon's base, she had lost all sense of place and self. Coming down the staircase from her room, she spied an affectionate young couple sitting together in the lobby. Something inside her snapped when she saw them. Perhaps she imagined it was Lon and his wife—or Johnny and Gisele Morhange. What happened next is described in a letter Philomene received from the Superintendent and Medical Director of Stockton State Hospital in Sacramento:

> Your daughter was committed to this hospital 3/30/48. . . . A peace officer . . . stated she came running down the stairs of the YWCA with few clothes on and said there was a hearse out front with a body in it . . . [She] imagines people trying to kill her . . . imagines that her food was being poisoned . . . thinks she was kidnapped and brought here. . . . [She has] no insight into her mental illness . . . imagines she is 5 months pregnant, and believes that Mr. [Lon] Jones put her in the hospital. . . . [She] will require electric shock therapy.[25]

After two months of confinement and treatment, Molly traveled by train to Bangor—confined in a straightjacket and accompanied by a hospital escort. Philomene, along with Jean and the Penobscot's Health and Welfare Supervisor, met her at the station, removed the jacket, drove her to Old Town, and took her across the river by canoe. Released into Philomene's care, Molly spent several days at home, "nervous but cooperative." Each night, unable to sleep, she walked about the house, talking to herself. Overcome by exhaustion, she would finally fall asleep, only to be awakened by an "old dream" that hints at her sense of being locked within herself—unable to dance or love her way to freedom: "J was carrying me all bandaged up in his arms. He put me down gently on my back on a white bedspread. . . . He looked at me wonderingly, then picked me up again not knowing what to do."[26]

Worried about Molly's condition, Philomene took her to Bangor State Mental Hospital and, with Molly's consent, committed her there for observation. In Philomene's hospital statement she declared that her daughter had "always been a happy go lucky type of girl and very active and enterprising. When she returned from France in July 1940 she was changed to a depressed and worried woman. She tried in every way to bring her French husband to this country, but she was unsuccessful." The doctor assigned to Molly's case recorded this diagnosis:

The patient suffered a severe shock due to her inability to make it possible for [her husband] to immigrate to the U.S., and finally his death in October 194[1]. Patient was rather depressed for a period of about seven months, however she recovered without any hospital treatment. . . . The writer would propose the diagnosis scizophrenia, paranoid type. Etiology: loss of husband 194[1], disappointing love affair; physical exhaustion; nearness of change of life, and unknown factors. . . . Patient's makeup: intellectually superior; temperamentally suspicious. Prognosis: may be favorable for recovery.[27]

Molly spent a full year in the mental institute. Upon her release, she insisted on returning to New York to look for work. Physically and mentally drained, she did not meet with success and at times roamed the streets with no place to stay. Once again, Louis Sobol wrote about her in his *Journal-American* column:

It has come to my attention that Molly Spotted Elk, once a famous dancer who got her start with the Texas Guinan troupe, is desperately ill and penniless. She is badly in need of good hospital care, of attention from doctors. Surely this genuine American girl—whose forefathers were famed Indian chiefs—occupying American soil long before Columbus spotted the precious land—surely this real citizen cannot be abandoned at this time. At one time she was the protegé of Anne Morgan—but Miss Morgan is gone. Who will help Spotted Elk now?[28]

Despondent about her mother's situation, eighteen-year-old Jean sent Molly a letter pleading with her to quit New York. This, in part, is what she wrote:

I thought of you so much on Christmas eve. I cried because I didn't know whether or not you even had a place to stay. . . . It is hell worrying about you out there. Not sure you have enough to eat, any money, whether you are warm. . . . Mommie, why don't you come home? Please mommie, don't be stubborn and foolish. I'll help you.[29]

Finally, Molly returned to the refuge of Indian Island—where no one was famous and no one could fall from fame. Usually dressed in flannel shirt and jeans, she spent her days quietly, reading, tending the garden, walking in the woods, making Indian dolls and baskets, starting but rarely finishing stories, and typing letters dozens of pages long to friends and government officials warning them about communism.[30] She exuded a preternatural quietude, haunting to those who did not know her well. Many children were afraid of her. But those who stepped through the penumbra of her world sometimes found themselves in a magical realm where ancient stories came to life, everything in the forest had a name, and one might catch fish by hand.[31]

In 1951, a one-lane bridge replaced the ferry bateau that linked Indian Island to Old Town. Most people called it progress. Horace called it "paradise lost."[32] On the one hand, it simply made coming and going to and from the island quicker and safer. But it also brought cars to the reservation, transforming forever the pace and silence of the place. And, symbolically, it signaled the end of an era, a point in time when most of the island folks had succumbed to the ways of the white world. Only a few stubborn oldtimers, including Horace, followed ancient rhythms, ignoring social pressures to define their lives by the standard work week and paycheck of dominant society. One can only guess how many, like Molly, wrestled mightily to reconcile contrasting ways of life, to carry precious pieces of their past into the future.

For Molly, genuine art and love had provided an ethereal bridge on which she traveled between two cultures on equal footing. When these collapsed, she fell into the gap, and lived the rest of her life sheltered in a reclusive realm of her own making. Although Molly surrendered her struggle, she never forgot the glorious, if fleeting, sense of belonging, of successfully linking the best of both worlds. Decades earlier she had told her diary, "the beautiful things live and heal the wounds of sorrow." If so, perhaps her introverted world, unlike the conflicting realm of hierarchical cultures, was a peaceful place.

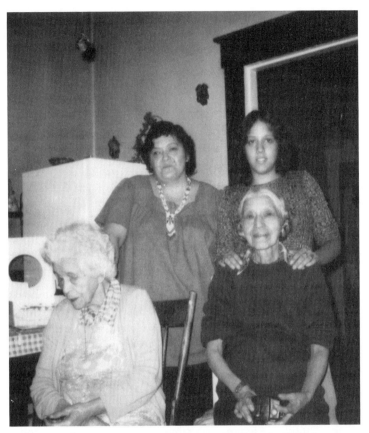

Four generations: Philomene Nelson, her daughter Molly Nelson
Archambaud, Molly's daughter Jean Archambaud Moore, and Jean's
daughter Barbara Moore. November 1976—about one year before
Philomene and Molly died.

In April 1953, Molly's daughter married Airman First Class
Harvey Moore, based at Dow Airforce Base in Bangor, and a
month later moved with him to New Hampshire. Jean and
Harvey soon had two children, John and Barbara. They were
adored by Molly, who cherished their occasional visits, and
regularly sent them care packages that, typically, included
books. In 1962, Horace passed away after a long illness, leaving

Philomene and Molly alone in the big house. Fifteen years later, at age ninety, Philomene died, and Molly found herself the sole inhabitant of the home she had bought for her family so long ago. By this time, people on the island showed an awakened interest in repressed Penobscot traditions and mounting indignation over the historic loss of native territory. This revitalization accompanied a successful campaign to win back a measure of Penobscot sovereignty and land. In the process, Penobscots gained federal recognition—formal acknowledgement of their status as a tribe, with all the attendant rights.[33] Most soon discovered that recognition by the United States government meant little without *self*-recognition, bringing to the fore the question of cultural identity, so long and intensely explored by Molly. Today's Penobscots, like Molly, have inherited a centuries-old battle to unearth the buried Indian heart and translate it into present-day terms. But, unlike Molly—born into an era when society-at-large viewed Indians as an inferior class of people whose traditions were backward, uncivilized, country-fair material—Penobscots today face a society in which notions of cultural superiority are no longer unquestioned.

Molly did not live to see the scope of these changes. Two weeks after her mother's death, she died of a fall at age seventy-three. It happened in the deep silent hours of a cold winter night. Unable to sleep, she roamed the house. Near the top of the back stairs, moonlight spilled through a window and seized her attention. Tripping over the brightness, she fell. *Down, down the narrow stairway . . . out the kitchen door, along the stream that crossed the island, past old Joe Hemlock's shack, and into the Penobscot River. Carried on the ancient current, she tumbled over the falls and flowed toward the river's mouth, passing the aged haunts of Chief Madokawando, his daughter Mathilde, and her French love St. Castin. The river poured her into the Atlantic, and she crossed the sea on heaving waves that tossed her onto the French Pyrenees at St. Jean de Luz. Tumbling down the mountside into a flower-strewn valley, she finally lay still beneath a canopy of ice-*

*chip stars in a pitch-black sky. She looked up at the moon, a
crescent light bending near the earth. Neebowset smiled. She
took his hand and they walked toward a forest remarkable,
where cypress, pine, and every arboreal form imaginable
stood together and reached for the sky. Then Molly turned,
and danced her way home.*[34]

POSTSCRIPT

I didn't see too much of my mother while growing up. She left me in the care of my grandmother on Indian Island while she worked in New York City. She'd come home once or twice a year for visits. Yet, memories of my times with her are vivid.

My memories of Mama and Daddy together are also vivid. There was love, laughter, protection, adventures, danger, mountain hiking, Boy Scout meetings and trips, fun times, hard times, and the war. But mostly, there was love, which they showed to each other in myriad ways, time and time again.

Except during our years in France, Mama was home again and gone again. But she regularly sent money to help support me. She provided me with clothes, toys, piano lessons, and, most of all, books. Contact with Mama always meant books—mailed to me when she was away, carried to me when she came home. She encouraged and delighted in my reading. She prompted and praised my poetry, drawings, and paintings—and saved most of them. When she was home on Indian Island, she told me Penobscot legends, sang songs in French and English, and played the piano. She taught me to sew by hand. She was always proud of the A's and B's I earned in school. Later in my life, she was the same with my children, saving the school papers, drawings, and cards they sent her. She knew I was providing them with books, so she didn't have to do that. Instead, she showed them secrets of the natural world.

After I was married and gone from the reservation, Mama's life was rather a lonely one. But she made the best of it. Resettled on the island, she wrote in her diaries, typed letters, and kept house. She voraciously read the Bangor, Boston, and New York newspapers, saving clippings about her old friends and acquaintances, and anything else of interest to her. She continued her research on the Maya and Inca; worked sporadically on her book about a rabbit and his ventures (which was never published); walked in the woods; made Indian dolls for pocket money (a pair of which is owned by the Smithsonian Museum); collected and studied rocks and stones; attended garage and rummage sales to gather antiques, material for her doll dresses, and items for her care packages to me. She was always busy, usually at her typewriter until late in the night, when exhaustion finally quieted her active mind into sleep. She watched TV when she could (which she hated to admit that she loved). She planted flowers and trees. She would come to visit us occasionally and stay for awhile. But she always missed the mental stimulation and sharing that she had with my father.

I was my mother's child. I had an insatiable curiosity, especially where she was concerned. So I drank in everything I heard about her. Being the very private person she was, she seldom talked about herself, her accomplishments, or her personal life. Most of what I learned about her came from my grandmother, her sisters and brothers, and others who had known her.

I learned the most about my mother after her death. She had saved a lifetime of letters, notes, diaries, photos, newsclips, and other keepsakes, and it fell to me go through them. Unfortunately, I did not save them all, but I looked at everything. As I journeyed through the remnants of her life, I made an important discovery. Growing up, I had wondered if my mother loved me, for she left me so often. Now I have no doubt, whatsoever, that she did.

Mama would have loved to read this book. She would have loved the writer. She is the type of person my mother appreciated. Her sensitivity, interest in my mother's life, and growing love for her subject confirm my original feeling that she, above many others who approached me, should be the one to present my mother's story.

My mother was a unique individual: a free spirit, a gentle, psychic, nurturing, self-depreciating, extremely sensitive, shy, retiring soul—thrust out into the harsh glare of the world because of necessity, to be watched. She preferred to be the watcher. Her soul danced on the winds of chance, and the winds of change swept her away. I loved her.

JEAN ARCHAMBAUD MOORE

Indian Island, Old Town, Maine

NOTES

Chapter 1

1. Molly's 1940 diary, 24, 25 June—just before her escape from Nazi occupation in France.

2. 1931 diary, 5–27 July.

3. "Former Old Town Girl Evacuee From France," *Bangor Daily News,* 23 July 1940; Jean Moore, interview by author, 8–13 Sept. 1989.

Chapter 2

1. Molly's 1934 diary, 17 March.

2. David Sanger explains that although burials dating back to the middle archaic period (7500 bp) have been found on Indian Island, the oldest habitation site found to date is in the 4000–5000 bp range. Yet sites immediately surrounding the island date back 8000–9000 bp. Sanger concludes, "We've got Indian Island bracketed back to 8000–9000 bp. So I've got no problem saying the island itself was probably inhabited that far back, even though there is not yet specific evidence" (interview by author, 28 Jan. 1993). Also, see Robinson, Petersen, and Robinson, regarding the early cultures of New England, including those along the Penobscot River 8000–9000 bp.

3. Speck 1940, 25; Hillman and Morris, 3; Webster, 227.

4. Speck 1940, 56.

5. Calloway, 1989, 18; Speck 1940, 25. For a detailed discussion of Penobscot family groups, totems, and territories, see also Speck 1940, 203–29.

6. Eckstorm 1932, 42–43; Speck 1940, 137–38; Whitehead, 12.

7. Frank T. Siebert, letter to author, 11 May 1993. This phrase describing January appears in American Friends Service Committee, which also attributes it to Siebert.

8. Speck 1940, 12.

9. Calloway 1989, 18; Speck 1940, 25.
10. Speck 1940, 35.
11. Calloway 1989, 17.
12. Speck 1940, 25.
13. Regarding Wabanaki attitudes toward ownership, see Sullivan 1970, 134–35.
14. Calloway 1989, 11; Snow, 147; Prins 1992. Snow says that Penobscots, along with the Abenaki, Pigwacket, Arosaguntacook, and Kennebec Indians, were collectively known as Eastern Abenaki. He contends that they occupied most of what is now Maine and spoke various dialects of the same language. To their west, in present-day New Hampshire and Vermont, lived the Western Abenaki tribes. And to the northeast, from Maine's northernmost coastal reaches to Canada's maritime provinces, lived the Passamaquoddy, Maliseet, and Micmac peoples. Prins's later research challenges this. According to him, at least from the mid-seventeenth century, Eastern Abenaki seeking refuge from Anglo-Iroquois aggression fled to the central Maine region, including Indian Island. The Abenaki newcomers encountered the river valley's original inhabitants, referred to by the French as Etchemin, and ancestral to today's Maliseet-Passamaquoddy tribes. With the arrival of the Abenaki, says Prins, many Etchemin moved northeastward. Those who stayed in the Penobscot Valley intermarried with and adopted the language (and cultivation practices) of the Abenaki refugees. The English, who named the inhabitants according to their locations, referred to all Indians living in the Penobscot River valley as Penobscots.

Chapter 3

1. From an untitled two-page lecture about Penobscots, written by Molly circa 1955 (among Molly's papers).
2. Among others see Calloway 1981, 444–45, and 1991, 35–36; Snow, 141; Speck 1940, 13.
3. For discussions of missions among Penobscots and other Wabanaki, see Leger; Sevigny; Morrison, 24–25, 74; Prins and Bourque 1987.
4. For overviews of the European struggle for control of Wabanaki Country, see, among others: Morrison; Williamson, 1932, 220–60.
5. Among many references, see Snow, 144; Speck 1940, 14.
6. For examinations of Abenaki/Penobscot relations and treaties

with Massachusetts and Maine, see Banks (unpublished manuscript), 5–43; Ghere; Verrill, 109–11.

7. In 1827 and 1828, pine shingles, nails, and boards were transported to Indian Island for building the first house on the island (Indian Affairs Documents, vol. 3, doc. 907). In 1828, Governor Attean moved into the first house with shingles (Indian Affairs Documents, J. Chamberlain's Report, doc. 275:13), Lorenzo cites the observations of a visitor who came to the island in 1857: "Now not a single wigwam remains on the principal island; every family inhabits 'the white man's house' . . . and possesses the most useful of the 'white man's things' . . . in dress too the change has been well-nigh universal in both sexes."

8. Thoreau, 5–6; Rivard, 42–44.

9. Lorenzo, 229–30.

10. According to Eckstorm, road-show Penobscot families at this time included the Mitchells, Neptunes, Newells, and Nicolas (253).

11. From a speech Hubbard made to the 31st legislature of Maine (Maine State Archives, Maine Public Documents 1851, vol. 1:45). According to Indian Affairs Documents, vol. V, the 1838 Treaty Annuity with the Penobscots consisted of over $2000 in provisions: 500 bushels corn, 15 bbls pork, 1 hogshead of molasses, 199 yards double width scarlet broadcloth, 50 blankets, 600 lbs of shot, 100 lbs of gunpowder, 150 lbs tobacco, 6 boxes chocolate, 50 silver dollars. With a population of about 100 families, that translates into $30 worth of goods per family. Based on the $22.92 average monthly pay of male laborers in Massachusetts in 1850 (Cole, 31), this amount equalled more than one month's wages.

12. Thoreau, 3, 5–7.

13. Ibid., 8.

14. Ibid., 109–11.

15. Ibid., 117.

16. The phrase "the Indian in our consciousness" comes from Lemaire, who used it as the title of his book, which explores in detail the myth of the noble savage and the ambiguous and conflicting projections of this myth onto American Indians by Europeans of the past and present.

17. Thoreau, 124, 140.

18. Ibid., 153–55.

19. Ibid., 178–79.

20. Ibid., 191–92.

21. Ibid., 192.

22. Ibid., 192–94.

23. The legends, as collected and written down by Molly, were donated to Northeast Folk Archives, University of Maine, Orono, by her daughter Jean Moore, in 1977. Molly's primary source was "old Joe Hemlock," whose memory reached back before the mid-1800s. In the preface to his 1893 book, *The Life and Traditions of the Red Man,* Penobscot Joseph Nicolar noted, "After forty years of search and study, I am satisfied that no more can be found, as the old traditional story tellers have all gone to the happy hunting ground" (4). Was he distinguishing a certain kind of storyteller no longer on hand in Molly's day?

Chapter 4

1. Molly Nelson 1938, unpublished manuscript, 3.

2. Mcfadden, 65–66. Mcfadden's profile of Molly's youngest sister, Eunice Nelson-Bauman, notes that Eunice's maternal grandmother delivered her; Eunice, in a telephone conversation with the author, 4 Oct. 1992, said she believed Molly came into the world via the same hands.

3. Speck 1940, 253.

4. Speck 1940, 252. Speck describes various Penobscot birthing traditions besides this one, including burying the afterbirth and cleansing the infant by giving it a "decoction of yellow ash leaves boiled very bitter and strong."

5. Glen Starbird, Penobscot tribal genealogist, provided this information in a conversation with the author, 24 July 1988. The intertribal marriage ratios come from Speck 1940, 15. Unfortunately, Speck's ahistoric perspective failed to capture the fact that what he calls "Penobscot:Penobscot marriages," are, in all likelihood, also mixed. A more detailed, less ethnically separatist analysis can be found in Harald Prins's "1900: Miscegenation in the Penobscot Community," an unpublished analysis of the 1900 Census list of Penobscot and Piscataquis Counties in Maine. According to his analysis, "In addition to a fairly widespread intermarriage with whites, there was also intermarriage with Indians from neighboring tribes. In total there were 14 Maliseets living on the Island, whose parents were both Maliseets. Two more were half Maliseets by way of their fathers, and one by way of the mother being Maliseets. In total, 17 'Penobscots' were minimally half Maliseet.

"Although a large number of Penobscots were directly related to the

Passamaquoddies, only eleven were full Passamaquoddies. In addition, there were nine Penobscots with Passamaquoddy mothers. Finally, there were ten Penobscots with Passamaquoddy fathers, although two of those had a white mother. In other words, 31 Penobscots were minimally half Passamaquoddy.

"One of the members of the Penobscot community at Indian Island was a St. Francis Abenaki, with both parents being Abenakis from Quebec Province. In addition, two had an Abenaki father, and one an Abenaki mother. This leaves a total of 4 Penobscots with minimally one parent being St. Francis Abenaki.

"At the Island, there were two Micmac women, both of whom had a Micmac mother and a white father, and who married Penobscot men.

"Finally, there was one Penobscot with a Huron mother, another with a Mohawk mother. One of the Indians at Indian Island, son of a Passamaquoddy mother, mentioned his father being a 'Norridgewock.' To conclude, one halfbreed stated that her mother was an Appalachic.

This leaves us with a total of 58 Penobscots who are minimally half Maliseet, Passamaquoddy, Micmac, Abenaki, Huron, or Mohawk. Twenty-seven of the Indians at the Penobscot village were not at all Penobscots."

6. Speck 1940, 223.

7. Speck 1940: 217–19.

8. Chamberlain.

9. Sadie Mitchel, interview by Northeast Archives of Folklore and Oral History, tape recording, University of Maine, Orono, 1967.

10. Herbert Adams, "Penobscots honor three authentic heroes," *Maine Sunday Telegram*, 10 Aug. 1986. Jim Hurley, in the *New York Daily Mirror*, 13 Oct. 1933, profiled Soxalexis.

11. Oldtown High School Records Ledger, 1891–1903.

12. Chamberlain.

13. Kenneth Cramer, Dartmouth archivist, letter to author, 9 March 1989; Barbara Krieger, Dartmouth archivist, letter to author, 10 Sept. 1993; Dartmouth archival records, Horace A. Nelson File; Hanover High School records.

14. Apid Nelson January, interview by author, 7 Aug. 1989.

15. This sketch of Horace and Philomene comes from interviews by the author with Jean Moore, 8–13 Sept. 1988, and Eunice Nelson-Bauman, 12–13 July 1988.

16. Jean Moore, interviews by author, 8–13 Sept. 1988.

17. Ibid. Also, according to Penobscot tribal genealogist Glenn Starbird, Molly's maternal grandmother "Mary is listed as an Indian in 1881 census—not necessarily because of her husband [Frank Saulis]; her mom was probably a Maliseet married to a Frenchman" (letter to author, 11 Feb. 1993).

18. Interviews by author: Jean Moore, 8–13 Sept. 1988; Eunice Nelson-Bauman, 12–13 July 1988.

19. Interviews by author: Jean Moore, 8–13 Sept. 1988; Apid Nelson January, 7 Aug. 1989; Eunice Nelson-Bauman, 12–13 July 1988. Although none of Molly's survivors recall for certain the location of the wedding ceremony, they all believe it took place on Indian Island, conducted by a priest.

20. Speck 1940, 255. Speck never found out what this term actually meant, although he wrote that some told him it was a corruption of the French *madame mariee*, meaning the woman is married. According to Frank Siebert (letter to author, 1 Feb. 1993), the term is actually an "archaic obscene word used in the vulgar wedding song." It translates, in its various conjugations: "I fuck her/him," or "You fuck her/him." I should note that Siebert translated this for me in Latin, in an apparent effort not to offend me.

21. Interviews by author: Eunice Nelson-Bauman, 6 Aug. 1993; Jean Moore, 8–13 Sept. 1988 and 5 Aug. 1993.

22. McFadden, 66; Jean Moore, interviews by author, 8–13 Sept. 1988 and 5 Aug. 1993; Eunice Nelson-Bauman (interview by author, 6 Aug. 1993) recalled going out with Philomene to gather flag root and balsam blisters. Flag root could be dried, ground, and made into a paste to treat burns, or sucked on to sooth sore throats, or boiled in water to ease aching muscles. Eunice also remembered Philomene applying balsam blisters to cuts as "a healing salve that inhibited scarring." Apid Nelson January also noted that Philomene had special healing gifts as the seventh daughter of a seventh daughter (interview by author, 4 Aug. 1989).

23. Jean Moore, interview by author, 8–13 Sept. 1988.

24. According to Jean Moore, Horace Nelson fathered two other girls about the same time he fathered Apid (interview by author, 8 Aug. 1992).

25. Glen Starbird, in his "History of Penobscot Legislators" (unpublished paper, 1989), notes that tribal representatives at that time were paid $120 for the entire Legislative Session.

26. Apid Nelson January, interview by author, 4 Aug. 1989.

27. Ibid.; Eunice Nelson-Bauman, interview by author, 12–13 July 1988.

28. Apid Nelson January, interview by author, 7 Aug. 1989.

29. Interviews by author: 7 Aug. 1989; Jean Moore, 8 Aug. 1992; Eunice Nelson-Bauman, 12–13 July 1988 and 6 Aug. 1993. According to Boyd, the Bangor Opera House began showing motion pictures in 1899. The city's first movie theater, The Nickel, opened in 1906, soon followed by the Gaiety Theatre which combined live vaudeville with short films. By the time Molly and Apid were in their late teens, a movie house had opened in Old Town.

30. Apid Nelson January, in a telephone interview by Jean Moore (conveyed by telephone to the author 4 Aug. 1989), made particular note of Philomene treating peptitus, tuberculosis, and gall stones. See also Jean Moore's unpublished family history.

31. Madas Sapiel, quoted in Lane, 8.

32. According to Harald Prins in his unpublished analysis of the 1900 census for Penobscot and Piscataquis counties in Maine, "Nearly 100 of the 157 Indian Island adults who responded to the 1900 census listed basketmaking as their primary occupation. Another thirty said they were day laborers, and ten worked as guides. Only one individual noted hunting as his employment, while one other said he made his living through a combination of hunting and guiding. Two stated that they were canoe builders"—a number that grew in the following years with the 1901 incorporation of Old Town Canoe Company. According to Chamberlain, writing at the turn of the century, "Penobscots support themselves chiefly by guiding tourists and sportsmen through the Maine forests and by the manufacture of baskets, snow-shoes and other wares. Some of the young men work in the lumber woods and the most energetic find employment in the spring at river driving, a very dangerous and laborious performance, demanding skill and courage as well as untiring energy. The women are expert basketmakers at which they have considerable skill." For first-hand information about Penobscot work activities in the early 1900s, see Ibelle.

33. Apid Nelson January, interview by author, 7 Aug. 1989.

34. Horace Nelson, 1939 alumni questionnaire, Dartmouth Archives; interviews by author: Jean Moore, 8 Aug. 1992; Apid Nelson January, 7 Aug. 1989; Eunice Nelson, 12–13 July 1988, said her father's erratic "work situation was hard on the family."

35. Jean Moore, interview by author, 8 Aug. 1992.

36. Apid Nelson January, interview by author, 7 Aug. 1989; Lane, 5.

37. Lane, 5; Apid Nelson January, interview by Jean Moore (conveyed to the author on Indian Island, 5 Aug. 1993).

38. Apid Nelson January, telephone interview by author, 7 Aug. 1989.

39. Jean Moore, interview by author, 8 Aug. 1992.

40. Ibid.; Apid Nelson January, interview by author, 7 Aug. 1989.

41. Lane, 14; Jean Moore, interview by author, 8 Aug. 1992.

42. Jean Moore, interview by author, 8 Aug. 1992.

43. Ibid.; Lane, 14; Molly Nelson, 1955 partial typescript of one of her lectures about Penobscot culture (among Molly's papers).

44. In Lane's 1979 interview with Molly's childhood friend Madas Sapiel, Madas recalled, "It was so beautiful then. The boat would land there, you know. All along the side [of the island] they had big trees. When we would come from over town shopping, we would sit down on the grass there and relax 'til we got ready to pick up our stuff and go. . . . 'Course the sisters and the priest—they had a beautiful place there. They had their own homes and then they had the church. They had a cement walk there from the path. We used to sit on their lawn and the people outside would be sitting there rocking. Indian men and women talking and making baskets. . . . getting ready for people to come over and buy their wares" (14).

45. Lane, 8; Ernestine Tomer, interview by author, 10 Aug. 1989.

46. Jean Moore, interview by author, 8 Aug. 1992.

47. Interviews by author: Jean Moore, 5 Aug. 1993; Wilfred Tomer.

48. Apid Nelson January, interview by author, 7 Aug. 1989.

49. Nelson, Molly, unpublished manuscript, 1938, 1–3. From this passage, it seems evident that Molly could speak Penobscot as a child. Her contemporary, Madas Sapiel, said in an interview that although she was not allowed to speak Indian at school, she did at home (Lane, 6–7). In the Nelson family, according to Molly's sister Eunice Nelson-Bauman (who is 15 years younger than Molly), the older children learned Penobscot at home, but as the years went by, it was spoken less and less in the household, and the younger ones learned only fragments of the language (interview by author, 18 Jan. 1993). Frank Siebert, letter to author, 11 May 1993, noted that Hemlock Joe was so-named because he once lived upriver on Hemlock Island.

50. Lawrence "Bill" Shay, interview by the author.

51. "Penobscotbelles," *Bangor Weekly Commercial*, 12 Jan. 1900.

52. Chamberlain, 2–3.

53. Interview by author: Jean Moore, March 1989; Apid Nelson

January, 4, 7 Aug. 1989. John Fysche, "History of Indian Island," *Lewiston Journal*, 1 Feb. 1940.

54. Gilbert Ketchum, interview by author.

55. Madas Sapiel, quoted in Lane, 8.

Chapter 5

1. Molly's 1922 diary, 4 July.

2. Green and Laurie, 3–4, 67.

3. McKenney; Jean Moore, interview by author, 10 March 1989.

4. 1929 diary, 19 March; John Fysche, "History of Indian Island," *Lewiston Journal*, 1 Feb. 1940; Jean Moore, interview by author, 17 March 1989; Apid Nelson January, interview by author, 4 Aug. 1989.

5. Madas Sapiel, quoted in Ibelle, 46–47.

6. Green and Laurie, 158, 248, 268. Boyd, in her flashback sketch of Maine theaters, notes: "The Bangor Opera House has been showing motion pictures since 1899. The city's first movie theater, the Nickel, opened in 1906. The Gaiety Theatre in Bangor will combine live vaudeville with short films, as will theaters throughout the nation. In 1911, the Bangor fire will destroy these two theaters, but three others—the Graphic, the Gem and the Union—will take their place" (7–8).

7. Boyd, 8.

8. Gilbert Ketchum, interview by author.

9. Old Town High School Records, 1917–1920.

10. Jean Moore, in a telephone conversation with the author, 26 July 1988, noted that although her mother's diaries from this period have not survived, she read them just after Molly's death: "In Mama's early diaries, which I threw out after reading, at age 14 she wrote of being on the road in Massachusetts, doing little vaudeville shows for women's clubs, churches, staying in boarding rooms, being lonely for her family, and sometimes mistreated by the people utilizing her talents."

11. 1923 diary, April (no specific date).

12. 1922 diary, March (the first Saturday after Good Friday).

13. Horace Nelson, letter to Molly, 29 Jan. 1922 (among Molly's papers).

14. 1922 diary, June (no specific date).

15. Apid Nelson January, interview by author, 8 July 1989; after I described a postcard of her and Molly, Apid offered this identification: "I was about fifteen [in that picture postcard]. There was a [pageant]

on the reserve [the day it was taken]. They danced, had big chow, and all kinds of races. Molly and I won the canoe race."

16. For a description of this delegation and other American Indians who went to Europe as performers and for other reasons prior to 1620, see Prins and McBride 1992, and Prins 1994b.

17. Penhallow, 26–27.

18. Viola, 141.

19. Vail, 170.

20. Viola, 143–53. Culhane, 34–45.

21. Vail, 182. Culhane, 100–107.

22. Culhane, 109–19.

23. Vestal, 250. See also Rosa and May, 83, 89–91, 149–53, and Culhane, 109–19.

24. Neihardt, 182; Rosa and May, 144.

25. Among these performers were: Penobscot Clara Mitchell-Neptune, who (according to Eckstorm 1978, 253) "traveled as far as New York and Philadelphia, taking part in primitive vaudeville shows of Indian life" in the mid-1800s; Micmac Jeremy Bartlett ("Dr. Lone Cloud"), medicine man for the (Kickapoo?) Medicine Company road show in the late 1800s; Penobscot Lucy Nicolar ("Watawaso"), a beautiful and elegant woman who charmed high society New York with song and lecture in the early 1900s before forming a troupe with Kiowa "Chief" [Bruce] Poolaw; Maliseet Henry Perley ("Red Eagle") from Greenville, Maine, whose early twentieth century performances in New England and abroad included a show called "The American Indian in Song and Story," in which he lectured while other Indians sang and danced.

26. Perhaps most famous of Lieurance's songs was "The Waters of Minnetonka"—one of several of his compositions that Watawaso recorded for the Victor Talking Machine Company. The company sent her on promotional singing tours across the United States. See Wiggins.

27. This sketch of Loring is based on Prins 1988, unpublished paper.

28. Sometimes only the stories were for sale. As a journalist writing for the *Bangor Weekly Commercial* (12 Jan. 1900) wrote in his article entitled "Penobscotbelles": "To many, 'Big Thunder' is the most interesting character on the island. If you give him a generous tip he will ask you to be seated, offer you a well-filled pipe, and after many long puffs, will tell you of the lost glories of his tribe, of its many interesting

traditions. . . . [He] will then turn to his relics . . . " This journalist noted that Loring's professed treasures included "the first iron axe and tomahawk that cut a Maine pine," "an old iron pistol, the first introduced to the Indians," "the knife with which his tribe took the last scalp," "stone bowls of famous pipes which were smoked at different treaties," and a "breast plate sent to his tribe by Queen Isabella of Spain." See also "Big Thunder, Mighty Medicine Man, Chief of the Tarrantines," *Lewiston Journal*, 6 May 1906 (Illustrated Magazine section).

29. Prins 1988, unpublished paper.

30. The rooming house was owned and run by Mrs. Lulu Morris, whose address Molly noted in the beginning of her 1926 diary.

31. 1922 diary, 5 July.

32. See Wiggins for a brief discussion of Lieurance. For a detailed discussion of Cadman, see Blackstone, who refers to him repeatedly throughout her book.

33. To ballyhoo is to arouse interest in an entertainment, typically by parading through public places in costume.

34. Green and Laurie, 59.

35. 1922 diary, 26, 30 May; 2, 7 June.

36. 1922 diary, 25, 31 May.

37. Horace Nelson, letter to Molly, 29 Jan. 1922 (among Molly's papers).

38. 1922 diary, 22, 26 May; 6 July.

39. 1922 diary, Aug. (no specific date).

40. Green and Laurie, 59.

41. 1923 diary, Jan. (no specific date).

42. 1923 diary, 26 March.

43. 1923 diary, Jan. (no specific date).

44. 1923 diary, March (no specific date).

45. 1923 diary, spring, various entries.

46. 1923 diary, Feb. (no specific date).

47. 1923 diary, late March (no specific date).

48. Reed, interview by author.

49. Powers, 557.

50. Needabeh.

51. This sketch of Camp Overlook is based on several newsclips in Reed's camp scrapbook.

52. Reed, interview by author.

53. Ibid. Speck 1940, 251, discusses Indian pronunciations of their Christian names.

54. This description of camp activities is based on Reed's camp scrapbook, which includes *The Sentinel* clipping regarding Molly's Harding poem.

55. Pettus, interview by author.

56. Reed, interview by author.

57. Ibid.; Pettus, interview by author.

Chapter 6

1. H. J. R. Tewksbury, "Indian Princess Will Paddle Own Canoe," *Portland Telegram,* 10 July 1927.

2. Apid Nelson January, interview by author, 4 August 1989.

3. Old Town High School Records, 1922–23.

4. Speck 1940, 1. Siebert 1932, 6; it should be noted that Siebert does not mention 1918 as a year in which Speck researched among the Penobscots.

5. See Blankenship, ed., *The Life and Times of Frank G. Speck.* In this book, Blankenship, who is Speck's grandson, includes a series of seven reminiscences by Speck's colleagues and friends; my description of him is drawn from two in particular: "Frank Speck: The Quiet Listener" (Edmund S. Carpenter 78–84) and "The Unforgettable Frank G. Speck" (C. A. Weslager 52–77). Several of the contributors also mention Speck's musical abilities, noting that he played harmonica, violin, mandolin, and piano. Commemorative articles other than those in Blankenship's book are noted in his preface, xiv.

6. Edmund Carpenter, letter to author, 16 May 1993.

7. Gilbert Ketchum, interview by author.

8. Speck 1940, 2, 4.

9. In his 1935 article "Penobscot Tales and Religious Beliefs," cowritten with Frank Gouldsmith, Speck noted, "Among the Penobscot younger generation should be mentioned the name of some in particular who have been consulted in the course of my study: *Molliedellis Nelson, Roland Nelson . . .* " (emphasis added).

10. Eunice Nelson-Bauman (interview by author, 12–13 July 1988) and Jean Moore (interview by author, 8–13 Sept. 1988) noted that Molly lived with the Specks, while Apid Nelson January (interview by author, 4 Aug., 1988) said that she believed Molly lived in a dormitory while at the university. Alberta Speck Hartman (interview by author) said that she was too young to recall whether Molly stayed in her household, but it was "quite possible." Frank S. [Billy] Speck (interview by author, 15 Oct. 1992) said, "I'm quite certain Molly stayed

with us. We had a trunk of hers in our basement for years. She was in and out." In a subsequent interview (27 April 1993) Billy said, "Molly would appear and disappear at our house when I was quite young. She slept on the sofa, or upstairs in the room where Gladys had stayed. There was nothing regular about her coming and going." The description of Speck's home comes from Carpenter (letter to author, 16 May 1993) and Blankenship, xii.

11. Edmund Carpenter, letter to author, 16 May 1993.

12. Alumni Records, Swarthmore and University of Pennsylvania.

13. Alberta Speck Hartman, interview by author. Frank S. [Billy] Speck (interview by author, 27 April 1993) commented, "I think my father had arranged through the faculty club to provide a place for one Indian student a year at the university." See also Blankenship, xiv, 80.

14. Fenton, 9.

15. Weslager, 75.

16. Alberta Speck Hartman, interview by author; Frank S. [Billy] Speck, interview by author, 15 Oct. 1992. Speck's effort to trace Indian ancestry in his family is corroborated by Weslager, 67. Siebert 94, touches on the issue of Speck's apparent romanticism concerning American Indians: "It has been stated by Morrison (1980) that Speck liked 'to play Indian' and had 'romantic' attachments to the Indian way of life. I believe this is a distortion or only half-truth and that his real motive was to project himself within Indian culture by participating in the activities of living Indians to obtain insights and data that otherwise would not be perceived in more formal and impersonal situations. In short, Speck was a devoted and indefatigable fieldworker, who took every opportunity he could to return to the Indians and gather new information."

17. Carpenter, 79.

18. Frank S. [Billy] Speck, interviews by author, 15 Oct. 1992 and 27 April 1993. In Pat Grandjean's article "The Elder," Gladys explains how Speck's family came to know Mrs. Fielding and the Tantquidgeons: "[Frank's] family used to have a summer home in Niantic" (94). See also Witthoft, 1–2.

19. Frank S. [Billy] Speck, interview by author, 15 Oct. 1992. Grandjean, 93.

20. Speck 1940, 1.

21. Grandjean, 95. Blankenship, xii.

22. Gladys Tantquidgeon, interview by author.

23. Carpenter, 80; Weslager, 57.

24. Frank S. [Billy] Speck, interview by author, 15 Oct. 1992.

25. Gladys Tantaquidgeon, interview by author.

26. Siebert points out the positive dimensions of Speck's work but criticizes him on various points including his uncritical acceptance of "primary data given him by Indian informants of greater or less competence." Siebert elaborated on this critique in letters to the author, 25 Sept. 1992, 11 May 1993.

27. Siebert 95.

28. Fenton, 9.

29. Dorothy Ranco, letter to Frank Speck; Edmund Carpenter, letter to author, 5 Oct., 1992, including comments regarding Frank Siebert's 1982 article on Speck.

30. Klein, 262.

31. Frank S. [Billy] Speck, interview by author, 15 Oct. 1992.

32. Many assume that the 101 Ranch was named for its size: 101,000 acres. But, by the time the ranch grew to be that big, the Millers had been using the name for years. It was chosen by their father after a group of his cowboys overcelebrated the end of a round up by wreaking havoc in the 101 Saloon in San Antonio, Texas. Colonel Miller paid all damages, then changed the family's road branch to 101, hoping to teach his crew a lesson. According to his son Zack, "They never forgot the lesson after those numbers had shimmered before their eyes day in and day out while pushing two thousand longhorns north under a blistering sun . . . " (Collings, ix).

33. Collings, vii–x, xii–xiv, 25–28, 39, 161; Brownlaw, 253–54.

34. Collings, xxi, xiii, 155, 184.

35. Apid Nelson January, interview by author, 4 Aug. 1989.

36. Collings, x–xii, 161–62, 174.

37. Collings, xiii, 166. Brownlaw, 254–57, 323. Friar and Friar, 122–23, 125–27.

38. Collings, 24–28, 168.

39. Collings, 37, 39.

40. Collings, 169–170.

41. Brownlow, 261.

42. Collings, 169.

43. Collings, 169; Brownlow, 254–57; Friar and Friar, 125.

44. Louis Reeves Harrison, "Bison-101 Headliners," quoted in Friar and Friar, 126–27.

45. Friar and Friar, 67–68.

46. Collings, xv–xvi.

47. Collings, xv.

48. For instance, she was listed on the "Home and School League" program in Philadelphia (9 April 1925) as "Miss Maullie Nelson (Nee-Bur-Ban)" (program among Molly's papers).

49. "Penobscotbelles," *Bangor Weekly Commercial,* 12 Jan. 1900.

50. "Spotted Elk, 'L'Elan mouchete'"; in this full-page Paris interview, Molly describes the competition as "a dance contest of the Oklahoma Indians in which 900 warriors and women participated."

51. According to unidentified newsclipping in Apid Nelson January's 1930s scrapbook.

52. This is an estimate, based on the fact that Buck Jones earned that much as a trick rider in 1917 while traveling with the Ringling Brothers Circus—prior to becoming a movie star. (See Brownlow, 323).

Chapter 7

1. H. J. R. Tewksbury, "Indian Princess Will Paddle Own Canoe," *Portland Telegram,* 10 July 1927.

2. Molly's 1927 diary, 1 Jan. Molly notes that she was ill during the previous New Year's season. In the interview by Tewksbury (ibid.), she mentioned both her illness and her writing.

3. 1945 diary, 31 January; in this entry, Molly reflects back on her initial arrival in New York. Her arrival time can also be determined from various entries in her sketchy 1926 diary and from the interview by Tewksbury.

4. This sketch of the Prohibition era draws upon Cashman, 29–30, 43–46, 54, 115–16, 204, and Coffey, 162, 316.

5. 1935 diary, 3 Feb.; 1945 diary, 31 Jan.

6. This brief sketch of MacLeary comes from several sources: Falk, 389; Remy, 27; Norma Champlin, Executive Secretary, San Antonio Art Legue Gallery-Museum, telephone conversation with author, 19 Aug. 1992. Champlin also provided several newspaper clippings about the artist (sources not identified) and two one-page biographical sketches of MacLeary. Alleyne Miller, Administrative Assistant, 20th Century Art, The Metropolitan Museum of Art, provided two obituary newspaper clippings on MacLeary (1971, sources not identified). Roger Reeves, MacLeary's nephew (now deceased), telephone conversation with the author. See also "Texas-Born Sculptress Pays Visit to Houston in Interest of Centennial." After writing this sketch of MacLeary, the author learned that one of MacLeary's relatives presented a paper about her: see Glaspy, unpublished paper.

7. H. J. R. Tewksbury. "Indian Princess Will Paddle Own Canoe," *Portland Telegram*, 10 July 1927.

8. "Introducing Mr. Foster and Mr. Loeb," *New York Times*, 8 Aug. 1926, sec. 7. This article details Foster's dance team and his rigorous training methods.

9. Ibid.

10. "Vaudeville Reviews: Hippodrome," *Variety*, 10 Jan. 1926.

11. Kann provides U.S. theater seating capacity listings, noting them by state and town. Molly's departure from Foster after only a few months means one of three things: she quit, she had been hired only as a substitute to fill in for one of his contract dancers, or (most likely) she had her own contract with Foster and he trained the chorus for the Aztec.

12. Green and Laurie, 270–72.

13. For a summary of this Metropolitan Pictures film, see Munden, 420.

14. From a newspaper advertisement found among Molly's papers (unidentified publication).

15. Molly identifies her only as Orcella.

16. 1926 diary, 20 Nov.

17. Various notations in Molly's 1926 diary make reference to sending money home—typically five dollars.

18. Jean Moore, interview by author, 26 March 1989. In the back of her 1926 diary, Molly notes Guaranteed Shoe Company, along with other "work" addresses.

19. This was not unusual. The *New York Times* profile of Foster, "Introducing Mr. Foster and Mr. Loeb," noted that his chorus girls were trained under "kindly though essentially military discipline . . . " They "not only play in every night performance . . . but they also work in the three matinees which are traditional at this house. Then, in addition, they are rehearsed and drilled on matinee days for an hour before the afternoon performance. These drills and rehearsals are in the nature of exercises to keep them in perfect condition . . . " A *Variety* article, "80 Publix Weeks for 4 Foster Girl Units," noted that picture houses typically required "four or more" daily performances of their chorus girls (12 Dec. 1927, 30).

20. 1926 diary, Dec., end of month memo.

21. For instance, included among addresses in Molly's 1926 diary is Lillian Seaman, Children's Book Dept., Macmillan. Her "poems published" reference appeared in "Indian Princess Will Paddle Own Canoe," *Portland Telegram*, 10 July 1927.

22. 1927 diary, 7 Jan.
23. 1926 diary, various entries.
24. 1927 diary, 9 Jan.
25. 1927 diary, 1 Jan.
26. 1926 diary, 17 Nov.
27. 1927 diary, 10 Jan.
28. For a sketch of Watawaso's life, based on an interview with her, see Wiggins. Information about Montague Chamberlain is on file in the Harvard University Archives. Chamberlain, who served Harvard simultaneously as Assistant Dean of Men, Secretary of the Lawrence Scientific School, and Clerk of the Summer School, was cherished by Harvard alumnae whose attendance overlapped with his work there in the 1890s. Records show that in 1924, Samuel F. Ratchelder (Harvard College class of 1893) raised funds to erect a headstone for "Monty," who, in his last years became destitute, and, upon his death, was buried in an unmarked grave in the family plot of an old friend. Seventy-two alumnae (nearly everyone who was approached) contributed, and a "fine 'bronze green' slate" headstone was very soon purchased and placed at his grave site. The inscription read: "Montague Chamberlain****Born at St. John N.B. 5 April 1844. Died at Boston, Mass. 10 February 1924****Sometime Recorder of Harvard College****This Stone Erected By Some of His Old 'Boys.'"
29. "Penobscotbelles," *Bangor Weekly Commercial*, 12 Jan. 1900.
30. Wiggins.
31. Blackstone, 31–32, 56–58.
32. Wiggins.
33. 1927 diary, 31 Jan. One journalist, writing about this revue, described the four members of "this gifted Indian troupe" in this way: Wantura "combined all the feminine graces—youth, talent, beauty, and a soprano voice of rare tonal beauty"; Molly was a "graceful" dancer-writer with a "studious nature" and "an innate understanding of the poetry of motion"; Watawaso was "an authority on Indian lore and a Victor record artist"; and their accompanist, Tommie Little Chief, was "a modern young fellow whose greatest enjoyment is a visit to the rendezvous of the jazz set. (From an unidentified 1927 clipping found among Molly's papers.)
34. Wiggins; 1926 diary, various entries between 7 March and 22 May.
35. Spitzer, 8–9.
36. Wiggins.

37. Kendall, 179.

38. From an unidentified newsclipping found among Molly's papers; the journalist reviewed her performance as a member of Wantura's Indian revue at the Montauk Theater during the last week in January 1927.

39. 1927 diary, 9 July.

40. 1927 diary, 29 Oct.

41. Green and Abel, 174.

42. *Variety,* Film House Reviews, 26 Oct. 1927.

43. 1927 diary, 13 Oct.

44. 1927 diary, 17 June.

45. Green and Laurie, 138.

46. 1927 diary, 18, 29 Aug.; 14, 16, 20 Oct.

47. 1927 diary, 16 Oct.

48. 1927 diary, 22 Oct.

49. 1927 diary, 16 Oct.

50. *Collier's Magazine,* 2 April 1927 (cover in Apid Nelson January's 1930s Scrapbook).

51. 1927 diary, 21–24 Jan.; 8 Oct.; 12 Dec.

52. 1927 diary, 18–21 Oct.

53. Higham, 108; Toll, 313, 319.

54. 1927 diary, 31 Oct.

55. 1927, 10 July.

56. 1927 diary, 17 Oct.; 13 Nov.

57. "Program of Wild West Show Today," *New Haven Journal-Courier,* 8 July 1927; 1927 diary, 8 July.

58. 1927 diary, 2 Oct.

59. 1927 diary, 15 Oct.

60. 1927 diary, 15 Aug.

61. 1927 diary, 10–12, 16, 22 Oct.

62. 1927 diary, 17 Oct.

63. 1927 diary, 18, 29 Aug.

64. 1927 diary, 18 Aug.; 12 Oct.

65. 1927 diary, 13 Oct.

66. 1923 diary, January.

67. 1927 diary, 15 Oct.

68. 1927 diary, 11, 16 Dec.

69. This unfinished poem, apparently authored by Molly, appears in the back of her 1927 diary.

70. 1927 diary, 18, 25 Nov.

71. 1927 diary, 13 Dec.

72. Spitzer, 192–93. Coffey, 122, 163. See also nightclub revue listings and reviews in 1926–1929 issues of *Variety*.

73. Cashman, 48. Coffee, 122–24, 200–202. Full biographies of Texas Guinan have been written by Louise Berliner and Glenn Shirley. Berliner's book captures the spirit as well as the facts of Tex's life.

74. Bolitho.

75. Slide, 65.

76. Coffey, 160–63, 173–75.

77. Berliner, 105.

78. Green and Laurie, 224. Stagg, 254.

79. 1 July 1928, 1.

80. In her 1929 diary, 30 Oct., Molly noted, "Brynie's birthday. . . . A year ago today . . . we had a wonderful evening together—playing music and cards. We were so happy. We made plans for the future." On 3 Jan. she wrote, "Here I am supposedly engaged to the scion [Cheedy] and friendly with the bush man." Molly made many references in her 1930 and 1931 diaries to the evolution of their friendship. On 6 Feb. 1931, she noted "Brynie—his friendship has weathered time. . . . He was my first boyfriend. Brynie engaged—again."

81. In his unpublished manuscript (1978a), Burden notes that he discovered Molly at Tex's (18). Molly, in a 1931 interview with *Pour Vous* in Paris ("Spotted Elk, 'L'Elan mouchete'"), said, "[Burden] came and asked me to play Neewa after having searched throughout the country for a young pure-blood female Indian . . . able to play the specific demands of that role. . . . Those who could have played it were afraid of the terrible cold, frozen ice wilderness, the lack of comforts, and the life without a maid."

Chapter 8

1. Molly Nelson, "Making *The Silent Enemy*," nine-page publicity narrative used in 1930 and 1931 by the film's publicist, Betty Shannon, 1930, 2 (among Molly's papers).

2. Burden, 1978a "The Silent Enemy," 1; this unpublished manuscript, which was in progress at Burden's death, was shared with me by his widow, Jean Burden Bostwick of Shelburne, Vermont in 1989.

3. This biographical sketch was compiled from several sources, in particular Burden 1960, and an interview with his sister Sheila Burden Lawrence. See also Brownlow, 548; Marion Carter "Luxury for

Indian Film: Three Scions of Wealth Return from Wilds of Quebec with tribal Movie," the *New York Journal* 6 May, 1930; Smith 1989, 165.

4. Among many articles about Burden's Komodo dragon expedition, see the *New York Times*, 2 February 1928, 13, an article noting that the lizards were then on display at the American Museum of Natural History in New York. See also Burden 1960, 169–93.

5. Brownlow, 548–50. Burden 1960. Smith 1982, 165; interview by author with Sheila Burden Lawrence. Burden's growing desire to preserve wildlife and draw public attention to its wonders later prompted him, along with his cousin "Sonny" L. V. Whitney and Ilia Tolstoy, to found Marine Land in Florida.

6. Brownlow, 539.

7. "Film Depicts Tribal Life of the Ojibways," *The Christian Science Monitor*, 19 May 1930; this insightful article draws much of its content from an interview with Douglas Burden. See also Brownlow, 529, 550; Burden 1978a, unpublished manuscript, 1–2; Smith 1989, 164.

8. Friar and Friar, 97–98.

9. Brownlow, 550. Burden 1978a, unpublished manuscript, 5. Smith 1982, 165. For an excellent two-volume synopsis of the *Jesuit Relations*, including excerpts, see Parkman. For the entire seventy-three-volume collection, see Thwaites.

10. Among others see Burden 1978a, unpublished manuscript, 3 and William Laurence: "A Camera Record of the Indian," the *New York World*, 11 May 1930.

11. This synopsis is based on the film itself, which was produced by Paramount and reissued in 1991 by Video Yesteryear (Sandy Hook, Connecticut).

12. Brownlow, 550. Smith 1989, 165.

13. Brownlow, 551. Burden 1978a, unpublished manuscript, 5.

14. For a thought-provoking peek at who has played which Indian(s) throughout film history, see Friar and Friar, especially: 134, 150, 154, 205, 214–15, 247–50. According to Russell Means, cofounder of the American Indian Movement and costar in the 1992 production of *The Last of the Mohicans* (playing the part of Chingachgook), "Every Indian film needs a white protagonist to be successful" (personal communication at the author's house in Manhattan, Kansas, 1 April 1993).

15. Burden 1978a, unpublished manuscript, 18. Smith 1989, 168.

Various interviews with Molly's daughter, Jean Moore. The amount of Molly's salary was determined by her 30 April 1930 renewal contract with Burden Pictures. Her initial August 1928 contract (not available) may have authorized a somewhat smaller figure.

16. Burden 1978a, unpublished manuscript, 13; Smith 1982, 168.

17. This biographical sketch was composed primarily from Yellow Robe's autobiographical article in "How the Silent Enemy was Made," Souvenir Edition, 1930, 4, 17 (in Burden's Clips Book). See also Yellow Robe's obituary in the *New York Times*, 8 April 1930; and Fiedler, 112–26.

18. From Yellow Robe's speech at the 1913 conference of the Society of American Indians (Friar and Friar, 67).

19. Burden 1978a, unpublished, 13; Smith quoted in Clifton, 168, 174.

20. This biographical sketch of Long Lance is based primarily on the works of his biographer, Donald Smith. For a full account of Long Lance's fascinating life story, see Smith's *Long Lance: The True Story of an Imposter*. For a more concise account, see Smith in Clifton, unpublished manuscript, 183–203.

21. Burden 1978a, unpublished manuscript, 2b, 3; Smith 1982, 166.

22. Burden, 1978a, unpublished manuscript, 2b. David McLaren, interview by author.

23. This sketch of Madeline Theriault's life is based on interviews with her, and on her autobiography, *Moose to Moccasins,* 12–31.

24. Theriault, 32–33.

25. For more information about Ojibwa life at this time, see Ruth Landes's *The Ojibwa Woman,* chronicling the lives of Western Ontario Ojibwa women who were born around the turn of the century. See also A. Irving Hallowell's *The Ojibwa of Berens River, Manitoba,* 1992, edited by Jennifer S. H. Brown, based on fieldwork conducted during the 1930s and 1940s.

26. Burden 1978a, unpublished manuscript, 3–4.

27. Theriault, 62–63.

28. Smith 1982, 166.

29. In our 5 March 1993 telephone conversation, Madeline Theriault noted that Burden paid her sixty dollars per month. In her autobiography (70), she notes that despite all the costume-making she did, her wages were the same as all the other Ojibwa "extras" in the film.

30. Burden 1978a, unpublished manuscript, 19. Background information about Benoit also appears in "How the Silent Enemy was Made," souvenir edition, 1930, 13 (in Burden's Clips Book).

31. Burden, in his unpublished manuscript (1978a), offers a wonderfully humorous account of how he discovered Cheeka (5–8).

32. Molly Nelson, "Making *The Silent Enemy*," 1 (among Molly's papers).

33. This description was compiled from several sources: Burden 1978 unpublished 27; Sheila Burden Lawrence, interview by author; David McLaren, interview by author; Molly, various notations in her 1929 diary.

34. Burden 1978a, unpublished manuscript, 9 and Burden 1978b, "Bob Hennessey: Buccaneer of the North," 1–2. Although sources variously note Hennessey's age in 1928 to be as young as eighteen and as old as thirty-one, Burden's unfinished manuscript about Hennessey gives a specific birth year: 1904.

35. This description of the camp layout at Rabbit Chutes derives from several sources: Sheila Burden Lawrence, interview by author; David McLaren, interview by author; Madeline Theriault, interviews by author, 3 May, 3 July 1993.

36. Theriault, 66–69.

37. Molly Nelson, "Making *The Silent Enemy*," 4–5 (among Molly's papers).

38. "Film Depicts Tribal Life of the Ojibways," *The Christian Science Monitor,* 19 May 1930. The fact that Burden sought input from Indians in the cast is corroborated by William Chanler's 30 July 1930 letter to Governor Milliken, which Burden includes in his 1978 manuscript about the film. It may be, however, that Burden consulted with Ojibwa men but not women. Madeline Theriault, Ojibwa extra and costume maker, commented in a telephone interview, 3 May 1993, that there were errors in filming that could have been avoided "if Burden had consulted us." When pressed for examples, she named only three: young children did not use snowshoes, natural wind never blew the snow as hard and thick as Burden's snow machine did, and no sane Ojibwa would ever try to take two bear cubs in a canoe.

39. 1929 diary, various entries. The description of Carver occurs in Molly's 30 March entry.

40. This brief critical commentary owes much to a letter from Dr. Jennifer Brown (Department of History, University of Winnipeg), a scholar on Ojibwa culture, who shared with me her critical insights and reservations about *The Silent Enemy* (7 Aug. 1993).

41. Brownlow, 558.

42. Burden 1978a, unpublished manuscript, 37–39.

43. Molly Nelson, "Making *The Silent Enemy,*" 3 (among Molly's papers).

44. Smith 1982, 168.

45. David McLaren, interview by author.

46. Burden 1978a, unpublished manuscript, 36–37.

47. Brownlow, 558–59; "How the Silent Enemy Was Made," 3, 8 (in Burden's Clips Book).

48. Brownlow, 556; Smith 1982, 169.

49. Smith 1982, 170.

50. 1929 Diary, 2 Feb.; Molly Nelson, "Making *The Silent Enemy,*" 5 (among Molly's papers).

51. Shirley Burden, interview by author.

52. Molly Nelson, "Making *The Silent Enemy,*" 5 (among Molly's papers).

53. Sheila Burden Lawrence, quoted in Burden 1978a, unpublished manuscript, 29–30. The references to Douglas and the Indian "squaw," and to Molly and Dul's singing, were inserted, based on my interview with Mrs. Lawrence, during which she recapped the evening's entertainment.

54. Burden 1978, unpublished manuscript, 10; Theriault, 74.

55. Burden 1978a, unpublished manuscript, 10.

56. David McLaren, interview by author.

57. Burden 1978a, unpublished manuscript, 10.

58. 1929 diary, 5–6 Feb.

59. 1929 diary, various entries, Jan.–Feb.

60. 1929 diary, various entries, Jan.–April.

61. 1929 diary, 21 Jan.; 7 May; 15 Aug.

62. Precisely when Molly found this letter is not clear, although it was certainly during the filming of *The Silent Enemy.* She refers to the letter some months later in her diary, 16 Aug. 1929.

63. 1929 diary, 8 May.

64. Letter quoted in Smith 1982, 169.

65. David McLaren, interview by author.

66. Madeline Theriault, interview by author, 3 May 1993.

67. 1929 diary, 5 April. Molly made dozens of references to "Mother" Nelson in this diary between January and April. She also wrote admiringly of her in "Making *The Silent Enemy,*" 6 (among Molly's papers).

68. Smith 1982, 175.

69. "Silent Enemy Music Score Synchronized by Experts." *Exhibitors Daily Review and Motion Pictures Today,* 14 May 1930.

70. Excerpted from the film *The Silent Enemy,* Paramount, reissued in 1991 by Video Yesteryear (Sandy Hook, Connecticut).

71. Barbara Johnson, "Maine Indian Princess of Many Talents Wins Fame in Motion Pictures," *Portland Sunday Telegram and Sunday Press Herald,* 8 June 1930.

72. 1930 diary, 17 Nov.

73. 1930 diary, 20 May.

74. Bruce Bliven, "Films, Russian and American," *New Republic,* 20 May 1930.

75. George Gerhard, "Reel Review," *New York Evening World,* 20 May 1930.

76. Robert E. Sherwood, "The Moving Picture Album," *Boston Herald,* 18 May 1930.

77. "Great Picture" (editorial), *New York Evening Post,* 20 May 1930.

78. Various newspaper clippings found in Molly's papers and Burden's *Silent Enemy* Clips Book.

79. Brownlow, 559–60; Burden 1978a, unpublished manuscript, 36–37; Sheila Burden Lawrence, interview by author; Smith 1982, 178.

Chapter 9

1. Molly's 1929 Diary, 30 Nov.; 8 Dec.

2. 1929 Diary, 18 May.

3. Contract between Burden Pictures, Inc. and Molliedell Nelson, dated 30 April 1929 (among Molly's papers).

4. This brief manuscript is among Molly's papers, along with a cover letter written by Betty Shannon. Molly mentions her "bush story" frequently in her 1929 diary.

5. 1930 diary, 21 March; 1931 diary, 3 Jan.

6. 1931 diary, 9 Feb.

7. 1929 diary, 14 Aug.

8. 1929 diary, 18 Nov.

9. 1929 diary, 23 Sept.; "Princess Spotted Elk, Who Played Neewa In 'The Silent Enemy' To Make Next Picture in Morocco," *Portland Sunday Telegram,* 24 August 1930.

10. 1929 diary, 21, 23, Sept.

11. Various 1929 diary entries, May–Sept.

12. 1929 diary, 16, 17, Sept.

13. Margin, John. "The Dance: A Vital Part of the Theater." *New York Times,* 6 Oct. 1929, sec. 9.

14. 1929 diary, 5 Oct.

15. "A Provincetown Tea," *New York Times,* 7 Oct. 1929; "Drama Group Quits For Lack of Funds," *New York Times,* 15 Dec. 1929; "The Provincetown Playhouse," *New York Times,* 16 Dec. 1929.

16. 1929 diary, 8 Oct.

17. 1929 diary, 7 Oct.

18. 1929 diary, 10 Oct.

19. 1929 diary, 11 Oct.

20. Berliner, 162.

21. 1929 diary, various entries, 20 Oct.–23 Nov.

22. 1929 diary, 20 Nov.

23. 1930 diary, 7 Jan.

24. 1929 diary, 16 June, 5 Dec.

25. 1929 diary, 24 May.

26. 1929 diary, 19 July.

27. 1929 diary, 24 July.

28. 1930 diary, 14 Jan.

29. Friar and Friar, 130–31.

30. 1930 diary, 24 Aug., 2 Nov.; Green and Laurie, 385; Friar and Friar, 13. In 1934, Hollywood produced its version of *Laughing Boy* — starring none other than Lupe Velez, who had also snatched the leading female role from Molly for *The Squaw Man* (see Friar and Friar, 183). Molly's sister Apid had a cameo role in *Laughing Boy* (according to unidentified newsclippings and Central Casting Corporation photographs in Apid Nelson January's 1930s Scrapbook).

31. An unidentified 1930 newsclipping among Molly's papers shows a photo of her, announcing that she will "again" be singing on "The Children's Hour."

32. 1930 diary, 12, 28 Feb.

33. 1930 diary, stories in progress noted in various entries.

34. 1929 diary, 19 Nov.

35. 1929 diary, end of Oct. memo.

36. 1930 diary, 26 Jan.

37. Ibid; 1931 diary, 16 Jan.

38. "Maine Indian Princess of Many Talents Wins Fame in Motion Pictures," *Portland Sunday Telegram,* 8 June 1930.

39. 1930 diary, 5 Feb.

40. 1930 diary, 10 March; 1931 diary, 4 Jan., 1 Feb., 20 March.

41. 1930 diary, 25 April.

42. 1930 diary, 19 Aug.

43. Shelton, xv.

44. Molly refers to St. Denis and Shawn several times in her diaries: 15 June, 30 Dec. 1929; 20 Feb. 1931. On 30 Dec. 1931, Molly wrote, "Over to the Forest Theater to see Ruth St. Denis—she sent me a note to come to see her later in the week. Was to have seen them [St. Denis and Shawn] last summer, but never had time."

45. Molly's training with St. Denis is noted in "Maine Indian Princess of Many Talents Wins Fame in Motion Pictures," *Portland Sunday Telegram,* 8 June 1930; 1929 diary, 30 Dec.

46. 1931 diary, 6, 16 Jan.; Lisan Kay, interview by author, 19 April 1989.

47. 1930 diary, 29 Dec.; 1931 diary, 2 Feb.

48. Molly sometimes noted in her diary that she wrote between shows (e.g., 21 July 1930), and publicist Betty Shannon, in a press release prepared for Walter Winchell upon Molly's 1934 return from France, noted that she "always had her portable typewriter with her in her dressing room" (release found among Molly's papers).

49. "Cabaret Reviews: Silver Slipper," *Variety,* 17 March 1927.

50. 1930 diary, 25 April.

51. 1930 diary, 30 May.

52. 1930 diary, 26 Sept.

53. Molly frequently made note in her diaries of "celebs" who came to the club (among many examples, 10 March, 1930).

54. For example, see Sobol's column, 27 Oct. 1930.

55. 1929 diary, 27 Dec.

56. 1931 diary, 15 Jan.

57. 1930 diary, 18 Feb.

58. 1929 diary, 30 Aug.

59. 1929 diary, 8 Aug. 18 Sept., 17 Oct.

60. 1930 diary, 28 Feb., 1 March.

61. 1930 diary, 26 July, 8 Aug.

62. 1930 diary, 7 July.

63. 1929 diary, 28 April; 1931 diary, 23 April.

64. 1931 diary, 9 Jan.

65. 1929 diary, end of the year memo; 1930 diary, 12 Jan., 13 July, 12 Aug.; 1931 diary, 21 Jan., 8 Feb.

66. 1930 diary, end of July memo.

67. 1929 diary, end of Sept. memo.

68. "Maine Indian Princess of Many Talents Wins Fame In Motion Pictures," *Portland Sunday Telegram*, 8 June 1930.

69. Smith 1989, 200.

70. Jean Moore, interview by author, 8–13 Sept., 1989. Molly's 1930 diary includes many references to Darly and Long Lance's affair; the excerpts cited come from 29 Jan. and 10 March.

71. 1930 diary, 20, 29 Oct.

72. 1930 diary, 22 Nov.

73. Jean Moore, interview by author, 8–13 Sept. 1989.

74. 1930 diary, 2, 20 Jan., 24 Feb., 2 July, 19 Sept., 27 Dec.; 1931 diary, end of Jan. memo, 10 Feb., 1 April.

75. 1930 diary, 14 July, 3 Nov.

76. 1931 diary, 7 April.

77. 1931 diary, 29 Jan.

78. "Maine Indian Princess of Many Talents Wins Fame in Motion Pictures," *Portland Sunday Telegram*, 8 June 1930.

79. Ernestine Tomer, interview by author, 10 Aug. 1989.

80. 1929 diary, 11, 15, 18 Dec.

81. Ernestine Tomer, interview by author, 10 Aug. 1989; 1929 diary, 25 Dec. Eunice Nelson, in a telephone conversation with the author, 4 Oct. 1993, noted, "Molly was so afire when she danced that one Christmas in our house she hit her forehead on the curlycue back of a chair and it sent her reeling."

82. 1929 diary, 24 Dec. Other evidence of Molly's penned protests, primarily in the form of letters, are among her papers. The earliest one I found was written during her year at the University of Pennsylvania—either fall 1924 or winter-spring 1925.

83. See, for example, "Veterans and Jobless Find That After All, They Had Cause To Be Thankful," *New York Evening Journal*, 28 Nov. 1930. This brief article included a large photograph, showing Molly among entertainers performing at a Thanksgiving dinner party given to "500 needy jobless men and their families" at the Hollywood Restaurant. Other references to charity events occur in her 1930 diary, 26 Oct., 10, 14, 27 Nov.

84. Information drawn from a society program found among Molly's papers: "A series of Four Evenings, Vocal, Piano, Chamber Music and Dance," presented by the Society of First Sons and Daughters of America, March 3, 10, 17, 24, 1937. Molly performed a warrior dance in this performance series.

85. Those most frequently noted include: Atalie Unkalunt, Watawaso (Lucy Nicola), Red Eagle (Henry Perley), TeAta (Mary Thompson), Joseph Shunatona, Needabeh (Roland Nelson), and Running Bear.

86. 1930 diary, 1 Feb., 6 June.

87. John del Valle, *New York Herald Tribune*, 17 Nov. 1940, quoted in Friar and Friar, 134.

Chapter 10

1. Molly's 1931 diary, 31 May, 11 June.

2. Molly makes no specific mention of this invitation in her diary, but it seems to have come in the first half of March. If it had come during January or February, her consistent diary entries during those months would surely have noted it. Among the scarce (less than a dozen) diary entries she made during March and April, she offered the first hint of the invitation in a 20 March notation: "At Miss Waters [for] voice, culture and French." Five days later she wrote, "very optimistic of trip." And on 2 April she stated, "studied French sayings and phrases." I surmise that Molly received the invitation at the Hollywood Restaurant because she performed there regularly during this period, and among her papers is a Hollywood table placard on which she made notes about the exposition and the Indian Band. It seems likely that the invitation came via O'Brien, who was in New York during most of February-April and during that time was in intense written negotiations with Bascom Slemp (the expo's U.S. Commissioner-General), attempting to secure a performance position for the Indian Band at the expo's U.S. exhibit.

3. The extensive letter/telegram exchange between O'Brien and Bascom Slemp (U.S.Commissioner-General to the 1931 Exposition), can be found at the U.S. National Archives, RG43, in the "Indian Band" and "Inauguration and U.S. Band" folders, box 9, file 1314. O'Brien's 23 Feb. 1931 letter to Slemp lists the band's credentials.

4. "Beautiful Maine Indian Princess Receives Great Praise in Paris," *Portland Sunday Telegram*, 14 June 1931.

5. Gridley offers a short profile of Joe Shunatona (109). In 1926, the year after her sojourn with the 101 Ranch in Shunatona's home state of Oklahoma, Molly included him and his wife Gwen in the address section of her diary for the first time. From 1929 through April 1931, she made frequent diary notes about visiting them in their New York apartment.

6. Molly made several diary notes (25 April–2 May 1931) about performing on board the Ile de France. Commissioner Slemp made note of Molly and the band's on-board performances in a letter to Mr. Seiper at the French Chamber of Commerce in New York: "Mr. Thomas O'Brien, Manager of the U.S. Indian Band, has informed me that you have been of great assistance to him in helping to obtain free passage for the band on the Ile de France. . . . I am sure his band will be a great attraction both on board ship and in Paris" (U.S. National Archives, RG43).

Also, the gravure section of the *New York Herald Tribune* included a photograph of the Indian Band performing on board the Ile de France, Molly and Shunatona dancing while other band members played their instruments (3 May 1931, sec. 9).

7. 1931 diary, 24 April.

8. 1931 diary, 25 April–May 2.

9. "Mercredi prochain sera inauguree l'Exposition Coloniale de Vincennes," *Le Petit Journal,* 3 May 1931 (author's translation).

10. Carlisle MacDonald, "Paris hears Indian Band: Redskins arrive with American Commissioner for Colonial Exhibit," *New York Times,* 3 May 1931.

11. 1931 diary, 2–3 May.

12. Among many descriptions of Paris at this time, see Bernier, 3–9, 39.

13. Greenhalgh offers an excellent and quite detailed overview of international expositions, exhibitions, and fairs from 1851–1939. See also Corbey 1991, 1–2.

14. Corbey 1991 (unpublished manuscript), 1, 3; Greenhalgh, 82–109.

15. Corbey 1991 (unpublished manuscript), 2, 9; Greenhalgh, 83–84.

16. Corbey 1991 (unpublished manuscript), 5–6.

17. Greenhalgh, 87, 96, 102. For an interesting discussion regarding the relationships between Western hegemony and ethnographic showcases at world's fairs, museums, and in photographic collections, see Corbey 1993 (unpublished manuscript).

18. Corbey 1991 (unpublished manuscript), 9; Greenhalgh, 84, 89, 100.

19. Case Four: "1904 St. Louis Louisiana Purchase Exposition," in World's Fairs 1851–1940, an exhibition of the Smithsonian Institution Libraries, Washington, D.C., 12 Feb.–26 Aug. 1992.

20. Bradford, 5–6, 123.

21. Greenhalgh, 108.

22. Rhoads to Slemp, 9 Feb. 1931; O'Brien to Slemp, 7 Feb. 1931; Slemp to O'Brien, 20 Feb. 1931 (U.S. National Archives, RG43.)

23. 1931 diary, various entries May–Aug.

24. 1931 diary, 29 June, 6 July.

25. Case Six: "Between the Wars," in World's Fairs 1851–1940, an exhibition of the Smithsonian Institution Libraries, Washington, D.C., 12 Feb.–26 Aug. 1992.

26. This brief description of the 1931 Expo draws from a multitude of sources, including various French newspapers; Greenhalgh, 69–70, 78; and the following rare books available at the library of the Smithsonian Africa Museum: *Exposition Coloniale Internationale Guide Officiel, Album-Souvenir de L'Exposition Coloniale Internationale, Paris 1931, Exposition Coloniale Internationale de Paris en 1931: Colonies et Pays D'Outre-Mer* (with beautiful illustrations by De G. Goor), and *Ministere Des Colonies Exposition Coloniale Internationale de 1931 Rapport General* by Marcel Olivier.

27. "President Doumergue Opens International Colonial Exposition," *Chicago Daily Tribune* 7 May 1931, European edition.

28. Now Musée des Arts Africains et Oceaniens.

29. This particular phrase was spoken by Italy's Prince di Scalea, quoted in "Colonial Exposition Opens at Vincennes In Splash of Color," *New York Herald,* 7 May 1931, European edition.

30. Ibid. Among many other articles on this event, see "Colorful Scenes Mark Long-Awaited Inauguration of Colonial Exposition," *Chicago Daily Tribune* (European edition), 7 May 1931 (European edition); Carlisle MacDonald, "France Opens Fair of All Its Colonies," *New York Times,* 7 May 1931; "C'est aujourd'hui que le President de la Republique inaugure officiellement l'Exposition Coloniale," *Le Petit Journal,* 6 May 1931; "M. Gaston Doumergue à inauguré l'Exposition Colonial," *Paris Soir,* 7 May 1931.

31. Quoted in papers around the world, including Carlisle Mac-Donald, "France Opens Fair Of All Its Colonies," *New York Times,* 7 May 1931.

32. "Colonial Exposition Opens at Vincennes In Splash of Color," *New York Herald,* 7 May 1931, European edition.

33. "Colorful Scenes Mark Long-Awaited Inauguration Of Colonial Exposition," *Chicago Daily Tribune,* 7 May 1931, European edition.

34. "Colonial Exposition Opens at Vincennes In Splash of Color," *New York Herald,* 7 May 1931, European edition.

35. Ibid.

36. "Beautiful Maine Indian Princess Receives Great Praise in Paris," *Portland Sunday Telegram,* 14 June 1931.

37. Ibid; the fifth paragraph in this excerpt draws heavily from the first two paragraphs of a *New York Herald* (European edition) article that appeared 7 May, 1931. However, the opening paragraphs in the *Herald* article did not mention American Indians and did not say that the "pale faced man and woman [seemed] colorless."

38. B. J. Kospoth, "Edge, Lyautey Open U.S. Site At Exposition," *Chicago Daily Tribune,* 27 May 1931, European edition. Among the many Paris dailies chronicling the opening of the U.S. exhibit, see: "2000 See 'Mt. Vernon' Opened at Vincennes By Edge and Pershing," *New York Herald,* 27 May 1931, European edition; "Cependant qu'on inaugure la Maison de Washington à Vincennes . . . " *Paris Soir,* 27 May 1931; "L'Inauguration De La Section Des Etats Unis A l'Exposition Coloniale De Vincennes," *Le Temps,* 28 May 1931; "Al'Exposition coloniale: Mount-Vernon Et Hawai A Vincennes," *Le Petit Parisien,* 27 May 1931.

39. "A l'Exposition Coloniale: Le Pavillon des Etats-Unis à été inauguré hier," *Echo de Paris,* 27 May 1931.

40. "American Indian Band to Return to U.S.," *Chicago Sunday Tribune,* 7 June 1931, European edition.

41. "Rambling Reporter at Vincennes Notes a Thing or Two—or Twenty," article from unidentified newspaper in the U.S. National Archives, RG43, file 1314, Box 9.

42. Molly's 1931 diary, 15 May–30 May. See also daily Empire Music Hall advertisements in various Paris newspapers during this period as well as Thomas O'Brien's "Statement re. Visit of the United States Indian Band to the International Colonial and Overseas Exposition," delivered with a cover letter to Commissioner Bascom Slemp, 19 Feb. 1932, U.S. National Archives RG43.

43. O'Brien, "Statement," U.S. National Archives, RG43.

44. "American Indian Band to Return to U.S." *Chicago Sunday Tribune,* 7 June 1931, European edition. "U.S. Indian Band Sails on France Today for Home," *Chicago Daily Tribune,* 9 June, 1931, European edition.

45. O'Brien, "Statement," U.S. National Archives, RG43.

46. O'Brien, ibid. In an undated letter to Slemp, probably late May 1931, O'Brien asked for "$300 so I can pay the Indian boys' hotel. Bills are two days overdue and I am sadly in need of this amount to keep

going." In another undated letter to Slemp, he suggested that Slemp contract the Indian Band to play at Mt. Vernon throughout the month of June—for room and board only. Slemp's reply to O'Brien (3 June 1931), stated: "We just cannot do this. We are making every effort to hold down expenses, sending people back home, and cutting down our payroll, in order to get through. . . . I advised you about this matter before you left the United [States], and we simply do not have the money." All three letters on file at the U.S. National Archives, RG43.

47. 1931 diary, various entries 25 May–9 June.

48. "No Misunderstanding Between U.S. Officials at Exposition and Departing Redskins Band," *Chicago Daily Tribune,* 8 June 1931, European edition.

49. 1931 diary, 9 June, memoranda page (between May and June).

Chapter 11

1. Molly's 1932 diary, end of year memo.

2. "Tex Guinan Barred in Havre," *New York Herald* (European edition), 30 May 1931.

3. "Texas Guinan Hears Sûreté Generale Will Ship Her Back Home Wednesday," *Chicago Daily Tribune,* 1 June 1931, European edition.

4. "Tex Guinan Barred in Havre," *New York Herald* 30 May 1931, European edition.

5. "Texas Sails Home," *Chicago Daily Tribune* 4 June 1931, European edition.

6. Press release about Molly, prepared by New York publicist Betty Shannon for Walter Winchell in the fall of 1934 (among Molly's papers).

7. Shirley, 105.

8. "Epitre à Miss Texas Guinan" by Paul Reboux, *Paris Soir,* 3 June 1931: 2 (author's translation).

9. Berliner 171–73. "'Too Hot for Paris,'" *New York Times,* 16 June 1931.

10. 1931 diary, 3–5, 7, 11.

11. Allan, 47–48; Bernier, 60, 67.

12. This description is based primarily on two interviews with Lisan Kay, March and 19 April 1989, with full verification from various entries in Molly's 1931 diary. The author visited Madame de La Tour's former residence on rue d'Algiers, which, indeed, proved to be as ample and elegant as Lisan described.

13. 1931 diary, 5, 23 May.

14. Morton, 14, 188.

15. *New York Herald,* 5 July 1931, European edition.

16. 1931 diary, 20 May.

17. 1931 diary, 14 Oct.

18. "News of Americans in Europe," *New York Herald* 9 May 1931, European edition; Molly's 1931 diary, 12 May. For a brief history of Les Ambassadeurs, see Flanner, 63–64.

19. "News of Americans in Europe," *New York Herald,* 19 June 1931, European edition; Molly's 1931 diary, 19 June.

20. 1931 diary, 23 Sept., 29 Oct.–15 Nov., 14 Dec.–7 Jan.

21. Every major Paris daily reviewed the film; for example see *Paris Soir* (10 Jan. 1931), *Ami du Peuple* (9 Jan. 1931), *Le Journal* (9 Jan. 1931); among the magazines that published major stories on the film, see *Pour Vous* (24 Nov. 1930 and 8 Jan. 1931), *Cine-Miroir* (19 Sept. 1930 and 9 Jan. 1931), and *Le Courier Cinematographique* (15 Nov. 1930).

22. 1931 diary, 12 Aug. Also, a Crystal Palace Theater flyer among Molly's papers shows that *The Silent Enemy* played there 7–13 Aug., 1931. She also noted going to see the film on 27 Aug. at the Cinema Odeon with "Ura," the *Pour Vous* journalist who wrote about her.

23. "Beautiful Maine Indian Princess Receives Great Praise in Paris," *Portland Sunday Telegram,* 14 June 1931.

24. Bernier, 31.

25. This sketch of Archambaud's journalistic pursuits for *Paris Soir* is based on a survey of his articles for that publication during the early 1930s. The following are those referred to here, in order of mention: "Une mission francaise va partir pour tenter de sauver des races condamnees," 18 March 1931; "'Si je ne suis pas le Nouveau Christ nous dit hier soir Krishnamurthi . . , je possède par contre le Bonheur parfait et la Vérité,'" 28 Oct. 1930; "La Trocadero poudreux devient sans qu'on sans doute à beau musée modern," 26 Oct. 1930; "La vicomtesse de Noailles patronne 'L'Age d'Or': Un film surrealiste à été presente ce matin," 23 Oct. 1930.

26. A photograph of Oskomon, Archambaud, and Molly sitting at the Rotonde and surrounded by curious onlookers can be found in Allan, 42.

27. Jean Archambaud, "Cependant qu'on inaugure la Maison de Washington à Vincennes: L'interview de Mais Vert," *Paris Soir,* 27 May 1931 (author's translation).

28. 1931 diary, 25 May.

29. 1931 diary, 26 May–10 June.

30. 1931 diary, 11 June.

31. Jean Archambaud to Molly, 13 June 1931 (among Molly's papers).

32. 1931 diary, 13 June.

33. 1931 diary, 30 June.

34. 1931 diary, 14, 15 June.

35. 1931 diary, 16 June. Molly's diary entries written in France, as in other places, typically described the local culture as well as her activities. While in France she noted, in her usual cryptic style, customs, history, historic sights, the contemporary political scene, qualities of various French cheeses, class divisions, major figures in literature, music and art (past and present) and their characteristics.

36. These excerpts are drawn from three 1931 diary entries: 21 June, 22 Sept., 4 Dec.

37. Jean Archambaud to Molly, 27 June 1931 (among Molly's papers).

38. 1931 diary, 27 June.

39. Trip details relayed in the following paragraphs are drawn from Molly's 1931 diary, 5–27 July.

40. Calloway 1991, 33–34; Trigger, 134–40.

41. Among many sources that make reference to St. Castin, see Munson's "St. Castin: A Legend Revised," and Webster, 192–94, for detailed synopses of his life.

42. 1931 diary, end of July memo.

43. 1931 diary, 13 Sept.

44. 1931 diary, 15 Sept.

45. 1931 diary, end of Oct. memo.

46. "Spotted Elk, 'L'Elan mouchete'"; Danse, 16 Dec. 1931.

47. 1931 diary, 30 Dec.

48. 1931 diary, 2–25 Sept. This trip was through the Massif Central and Evennes Mountains along the Alliez River in Auvergne and Languedoc provinces.

49. 1931 diary, 22, 30 Sept.

50. See Paris Soir, 20 Jan. 1931, for a description of this club.

51. Among many of Molly's 1932 diary references to her own performances, see 14, 22, 24 Feb.; 2, 6, 9–10, 15, 17, 19 March; 19, 29 May; 25 June; 29 July–11 August; 19–25 Sept; 13–20 Nov.

52. 1931 diary, 20 Dec. Lisan Kay, interview by author, March 1989.

53. 1933 diary, 26 May.

54. Flanner, 81, 118–19; Morton, 80, 94, 208.

55. 1933 diary, 28 July–3 Aug. Verified by a promotional poster for the Ranch during Molly's engagement there (among Molly's papers).

56. Allan, 59.

57. Haney, 63.

58. 1933 diary, 6 June.

59. Haney, 62.

60. "Spotted Elk, 'L'Elan mouchete'" (author's translation). Molly's 17 Sept. 1931 diary entry about this article illustrates how private she was: "the content was good . . . but it is written in the French manner, rather personal even to my pastimes, likes & dislikes—and my opinions of my stay so far here. One has to be diplomatic."

61. Lisan Kay, interview by author, March 1989.

62. Allan, 60.

63. Among others, these engagements are mentioned in the following diary entries: 6 Oct. 1931, 2 March 1932, 12 Oct. 1933, 11 Jan. 1934.

64. This comment, one of many written by Molly regarding Jean's insight and helpfulness with her work, is drawn from her 1932 diary, 22 Feb. In a 7 Sept. 1931 entry, she describes how she bought an African tom-tom for 150 francs and taught Jean to play it: "Kept neighbors up with tom tom, songs and much laughter—but who cares?" References to Jean playing the tom-tom for Molly's performances are found in the following entries: 6 March and 25 June 1932, 17 March and 26 May 1933.

65. Clifford, 121–22.

66. For example, see *Paris Soir,* 26 Oct. 1930, 5 Nov. 1930, 1 May 1931; *Le Petit Journal,* 8 Oct. 1933.

67. Among various newspaper references to this exhibit, see *Le Petit Journal,* 20 May 1931. For a biographical sketch of Coze, see Samuels and Samuels, 112.

68. 1931 diary, 2, 7, 13 May.

69. 1934 diary, 16 Jan.

70. These excerpts are drawn from the following diary entries: 7 May, 9 June, 13 Aug., 11 Oct. 1931; 1, 2 Sept. 1932; 27, 28 May, 10 June, 2 Oct., 7 Oct. 1933. The article Molly refers to in her 7 Oct. 1933 entry appeared in *Le Petit Journal* 8 Oct. 1933. Gridley mentions Molly's "ethnological work at the Trocadero" (111).

71. Clifford, 121–22.

72. 1932 diary, 9 Dec.; in this entry Molly notes that everyone expected Kateri "to be canonized next year."

73. 1932 and 1933 diaries, various entries, including 6, 11 Oct.

74. "Princess Spotted Elk interprets Indian dance at Chicago fair," *Portland Sunday Telegram,* 15 Oct. 1933.

75. This profile draws primarily from two sources: the introduction and Mary's contribution in a 1937 book of essays by leading foreign correspondents, edited by Eugene Lyons; and the *New York Times* review of this volume, "Fifteen Writers on a World-wide Quest," by R. L. Duffus, 18 April 1937, sec. 7.

76. 1932 diary, 12 May; on 14 May, Molly noted that Jean was doing an article about Tex. Berliner (179) and Shirley (112) describe Tex's "glorious" ten-day sojourn in Paris during the spring of 1932.

77. 1932 diary, 25 Aug., 29 Sept.

78. 1931 diary, 4 Aug.

79. 1934 diary, 21 and 28 Jan.

80. Lisan Kay interviews, March and 19 April 1989.

81. Diaries, 1931–1934, various entries.

82. *New Yorker,* 9 Feb. 1929.

83. Longstreet, 420–21.

84. 1932 diary, 23 Oct., 25 Dec.

85. 1932 diary, 12 Oct.

86. "Princess Spotted Elk interprets Indian dance at Chicago fair," *Portland Sunday Telegram,* 15 Oct. 1933.

87. 1932 diary, 26, 28, 29 Dec. 1933 diary, 2, 4, 5, 6 Jan.; 29 Feb., end of Feb. memo; 20 March; 10, April.

88. 1933 diary, 11 April.

Chapter 12

1. Molly's 1934 diary, 4 April.

2. Bernier, 7, 83–84, 106–107; Bury, 125, 141; Calvocoressi, 317.

3. 1933 diary, 12 April; 1934 diary, end of June memo.

4. Bataille and Sands, 4–6; Hallowell 1955, 132–41.

5. Eunice Nelson-Bauman, interview by author, 4 Oct. 1992.

6. 1933 diary, 13 April.

7. 1933 diary, 22, April, 15 May.

8. 1931 diary, 2, 3 July.

9. 1931 diary, 4 July, end of Aug. memo; 1933 diary, 3 Jan., 16, 18 April.

10. 1931 diary, 6 Dec.; 1932 diary, end of July memo, 12, 26, 27 Aug.

11. 1932 diary, 28 Oct.

12. 1932 diary, 29 Nov.

13. Among various notes about film opportunities, are diary entries on 21 April 1933 and 22 Feb. 1934.

14. 1932 diary, 13 Aug.; "Princess Spotted Elk Interprets Indian Dance at Chicago Fair," *Portland Sunday Telegram*, 15 Oct. 1933.

15. Bernier, 43, 64.

16. 1934 diary, 21 March.

17. 1934 diary, 17, 22, 24 Jan. Molly wrote that her dancer-friend Aloma earned forty francs a day as a principal dancer at the Folies.

18. 1934 diary, 22 Jan.

19. Bernier, 32, 81–82.

20. 1931 diary, 1 Aug.

21. Molly's comments about *L'Ami du Peuple* appear in the following entries: 1933 diary, 6 Nov., 3, 15, 24 Dec.; 1934 diary, 2 Feb. For brief references to Coty, his paper, and Croix de Feu, see Flanner, 138, and Bury, 142. Jean's friend Raymond Gast, in a 29 May 1968 letter from Paris to Molly's daughter Jean Moore, noted that Jean had worked for *Le Petit Journal*, where his father served as editor.

22. 1934 diary, 14 Jan.

23. 1932 diary, 30, end of month memo, Sept.

24. 1934 diary, 21 Feb.

25. 1933 diary, end of May memo.

26. 1933, 26 Dec.

27. 1933, 28 Nov.

28. 1933 diary, 13, 19, 21, 23, Dec.; 1934 diary, 4, 5 Jan., 14 March. The Indian words are Maliseet and are written in Molly's own orthography. Maliseet language experts offered various but similar translations. According to Penobscot Alan Sockabsin, who speaks Maliseet, they translate as follows: *Nit-tam-swew!* (Praying to the Power!) *Wenooch-uk!! Ski-gin-uk ma-we-ah-sin!* (Whitemen!! Indians ask that things be made better!) *Biskit-poor kat* (It's pitch black and there is no light ahead). Linguist Phil LeSourd of Provincetown, Mass., offered this orthography in a letter to Dr. Karl V. Teeter (29 Nov. 1993): *Nit-te msiw! Wenuhcok! Skicinuwok mawiyahsin[uk]! Piski-tpuhkot,* which he translates, "That's it! [Literally, "that's all"] White people!! Indians work together! The night is dark." In a letter to the author (22 Nov., 1993), Dr. Karl Teeter of Cambridge, Mass., offered a similar translation, although he deciphered *ma-we-ah-sin* as "there is a meeting." Indian phrases appear in about five of Molly's diary entries each year.

29. 1934 diary, end of Feb. memo.
30. 1934 diary, 3 April.
31. 1933 diary, 3, 20 Jan.
32. Lisan Kay, interview by author, 19 April 1989.
33. 1934 diary, 23 Jan.
34. 1933 diary, end of Aug. memo; 6, 26 Sept.; 20, 24–27, 30 Oct. 1934 diary, 15 Feb.
35. Bernier 7, 106–107, 140–41; Safran, 8.
36. Bernier, 7, 56, 85–86; Bury, 142.
37. Bury, 141–42; Calvocoressi, 317–18; Paxton, 243–49, 273–75; Safran, 68–69; Tint, 53.
38. 1934 diary, 20 April.
39. Bury, 142–43; Paxton, 244; Tint, 53–54.
40. Bury, 142–44; Hartley, 44; Paxton, 243–49.
41. 1934 diary, 21 March, 20 April.
42. 1934 diary, 8 Feb.
43. 1934 diary, 12–16 Jan., 12 Feb.
44. 1934 diary, 11 January.
45. 1934 diary, 13 Jan.
46. 1934 diary, 25 March.
47. Jean Moore, interview by author, 8–13 Sept. 1988.
48. 1934 diary, 23 March, 7 April.
49. 1934 diary, 8 Jan.
50. 1934 diary, 25 Jan.
51. 1934 diary, 9 April.
52. 1934 diary, 10, 13 April.
53. 1934 diary, 14 April.
54. 1934 diary, 16 April (italics added).
55. 1934 diary, 14 April.
56. 1934 diary, 9 Feb.
57. 1934 diary, 24 April.
58. 1934 diary, 22, 23 April.
59. 1934 diary, Jean's entry in Molly's end of April memo.
60. 1934 diary, end of April memo.

Chapter 13

1. Molly's 1934 diary, end of May memo.
2. 1934 diary, 30 April.
3. Molly logged the ship's location daily. The first two weeks on

board and in northern European ports are recorded in her 1934 diary, 24 April–6 May.

4. 1934 diary, 7 May.

5. Jean Archambaud to Molly, 8 May 1934 (among Molly's papers).

6. 1934 diary, 16 May.

7. Jean Archambaud to Molly, 19 May 1934 (among Molly's papers).

8. 1934 diary, 27 May.

9. Jean Moore, interview by author, 8–13 Dec. 1988.

10. 1934 diary, 27 May; Jean Moore, interview by author, 8–13 Sept. 1988.

11. Gridley profiles Ross (102); Friar and Friar list Thorpe's films (186).

12. 1934 diary, 30 May.

13. 1934 diary, 29 May.

14. 1934 diary, 31 May.

15. 1934 diary, 1 June.

16. Jean Archambaud to Molly, 27 June 1934 (among Molly's papers).

17. 1934 diary, 2 June; Jean Archambaud, in a 6 July 1934 letter to Molly, wrote: "There is a link somewhere and now I have a brown baby of my own and brown wife; it's too beautiful to be true. I can only thank God for his kindness." (Letter lost, but quoted in Molly's 1934 diary, 18 July.)

18. 1934 diary, 7 June.

19. 1934 diary, 6 June.

20. 1934 diary, 6, 9 June.

21. 1934 diary, 22 June. Jean Moore, interview by author, 8–13 Sept. 1988.

22. 1934 diary, 22, 25 June; 8, 10 Aug.

23. Apid Nelson January, interview by author, 4 Aug. 1989; Jean Moore, interview by author, 8–13 Sept. 1988.

24. 1934 diary, 12 Aug.

25. 1934 diary, 19 July.

26. 1934 diary, 7 Sept.

27. 1934 diary, 26 June; 1, 24 Aug., 26 July; 1 Aug.

28. 1934 diary, 26 June; 1, 24 Aug.; 26, 30 July; 23, 7 Aug.

29. 1934 diary, 31 July.

30. 1934 diary, 18 Aug.

Chapter 14

1. Molly's 1935 diary, 1 Jan.

2. "Princess Spotted Elk Interpets Indian Dance at Chicago Fair," *Portland Sunday Telegram*, 15 Oct. 1933. This lengthy feature article about Molly noted, "To a Maine princess, Molly Spotted Elk of Indian Island, chosen from the many tribes of the United States, has fallen the honor of representing the Indian dance at the Exposition of Progress." The exposition ran for two seasons, May–Nov. 1933 and May–Oct. 1934.

3. 1934 diary, 25 June.

4. This description of the Nelson home comes from an article by John Fysche ("History of Indian Island," unidentified newspaper, 1 Feb. 1940, among Molly's papers) who visited the home in 1940, from interviews with various family members, and from the author's 1993 tour of the house with Jean Moore. "Gee-gis" is Molly's own orthography for the Penobscot term for baby; Frank Speck (1940, 253) spelled it "dji'jis."

5. Philomene's treatment of little Jean is noted in Molly's 1935 diary, 8, 15 Jan. The other activities noted here are mentioned in various 1934 and 1935 diary entries.

6. For an enlightening illustration of intentional underemployment among Wabanaki Indians as a means of resisting total "commodification" of their lives, see Prins 1994. For more details about Indian Island life at this time, see Speck 1940, 301–11.

7. 1934 diary, 16 Feb.

8. 1935 diary, 16 Jan.

9. Jean Moore, interview by author, 8–13 Sept. 1988. Verified by Apid Nelson January by telephone, 7 Aug. 1989.

10. 1935 diary, 4 Jan.

11. Eunice Nelson, interview by author, July 1988.

12. Jean Moore, interview by author, 8–13 Sept. 1988.

13. 1934 diary, 16 Feb. The adjective "skeptical" is drawn from a 16 Jan. 1935 entry about Blun.

14. Jean Moore, interview by author, 8–13 Sept. Verified by Eunice Nelson-Bauman in a telephone conversation with the author, 10 Nov. 1993.

15. 1935 diary, 16 Jan.

16. 1934 diary, 5, 6, 30 Nov.

17. 1934 diary, 17 Nov.

18. 1934 diary, 25 Nov.

19. Jean Archambaud to Molly, 6 Nov. 1934 (among Molly's papers).
20. 1935 diary, 7 Jan.
21. 1935 diary, 19, 20 Jan.
22. 1935 diary, 21 Jan.
23. 1935 diary, 3 Feb.
24. 1935 diary, 19, 20 Feb.
25. Ruth McKenney, "Wampum is Thicker Abroad Indian Princess Reveals: Molly Spotted Elk Returns From Fruitful Four-Year Tour of Europe," New York *Post*, undated clipping among Molly's papers.
26. 1935 diary, 22, 23 April.
27. 1935 diary, 28 April.
28. 1935 diary, 3, 6, 16, April.
29. 1934 diary, 27 July.
30. 1935 diary, 14 May.
31. 1935 diary, 21 May.
32. 1935 diary, 9 Feb.
33. 1935 diary, 5 July.
34. 1935 diary, 23 Jan.
35. 1935 diary, 8, 28 June; 26, 9, 11, 19, 27 July; 2 Sept.; 20 Aug.; 21, 23 Sept.; 17 July; 7 Aug.; 3, 17 Oct.; 16 July; 9, 26 Aug.
36. 1935 diary, 30 June–2 July.
37. 1935 diary, 11 June.
38. Jean Archambaud to Molly, 23 April 1935 (among Molly's papers).
39. 1934 diary, 29 Nov.
40. This paragraph is compiled from three letters by Jean Archambaud to Molly: 12 March 1935; 29 June 1936; January 1936 (all among Molly's papers).
41. 1934 diary, 29 Nov.
42. Compiled from two lengthy letters Jean Archambaud wrote to Molly recapping his relationship with Gisele Morhange: 19 June 1936, 23 April 1935 (both among Molly's papers).
43. Jean Archambaud to Molly, 23 April 1935 (among Molly's papers).
44. Jean Archambaud refers to Molly's saying this in his 20 July 1935 letter to her (among Molly's papers).
45. The last three paragraphs are based on Jean Archambaud to Molly, 20 July 1936 (among Molly's papers).
46. There are frequent references to this problem in Molly's diaries and Jean's letters. For instance on 20 July 1935, Jean wrote: "I think I

did not get all your letters. And you certainly did not get all of mine. I know because sometimes you refer to things I never read." To keep track of what mail got through, their letters often included a list of letters received from each other.
47. 1935 diary, 27 June.
48. Jean Archambaud to Molly, 5 July 1935 (among Molly's papers).
49. 1935 diary, 28 June.
50. 1934 diary, end of April memo.
51. 1935 diary, 22, 28 June.
52. 1935 diary, 8 Aug., 1 Sept.
53. 1935 diary, 10, 17 Aug.
54. 1935 diary, 2 Nov.
55. "Indian Dancer at the Casino: Princess Spotted Elk, Formerly of the Movies, Featured," *Bangor Daily News,* 29 Oct. 1935.
56. Eunice Nelson-Bauman, interview by author, 4 Oct. 1992.
57. 1935 diary, 25 Nov.–31 Dec.
58. "The Lee Side o'L.A.: Indian Girl Reporter on Paris Night Newspaper Dancing Here," *Los Angeles Times*, 1936 (clipping among Molly's papers; no specific date).
59. Jean Archambaud to Molly, January 1936 (among Molly's papers).
60. Jean Archambaud to Molly, 19 Nov. 1936 (among Molly's papers).
61. Jean Archambaud to Molly, 25 Nov. 1935 (among Molly's papers).
62. Jean Archambaud to Molly, 17 Nov. 1936 (among Molly's papers).
63. Ibid.
64. 1937 diary, 23 Jan.
65. 1937 diary, 23 Jan.
66. 1937 diary, 1 Feb.
67. 1937 diary, 17 April.
68. Lisan Kay, interview by author, 19 April 1989.
69. 1937 diary, 9 April.
70. 1937 diary, 3, 4 March.
71. 1937 diary, 6, 12, 9 March.
72. 1937 diary, 21, 28 April.
73. *New York Evening Journal,* 8 April 1937.
74. 1937 diary, 14 April.
75. 1937 diary, 9 April.

76. 1937 diary, 15, 16 May.
77. *Portland Press Herald*, 22 May 1937.
78. 1937 diary, 29 May.
79. 1937 diary, 21 June.
80. 1937 diary, 6 Aug.
81. 1937 diary, 28 Sept.
82. Jean Archambaud to Molly, 13 June 1937 (among Molly's papers).
83. "Old Town Indian Girl A Sensation As Native Dancer," *Portland Sunday Telegram*, 30 Dec. 1937. The first line of the article notes: "The following article is clipped from a New York newspaper of recent date."
84. Etienne and Louise Archambaud to Molly from St. Martin de Ré, 15 Nov. 1937 (among Molly's papers).
85. Jean Archambaud, letters to Molly; the first three paragraphs come from a letter written 13 May 1938, but never mailed. This letter offers more detail on Jean's bout with septicemia than his 17 June 1938 letter, which starts out with a brief sketch of his illness, then moves on to other topics. The balance of this quotation comes from the latter letter. Both letters are among Molly's papers.

Chapter 15

1. Molly's 1940 diary, 24 June.
2. Jean Moore, interview by author, 8–13 Sept. 1988.
3. Ibid.
4. Molly to Philomene Nelson, 15 July 1938 (among Molly's papers).
5. Jean Archambaud to Molly, 23 June 1936 (among Molly's papers).
6. Molly, in a 15 June 1940 letter (apparently a preliminary draft) to Mr. Taylor at the American Consulate, noted that her husband wrote stories for "'Junior,' a weekly sheet for boys." Jean, in his 16 June 1937 letter to Molly, noted that "the [publishing] house I am working for will publish any adventure story for boys that you can send. What will you accept? Would 50 dollars suit you. In France, we count by lines. The story must be 150, 300 or 600 [lines]. Here is a field for you. Send me the story. I will translate it." (Both letters among Molly's papers.)
7. Philanthropist Anne Morgan, daughter of banker J. P. Morgan, hints at this ongoing association in her 15 Nov. 1939 letter to Molly,

noting that "Mrs. Ames of the Danse Internationale is arriving here next week to work with us, so you will see two very warm friends when you arrive" (among Molly's papers).

8. Jean Moore, interview by author, 8–13 Sept. 1988.

9. Ibid.

10. Ibid.

11. Jean Archambaud to Molly, undated, circa Oct. 1938 (among Molly's papers).

12. Jean Moore, interview by author, 8–13 Sept. 1988.

13. Jean Archambaud to Molly, 23 July 1939 (among Molly's papers).

14. Author's translation (letter among Molly's papers).

15. Jean Archambaud to Molly, 23 July 1939 (among Molly's papers).

16. Barber, 68.

17. Jean Archambaud, later writing to Molly from another refugee center in Toulouse (11 Sept. 1940), noted, "For our work, same as in Royan, we get room and board."

18. "Anne Morgan is Dead at 78, Philanthropist, Civic Leader," *New York Herald Tribune*, 30 Jan. 1952. Molly's 1931 diary, 20 May, notes meeting Anne Morgan for the first time.

19. Anne Morgan to Molly, 3 Nov. 1939 (among Molly's papers).

20. Anne Morgan to Molly, 15 Nov. 1939 (among Molly's papers).

21. A pass ("sauf conduit . . . aller et retour à Paris") issued to Molly in Royan by the Department de la Charente-inferieure, Service des Etranger, shows that they traveled from Royan to Paris and back at this time (among Molly's papers).

22. Molly's 15 June 1940 letter to Mr. Taylor of the American Consulate in Bordeaux, notes Jean's exam results.

23. 1940 diary, 12 June.

24. Jean Moore, interview by author, 8–13 Sept. 1988.

25. Henry Waterman, American Consul, American Consulate, Foreign Service of the U.S. State Department, 3 June 1940 letter to Molly (among Molly's papers).

26. Molly's 15 June 1940 draft letter to Mr. Taylor at the American Consulate in Bordeaux (among Molly's papers).

27. Shirer, 23.

28. Barber, 33.

29. Bauer, 232.

30. Shirer, 24–26, 126; Bauer, 66–68.

31. 1940 diary, 12 June.

32. Barber, 39, 42–43.

33. This rough draft of a letter is among Molly's papers.

34. Barber, 199–200.

35. 1940 diary, 22 June.

36. 1940 diary, 15 June.

37. Jean Moore (interview by author, 8–13 Sept. 1988) recalls returning to the bungalow with her parents after an evening of card playing with friends and finding that "everything in the house had been ransacked, the beds torn apart. We came back to [such a] mess over and over again. . . . Apparently they wanted [my father's navy] manuscript."

38. Bauer, 138–39.

39. This quotation comes from a story based on an extensive interview with Molly: "Former Old Town Girl Evacuee From France," *Bangor Daily News*, 23 July 1940.

40. Molly's paranoia concerning Communism was verified by many people, including Eunice Nelson-Bauman (interview by author, 12–13 July 1988) and Jean Moore (interview by author, 8–13 Sept. 1988).

41. Barber 296, 303; Calvocoressi, 321.

42. Barber notes the gestapo's round up and arrest of "dangerous newspaper agitators" (235), and the fact that German spies were well acquainted with who was who among French journalists: "Lt. Joseph Schliess, of the German army, member of a wealthy German publishing family, one time model liftman at *Paris Soir* [where Johnny worked] had been planted as a spy years previously in readiness for this very moment [of Nazi occupation of Paris] and almost immediately he started to plan a Nazi version of *Paris Soir* for the following day" (163). Jean Moore noted, "My father had to leave us because he was being told the Germans were going to take him prisoner . . . because of his activity as a journalist" (interview by author, 12–13 July 1988).

43. Jean Moore, interview by author, 12–13 July 1988.

44. 1940 diary, 24 June.

45. Ibid.

46. Jean Moore, interview by author, 12–13 July 1988.

47. 1940 diary, 25 June.

48. 1940 diary, 30 June.

Chapter 16

1. Molly's 1929 diary, 20 March.

2. This recapitulation of Molly and Jean's journey was compiled

from various sources: Jean Moore, interview by author, 8–13 Sept. 1988; promissory notes issued by the American Consulate in Bilbao, Spain (among Molly's papers); two newspaper articles based on interviews with Molly just after her return: "Mrs. Archambaud, Old Town Girl, Evacuee From France With Child," *Penobscot Times,* 25 July 1940; "Former Old Town Girl Evacuee from France," *Bangor Daily News,* 23 July 1940.

3. "Former Old Town Girl Evacuee From France," *Bangor Daily News,* 23 July 1940. For another interview with Molly concerning her evacuation, see "Mrs. Archambaud, Old Town Girl, Evacuee From France With Child," *Penobscot Times,* 25 July 1940—based on a 5:30 P.M. radio interview by station WABI, 24 July 1940.

4. Jean Moore, interview by author, 8–13 Sept. 1988.

5. John Fysche, "Penobscot Indians Live Like White Neighbors, Observe Tribal Traditions," *Lewiston Journal,* 18 Nov. 1939, Illustrated Magazine Section. See also Speck 1940 for a view of the cultural and economic consistencies and changes on the island during the 1920s and 1930s (301–11).

6. Madeline Shay, interview by author, 8 August 1992. Madeline became one of the finest basketmakers on the island. Before her death in 1993, she taught several years in the Master-Apprentice program sponsored by the Maine Arts Council, working closely with one student per year. Among her students was Darly's granddaughter, Theresa Secord Hoffman.

7. Barber, 296; Calvocoressi, 321.

8. Jean Archambaud, to Molly, 11 Sept. 1940, except for paragraph two, which is from a 16 Oct. 1940 letter.

9. Molly, letter (unfinished, unmailed) to Jean Archambaud in Bagneres de Luchon, 11 Jan. 1941; Jean Archambaud, letters to Molly, 24 Jan. 1941 and 10 March 1941 (all three letters among Molly's papers).

10. Tint, 94.

11. Jean Archambaud, letter to Molly, 24 Jan. 1941. The location of Jean's brother, Jacques, is stated in a 23 Aug. 1941 letter from Jean to Molly (both letters among Molly's papers).

12. Program and unidentified newsclipping from this tour (among Molly's papers).

13. Louis Sobol, "New York Calvalcade," *New York Journal-American,* 29 May 1941.

14. Jean Archambaud to Molly, 22 May 1941 (among Molly's papers).

15. Jean Archambaud to Molly, 16 Oct. 1940 (among Molly's papers).

16. Jean Archambaud to Molly, 20 July 1941 (among Molly's papers).

17. Jean Archambaud to Molly, 24 Sept. 1941 (among Molly's papers).

18. A. Rolland to Molly, 9 Dec. 1941 (among Molly's papers).

19. E. Baldwin, Executive Secretary, American Red Cross, Penobscot County Chapter (Bangor), letter to Molly, 14 July 1941; Vice Consul, Consulate de France (Boston), letter to Molly, 11 Aug. 1942.

20. A. Rolland (Bagneres de Luchon) to Molly, 20 April 1942 (among Molly's papers).

21. Excerpt from untitled and apparently unfinished poem by Molly (among Molly's papers).

22. Ernestine Tomer, interview by author, 10 Aug. 1989.

23. YMCA Sloan House Business Secretary Ralph McKee (New York), a 15 Sept. 1947 "to whom it may concern" letter regarding Molly.

24. This brief overview is based on the 1945–48 diaries, two undated letters from Lon Jones to Molly (among Molly's papers), and comments of Jean Moore (interview by author, 8–13 Sept. 1988).

25. R. B. Toller, M.D., to Philomene Nelson, 20 April 1948 (among Molly's papers). Molly transcribed this letter in her 1948 diary, 2 Sept. The bus ride description is also based on Toller's letter.

26. 1948 diary, 29 Oct.

27. Bangor State Hospital Records on case no. 11,590, 1948–49.

28. Louis Sobol, *New York Journal-American,* 6 March 1951.

29. Jean Archambaud (Moore) to her mother Molly, 7 Jan. 1953 (among Molly's papers).

30. Jean Moore, interview by author, 8–13 Sept. 1988.

31. Tim Nicola, during a 10 Aug. 1991 interview with the author, described his fond memories of Molly teaching him about nature and how to fish by hand when he was a child in the 1960s. Jean Moore made many references to Molly's nature activities with her children in the 1950s and 1960s.

32. Jean Moore, interview by author, 8–13 Sept. 1988.

33. For a detailed description of the 1980 Maine Indian Claims Settlement (involving the Penobscot, Passamaquoddy, and Maliseet), see Brodeur. For a quick overview of Penobscot cultural and political changes from the time of initial European contact through today, see Prins 1994a.

34. Perhaps, for academic readers, this conclusion requires an explanation. Molly was a hiker. When I started this book, I swam regularly. By the time I finished it, I had surrendered swimming for daily hikes through the Flint Hills of Eastern Kansas. The switch was not conscious, but looking back, I believe I traded water for soil because putting foot to ground made me feel closer to Molly. She was not an easy woman to know, for she was intensely private, even in her diaries. Always, when I walked, I imagined her with me, challenging me up the slopes with her strong graceful stride. Watching her in my mind's eye, I struggled to glimpse her soul—a soul so different from my own. Molly frequently had visions, but I did not—until I started hiking in her mental company. Just before I began the last chapter of her life, this final paragraph came to me in a vision in the hills. At that moment, I felt as if Molly's soul and my own had finally met. Some readers of my manuscript suggested I change or delete it. I could not.

BIBLIOGRAPHY

Public Documents

Indian Affairs Documents from the Maine Executive Council Committee on Indian Affairs. 1820–1910. This ten-volume compilation of materials regarding Maine Indians, bound circa 1975 by the Maine State Library, was culled from various sources: Maine Executive Council Committee on Indian Affairs Reports, Registers, Journals, and Correspondence; Indian Agent Reports; and Maine State Legislative Documents.

Maine State Archives. Maine Public Documents. 1851. Vol 1.

United States National Archives. RG43. Record of International Conferences, Commissions, and Expositions. File 1314: Records of the Commission Representing the International Colonial and Overseas Exposition at Paris in 1931.

Newspapers

Ami du Peuple (Paris), Jan. 9, 1931.

Bangor Daily News (Maine), Aug. 4, 1930; Oct. 29, 1935; July 23, 1940.

Bangor Weekly Commercial, Jan. 12, 1900.

Chicago Daily Tribune (European Edition), May 7, 27, June 1, 4, 8, 9, 1931.

Chicago Sunday Tribune (European Edition), June 7, 1931.

Christian Science Monitor, May 19, 1939.

Echo de Paris (Paris), May 27, 1931.

Le Journal (Paris), Jan. 9, 1931.

Le Petit Journal, (Paris), May 3, 1931; Oct. 8, 1933.

Le Petit Parisien (Paris), May 27, 1931.

Le Temps (Paris), May 28, 1931.

Lewiston Journal, May 5, 1906; Nov. 19, 1939; Feb. 1, 1940.

New Haven Journal-Courier, July 8, 1927.

New York Daily Mirror, Oct. 13, 1933.

New York Evening Journal, April 8, 1937.

New York Evening Post, May 20, 1930.

New York Evening World, May 20, 1930.

New York Herald (European Edition), May 7, 9, 27, 30, June 19, July 5, 1931.

New York Herald Tribune, Jan. 30, 1952.

New York Journal, May 6, 1930.

New York Journal-American, May 29, 1941; March 6, 1951.

New York Times, Aug. 8, 1926; Feb. 2, July 1, 1928; Sept. 8, Oct. 6, 7, Dec. 15, 16, 1929; April 8, 1930; May 7, June 16, 1931; April 18, 1937.

New York World, May 11, 1930.

Paris Soir, Oct. 23, 26, 28, Nov. 5, 1930, Jan. 10, 20, March 18, May 1, 27, June 3, 1931.

Penobscot Times (Maine), July 25, 1940.

Portland Press Herald (Maine), May 22, 1937.

Portland Telegram (Maine), July 10, 1927.

Portland Sunday Telegram (Maine), June 8, Aug. 24, 1930; June 14, 1931; Oct. 15, 1933; Dec. 30, 1937.

Voila (Paris), Sept. 23, Oct. 6, 1932.

Books and Articles

Allan, Tony. 1977. *Americans in Paris: An Illustrated Account of the Twenties and Thirties.* Chicago: Contemporary Books.

American Friends Service Committee. 1989. *The Wabanakis of Maine and the Maritimes: A Resource Book about Penobscot, Passamaquoddy, Maliseet, Micmac, and Abenaki Indians.* Bath: Maine Indian Program, New England Regional Office of the American Friends Service Committee.

Barber, Noel. 1976. *The Week France Fell.* New York: Stein and Day.

Bataille, Gretchen, and Kathleen Mullen Sands. 1984. *American Indian Women Telling Their Lives.* Lincoln: University of Nebraska Press.

Bauer, Eddy. 1978. *World War II Encyclopedia.* Edited by Peter Young. H. S. Stuttman.

Berliner, Louise. 1993. *Texas Guinan Queen of the Night Clubs.* Austin: University of Texas Press.

Bernier, Olivier. 1993. *Fireworks at Dusk: Paris in the Thirties.* Boston: Little, Brown and Co.

Blackstone, Tsianina. 1968. *Where Trails Have Led Me.* Burbank, Calif.: Tsianina Blackstone.

Blankenship, Roy, ed. 1991. *The Life and Times of Frank G. Speck.* Philadelphia: University of Pennsylvania Press Publications in Anthropology.

Bolitho, William. 1931. Two Stars. *Delineator,* 15 January, 118.

Boyd, Stephani. 1989. One Hundred Years Ago: The Moving Image. *Northeast Historic Film Moving Image Review,* Winter 1989: 3, 7–8.

Bradford, Phillips Verner and Harvey Blume. 1992. *Ota Benga: The Pygmy at the Zoo.* New York: St. Martin's Press.

Brodeur, Paul. 1985. *Restitution: The Land Claims of the Mashpee, Passamaquoddy, and Penobscot Indians of New England.* Boston: Northeastern University Press.

Brownlow, Kevin. 1979. *The War, The West, and The Wilderness.* New York: Alfred A. Knopf.

Burden, Douglas. 1960. *Look to the Wilderness.* Toronto: Little, Brown and Company.

Bury, John P. T. 1972. *France: The Insecure Peace, From Versailles to the Great Depression.* New York: American Heritage Press; London: MacDonald.

Calderwood, Neil M. 1993. One Hundred Years: Island Movie Music. *Northeast Historic Film Moving Image Review,* Winter 1993: 4–5.

Calloway, Colin G. 1989. *The Abenaki.* New York and Philadelphia: Chelsea House Publishers.

———. 1990. *The Western Abenakis of Vermont, 1600–1800.* Norman and London: University of Oklahoma Press.

———. 1991 *Dawnland Encounters: Indians and Europeans in Northern New England.* Hanover and London: University Press of New England.

Calvocoressi, Peter, with Guy Wint and John Pritchard. 1989. *Total War.* New York: Pantheon Books.

Carpenter, Edmund S. 1991. Frank Speck: The Quiet Listener. In *The Life and Times of Frank G. Speck,* edited by Roy Blankenship, 78–84. Philadelphia: University of Pennsylvania Press.

Cashman, Sean Dennis. 1981. *Prohibition: The Lie of the Land.* New York: The Free Press.

Chamberlain, Montague. 1898. The Penobscot Indians: A Brief Account of Their Present Condition. *The Cambridge Tribune,* 8 February. Reprint, Augusta: Maine State Library.

Clifford, James. 1983. Power and Dialog in Ethnography: Marcel Griaule's Initiation. In *Observers Observed: Essays on Ethnographic Fieldwork,* edited by G. W. Stocking, Jr., 121–156. Madison: University of Wisconsin Press.

Clifton, James A. 1989. *Being and Becoming Indian.* Chicago: The Dorsey Press.

Coffey, Thomas, M. 1975. *The Long Thirst: Prohibition in America 1920–1933.* New York: W. W. Norton & Co.

Cole, Donald B. 1963. *Immigrant City, Lawrence Massachusetts 1845–1925.* Chapel Hill: The University of North Carolina Press.

Collings, Ellsworth, with Alma Miller England. 1971. *The 101 Ranch.* Norman: University of Oklahoma Press.

Culhane, John. 1989. *The American Circus.* New York: Henry Holt and Co.

Eckstorm, Fannie. 1932. *The Handicrafts of the Modern Indians of Maine.* Lafayette National Park Museum Bulletin III. Bar Harbor, Maine.

———. 1978. *Indian Place Names of the Penobscot Valley and the Maine Coast.* Orono: University of Maine at Orono Press.

Fenton, William. 1991. Frank G. Speck's Anthropology (1881–1950). In *The Life and Times of Frank G. Speck,* edited by Roy Blankenship, 9–37. Philadelphia: University of Pennsylvania Press.

Fiedler, Mildred. 1975. *Sioux Indian Leaders.* Seattle: Superior Publishing.

Flanner, Janet. 1972. *Paris Was Yesterday 1925–1939.* Edited by Irving Drutman. New York: The Viking Press.

Friar, Ralph and Natasha Friar. 1972. *The Only Good Indian . . . The Hollywood Gospel.* New York: Drama Bk. Pubs.

Ghere, David L. 1984. Assimilation, Termination, or Tribal Rejuvenation: Maine Indian Affairs in the 1950s. *Maine Historical Quarterly* 24, no. 2: 239–64.

Grandjean, Pat. 1992. The Elder. *Connecticut Magazine,* August, 92–97.

Green, Abel and Joe Laurie Jr. 1951. *Show Biz from Vaude to Video.* New York: Henry Holt and Co.

Greenhalgh, Paul. 1988. *Ephemeral Vistas, The Expositions Univer-selles, Great Exhibitions, and World's Fairs, 1851–1939.* Man-chester, U.K.: Manchester University Press and New York: St. Martin's Press.

Gridley, Marion. 1936. *Indians of Today.* Crawfordsville, Ind.: The Lakeside Press.

Hallowell, A. Irving. 1992. *The Ojibwa of Berens River, Manitoba.* Edited by Jennifer S. H. Brown. New York: Harcourt Brace Jovanovich College Pubs.

————. 1955. *Culture and Experience.* Philadelphia: University of Pennsylvania Press.

Hammond, Bryan and Patrick O'Conner. 1988. *Josephine Baker.* Lon-don: Jonathan Cape.

Haney, Lynn. 1981. *Naked at the Feast: A Biography of Josephine Baker.* New York: Dodd Mead.

Hartley, Anthony. 1971. *Gaullism: The Rise and Fall of a Political Movement.* New York: Outerbridge G. Dienstfrey.

Higham, Charles. 1972. *Ziegfeld.* Chicago: Henry Regnery Co.

Hillman, A. Merle, and Lillian Morris, eds. 1965. *Old Town, Maine: The First 125 Years 1840–1965.* Old Town, Maine: City Coun-cil.

Ibelle, William. 1983. In Search of 20th Century Penobscot: Madas Sapiel, an Elder. *Salt Journal of New England Culture* 5, no. 4: 45–49.

Kann, Maurice, ed. 1928. *Film Daily 1928 Yearbook.* New York and Los Angeles: The Film Daily.

Kendall, Elizabeth. 1979. *Where She Danced.* New York: Alfred A. Knopf.

Klein, Barry T., ed. 1986. *Reference Encyclopedia of the American Indian.* New York: Todd Publications.

Lance, Chief Buffalo Child. 1928. *Long Lance.* New York: Farrar & Rinehart.

Landis, Ruth. 1971. *The Ojibwa Woman.* New York: W.W. Norton & Co.

Lane, Sheryl. 1979. We Don't Make Baskets Anymore. *Salt Journal of New England Culture* 4, no. 4: 4–16.

Leger, Mary Celeste. 1929. *The Catholic Missions in Maine, 1611–1820.* Washington, D.C.: Catholic University of America, Stud-ies in American Church History, 8. (Copy at Maine State Library, Augusta).

Lemaire, Ton. 1986. *De Indiaan in Ons Bewustzijn* [The Indian in

Our Consciousness]. Baarn, the Netherlands: Uitgeverij Ambo bv.

Longstreet, Stephen. 1972. *We all Went to Paris*. New York: Macmillan.

Lorenzo, S. 1857. Indian Tribes of New England. *Christian Examiner and Religious Miscellany* 62 (March): 210–37.

Lottman, Herbert R. 1982. *The Left Bank: Writers, Artists, and Politics from the Popular Front to the Cold War*. Boston: Houghton Mifflin Co.

Lyons, Eugene, ed. 1937. *We Cover the World, by Sixteen Foreign Correspondents*. New York: Harcourt, Brace & Co.

McFadden, Steve. 1991. *Profiles in Wisdom: Native Elders Speak About the Earth*. Santa Fe: Bear & Co.

McLaren, David. 1992. *Turn of the Century: Stories About Northern Pioneers From the Early 1900s*. Cobalt, Ontario: Highway Book Shop.

Morrison, Kenneth M. 1984. *The Embattled Northeast*. Berkeley, Los Angeles and London: University of California Press.

Morton, Brian N. 1984. *Americans in Paris*. Ann Arbor, Mich.: The Olivia & Hill Press.

Munden, Kenneth W., ed. 1971. *The American Film Institute Catalog of Motion Pictures Produced in the United States: Feature Films 1921–1930*. New York and London: R.R. Bowker Co.

Munson, Gorham. 1965. St. Castin: A Legend Revised. *Dalhousie Review* 45: 338–60.

Needabeh [Roland Nelson]. Circa 1935. *The Unwritten Indian: A Brief Historical Sketch of the Penobscot Tribe of Maine*. Canton, Maine: The Pinewood Press Publishers. (Available in the Frank G. Speck Files, American Philosophical Society Library, Philadelphia.)

Neihardt, John G. 1959. *Black Elk Speaks*. New York: Washington Square Press.

Nelson, Eunice. 1982. *The Wabanaki: An Annotated Bibliography*. Cambridge, Mass. American Friends Service Committee.

Nicolar, Joseph. [1893] 1979. *The Life and Traditions of the Red Man*. Reprint, Fredericton, New Brunswick: Saint Anne's Point Press, 1979.

Parkman, Francis. 1897. *The Jesuits in North America*. Boston: Little Brown and Company.

Paxton, Robert O. 1975. *Vichy France: Old Guard and New Order, 1940–1944*. New York: The Norton Library.

Penhallow, Samuel. 1878. Indian Wars. *New England Historical and Genealogical Register* 32.

Powers, William K. 1988. The Indian Hobbyist Movement in North America. In *History of Indian-White Relations*, 557–61, edited by Wilcomb E. Washburn. vol. 4, *Handbook of North American Indians* Washington, D.C.: Smithsonian.

Prins, Harald E. L. 1992. Cornfields at Meductic: Ethnic and Territorial Reconfigurations in Colonial Acadia. *Man in the Northeast* 44 (fall): 1–18.

———. 1994a. Penobscot. In *Native America in the Twentieth Century: An Encyclopedia*. New York: Garland Publishers.

———. 1994b. To the Land of the Mistigoche: American Indians Traveling to Europe in the Age of Exploration. *American Indian Culture and Research Journal* 17, no. 1: 175–95.

———. Tribal Network and Migration Labor: Micmac Indians as Seasonal Workers in Aroostook's Potato Fields. In *Native Americans and Wage Labor,* edited by Martha Knack and Alice Littlefield. In Press. Norman and London: University of Oklahoma Press.

Prins, Harald E. L., and Bruce J. Bourque. 1987. Norridgewock: Village Translocation on the New England-Acadian Frontier. *Man in the Northeast* 33(spring): 137–58.

Prins, Harald E. L., and Bunny McBride. 1992. "Discovering Europe 1493." *World Monitor,* November, 58–62.

Rigdon, Walter, ed. 1966. *Biographical Encyclopedia and Who's Who in the American Theater.* New York: J.S.H. Heineman.

Rivard, Paul E. 1990. *Maine Sawmills: A History.* Augusta: Maine State Museum.

Robinson, Brian S., James B. Petersen, and Ann K. Robinson, eds. 1992. *Early Holocene Occupation in Northern Maine,* Occasional Publications in Maine Archaeology no. 9. Augusta: Maine Historic Preservation Commission.

Rosa, Joseph G., and Robin May. 1989. *Buffalo Bill and His Wild West.* Lawrence: University of Kansas Press.

Russell, Don. 1970. *The Wild West: a History of the Wild West Shows.* Fort Worth, Tex.: Amon Carter Museum of Western Art.

St. Denis, Ruth. 1939. *An Unfinished Life.* New York: Harper & Brothers.

Safran, William. 1977. *The French Polity.* New York: David McKay Company.

Samuels, Peggy, and Harold Samuels. 1985. *Samuels' Encyclopedia of Artists of the American West*. Edison, NJ: Castle, Book Sales Inc.

Shay, Florence Nicola. Circa 1945. *History of the Penobscot Tribe of Indians*. (Available in Frank G. Speck Files in the American Philosophical Society Library, Philadelphia.)

Shelton, Suzanne. 1981. *Divine Dancer: A Biography of Ruth St. Denis*. Garden City, New York: Doubleday & Co.

Shirley, Glenn. 1989. *"Hello Sucker!" The Story of Texas Guinan*. Austin, Tex.: Eakin Press.

Siebert, Frank T. 1982. "Frank G. Speck, Personal Reminiscences." In *Papers of the Thirteenth Algonquian Conference*, edited by William Cowan. 91–136. Ottawa: Carleton University.

Silent Enemy Music Score Synchronized by Experts. 1930. *Exhibitors Daily Review and Motion Pictures Today*, 14 May.

Sévigny, P.-André. 1976. *Les Abénaquis: Habitat et Migrations (17e et 18e siecles)*. Montreal: Les Editions Bellarmin.

Shirer, William L. 1969. *Collapse of the Third Republic*. New York: Simon & Schuster.

Slide, Anthony. 1983. *The Vaudevillians: A Dictionary of Vaudeville Performers*. Westport, Conn.: Arlington House.

Smith, Donald. 1982. *Long Lance: The True Story of an Imposter*. Lincoln: University of Nebraska Press.

———. 1989. From Sylvester Long to Chief Buffalo Child Long Lance. In *Being and Becoming Indian: Biographical Studies of North American Frontiers*, edited by James A. Clifton, 183–203. Chicago: The Dorsey Press.

Snow, Dean R. 1978. Eastern Abenaki. In *Northeast*, 137–47, edited by Bruce Trigger. Vol. 15, *Handbook of North American Indians* Washington, D.C.: Smithsonian Institution.

Speck, Frank G. 1915. Myths and Folk-lore of the Timiskaming Algonquin and Timagami Ojibwa. Canadian Department of Mines, Geological Survey Memoir No. 71, Anthropological Series No. 9.

———. 1940. *Penobscot Man: The Life History of a Forest Tribe in Maine*. Philadelphia: University of Pennsylvania Press.

Speck, Frank G. and Goldsmith, Frank. 1935. "Penobscot Tales and Religious Beliefs," *Journal of American Folklore* 48: 1–107.

Spitzer, Marian. 1969. *The Palace*. New York: Atheneum.

"Spotted Elk, 'L'Elan Mouchete': La petite Indienne de L'Ennemi silencieux nous dit . . . " 1931. *Pour Vous*, 17 September, 6.

Stagg, Jerry. 1968. *The Brothers Shubert*. New York: Random House.

Sullivan, James. [1795]. 1970. *History of the District of Maine*. Reprint, Augusta: Maine State Museum.

Theriault, Madeline Katt. 1992. *Moose to Moccasins*. Toronto, Ontario: Natural Heritage/Natural History.

Thoreau, Henry David. 1966. *The Maine Woods*. New York: Thomas Crowell.

Tint, Herbert. 1970. *France Since 1918*. New York and Evanston: Harper & Row.

Trigger, Bruce G. 1985. *Natives and Newcomers: Canada's "Heroic Age" Reconsidered*. Kingston and Montreal: McGill-Queen's University Press.

Thwaites, Reuben G., ed. 1896–1901. *The Jesuit Relations and Allied Documents: Travel and Explorations of the Jesuit Missionaries in New France, 1610–1791*, the original French, Latin, and Italian texts with English translations and notes. 73 vols. Cleveland: Burrows Brothers. (Reprinted: Pageant, New York, 1959.)

Toll, Robert C. 1976. *On with the Show*. New York: Oxford University Press.

Vail, Robert W. G. 1934. Random Notes on the History of the Early American Circus. In *Proceedings of the American Antiquarian Society*, New series, Vol. 43, Part 1, 116–85. Worcester: The Society.

Verrill, A. Hyatt. 1933. *Romantic and Historic Maine*. New York: Dodd, Mead & Co.

Vestal, Stanley. 1989. *Sitting Bull: Champion of the Sioux*. Norman: University of Oklahoma Press.

Viola, Herman J. 1981. *Diplomats in Buckskin*. Washington, D.C.: Smithsonian Institution Press.

Vogel, Virgil J. 1972. *This Country Was Ours: A Documentary History of the American Indian*. New York: Harper Torchbooks.

Webster, John Clarence. 1934. *Acadia at the End of the 17th Century: Letters, Journals and Memoirs of Joseph Robineau de Villebon, Commandant in Acadia, 1690–1700 and Other Contemporary Documents*. St. John, New Brunswick: The New Brunswick Museum.

Weslager, C.A. 1991. The Unforgettable Frank G. Speck. In *The Life and Times of Frank G. Speck*, edited by Roy Blankenship, 52–77. Philadelphia: University of Pennsylvania Press.

Whitehead, Ruth Holmes. 1980. *Elitekey: Micmac Material Culture from 1600 to the Present.* Halifax: Nova Scotia Museum.

Witthoft, John. 1991. Frank Speck: The Formative Years. In *The Life and Times of Frank G. Speck,* edited by Roy Blankenship, 1–8. Philadelphia: University of Pennsylvania Press.

Wiggins, John R. 1966. Indian Princess. *Down East,* November: 28–30.

Williamson, William D. 1832. *The History of the State of Maine from Its First Discovery, A.D. 1602, to The Separation, A.D. 1820, Inclusive.* Vol. 1. Hallowell, Maine: Glazier, Masters & Co.

———. 1846. Notice of Orono, A Chief at Penobscot. Boston: *Collections of the Massachusetts Historical Society* Vol. IX, 3rd Series: 82–91.

Unpublished Papers

Banks, Ronald. 1977. Historical Summary: Relations Between the Penobscot Tribe and the Province and State of Massachusetts up to 1796. (Photocopy in the files of Harald E. L. Prins, Manhattan, Kans.)

Burden, Douglas. 1978a. "The Silent Enemy." Manuscript in progress at Burden's death. (In the possession of his widow, Jean Burden Bostwick, Shelburne, Vt.)

———. 1978b. Bob Hennessey: Buccaneer of the North. Manuscript in progress at Burden's death. (In the possession of his widow, Jean Burden Bostwick, Shelburne, Vt.)

———. "The Silent Enemy" Clips Book, 1930–1932. (In the possession of his widow, Jean Burden Bostwick, Shelburne, Vt.)

Corbey, Raymond. 1992. Survey and Surveillance. Paper presented at the annual meeting of the American Anthropological Association.

Corbey, Raymond, with Steven Wachlin. 1991. Ethnographic Showcases, 1870–1930. Working paper, Department of Philosophy, Tilburg University, The Netherlands.

Glaspy, Sugar. 1979. Aspiration: The Story of Bonnie MacLeary. Paper presented at the Texas State Historical Association.

January, Apid (Winifred) Nelson. 1930's Scrapbook. (In the possession of Molly's daughter, Jean Archambaud Moore, Indian Island, Old Town, Maine.)

Moore, Jean Archambaud. 1990. The Nelson Family History. (Photocopies in the possession of various family members on Indian Island, Old Town, Maine.)

Nelson [Archambaud], Molly [aka Mary Alice Nelson, Molliedellis Nelson, Molly Spotted Elk]. Diaries: 1920, 1921, 1922, 1926, 1927, 1929, 1930, 1931, 1932, 1933, 1937, 1940, 1944, 1946, 1947, 1948, 1951, 1951, 1959. (In the possession of her daughter, Jean Archambaud Moore, Indian Island, Old Town, Maine.)

————. Personal Papers. These include letters, newsclippings, manuscripts, photographs, and research notes. (In the possession of her daughter, Jean Archambaud Moore, Indian Island, Old Town, Maine.)

————. 1938. Katah-din: Wigwam's Tales of the Abnaki Tribes. Unpublished ms. Accession no. 1115, Northeast Archives of Folklore and Oral History, University of Maine, Orono.

Prins, Harald E. L. 1987a. A Case Study in Political Ecology—Penobscots in Maine. Working Paper.

————. 1987b. 1900: Miscegenation in the Penobscot Community. Working paper.

————. 1988. Public Performance and Ethnic Identity: Chief Big Thunder and the Peddling of Native American Culture. Paper presented at the annual meeting of the American Society for Ethnohistory.

Reed, Dorothy Crocker. 1923. Camp Overlook Scrapbook. (In the possession of Mrs. Reed, Methuen, Mass.)

Starbird, Glen. History of Penobscot Legislators. In the files of the Penobscot Nation Department of Trust Responsibilities.

Interviews

Bostwick, Jean Burden, Shelburn, Vt., 31 March 1989.

Burden, Shirley, New York, N.Y. (telephone), April 1989.

Champlin, Norma, San Antonio, N. Mex. (telephone), 19 Aug. 1992.

Hartman, Alberta Speck, Wilmington, Del. (telephone), 15 Oct. 1992.

January, Apid Nelson, Canoga Park, Calif. (telephone), 8 July, 4, 7 August, 1989.

Kay, Lisan, New York, N.Y. (telephone) March, New York, N.Y. 19 April 1989.

Ketchum, Gilbert, Indian Island, Old Town, Maine, 24 July, 1988.

Lawrence, Sheila Burden, Shelburne, Vt., 31 March 1981.

McLaren, David, North Cobalt, Ont. (telephone), 19 January 1993.

Moore, Jean Archambaud.

    Murfreesboro, Tenn., tape recording, 8–13 Sept. 1988.

Indian Island, Old Town, Maine, 7–8 Aug. 1992, 4–5 Aug. 1993, 5–8 Aug. 1994.

Various telephone interviews, Murfreesboro and Indian Island, 1988–94.

Nelson, Clara, Indian Island, Old Town, Maine, 8 July 1992.

Nelson-Bauman, Eunice.

Hallowell, Maine, 12–13 July 1988.

Indian Island, Old Town, Maine, 24 July 1988, 10 August 1989, 8 August 1992, 4–5 August 1993.

Various telephone interviews, Indian Island 1989–1994.

O'Brien, Margaret, Paris, 25 June 1989.

Pettus, Elizabeth Jennings, Lafayette, La. (telephone), 20 Aug. 1992.

Reed, Dorothy Crocker, Methuen, Mass. (telephone), 20 Aug. 1992.

Reeves, Roger, Harrisburg, La. (telephone), 22 Aug., 1992.

Sanger, David, Orono, Maine (telephone), 28 Jan., 1992.

Shay, Madeline, Indian Island, Old Town, Maine, 8 August 1992.

Shay, Lawrence ("Bill"), Indian Island, Old Town, Maine, 8 August 1992.

Speck, Frank S., Green Valley, Ariz. (telephone), 15 Oct. 1992, 27 April 1993.

Starbird, Glen, Indian Island, Old Town, Maine, 24 July 1988, 7 August 1992.

Tantaquidgeon, Gladys, Uncasville, Conn. (telephone), 15 Oct. 1992.

Theriault, Madeline, North Bay, Ontario (telephone), 5 March, 3 May, 3 July 1993.

Tomer, Ernestine, Indian Island, Old Town, Maine, 10 August 1989, 8 August, 1992, 5 August, 1993, 23 January, 1993 (telephone).

Tomer, Wilfred, Indian Island, Old Town, Maine, 5 August 1993.

INDEX